The

British Commonwealth

and

International Security

The
British Commonwealth
and
International Security

*The Role of the Dominions,
1919-1939*

By
GWENDOLEN M. CARTER
SMITH COLLEGE

*Issued under the auspices of
the Canadian Institute of International Affairs*

GREENWOOD PRESS, PUBLISHERS
WESTPORT, CONNECTICUT

NOTE

The Canadian Institute of International Affairs is an unofficial and non-political organization founded in 1928. The Institute has as its objects to promote and encourage in Canada research and discussion in international affairs and to give attention to Canada's position both as a member of the international community of nations and as a member of the British Commonwealth of Nations.

The Institute, as such, is precluded by its Constitution from expressing an opinion on any aspect of public affairs. The views expressed, therefore, are those of the writer.

Originally published in 1947
by The Ryerson Press, Toronto

First Greenwood Reprinting 1971

Library of Congress Catalogue Card Number 71-114494

SBN 8371-4731-X

Printed in the United States of America

To my Father and Mother
whose interest, encouragement, and help
made this a work of partnership.

FOREWORD

THE present volume on the British Commonwealth and international security is the second of a series of monographs in process of being prepared by the Canadian Institute of International Affairs on different aspects of international relations. The years from 1919 to 1939 saw the birth of a League of Nations designed to promote international co-operation and to achieve peace and security among nations; they saw nation after nation advocate a progressive weakening of commitments under the League Covenant, even while storm clouds loomed high over both eastern and western horizons; they witnessed the failure of the powers, great and small, to permit collective security a fair trial out of jealousy for their independent sovereignties; and hence they witnessed a sequence of international crises in China, in Ethiopia, in the Mediterranean, in Spain, in the Rhineland, and in Central Europe, all revealing the imminent danger of military aggression on a world-wide scale. Dr. Gwendolen Carter's study examines the policies of the members of the British Commonwealth in these recurring crises and the degree and significance of their participation in the vain efforts of the League to establish international security. In doing so, it portrays the maturing experience of the Dominions in international affairs, and in particular presents a valuable analysis of Canada's external policies in the years between the wars.

ALEXANDER BRADY,
Chairman of the Research Committee,
Canadian Institute of International Affairs.

PREFACE

THIS study deals with the efforts to achieve security in the inter-war period of the members of the British Commonwealth of Nations, in particular Canada, Australia, New Zealand, South Africa, and the Irish Free State. The emphasis is therefore primarily political and international. Internal developments, constitutional evolution within the British Commonwealth and economic factors have been included only in as far as they seemed to bear directly upon the primary issues.

This concentration upon international political developments has seemed justified not only in terms of the comparative unity of the subject but also because these developments have generally received less attention in studies on these countries than have internal problems, constitutional relations and economic trends. Moreover, it is believed that issues of international security have had a more significant impact on individual Dominions and on the evolution of the British Commonwealth than has customarily been recognized.

Each of the five countries whose policies form the basis for this study has distinctive external problems and characteristic features of life which mould its reactions to international developments. Canada's outlook is inevitably affected by its common boundary with a powerful neighbour. Australia is too close to the mainland of Asia not to be intimately concerned with the politics of the Far East. New Zealand's isolation coupled with the closeness of traditional ties with Great Britain have kept it in the past from being as conscious of regional influences as Australia and concentrated rather on retaining the British connection. South Africa, the only home of European peoples in its continent, has faced in an acute form the problems of race and colour within and without its own boundaries. The proximity of the Irish Free State to Great Britain has meant its security from all except that country. Its concentration has been upon ending the partition of the island between itself and Ulster, the majority of whose people have been unwilling to forego the intimate relationship with Great Britain which is no longer maintained in the south.

Not only strategic position but local environment and demography have shaped the characteristic life of these countries. Canada, larger in area than the United States, has had to face problems of geography and racial divisions in developing towards nationhood. Its five great regions stretching from ocean to ocean have been tied together by the bonds of transportation. The efforts to devise policies which would command the allegiance of both its English- and French-speaking groups, of which the latter form one-third of its eleven and a half million people, have taxed the ingenuity of its statesmen.

Australia, slightly smaller than Canada, is a continent almost equal in extent to the United States. The few scattered ports of its long coast line have become huge cities containing one-half of its seven million people. Like New Zealand, its population is almost wholly British in origin but unlike the latter it was drawn largely from the dissatisfied or disadvantaged groups of the British Isles, including many of those who were driven from Ireland by economic want in the nineteenth century. In contrast, New Zealand's people have sprung from the planned middle-class emigration of the 1840's to found an "England" in the south Pacific. Their long, narrow islands, with mountains stretching almost their length separating the fertile lands of east and west, and with an unusual extent of sea-coast, have fostered external rather than internal trade. The emphasis on pastoral and agricultural occupations of its million and a half people encouraged a type of direct democracy which early resulted in advanced social legislation and a jealous safeguarding from competition of standards of living through state action. In comparison with Canada which was backward among industrialized countries in developing a strong labour movement, New Zealand and Australia reflected in their social programmes the pressures of labour organized both for economic and political action.

South Africa, which acquired its unity and Dominion status in 1910, has an area five times that of Great Britain. Within it, the native population of the Union, itself an immigrant group from the north, outnumbers the million and a quarter whites by six to one. They in turn are subdivided between British and Afrikaans, of which the latter form the majority, and have provided the political leaders of the Union since its inception.

The Irish Free State, or Eire (Ireland) as it has been known since 1936, is itself a mother country which has sent as many of its people beyond the seas to the United States, Australia, and Canada as have stayed at home. The three million who form its present-day population are predominately Catholic in belief and homogeneous in race, largely dependent on external trade with Great Britain yet increasingly committed to planned programmes to provide immediate employment.

Such distinctive characteristics and problems give rise inevitably to separate national reactions. Yet despite these differences whose reality has been reflected continuously in policy, there have also been similarities in position and outlook, particularly of Canada, Australia, New Zealand, and South Africa. The Irish Free State was always an anomaly within the grouping whose identification with the others between 1922 and 1936 was a matter of political necessity rather than of desire. But the other four have common experiences, influences, and aims. These come not only out of their growth from dependence to independence but also from problems common to communities whose populations are small in comparison with the area and resources which they develop. It is these common features of their positions and problems which provide the justification for their treatment as a group in the period in which they, in company with many other countries, participated in the first great attempt to answer the problem of security through international action.

*　　*　　*　　*

Though the basic material for this study has been drawn from published sources, the work as a whole owes much to the knowledge and insight of many people who were directly concerned with the events which it considers. Grateful thanks are extended to those delegates to the League of Nations, diplomatic representatives, members of the League Secretariat and International Labour Organization, and of government departments and offices in Ottawa, London, Dublin, Washington, and New York, who in the course of the past ten years so generously shared their experiences with the author. It was also most helpful to be able to make use of the private papers of Sir Robert Borden, the Hon. C. J. Doherty, and Mr. Newton W. Rowell through the kindness of Mr. Henry Borden, Mrs. Wingate, and Mrs. Rowell. In checking newspaper material, the files of the Royal Institute of International Affairs, London, and of the League of Nations Library, Geneva, were particularly useful.

During the years of collecting material, the author was generously aided by grants from the Bureau of International Research, Harvard University-Radcliffe College, and the Canadian Institute of International Affairs and in particular by a travelling fellowship from the Royal Society of Canada which made possible a year's study abroad in 1937-1938. Some passages in this book have already appeared in a chapter entitled "The Dominions and World Security," in *The Quest for Political Unity in World History*, edited for the American Historical Association by Stanley Pargellis (Washington, 1944), and in two articles, "Canada and Sanctions in the Italo-Ethiopian Conflict" and "Some Aspects of Canadian Foreign Policy after Versailles," printed in the *Annual Report* of the Canadian Historical Association, 1940 and 1943. Permission has been kindly given to reprint this material.

Special appreciation is extended to the teachers, colleagues, and friends who have given so unstintingly of their time and support during the years in which this study was under preparation. Professor W. Y. Elliott of Harvard University helped the work to take form. Miss Louise W. Holborn suggested the subject and has watched it develop through all its stages. Miss Claire Mali has been indefatigable in checking references. Dr. Lawrence Burpee, Professor George deT. Glazebrook, Professor Hajo Holborn, and Dr. Felix Gilbert gave much useful advice while the manuscript was in progress and also read the finished work as did Dr. C. C. Lingard, and Mr. P. E. Morison of the Australian News and Information Bureau. All this is acknowledged with gratitude not only for what it has meant in connection with the present work but also for the tangible evidence it provided of the reality of the community of scholars.

G. M. C.

Northampton, Massachusetts.
Autumn, 1946.

Contents

INTRODUCTION

MORE than other small states, Canada, Australia, New Zealand, and South Africa have considered security in terms of world security. Their global distribution has laid them open to the impact of events in North America, Africa, or Asia. Their need of outside markets for their raw materials, agricultural and dairy products, or specialized manufactures, has made them dependent upon the free flow of international trade. Their intimate association with a great power of world-wide interests and commitments had made them susceptible to the currents of world history. Each has distinctive internal problems and strategic concerns which limit its sphere of action. But the common features of their position and the imperatives of growth have created in all the overseas Dominions a certain unity of international outlook. This outlook has been reflected in their security policies which have moulded the character of the British Commonwealth of Nations and helped to shape the growth of international organization.

The characteristic external policies of the Dominions developed empirically in the period preceding 1914, a period characterized by the relative security of the *pax Britannica*, based on sea power and financial strength. This security made it possible for the Dominions to concentrate almost exclusively upon their internal development, to which external policies could generally be subsidiary. Unprecedented economic expansion provided markets for the primary products of the Dominions and the wealth needed to support advanced programmes of social legislation in Australia and New Zealand, the vast railway lines which bound the Canadian provinces together, and machinery which could tap South Africa's underground resources. Side by side with large-scale construction work went programmes of immigration and protective tariffs which formed the framework for the building of distinctive social and economic structures. Political programmes were in general the expression of these social and economic aims. There was little outside check upon them for, in a setting of general peace and British predominance, the Dominions were allowed to broaden the interpretation of responsible government to an accepted autonomy in internal affairs. This autonomy was extended also to certain restricted external relations such as those of Canada with the United States. General harmony between the limited interests of the Dominions, which were firmly rooted in their local situations and the world-wide commitments of Great

xvi INTRODUCTION

Britain, was secured within the flexible framework of an extra-constitutional body, the Imperial Conference.

Before 1914, the Dominions accepted Great Britain's exclusive control of imperial foreign relations as a concomitant to the maintenance of security. Dominion claims to influence foreign policy were infrequent and dictated only by local strategic issues such as German expansion in the south Pacific, which was vigorously but unsuccessfully opposed by Australia and New Zealand in imperial discussions. On the other hand, the Dominions exhibited relatively little feeling of responsibility for the empire. No contributions to imperial defence were customarily made by any Dominion nor were they asked for until the threat of general war became obvious. Moreover, in the isolated and local wars of the nineteenth century, the Dominions established the precedent that the extent and character of their participation should be determined by themselves, though they accepted the obligation to support Great Britain in any major conflict.

When serious danger threatened the security of the sea lanes which bound the empire together, it came from Europe, a fact of considerable importance for future empire relationships. True, the menace of the German colonies in the Pacific underscored the value of an Australian navy which came into existence in 1909 for the specifically reserved purpose of defending Australian waters. New Zealand, twelve hundred miles further to the south-east, made its contribution to British naval strength through the gift of a battleship. Canada's naval programme fell between the two approaches of a direct contribution and a separate navy and achieved neither. No Dominion felt the pressure of direct and overwhelming danger to itself except in the dim possibility of British defeat.

Yet the Dominion contribution in the war of 1914-1918 was of almost decisive importance. The Dominions put more men in the field and suffered heavier losses than any but the major Powers. The Canadian Army, which represented the military effort of eight million people, lost more men than did the American Army. Naval forces were developed; heavy contributions were made to the Royal Flying Corps; and Canada, in particular, became a great base for the production of supplies. The invitations to Dominion statesmen to share in the direction of the war, from 1916 on, through participation in the Imperial War Cabinet, were a well-earned recognition of the importance of the material aid of their countries.

It is a truism that the war brought the Dominions to a new stage of self-consciousness and self-confidence. But they suffered heavily in men and public debt and above all in the bitter wartime conscription

controversies within South Africa, Australia, and Canada which threatened to break their thinly woven unity. The voluntarily accepted
strain on the resources of the Dominions had proved that except in their
delicate social structures, the foundations were firmly laid. War needs
stimulated vast superstructures of production, however, which imposed
a heavy economic burden, and war losses complicated the effort to carry
this burden. Above all else, the Dominions desired a return to normalcy
after the war that they might have time to restore desired conditions of
living, continue with their social aims, and re-establish the lines of trade
which supported the ambitious programmes of their still scattered and
somewhat undeveloped communities.

The pervading question after 1918 was: how could the security of
the period before 1914 be regained? Was it by avoiding responsibilities or by assuming them? If by assuming them, within what type
of organization should it be—in the British Empire, now being transformed into a British Commonwealth of Nations, or in the new international organization, the League of Nations? Could either one or a
combination of these offer the re-establishment of world security and a
framework within which the Dominions could continue their normal
lines of development?

These were the questions which animated the policies advocated
or attempted by individual Dominions in their search for security
between 1919 and 1939. In part these policies were moulded by local
situations and long-established aims; in part by traditional loyalties.
New idealism and new hopes helped to modify or direct them. Fear of
involvement in another war was still more influential. The impact of
events acted as a slow but powerful educative force whose ultimate
effect cannot yet be gauged.

In the inter-war period, the distinctive external problems and aims
of Canada, Australia, New Zealand, and South Africa became more
obvious. So, too, did the differences in interpretation of interest and
the means to secure it which political parties reflected in their programmes. In the forcing house of international tension the interaction
of racial and cultural background, of ideals, and of geographical environment developed external policies characteristic of major groups in each
Dominion. Only rarely were these policies able to command the
allegiance of a whole Dominion. Nor did the apparently similar ideological bases of parties carrying the same name in different Dominions
result in similar views. This was true even in Australia and New
Zealand, the most isolated strategically, the most British in race and
tradition among the Dominions. Where the more conservative parties
in Australia were to be dubious of the potentialities of the League

as a means of security and were to use the British connection to restrain Great Britain from policies dangerous (in their view) to the Empire lifeline and to the peace of the south-west Pacific, the comparable groups in New Zealand were to maintain an attitude of support for Great Britain almost regardless of the issue. The Labour Parties in the two countries were to differ as sharply. In the thirties, parliamentary Labour in Australia wavered between isolationism and opposition to the League as an "imperialist" tool on the one hand and modified Empire solidarity on the other. In New Zealand, the Labour party when it came into power in the middle thirties added to its customary independent attitude towards Great Britain a wholehearted conversion to the principles of collective security which made New Zealand temporarily the most forthright supporter of the League of Nations.

The bi-racial character of both Canada and South Africa made more difficult the evolution of characteristic party policies in those countries. Both French Canadians and Afrikaans were rooted in their own countries alone and suspicious of involvement in British wars. But where the Afrikaans were to support international action as the best defence of a small country, the French Canadians could feel that isolation and lack of commitments were an adequate protection. In South Africa where Afrikaans-speaking leaders were to be always in power, the emphasis was to shift between Smuts' "holism" in which both Commonwealth and League played essential rôles in the development of an international society and Hertzog's more restrained acceptance of the relationship with Great Britain (once it had been placed on what he considered a satisfactory plane of equality) as long as it concerned issues directly affecting his country. In Canada, the French-speaking formed a solid block inside the Liberal party whose leader, Mr. Mackenzie King, was to steer a cautious way between the general French Canadian desire for separation from the affairs of Europe and the view of other Liberals including his own that separateness of policy should be conditioned by directness of interest. His distinction, therefore, somewhat like that of Hertzog, was to be between issues relating only to imperial interests with which he believed Canada was not directly concerned and Great Britain's own security which he saw was vital to Canada as an essential safeguard of the North Atlantic. This modified support of Great Britain was to be coupled with modified support of the League of Nations. There was to be no leader in Canada who supported the League in the way in which Smuts or even Hertzog did. That was to be left to private groups. Nor was any Canadian to preach the doctrine of the Commonwealth with the insight and convincing quality of Smuts. Solidarity with Great Britain was to be the particular programme of the Conservative party in Canada but perhaps less in the spirit of Smuts than of the Dominion party in South Africa. Among those who were to hold aloofness to be a policy in itself, the Canadian Co-operative Commonwealth Federation (C.C.F.) party cannot be overlooked. Particularly in the late thirties it showed signs of veering towards the programme of neutrality long dear to the heart of the Nationalist group in South Africa which acknowledged Malan as their leader after Hertzog became more moderate. This was perhaps the only point on which the two parties met, however, for there was little of concern for labour in Malan's platform while the purpose of the C.C.F. was to unite labour and farmers in support of a moderate socialist programme.

Not without general influence but springing from different roots were the platforms of the parties of the Irish Free State which between 1922 and 1936 was to be in fact as in theory one of the Dominions of the Crown. Never forgetful of its unhappy history, Irish Free State policies within the Commonwealth were to act to accelerate the process of constitutional change so marked in the twenties. Under the leadership of Cosgrave's United Ireland party which was to accept the settlement with Great Britain and act loyally to work it out through constitutional channels, the Irish Free State first undertook an active rôle in the League which it considered a counterbalance to the British connection. De Valera and his *Fianna Fail* party which came into power in 1932 were to intensify the process of decentralization by working for an "internal republic" associated with the Commonwealth only through legislative act. In the League, the position of a small independent state was to be assumed until such time as the failure of collective security became apparent. Thereafter Eire's geographical position was to afford it relative security despite its refusal of external responsibilities.

These attitudes were to exist almost unchanged throughout the period of acknowledged Dominion status of the Irish Free State. They came from the past and if anything were to be intensified by current developments. But in the overseas Dominions attitudes were to be slower in evolving. Policies were to become crystallized in some cases only with growing insecurity in the thirties.

Yet behind the variety of responses with which different groups in the individual Dominions were to react to international developments in the inter-war period was one common aim, to avoid involvement in another war. This was the motive which led some to put their faith in the League, first as an international stabilizer and later as the rallying point for collective security. Equally it led others to attempt to weaken the commitments of the Covenant lest they prove too serious a limitation on freedom of action in given situations. Some sought their end by supporting the British connection as their best hope of warning off potential aggressors. Others felt it could best be achieved by freedom from British commitments lest they be involved thereby in conflicts which did not touch their immediate interests. Support of complete isolation was to be rare except under the shadow of impending war, but there was general desire to avoid taking action in a situation which did not seem to be of direct concern. Only gradually and partially was it learned that in an interdependent world, any international situation may have a direct influence on any country; that the direct concern for world security of every overseas Dominion demanded in turn positive policies in all matters affecting world security.

At the end of the first world war, the overseas Dominions assumed for the first time the international status and responsibilities of separate states. Their leaders became full participants in the first broadly collective effort to shape the future by international machinery. More than did their people as yet, Dominion leaders sensed and reacted to the great forces of the time, nationalism and internationalism. Nationalism spurred their demands for separate status at the Peace Conference and animated their defence of characteristic programmes and purposes. But internationalism appealed both to idealism and to interests. They were starting the long search, whose end is not yet within sight, for a synthesis between nationalism and internationalism which would make possible the development of the potentialities of individual countries within the context of world security.

The Commonwealth and International Security

CHAPTER I
SHAPING THE LEAGUE OF NATIONS

The Covenant and the First Assembly

THE experience of the first world war in a century made urgent the task of re-establishing peace on a foundation capable of withstanding the pressures of a dynamic, industrial society. Should this be done by reinforcing the strategic and economic position of the Allies, thereby making their superiority overwhelming in the balance of power? Or should the attempt be made to establish conditions which would be lasting because they were based on principles whose justice was commonly accepted? Between these two approaches, the members of the Paris Peace Conference trod a wavering path. The Treaty of Versailles, their major accomplishment, embodied some provisions clearly designed to uphold the superior position of the victor nations. But it also included the Covenant of the League of Nations.

The conception that international organization could be the means through which nations would adjust their differences without recourse to war was not new. After the Napoleonic Wars, a league of Great Powers had been organized though it soon became an instrument of repression and collapsed. But during Word War I far broader plans had been evolved embodying the concept of a League democratic in character, open to all self-governing countries, and designed to promote international co-operation and achieve international peace and security. These plans as modified by the clash of opinion at Paris took shape in the League of Nations.

The Covenant which provided the form of the League and the principles under which it should act was a composite document reflecting the different approaches to peace of those who shaped it. The British were chiefly interested in providing means whereby nations would be brought together regularly for consultation on issues of international concern. President Wilson believed that peace must be guaranteed and that the French demands for security might be met thereby. The Italians and Japanese wished international endorsement of what they considered principles of social justice such as access to raw materials and acceptance of racial equality. Out of the interaction of these and other views came the constitution of the League which was to be the chief new element in the international situation.

Through the League of Nations, nations were to be brought together at regular intervals for informed discussion of common problems. Each of these nations pledged itself to respect the territorial integrity and political independence of all other member states. If disputes arose, each agreed to submit them to arbitration or conciliation procedures. If aggression should occur in violation of the pledges assumed under the Covenant, each member was to undertake economic action against the guilty party. If the Council so recommended, military measures might also be required. Thus the Covenant combined two types of restraint against breaking the peace: individual pledges to adhere to fixed standards of conduct, and mutual guarantees of action against an aggressor. At the same time, the Covenant also embodied the goal of general disarmament which might be expected to relieve international tensions. It introduced the principle of trusteeship for dependent territories removed from the control of former enemy countries. Even more significant seemed the article providing for reconsideration of situations known to threaten peace. If these provisions could be made effective, and generally satisfactory, there might be no need to fear recourse to more stringent measures for preserving peace.

Those who believed most ardently in the potentialities of the League of Nations were willing to sacrifice much at the Paris Peace Conference to secure its acceptance. Their hope was that it would gradually be able to overcome the distrust characteristic of the pre-war struggle for power and to modify the results of earlier nationalistic aggrandizement. But there were others, notably the French, who were sceptical of its value. They questioned its potential power and were fearful lest it induce a false sense of security which would undercut reliance on older and better established means of national self-preservation. Not the French alone favoured accepting the Covenant only if they were able to establish prior conditions of security through territorial acquisitions and reservations on traditional policies.

Throughout the Paris Peace Conference, there was bargaining over the provisions of the Treaty of Versailles and compromises within the Covenant itself, seeking a mean between national and international interests. In the end, no one was completely satisfied. But at least a new conception of the purposes of international action had been introduced which forced a reconsideration of characteristic policies and provided a new standard of reference for them. New machinery had been set up through which both great and small powers would be able to express their opinions and have some influence on the course of international action. A means to shape the future had been established. Its effect was to be dependent on the way in which it would be used.

A. *The Dominions and the Covenant*

In the plans, discussions, and clash of ideas out of which the Covenant developed, Dominion statesmen had a larger part than the representatives of other small states. In London, they had a share in British discussions on the terms of peace and on future international organization both in the Imperial War Cabinet, through which from 1916 on they had assumed a part in moulding the strategy of the war, and in the Imperial Conference of 1918. At Paris, where the Imperial War Cabinet functioned as the British Empire Delegation, Dominion representatives played a dual rôle as members of that group and as spokesmen for their own countries. At times, Dominion leaders spoke for the British Empire Delegation and General Smuts served as its representative on the Commission which drafted the Covenant of the League of Nations. At no time, however, did they forget the interests and desires of their own countries. Under the lead of Sir Robert Borden, Prime Minister of Canada, they had insisted on obtaining separate representation and voting power at the Paris Peace Conference for the individual Dominions, thereby establishing a useful precedent for separate membership in the League of Nations. They thus found themselves in the favourable position which they were to retain in the inter-war period of being able to express their points of view directly in the international gathering, as far as that was open to the representatives of any small state, and at the same time to exert direct influence upon one of the major powers, Great Britain.

During the discussions on international organization which preceded the end of the war, Dominion representatives already proved effective. Under the leadership of Mr. Massey of New Zealand, they were responsible for reinserting in the British draft for the Covenant the provision for general disarmament which had been omitted because of Foreign Office opposition.[1] General Smuts' *The League of Nations: A Practical Suggestion* was perhaps most significant in its timing for it appeared at a moment when British statesmen were wavering in their attitude towards an international organization and with its challenging picture of current trends clinched their support.[2] Though President Wilson's drafts modified by British plans formed the basis for the Covenant, Smuts' proposals introduced the conception of trusteeship, though he envisaged the mandate principle as applying not to colonies but to the states carved out by the new territorial settlement over which according to his suggestion the League would have had authority as the residual legatee of the peace treaties.

Subsequently at the Paris Peace Conference, Smuts adopted a more nationalistic emphasis and joined the Australian and New Zealand representatives in unsuccessfully opposing the extension of the mandate principle to the territories adjacent to their respective countries which they had seized from Germany in the course of the war. It was as an alternative to annexation that he evolved the "C" type of mandate in which territories were governed as integral parts of the mandatory power with the same tariff and immigration restrictions.[3]   Mr. Hughes, the Australian Prime Minister, was the moving spirit of the Conference in opposition to the "racial equality" clauses proposed by the Japanese which he feared might challenge the "White Australia" principle. The Canadians, with no territorial claims to support, sought rather to clarify the meaning of the clauses of the Covenant which were concerned with the maintenance of peace, to introduce a distinction between the obligations assumed by small and great powers, and to prevent the Covenant from stratifying existing territorial arrangements.

Though the efforts of Dominion representatives met with varying success, the views they maintained on the issue of security were to prove generally characteristic of thinking in their home countries. In their emphasis on disarmament, Dominion statesmen were making the first among many attempts to reduce the menace of competitive building of armament. It was part of the emphasis on security *against* war which marked so many of their policies. So, too, in a measure was the Canadian opposition to universal commitments though here the motive was even more to avoid too widespread responsibilities. Even more characteristic was the insistence of all the Dominions on safeguarding rights of domestic jurisdiction, particularly over trade and immigration. Less justifiable was the attempt by Australia, New Zealand, and South Africa to annex the near-by territories which they had wrested from Germany during the war. Particularly in the way in which it was handled, this claim created ill feeling within the Peace Conference and complicated the efforts to develop an inclusive international organization.

President Wilson agreed with Allied leaders that Germany should be stripped of its colonies but he was equally determined that they should be placed under mandate. Originally his thought was that they "should be declared the common property of the League of Nations and administered by small nations,"[4] but this ran counter to claims based on conquest and possession and was soon seen to be impractical. In fact, though the British Prime Minister, Lloyd George, was not particularly eager to extend the Empire, Australia, New Zealand, and South Africa claimed the right to annex New Guinea, Samoa, and Southwest Africa respectively as early as the spring of 1917.[5] The Imperial War Cabinet accepted the mandatory principle in general in December, 1918, but felt that these territories should be excluded from its effect on the ground that they were essential to the security of the respective Dominions. Hughes particularly emphasized that his demand for New Guinea was put forward in "the interests of Australian security and not in the interests of the British Empire."[6] This distinction was presented to Wilson on his visit to London that month, at which time he was also made aware of the promises to Japan of the German islands north of the equator.

To neither point was Wilson willing to accede and the struggle was carried over to Peace Conference sessions where Hughes' intransigeance delighted Clemenceau, who called him "a cannibal,"[7] exasperated Wilson, who demanded at one point whether the Dominion premiers were presenting the Conference with "an ultimatum"[8] (to which Hughes, whose hearing apparatus had temporarily ceased functioning, agreed), and paved the way for similar Japanese demands. At one moment only the British appeared willing to hold territories under mandate as the French, who feared limitation on their power to raise native troops, joined in the attack. A combination of pressure and compromise was to be necessary to save the principle of trusteeship.

Borden, who feared that large-scale acquisitions of territory to the Empire might lead to Anglo-American friction, had somewhat reluctantly acquiesced in the demands of the other three Dominions if they were necessary for future imperial security.[9] But as the tension between Wilson and Hughes grew high, Borden took on the rôle of peacemaker, in which he was joined by Lloyd George and ultimately by all the Dominion representatives except Hughes. Compromise was secured on the basis of Smuts' proposal of a "C" type of mandate which was to be governed according to the laws of the mandatory state. By placing the territories under dispute in this category, and also the islands desired by Japan, Wilson's principle was upheld while at the same time the territories virtually became part of the mandatory states. Moreover, this also produced a practical compromise on the other issue dividing Wilson and the three Dominion premiers; his insistence that the mandate principle should be accepted before the territories were actually apportioned. Though again in form Wilson's point was upheld, the fact that "C" mandates were so designated in part because of their contiguity to the mandatory power answered indirectly the claims of these Dominions to maintain control of the territories their troops had captured.

In this early conflict between principle and national security, some at least of the Dominion premiers showed themselves more concerned with the latter than the former. This was hardly a surprising result of a long period of anxiety lest these territories be used as jumping-off places for attack against their countries, and of the first flush of nationalistic fervour over success in conquering them, but it was an unfortunate example to other more dangerously placed countries. That the Canadians were more restrained was partly because there was no former German territory close to Canada. However, Borden's strongest reason for seeking compromise was to avoid friction with American representatives.

In a second bitterly contested issue—the Japanese request that the Covenant should endorse the principle of racial equality—Hughes scored practically singlehanded a victory whose implications were no less unfortunate than had been his efforts in support of annexation. The Japanese motive was largely prestige though partly to secure a bargaining point in regard to their claims to Shantung. The acceptance of an innocuous resolution or phrase on the subject which could not possibly have had any legal effect on immigration regulations would have met the situation, as Colonel House and most British and American delegates realized. But Hughes was adamant in regard to any proposal touching this subject and threatened to start a public agitation in the Dominions and the United States if it were considered. This time Borden was unsuccessful in securing a compromise, though he tried with others to find a wording which Hughes would accept.[10] Smuts told the Japanese delegate, "Your position is incontestable," but added, "if you persist in your motion, for which I have much sympathy, and if Hughes of Australia opposes it, as he undoubtedly will, I shall have to fall in line and vote with the Dominions, like a 'good Indian.'"[11] The other British representatives found themselves in the same dilemma. Wilson, who favoured accepting some moderate phrasing, was warned by House against doing so lest Hughes carry out his threat. The Japanese brought up their motion in Committee and, on demanding a vote, secured a majority in favour with none openly opposed. But British and American representatives abstained from voting and the President interpreted this to mean that unanimity had not been secured and therefore that the motion had not passed. In this way Hughes secured his end though at the expense of injuring Japanese feelings and of strengthening their position in the Shantung question.

The opposition to the racial equality clause was far more the work of a single person, Hughes, than had been the efforts to annex former German territories. But while in the latter issue collective pressure could be brought to bear, the greatest caution had to be exercised in a matter so potentially explosive as the race question and immigration, to prevent public prejudice from being aroused. This was Hughes' trump card, and he made effective, if dangerous, use of it.

Though alone in the extremes to which he went over the Japanese request, Hughes' position in as far as it aimed to protect rights of domestic jurisdiction was characteristic of both Dominion and American thinking. The Canadian Privy Council cabled Sir Robert Borden during the Peace Conference asking that all signatories to the Covenant should clearly recognize that: "(1) The right of each nation to regulate and control the character of its own population by restriction of immigration is maintained unimpaired, and that such control is recognized as a matter of purely domestic concern and not one in which the League of Nations is concerned; (2) This Covenant does not in any way interfere with the fiscal freedom of Canada nor with the control or regulation of its own tariffs."[12] The American Senate was to be no less outspoken in its reactions.

In the immediate situation, both the emphasis on annexation and the opposition to mentioning racial equality helped to weaken the moral basis of the discussions on the Covenant. They showed the disposition to put territorial expansion in the interest of national security, and safeguarding of domestic jurisdiction higher than the establishment of effective international organization. Implicit in both contentions was the desire to make individual decisions in matters of direct concern, rather than to submit to collective judgment. Colonel Bonsal linked the Australian stand on the racial equality clause with an amendment to Article V, introduced by Wilson, which specifically noted that Council and Assembly decisions required the agreement of all members represented at the meeting unless express provisions provided otherwise.[13] This kind of *liberum veto* was generally endorsed by Dominion representatives.

Not only was there reluctance to countenance without consent positive action through which a country's freedom of action might be affected but also, at least on the part of the Canadians, concern lest the guarantees of the Covenant place too heavy demands on individual countries. The most significant of Canadian comments on the draft of the Covenant, and one which time was to prove had the support of all major groups in the country, sought the deletion or substantial amendment of Article 10 guaranteeing the territorial integrity and political independence of members of the League.   In the opinion of the Canadian Prime Minister, Sir Robert Borden, the article involved accepting the justice of and guaranteeing "all existing territorial delimitations."[14] Whether right or not in his interpretation of its scope,[15] there could be little doubt of the wisdom of his comment that there "may be national aspirations to which the provisions of the peace treaty will not do justice and which cannot be permanently repressed," a fact which he believed made the guarantee too far-reaching.   Mr. Doherty, the Canadian Minister of Justice, went still further in attacking the obligation of Article 10 "both generally, and from the point of view of countries in the condition and stage of development of Canada in particular."[16] In general he opposed it as embodying an "absolute obligation of mutual protection of existing possessions," which implied, he maintained, a complete stabilization of the *status quo* without reference to the justice of particular titles of possession.   Pointing out that territorial disputes were the most common cause of war, Doherty felt that the inflexibility of the guarantee would be inclined to lead to wars rather than to prevent them.   If, however, such a guarantee were to be made, Doherty proposed that it should be by the Great Powers and specifically limited to the territorial settlement of the Peace Treaties.   In any case, he opposed placing the obligation on Canada, partly because it had had no responsibility in arranging the territorial settlement, partly because it was a nation "still in process of formation," partly because it imposed a mutual guarantee in which he believed the inequality between the risks run and the burdens imposed worked greatly to the detriment of Canada.

Implicit in the Canadian contentions was the belief, which may well be questioned, that guarantees are dangerous because they freeze the *status quo*.   The emphasis on differentiation of function was a not unnatural attempt to reproduce in the League a distinction present in the British Commonwealth relation.   Comments on other articles endorsed the fact that it was a "Covenant of peace and not of war," with "discussion, publicity, and mediation" the "best means of reducing to a minimum" the possibility of the outbreak of war.[17]   Noting the "gap in the Covenant" which permitted war under certain circumstances, Borden considered it might be closed by additional safeguards including the control of the results of war through a form of nonrecognition by withholding permission to legalize treaties of peace through League registration until they had been approved by the Council.   He did not deny the possibility that force might have to be exercised through the League nor believe that in all cases war could be prevented, but his emphasis was upon avoiding its outbreak.

Less comprehensive but no less characteristic were Hughes' comments[18] opposing an automatic commitment to take forcible action such as he assumed Article 16 implied in case a state resorted to war, and criticizing such "expressions and phrases" in the Covenant as suggested that the League might become a super-state. He proposed that Article 16 should include an "affirmation of the *right*" rather than the duty to "make war against a covenant-breaking State," thereby leaving the decision to be made in the light of existing circumstances. As to the form of the League, he considered it should be a "standing international Conference" whose recommendations would be binding only as individual countries agreed to accept them.

The general emphasis of the comments and action of Dominion leaders at the Peace Conference was upon preserving long-cherished rights of individual decision. Over and beyond this stood their conception of a League through which wars might be prevented by the provision of means for peaceful settlement of disputes. Mediation and conciliation rather than coercion had their support. Canadian leaders in particular opposed League guarantees of rigid territorial arrangements lest they bottle up resentment to the point where the explosion of war became inevitable.

As Borden said, it was a "League of peace and not of war" which they desired. The meaning of this they interpreted out of their own experience as involving opportunities for growth, particularly for countries in the process of development; suggestions as to advisable policies rather than fixed commitments; emphasis on conciliation rather than force. In the end, they probably hoped for an international organization which would duplicate the purpose of the pre-war British Empire as far as the Dominions themselves had been concerned. Thus they hoped that it would provide general security while asking of them only limited and occasional aid; that it would leave them free to pursue their social and economic policies so that their problems of growth could be worked out in a self-determined framework; that in return for general co-operation, their parliaments should retain the ultimate decision on the degree of participation in a given situation.

Dominion points of view received more sympathetic response from the British delegation than from either the American or the French. The claims of the Dominions for representation at the Peace Conference and for separate membership in the League of Nations and the International Labour Organization would have had slight chance of acceptance, despite their war record, without British support.[19] The Australian, New Zealand, and South African demands to control their adjacent territories taken from Germany received Lloyd George's blessing, except that he insisted with Wilson that the lands must be held as mandates. On the racial equality issue, the Commonwealth stood together, however reluctantly. On the other hand, while Lord Robert Cecil, the leading advocate of the League on the British delegation, agreed with the Canadian view of Article 10,[20] there was no formal British opposition to the guarantee. Though Doherty was to maintain that the Canadians came "within an ace of succeeding" in securing its elimination at the Peace Conference,[21] President Wilson considered Article 10 to be the heart of the Covenant and a necessary satisfaction of French claims for security. The French, themselves, looked on it as little enough indication that the League was to be one means of enforcing peace.

Despite the fact that the Covenant did not provide their ideal of a League, membership meant the fulfilment of one major aim of Dominion leaders; international recognition of the self-governing status of their countries. The full effect of the recognition was somewhat marred by the inclusion in League membership of India which was still obviously not fully self-governing and which acquired membership only through its signature of the Treaty of Versailles. On this and other counts, more than American Senators were sceptical about the "six British votes." From the point of view of the Dominion leaders, however, League membership was the natural outcome of the responsibilities their countries had assumed during the war, and, in broader perspective, of the long evolution towards full handling of their own affairs. They were prepared to let future action prove the validity of their demands for recognition.

When League membership was considered in Dominion parliaments, there was less unanimity of opinion regarding its value. Comparatively little had been done to familiarize their people with its purposes and form and even in Canada, which had felt the effects of the discussions in the United States on a League to Enforce Peace and where there had been more general consideration of the issues involved than in any other Dominion, there was little accurate knowledge and less thought through conviction on its behalf.[22] Canadian Liberals feared it might saddle their country with new international responsibilities, implicate it in European politics, and override the ultimate authority of the Canadian Parliament.[23] South African Nationalists voiced suspicions of it as a mere alliance of Great Powers and feared that it might embroil them in European quarrels though they appreciated its endorsement of the rights of small nations.[24] Some New Zealanders opposed holding mandates lest British unity should be weakened thereby. Australians appeared less concerned with League membership as such than with the disposition of German territories, some speakers maintaining that they only extended Australian responsibilities, others that control through mandates was an unfortunate limitation, and still others that all former German territories should have been internationalized so that Japan would not have extended its control to the equator.[25]

To these varied comments and objections, there were two general answers reiterated over and over again in Dominion Parliaments by those who had been at the Peace Conference: membership is a necessary symbol of status, and whatever its disadvantages, they are far outweighed by its advantages. Canadian Conservatives upheld the value of "Britannic equality." Perforce they found themselves defending the obligations of Article 10 (since the memoranda in which they had opposed it at the Peace Conference were still secret), though maintaining that Canada would have the ultimate decision regarding the extent of its action in case the Council should find an unjust aggression had occurred. Smuts placed an even stronger emphasis on prestige than did the Canadians and on the necessity of sharing in international affairs in the future.[26] Hughes maintained that League membership was necessary in order to acquire control of mandated territories and that only through their control could the "White Australia" principle be maintained.[27] Massey appealed for support of the newly-born international organization but not to the extent of feeling it could act as a substitute for the protection of the British Navy.[28]

The issue of the interconnection of British Commonwealth and League of Nations relations gave rise to very differently motivated questions in the New Zealand and South African Parliaments. Why should not the League be a substitute for the British connection? asked South African separatists. Is there not danger that the League will weaken the British connection? asked New Zealand imperialists. We need both, replied their leaders, the League for general co-operation but the Commonwealth for more immediate interests and security. The Dominions and Britain form "an inner league," said Smuts, which provides an essential core to the international League of Nations.

Broadly the answer was satisfying. There were obvious mutual advantages in Commonwealth membership in the League of Nations. The Commonwealth had been the most successful and the most universal league for mutual security yet developed. Yet the strain placed by the war on the national unity of Canada, Australia, and South Africa pointed to the urgency of finding some means whereby the danger of future British wars might be lessened. League membership by attempting "to anchor foreign policy to justice"[29] might undercut Dominion suspicions of "British imperialism" and make it easier to secure co-

ordinated policies. Moreover, Geneva provided a centre for Commonwealth consultations at which British and Dominion statesmen could
meet on terms of equality and, unlike London, without arousing fears
of Empire centralization or domination by Great Britain.[30]   These were
positive advantages which, if the League had developed as its pro-
tagonists hoped, might have been even more fruitful than they proved
in practice.

Yet it is also clear that these features of the new situation appeared
most advantageous to those parts of the Commonwealth which had
least fear of immediate danger, Canada and South Africa.   Their desire
for an outside source of reference, a neutral place for discussions, and a
restraint upon British policy was reinforced by the differences in
attitude towards the British connection between the major racial groups
on which their countries were built, but it had a basic foundation in their
feeling of security.   In contrast, Australia and New Zealand, two
comparatively small white communities not far from the great masses
of Oriental peoples, tended to feel their isolation as a danger rather
than a blessing.   "We are only 5,000,000 people," said Hughes to the
Australian Parliament, "and we arrogate the right to say to the whole
world, 'You cannot come in here without our consent.'"[31]   Later he
wrote, "Australia, as a portion of the Empire, was powerful enough to
induce the Conference to support its national policy ('White Australia').
Australia outside the Empire would, although the nation were armed
to the teeth and prepared to . . . fight to the last ditch for what it
believed essential to its national existence, have failed to turn the
Conference from what was only too obviously its settled purpose."[32]
Here the prime concern was to maintain British support of policies
considered vital to the national life and in time of need, British aid in
defence.   No wonder that at times League membership assumed
different meanings to different Dominions nor that, particularly in
times of crisis, their policies were sharply to diverge.   "Security *from*
war" was a platform on which all the Dominions could meet, but
geographical position was to lead to different interpretations of its
meaning in specific cases.

In the more immediate situation, two issues were raised by the
coincidence of Commonwealth and League membership; whether the
"British Empire" member on the Council of the League of Nations
represented the whole Empire or only Great Britain; and the objection
to "six British votes" raised by the majority group of the Republican
senators in the United States and used by them as the basis for the
Lenroot reservation to the Treaty of Versailles, which attempted to
exclude the Dominions from distinctive representation in the League.

The first was a technical matter which caused little concern except to legalists. The second aroused indignation among the Dominions, particularly in Canada, and from the side of the United States represented a feeling which aided in securing American rejection of membership in the League of Nations.

The question of selecting the "British Empire" member on the Council was considered early in 1919 by the Committee to consider the position of the Dominion and Indian Governments in the formation of a League of Nations of which Smuts, Doherty, and Cecil were members and whose meetings were held parallel to the sittings of the Imperial War Cabinet in London. According to Doherty, there was general agreement in this Committee that there "must be" participation by Dominion and Indian representatives in the choice of the Council member.[33] No steps were taken, however, to devise means whereby this participation might be made effective and in default of action, the "British Empire" member on the Council became and remained always the nominee of Great Britain alone. This was a natural result both of its position as a Great Power and of the opposition of the Dominions to imperial centralization. But it did not solve the issue for Doherty, who continued to maintain that "quite irrespective of whether we do or do not demand the right to join in the selection of the representative or of whether we do or do not admit the fact, any representative of the British Empire as a whole must necessarily represent all of its parts." As long as Canada remains in the Empire, he declared, "then we are responsible for what *it* does. . . ." The alternatives are either to "fall back to the status of voiceless dependence from which we have so loudly boasted we had emerged" or to move towards separation "if we claim not to be bound by whatever the Empire acting through that representative may do." It was the dilemma of most legalists in confronting the counter claims of union and diversity. Borden had a better answer to the situation when he secured from Wilson, Lloyd George, and Clemenceau, a declaration stating that the Dominions were eligible for membership as non-permanent members of the League Council.[34] Though at the time the motive was recognition of status rather than expectation of seeking office, it was a more logical outgrowth of separate membership in the Assembly than could be any attempt in practice or logic to reunite Commonwealth countries in the Council. Moreover, from another angle, which Rowell and Smuts were quick to recognize, an attempt to have a "British Empire seat" on the Council would have meant committing the Dominions to the world-wide responsibilities of Great Britain for which none of them was prepared.[35]

Dominion participation in the choice and direction of the "British Empire" member of the Council would have meant a unity in Commonwealth policy achieved by a limitation on Great Britain's freedom of action. The American attempts to block the separate representation of the Dominions in the League would have resulted in imposing a far more rigid straitjacket of Commonwealth unity, by denying to the Dominions the League platform for the expression of their separate views.

Though overcome at the Paris Peace Conference, American objections to Dominion membership in the League took form in the Senate debates on the Treaty of Versailles in the Lenroot reservation which was accepted by majority vote of the Senate. This declared that the United States would not be bound "by any election, decision, report, or finding of the Council or Assembly" in which more than one vote was cast by "any member of the League and its self-governing Dominions, colonies, or parts of the Empire in the aggregate or in any dispute between the United States and a member of the League if such member or any self-governing Dominion, colony, Empire, or part of Empire united with it politically has voted." The first provision was a direct attack upon separate membership and voting by the Dominions in the League and as such was resented by outstanding Canadians like Newton W. Rowell, President of the Privy Council in the Unionist Government and acting Secretary of State for External Affairs at the time the Lenroot resolution was under consideration. He accepted the second part of the resolution—that in a dispute between the United States and any part of the British Empire, no other part of the Empire would have a vote—as expressing "what we understand to be the effect of the Treaty as it now stands." But the effect of the resolution as a whole would be to force the Dominions out of distinctive representation in the League. "We fully recognize," he declared, "the right of the United States to lay down the conditions upon which she is willing to ratify the Treaty and enter the League of Nations; but if one of the conditions imposed is that Canada and the other Dominions shall be denied their status and voting rights as members of the League, the United States will recognize that it is equally the right of Canada to oppose the acceptance of such a condition. . . . Canada cannot and will not assent to any impairment of her status or voting rights under the Treaty."[36]

In an argument widely endorsed in the Dominion, Rowell maintained that Canada was entitled to membership in the League and to a vote in the Assembly "(1) because she is a free self-governing nation, one of the nations of the Britannic Commonwealth; (2) because of her proved interest in the cause of Peace and the part she has played in promoting the settlement of international disputes by peaceable means and (3) because of her part in the war and her contribution toward the re-establishment of world peace."[37] He pointed out that no other nation had objected to Dominion membership and that within the United States itself not only Administration followers but the Republican minority on the Committee on Foreign Relations had supported it. From the report of the latter group he cited the comparison between giving League membership to Hedjaz, Panama, Honduras, and Uruguay, each with populations under a million and no share in the war to their credit, and attempting to withhold it from Canada, with its eight and a half million people and its major contributions to the war. On another angle Colonel House was to say later, in words not unlike those used by the Republican minority report: "as for the Empire's six votes, supposing they can be held together on occasions, we could always have brought against them in counter-balance many more from the Pan American Republics."[38] This was obvious, but more important was the other aspect of the situation which House was shrewd enough to gauge: ". . . as time goes on, the Dominions—and especially those with Pacific interests—will be inclined to adopt our policies rather than England's. They are really much closer to us than to England in questions of international policy . . . allowing the Dominions and India the status of independent powers in the League . . . will encourage them to think for themselves, for their own interests."

From the American side, the issue of separate Dominion membership was only one of the objections to participation in the League, though it was one which received fairly wide currency. Lodge maintained that "England has five votes to one vote of any other country," though he also declared that the Dominions would be "far more worthy and more valuable members of a League of Nations than some of the nations which I think will find their way into the body."[39] American feeling about Dominion membership was far from unanimous, as the report of the Republican minority and the attitude of Colonel House and others demonstrated. The far-sighted were aware that fears were groundless not only because the issue of "votes" in the Assembly was unimportant since all action except procedural had to be by unanimous consent, but more particularly because of the independence of attitude of the Dominions. They saw that the provision of a new and international platform for Commonwealth members would intensify this independence. Moreover, as House had recognized, the natural reactions of the Dominions were very similar to those of the United States. It was similar feelings of security and isolation from danger which led Canadians at the Peace Conference to the same reaction against Article 10 as Republican senators were subsequently to voice.

Hughes' attack upon the Japanese "racial equality" clause was inexcusably blatant, but the attitude underlying it was not essentially different from American reactions.[40] More constructively, the emphasis on mediation and judicial processes which marked Dominion comments on the Covenant were American in spirit. It is unfortunate that this similarity of viewpoint should not have been more widely recognized.

From the side of the Dominions and particularly of Canada, American opposition to their separate League membership was irritating and disappointing, but the decision of the United States not to enter the League was a bitter blow. Senator Dandurand, Canada's chief delegate to the meetings of the Assembly in the early years of the League, had opposed ratification by Canada of the Treaty of Versailles until after it was sure that all the principal nations and especially the United States would join the League.[41] But though his suggestion was not heeded, it was with very different feelings that Canada, and in fact all British countries, faced their membership in the League of Nations when they knew the United States would not be among its members. There was much less chance thereafter that the hesitant attitude towards the League of some groups and officials in each of the Commonwealth countries would be transformed into the enthusiastic support needed to make a success of this experiment in international co-operation and mutual support.

B. *The Dominions and the First Assembly*

The consideration of the Covenant had been of international organization in theory: the first meeting of the Assembly was to begin the experience of general international organization in action. The Council had been in session a number of times discussing critical issues of the immediate post-war period. Its comparatively small size and its nucleus of members which had worked together as Allies during the war and were still in constant contact through the Supreme War Council had aided the Council in developing some corporate sense and considerable feeling of its own importance. It was a far more difficult task for the Assembly with its large and varied membership to develop a sense of *esprit de corps*, to evolve a satisfactory system whereby its members could work together, and to carve out a distinctive rôle for itself in international action. In all these respects, developments during its first meeting were to be decisive for its future character and significance.

At eleven o'clock on the morning of November 15, 1920, the Assembly of the League of Nations meeting in the Salle de la Reformation in the heart of Geneva was called to order for the first time in its history.

On a high platform sat the presiding officer with the chief members of the secretariat on either side and behind him; in the lower gallery extending around three sides of the hall were some two hundred journalists, representing the press of many countries, including the United States; at the end sat diplomats and distinguished visitors; in the upper gallery crowded those members of the general public who had been able to push themselves in. On the floor of the hall, the desks of the forty-one delegations were arranged in eleven rows by alphabetical order, "thus avoiding all questions of precedence," as Sir George Foster wrote in his diary.[1] First among them was "Afrique du Sud," with Sir Robert Cecil at the end of the row next to the platform, a position which facilitated his frequent interventions in debate. Next but one came the Australian delegation. In the second row, directly behind the South Africans, sat the Canadian delegation, with the British on their right. Sir James Allen of New Zealand was farther to the rear.

In a group which included some of the most outstanding European figures of the day, the delegations from the Dominions ranked well, comprising in the aggregate the ablest representatives these countries ever sent to an Assembly. None of the Dominion Prime Ministers who had been at the Peace Conference were present but the two most outstanding, Smuts and Borden, had representatives in the respective delegations who reflected very nearly their points of view. Sir Robert Cecil (whose mistrust that Lloyd George's ministry wholeheartedly supported the League had led him to refuse a place in it[2]) had accepted with enthusiasm Smuts' suggestion to serve on the South African delegation to the Assembly and in a very direct sense looked on himself as representing Smuts' personal point of view on the issues which were raised there.[3] Newton W. Rowell, a prominent Canadian Liberal (who had served under Borden in the Unionist Government but withdrew when Arthur Meighen formed a predominantly Conservative Ministry), shared Borden's point of view on the status the latter had won for Canada at the Peace Conference and was looked to by Borden to maintain it at the first meeting of the Assembly.[4] Charles Doherty and Sir George Foster, the other members of the Canadian delegation, had both been at the Peace Conference and the former, though not the latter, had a firm belief in the new international rôle of the Dominions. An experienced English observer believed the Canadians to be "the strongest and best balanced of all the Dominion delegations" and ranked Rowell as "among the eight or ten leading figures" of the Assembly.[5] The breadth of subjects to be considered and lack of restraint by rigid instructions was to make possible the full expression of personal capacities, though the viewpoints expressed during the

Assembly meetings by representatives of the Dominions were generally characteristic of the attitudes of their countries.

On this occasion, though not subsequently, the Dominion delegations had met with the British in London for consideration of the issues likely to be raised at the Assembly meeting and for exchange of information.[6] No attempt had been made to lay down a single line of policy, however, and the Assembly was to be treated to the unexpected spectacle of some open divergences in opinion between the representatives of Dominion countries and of Great Britain.

When the Assembly first met, it had no officers, no committees, no rules of procedure, no accepted plan of work. Like any good constitutional instrument, the Covenant had left unsettled many questions of function and of relationship with the second major organ of the League, the Council. These issues had to be settled before the Assembly could proceed to develop its spheres of action and means of implementing it, and it was in regard to these questions that Dominion representatives, in particular Rowell, began to emerge as significant figures in the Assembly.

The Australian delegation made its special contribution in the formulation of rules of procedure.[7] Doherty objected to the lack of prior notification on motions.[8] Cecil and Allen pressed for publicity for the proceedings of Committees and, though temporarily unsuccessful due to opposition by the Italian, French, and British delegates, it was decided that the minutes of the Committees should be published. In the long run, their proposals that the press[9] and general public should be admitted to Committee meetings became the practice of the Assembly. The most significant preliminary question to be determined, however, was that of the relation between the Assembly and the Council. What Cecil called "a silly controversy" over the respective jurisdictions of these two bodies had led the representatives of some of the major members of the Council to refrain from taking part in the opening debate of the Assembly on the work of the Council, lest they appear to sanction the view that the Council was responsible to the Assembly.[10] The issue of jurisdiction was referred to the First Committee, where Rowell's willingness to take the lead in discussion resulted in his being associated with the French delegate, Viviani, as Rapporteur on the subject.

In the Assembly discussions of the work of the Council, Cecil had opposed applying the analogy of Cabinet and Parliament to the relationship of the Council and Assembly[11] and Rowell had challenged sharply the implication in the statement of the Italian delegate, Tittoni, that the Council was a body "of Elder Statesmen chosen because of their experience and ability" whose members "do not consider themselves as mouthpieces of their Government or their countries but as Magistrates." Rowell believed it would be dangerous to accept the view that countries were not responsible for the declarations of their representatives and he challenged the Council members not only to assume responsibility for their statements but also to back up their own decisions with whatever force was necessary.

Against Tittoni's opposition, which was repeated in the Committee, Rowell carried his point that not the individual delegates but the States represented on the Council "should be held accountable" for their decisions.[12] In regard to general relations between the Assembly and the Council, it was agreed that the League of Nations had no analogy in constitutional law and that it was a single organism having at its disposal two bodies through which its work could be done. This did not dispose, however, of the knotty problem of concurrent jurisdiction, on which Rowell was only to be able to persuade Viviani to his point of view, after considerable effort.

In the Committee, Rowell had agreed that an attempt should be made to determine which body should perform certain functions which had not been clearly allocated to either Council or Assembly, but after reading Viviani's draft of the report on jurisdiction, he came to the conclusion that it would be unwise to attempt "a very precise definition." Because of the continuing activity of the Council, Viviani had drawn the conclusion that except for the appointment of various officers "all questions of control" not clearly designated to either body belonged to the Council. To this, Rowell could not agree, and he prepared a statement of his lack of concurrence with this part of the Report. Delay in the schedule of the Assembly provided more time for discussion, however, and in the intervening period Rowell persuaded Viviani that it would be better to omit the statement.[13] The Report, as accepted by the Committee, declared that neither body was to render a decision in a matter "expressly committed" to the other, but no attempt was made to define the basis of jurisdiction in other questions. Thus the way was left open for the Assembly to take whatever share in League activities its members were willing to assume.

The basis of Rowell's action had been his desire to build up the authority of the Assembly. He spoke frankly in the plenary session of his personal agreement with the "substantial body of opinion . . . which would magnify the functions of the Assembly."[14] Recognizing, however, that agreement could not have been reached on a resolution which enlarged the functions of either Council or Assembly, he had recourse to a typically Anglo-Saxon expedient of avoiding precise definition lest it subsequently form a limitation on the powers of the Assembly.

The stand which Rowell had taken was both important and characteristic. The emphasis on the responsibility of states for the declarations of their representatives, either in the Council or the Assembly, was an attempt, not always successfully implemented, to secure a close relation between international utterances and national policy. This was particularly necessary in regard to the Great Powers if the smaller ones were to be able to look to them for leadership. The aim of making the Assembly an important element in League affairs was significant for all smaller states, for only in the Assembly were they sure to be represented. The British Empire representative on the Council, as has been said, was in practice always the representative of Great Britain alone. Even after 1926 when one of the Dominions always held a seat on the Council, there was no feeling that it represented in any way the other Dominions. It was only in the Assembly, therefore, that Canada could be sure of exerting influence. Thus the desire to protect the control of its own affairs, which played a significant rôle in Commonwealth relations, was a contributory motive for supporting the power of the Assembly. Lastly, from the point of view of the League as a whole, the move to prevent premature curbing of the authority of the Assembly was decisive in preparing the way for it to develop into a strong representative body with direct responsibility in any issue which properly belonged under the Covenant and was not within the express jurisdiction of the Council.

The activities which the Assembly undertook in 1920 went far towards giving effect to this claim to full co-ordinate authority. It examined and revised the statute of the Permanent Court of International Justice and decided that the Court should come into existence when the protocol had been ratified by a majority of the members of the Assembly. It created three new technical organizations for health, economics and finances, and transit and communications. It brought the control of the opium and white slave traffic under the supervision of the League. It proved itself more successful than the Council in raising funds to combat the typhus epidemic in Eastern Europe. It endorsed the work for refugees undertaken by Fridtjof Nansen at the request of the Council, though without assuming financial responsibilities. It initiated a modest plan for the reduction of armaments and considered recommendations regarding economic sanctions. Against the wishes of the Council, it investigated policy relating to the war between Poland and Soviet Russia, though without claiming power to act. In regard to the perennially difficult situation in Armenia, it undertook special negotiations under the leadership of Cecil and despite the ultimate necessity of suspending activity due to uncertainties regarding Armenia's relations with Soviet Russia, the move itself produced a spirit of *esprit de corps* in the Assembly which marked all its work thereafter.[15]

In one issue placed on its agenda by the Council, that of mandates, the Assembly found itself unable to implement effectively its claim to concurrent jurisdiction. According to the Covenant, the "degree of authority, control, or administration to be exercised by the Mandatory shall, if not previously agreed upon by the Members of the League, be explicitly defined in each case by the Council." Before the Assembly met, both Cecil and Sir James Allen had publicly interpreted "Members of the League" to mean the Assembly,[16] and Doherty and others were to maintain the same point during its meetings. The Council, however, flatly refused to provide the Assembly with copies of the draft "A" and "C" mandates which were in its hands. Cecil, as rapporteur of the Committee which had hoped to consider the draft mandates, spoke with feeling in the last meeting of the Assembly regarding the unco-operativeness of the Council, and was strongly supported by Doherty, who expressed his disappointment that there had been "such inadequate opportunities . . . to consider this most important subject" of mandates. Balfour, representative of Great Britain and speaking for the Council, replied sharply that its freedom of action could not be limited by the Assembly.[17] A hot exchange between Cecil and Balfour nearly marred the close of the session and, in general, the handling of the mandate issue by the Council left a feeling of considerable dissatisfaction among the members of the Assembly.[18]

As far as the League was concerned, the issue illustrated the unwillingness of the Council to allow the Assembly influence in a matter touching the territorial interests of Council members. In part the same division was present in the Commonwealth between those countries whose chief concern was the holding of the mandates[19] and those which were more interested in the position of the Assembly. In comparison with Peace Conference discussion on the same subject, however, it is interesting to note that Cecil, though on the South African delegation, and apparently also Sir James Allen of New Zealand as well as Doherty, upheld the Assembly, while it was the British and Australian members who supported the exclusive action of the Council.[20]

The Canadian delegation had taken a leading rôle in preventing the work of the Assembly from being circumscribed by definition. It was equally concerned that the energies of the League should not be spread over too wide a sphere of action to be effective. "May I very respectfully submit to the Assembly," said Rowell in his opening speech in the Plenary Session, "that it is important we should keep in view the distinction between the primary and secondary functions of the League of Nations."[21] The primary functions he believed to be the prevention of war and the provision of other means of settling international disputes. The secondary functions were those relating to health, transport, and other matters cited in Article 23 as suitable subjects for international conventions. His fear was that undue emphasis upon the secondary functions would result in the neglect of the League's primary purpose. In this he differed from certain Continental statesmen, in particular Tittoni (Italy), Lafontaine (Belgium), and Ador (Switzerland), who held that these so-called "secondary" functions referred in fact to a basic cause of war, the inequalities in the economic situation of countries.

The issue was argued mainly in relation to a matter over which there had been much concern since the conclusion of the war, the distribution of raw materials. An Italian draft for the Covenant, which was never formally considered at Paris, had included a clause concerning the necessity of controlling the international distribution of foodstuffs and raw materials.[22] Wilson's draft of January, 1918, had referred to the desirability of removing economic barriers and establishing equality of trade conditions among all nations associating themselves in the maintenance of peace,[23] but following opposition at the Conference had been superseded by a rather vague British formula which eventually became part of Article 23.[24] Acute difficulties in obtaining raw materials, partly due to inflation, partly to the problems involved in starting civilian production again and in re-establishing normal transportation facilities, coupled with serious unemployment, kept the issue to the fore, however, and led to numerous appeals for international intervention.[25]

With one of these appeals, brought to the International Labour Conference at its first annual meeting in Washington, November, 1919, by the Italian workers' delegate, Digno Baldesi, Rowell had already been concerned. Baldesi had proposed that the Conference should bring to the notice of the League of Nations the importance of "an equitable distribution of raw materials in preventing unemployment" and the advisability of "setting up" a "Permanent Committee" to "guarantee this equitable distribution among the various countries, according to their present need and future industrial requirements."[26] Rowell, acting as the Canadian Government delegate, had been one of the most active in opposing the suggestion, which he considered impractical as well as outside the jurisdiction of the Conference. Considerable feeling was displayed in the discussion and the motion was only defeated by forty-three votes to forty. This experience formed the backdrop for Rowell's statements on the subject at the First Assembly.

The issue was first raised there by the Belgian delegate, who maintained in the plenary session that the League of Nations should deal especially with the issue of armaments and with economic problems. Among the latter he ranked raw materials which, he declared, should no longer be considered the possession of the country within which they were found but "must be at the disposal of all mankind, under conditions of as great equality as possible."[27] Rowell, who spoke next, undertook to answer this directly. ". . . it is important," he maintained, "that we should not seek . . . to promote proposals here or elsewhere which cannot possibly be realized because they are outside the scope of the Covenant." To submit to them would be for countries to lose "control of their own internal affairs," than which nothing could be more strenuously opposed "on our side of the Atlantic." American membership in the League could never be looked for, he believed, so long as there was any suggestion that the League might interfere with domestic affairs, such as the question of raw materials. That it was a matter of "tremendous importance" to all nations, he did not deny, but to consider their distribution to be a function of the League, he felt to be a gross misreading of the Covenant.[28] This is the statement which Tittoni declared "expressed so categorically a *non possumus* in connection with the matter of raw materials and their proprietary rights for the nation which possesses them." Later in his speech, Tittoni appealed with exaggerated eloquence "to those Powers who are the fortunate possessors of raw materials, to those Powers who are rich, not to wait for the request from the poorer Powers and the Powers who are dependent upon them, but to come before this Assembly and say that they will waive their national interests and national egoisms in the general interest of humanity, justice and equality."

The division of opinion regarding the functions of the League was equally obvious in the Second Committee, where the issue was again raised.[29] No conclusion was reached, however, and the opposition of the Canadian, Australian, and Indian representatives in the Committee prevented any resolution from being presented which implied that raw materials were a subject for international regulation.

Rowell's attitude to the issue was based on three major considerations. First and foremost, he did not believe that the Covenant provided for action of this type. A reading of the relevant article on which proponents of action based their claim makes it difficult not to accept his contention. Article 23 began, "Subject to and in accordance with the provisions of international conventions existing or hereafter to be agreed upon, the Members of the League"; and continued in section (e) "will make provision to secure and maintain freedom of communications and of transit and equitable treatment for the commerce of all Members of the League." It was difficult, particularly for a lawyer, to read into this a justification for international regulation of raw material. Even if agreement were reached that such a subject did fall under this article, action could be taken only through international covenants and by the express consent of the governments concerned. Secondly, Rowell quite frankly believed that it was not a feasible approach to the issue because it would require a degree of regimentation in economic life and of outside control in internal affairs for which the Canadian people were not prepared. In the third place, Rowell still hoped for American membership in the League and as he said later, "any suggestion that the League of Nations sought to control or regulate the distribution of raw materials would put a weapon in the hands of the opponents of the League in the United States which might destroy any chance of the United States entering the League."[30] It was not the only occasion on which Canadian representatives constituted themselves the spokesmen for North America and endeavoured to prevent any steps being taken which they felt might militate against eventual American entry into the League.

The Canadian stand on raw materials at the First Assembly has been cited frequently as evidence of an unenlightened and selfish attitude towards an issue of international concern. Particularly was it attacked at the time of the Italo-Ethiopian conflict when it was suggested that the Canadian action in blocking inquiry into the question of raw materials had been a contributory cause of Italian expansionism.[31] In evaluating this contention, it is important to note that in fact the inquiry into raw materials was not blocked but was continued and that an elaborate report on the subject by Professor Gini was presented to the Second Assembly.[32] By that time, however, it was not difficulty in securing raw materials which was the problem, but difficulty in disposing of them. Hence, there was a change in approach which Rowell fully endorsed. Restrictions on the distribution of raw materials were seen to have been a by-product of the general system of trade barriers in existence after the war. In regard to these trade barriers, Rowell later quoted with approval the Report of the Economic and Financial Committee to the Assembly in 1921 which, while recognizing "the incontestable right which states have to dispose freely of their natural resources or of the output of their countries in respect of raw materials," warned against restrictions or differential regulations which might injure the production of other countries. "Had this position been taken at the First Assembly," Rowell maintained, "there would have been no occasion for any difference of opinion."[33]

It is unfortunate that a wider exploration of the economic problem did not take place at the First Assembly and that the issue of raw materials was not placed in the general setting where it belonged. Exaggerated claims were met by a sharp response which was justified by the legal context and the practical circumstances. But further consideration might have revealed more basic issues and pointed towards positive means of meeting them. In considering the Canadian attitude, however, it is important that, neither in practice nor in declarations at home or at the League, was any attempt made to support a principle of exclusive or widely differential regulations in regard to exports.

In addition to questions of function and the means by which its activities should be carried out, the First Assembly had also to consider a number of applications for membership in the League which confronted it with the necessity of laying down certain principles in the light of which the requests could be considered. In general the representatives of the Dominions favoured broadening the membership of the League to make it as nearly universal as possible. With the exception of the Australian delegate,[34] they voted for the admission of ex-enemy states like Austria and Bulgaria. Sir Reginald Blankenberg asked on behalf of South Africa for the "most sympathetic consideration to Germany" and also to the applications of other states capable of assuming membership.[35] Rowell subsequently spoke of the necessity of the League including "all the ex-enemy states" when they could meet the conditions for membership.[36] In regard to Georgia and Armenia, there was division of opinion between Fisher of Great Britain, who successfully opposed immediate action because of the uncertainty of Russian policy towards them, and Cecil, who felt the risk of having to extend protection was not great and that there was considerable advantage in "preventing yet another state going Bolshevik."[37] Regarding the Baltic states, there was more agreement that their proximity to the Soviet Union made it too hazardous to extend League protection under Article 10, a point stressed by Rowell, who pointed out the special interest of Canada in any question concerning Russia.[38] The most spectacular incident, however, concerned the admission of Albania which Cecil and Rowell succeeded in securing despite the opposition of the Great Powers.

The proposal had been made that Albania's request should be deferred until its international status had been decided.[39] Parts of Albania, which had only acquired its independence in 1913, had been promised Italy in the Secret Treaty of London under which it entered the war on the Allied side.   At the peace conference, Italian delegates attempted to acquire Albania as a mandate, since their troops were still occupying the country, or as an alternative to share in a partition of it with Greece and Yugoslavia.   Cecil's reaction was that the decision of the Assembly should not be subordinated to that of a group of powers, and Rowell supported him in maintaining that neither the Secret Treaty of London nor the occupation of Albanian territory had been able to deprive it of its position as an independent state.   Cecil secured the defeat of the proposal that the representatives of the Great Powers should make the final decision regarding the status of Albania, but he was not able to gain Committee support for immediate admission, which was rejected by thirteen votes to eight.   In the plenary session, however, Cecil as rapporteur presented not only the majority report but signified his own dissent from it.   His belief was that Albania's admission would help to pacify the Balkans, that it was important not to discriminate against a Mohammedan state, and that the strong nationalistic feeling of the Albanian people justified consideration.[40]   Rowell emphatically supported him.[41]   Probably following private consultations, the British and French representatives now expressed their willingness to vote for Albania's admission and the Committee's decision was reversed.   The action had demonstrated the effectiveness of an appeal to opinion within the Assembly.   It may have helped to prevent a partition of Albania, although it did nothing to ensure that country a smooth or economically independent future.

One particular issue raised in connection with the admission of states threw light on Canadian reactions to the important issue of minorities.   Cecil made the proposal that the League should not accept new members unless they were prepared to accept the equivalent of minority treaties.[42]   In the Fifth Committee, to which this resolution was referred, it was strongly opposed by Rowell on the grounds that it modified the Covenant by imposing an additional provision for membership, and that the provision would be "wholly inapplicable" to countries outside of Europe.   "The effect of such a policy," he declared, "would be to perpetuate in Canada the division which had marred Europe," and he added, "Moreover, the policy could not be carried out in the United States."[43]   His attitude was sharply attacked by Beneš (Czechoslovakia), who maintained warmly that "in Europe the policy of suppressing nationalities—a policy which was no doubt justified in America—has been the real cause of the World War."   The matter was finally disposed of through an innocuous resolution, but it was significant in illustrating the difference in attitude between European and non-European states towards the minority question.   It provided one more indication, also, both of the similarity of Canadian and American attitudes and of Canada's desire to prevent any development which might lessen the chance of eventual American participation in the work of the League.

Both the strengths and limitations of the Assembly as an international force had become clear in these first decisive sessions. As a sounding board, as a platform from which to marshal public opinion, the potentialities of the Assembly were evident. The very fact that the Council had been unwilling to submit the draft mandates to the Assembly showed an awareness of the force of this influence. But it showed, too, the weakness of the Assembly in relation to issues touching the vital interests of member states, particularly of the Great Powers. The skirmish over Albania demonstrated the possibility of bending the purposes even of Great Powers once the issue was open to publicity. But it showed the dependence of the Assembly upon strong and courageous leadership.

Rowell had taken the lead in preventing the functions of the Assembly from being circumscribed by definition. The Assembly itself had ranged far in the field of international affairs. But though precedents had been established, a continued drive would be needed to maintain them. The League was taking shape as an instrument to be used by its members. Their interpretation of what its functions should be was to be decisive for its future.

The active share which representatives from the Dominions had taken in shaping the work of the Assembly provides a fairly clear picture of their general conceptions of the functions of the League. The importance of concentrating upon what Rowell called its primary function, the provision of substitutes for war by devising other means for settling international disputes was endorsed by all the Dominion representatives. Hence they put great stress upon the creation of the Permanent Court of International Justice which Rowell was to call "the greatest single achievement of the First Assembly."[44] Like most of the delegations of the smaller states, the Canadians had strongly favoured establishing compulsory jurisdiction of the Court. The objections of the British and representatives of other Great Powers had led to a compromise establishing voluntary jurisdiction except for such states as wished by signing the so-called "optional clause" to signify their intention of accepting compulsory jurisdiction in any or all of the classes of legal disputes defined in the Statute. Despite their own unanimous support of compulsory jurisdiction, the Canadian delegation agreed to this because of the British unwillingness to sign at that time, but they maintained their hope that eventually the Court would so establish itself in public confidence that it would be possible to have compulsory jurisdiction accepted later.[45]

With his emphasis on the Court, Rowell coupled "progress in disarmament, and full publicity for treaties." The emphasis was on security *against* war, by limiting the race in armaments and by lessening the opportunities to plan for aggression or, as Borden had suggested earlier, to benefit by it. Publicity in itself was looked on as a safeguard and the efforts of Dominion representatives to secure the entrance of the press and public to League meetings and of Rowell to explain issues to American and Italian newspapermen were constructive means of securing it.

There was no similar enthusiasm for more forcible means of preventing conflicts. In the last days of the session, Doherty introduced the first of a number of public attempts to secure the elimination or substantial amendment of Article 10 against which he and Borden had written during the Peace Conference, though they had had to support it in the face of Liberal opposition in Parliament in the debates on the Peace Treaty. It was a negative way of expressing fear at the possibility of having to take action to protect League members. It indicated at least a seriousness about League responsibilities, also evidenced in the consideration of the admission of new members to the League, but no enthusiasm for the idea of mutual guarantee, from which Canada, in particular, could anticipate little aid and considerable risk.

In regard to the so-called secondary functions, of promoting co-operation between countries in activities transcending national boundaries, the Dominion representatives also had generally similar views. While approving such measures in themselves, they insisted that they could not be imposed by international action but only after careful consideration and decision by individual countries. The attitude found clear expression in the discussions over raw materials and in the interrelated consideration of technical organization.[46] Supported by Millen (Australia), Rowell succeeded in the plenary session of the Assembly in reversing the unanimous recommendation of a Committee to make the technical organizations permanent, and substituted an agreement that they should remain temporary at least until they had had one year's experience. Behind Rowell's action were both his suspicion, subsequently proved unjustified, that the technical organizations might assume too wide functions, and his fear that they would be in fact "European" rather than "international" organizations because of the difficulty overseas countries would have in sending representatives to a number of annual meetings. "It is not that we have not the greatest respect and admiration for the European statesmen," he pointed out, ". . . but they do not understand our viewpoint." Even the statesmen of Great Britain "for whom we have respect, admiration and affection" are not allowed "to settle any of our Canadian affairs. We settle those ourselves. Much less," he concluded, "are we prepared to turn over the settlement of those matters to a general European committee."[47] Time was to show that the implications were not well founded, though naturally the committees tended to deal more with European problems than those of overseas countries, but the attitude behind it was instructive. The unnecessarily sharp terms in which Rowell reiterated his point caused resentment among his European listeners but few failed to recognize the importance, not only from the Dominion point of view but also that of the future of international organization, of avoiding the impression, as Cecil put it, "that the League of Nations was a League of Europe and not a League of the World." The willingness of the Assembly to bow to Rowell's wishes and not to make the organizations permanent until the following year was an indication of the general recognition of the importance of his point, not in itself but in what lay behind it: the fear of being influenced by decisions important for national life without having adequate opportunity to participate in their formulation or to reject them if desired.

In general, the attitudes and policies of the Dominions seem to have been more nearly akin to those of the Scandinavian countries than to other small powers in the League. Their need for international recognition was greater than that of Norway or Sweden; their need for international collaboration was probably less. Both groups of countries tended to feel that they had more to contribute than to gain from their international association and therefore to be reluctant to assume new responsibilities, especially those involving the use of force. On the whole, the members of both groups exhibited wholehearted belief in the principles of international co-operation and exemplary individual conduct if their own standards of behaviour were the criterion.

In this formative period of the League, the Dominions had been at least as influential as any other group of smaller countries. They had helped to contribute to the strengthening of the Assembly as a force in League affairs. They had been strict constructionists, generally opposing efforts to broaden the functions of the League, particularly in any way which would threaten their control over their own affairs. They had effectively demonstrated an independence of action which more than justified their claims to membership in the League.

During the First Assembly, individual Dominions had not diverged as markedly from each other in attitude and emphasis as they had done in response to the territorial issues raised during the Peace Conference. There was some evidence, however, of distinctive points of view. Canada had constituted itself the spokesman for North America and was, in fact, to be the only representative from that area until the entry of Mexico into the League in 1936. Australia and New Zealand had endorsed the Chinese proposal regarding non-European representation. On the whole, however, the issues raised in the First Assembly were those on which the Dominions tended to have similar rather than divergent points of view. This was not always to be the case in regard to League questions any more than it was on issues of Commonwealth relations and policy or of imperial defence, which were already pressing in upon the Dominions.

Behind most considerations of League form and policy by Dominion or other statesmen lay traditional conceptions of national security and national interests. No countries were willing to go more than a limited distance in modifying these conceptions in the interest of international organization. Lack of American participation in League work put a further restraint both because it meant the League was less powerful and because every change in the Covenant had to be weighed in terms of its possible effect on the subsequent entry of the United States. Facing this situation, Dominion representatives, particularly those whose countries were in exposed positions, could not help but be aware that while the League might be an outer line of defence in case of danger, it was very remote compared with the aid they might expect from within the Commonwealth and particularly from Great Britain. Interested as they might be in recognition through League membership and in what the League might be able to do to keep future wars from arising, governments in the Dominions like those of other countries were more interested in specific means of defence. The British Navy still bulked largest in their considerations of security though no longer in so unquestioning a manner as in the past.

REFERENCES FOR CHAPTER I

SECTION A.   THE DOMINIONS AND THE COVENANT

1. Viscount Cecil, *A Great Experiment* (London, 1941), p. 61.

2. J. C. Smuts, *The League of Nations, A Practical Suggestion* (London, 1918; New York, 1919). In a famous passage, he wrote, "For there is no doubt that mankind is once more on the move. The very foundations have been shaken and loosened, and things are again fluid. The tents have been struck, and the great caravan of humanity is once more on the way. Vast social and industrial changes are coming—perhaps upheavals which may, in their magnitude and effects, be comparable to war itself. A steadying, controlling, regulating influence will be required to give stability to progress, and to remove that waste-

ful friction which had dissipated so much social force in the past, and in this war more than ever before." The main features of his proposal were that the League should be composed of a General Conference, representative of nations rather than governments, which would formulate proposals to be presented to countries for ratification, a Council to act as the executive committee of the League, an Arbitration Court to which questions of law would be automatically referred, and an international secretariat. The states composing the League were to give up compulsory military training, to nationalize the manufacture of armaments, to limit their militia and armaments as determined by the Council, and to pledge themselves not to go to war without submitting the issue to arbitration or inquiry by the Council, or against any state submitting to a Council award. In case a state should break its pledge, the plan provided for economic and financial sanctions with military action as necessary, and for permanent demilitarization of the state thereafter.

3. David Hunter Miller, *Drafting of the Covenant* (New York, 1928), I, 110.

4. Paul Birdsall, *Versailles Twenty Years After* (New York, 1941), p. 42.

5. David Lloyd George, *The Truth about the Peace Treaties* (London, 1938), I, 63-4. The American edition is *Memoirs of the Peace Conference* (New Haven, 1939). The page references are taken from the English edition.

6. Birdsall, *op. cit.*, p. 46.

7. Lloyd George, *op. cit.*, I, 516.

8. David Hunter Miller, *My Diary at the Conference of Paris* (privately printed, 1928), XIV, 92-3, and Lloyd George, *op. cit.*, I, 541-42.

9. G. P. deT. Glazebrook, *Canada at the Paris Peace Conference* (Toronto, 1942), pp. 39-40.

10. *Ibid.*, p. 72.

11. Stephen Bonsal, *Unfinished Business* (New York, 1944), pp. 169-70 (diary entry for March 29, 1919). In a later book, *Suitors and Suppliants: The Little Nations at Versailles* (New York, 1946), p. 229, Bonsal printed a diary entry for March 16, 1919, on the violence of Hughes' feelings and the reactions they produced. ". . . morning, noon, and night [Hughes] bellows at poor Lloyd George that if race equality is recognized in the preamble or any of the articles of the Covenant, he and his people will leave the Conference bag and baggage. Even the President, usually so restrained not to say formal in his language, says Hughes is 'a pestiferous varmint'—but still he represents a continent."

12. *Canada, Sessional Papers*, Special Session, 1919, 41.

13. Bonsal, *op. cit.*, pp. 210-11 (entry for April 28, 1945).

14. Extracts from Sir Robert Borden's memorandum are printed in R. A. MacKay and E. B. Rogers, *Canada Looks Abroad* (London, New York, Toronto, 1938), Appendix A, pp. 325-27, and it is in full in Miller, *Drafting of the Covenant*, I, 354-362.

15. David Hunter Miller believed it to be founded "*in part*" on a misconception. He, himself, interpreted Article 10 as meaning "merely that forcible annexation shall not result from 'external aggression.'" *Ibid.*, I, 354.

16. League of Nations, Committee on Amendments to the Covenant, *Memorandum submitted by the Canadian delegation* (C. 215, M. 154, 1921). Reprinted in G. P. deT. Glazebrook, *Canada at the Paris Peace Conference* (Toronto, 1942), Appendix C. The memorandum was not made public until 1921.

17. Sir Robert Borden's memorandum, cited above.

18. Miller, *Drafting of the Covenant*, I, 363-368. "Notes on the Draft Covenant," by W. M. Hughes. Miller's personal comment was that they "were written from a rather hostile point of view . . ."

19. Dominion membership in the League was first specifically provided for in the British Draft Convention of the Covenant of January 20, 1919.

32   THE COMMONWEALTH AND INTERNATIONAL SECURITY

20. Cecil, *op. cit.*, p. 77, felt "it seemed to crystallize for all time the actual position which then existed." He declared that the article was agreed to, subject to the provision for peaceful change embodied in Article 19.

21. *Journal of the Parliaments of the Empire*, 1921, II, 794-5. Subsequently cited as *J.P.E.*

22. A study of newspaper comments on the idea of a League of Nations is contained in Shirley Saul Gordon, *Canadian Public Opinion on the League of Nations*, 1914-1920 (University of Toronto, unpublished thesis).

23. *J.P.E.*, 1920, I, 87-105, 322-327, 464-469. In the course of discussion, Mr. Fielding of the Liberal party moved an amendment seconded by M. Lapointe, "that in giving such approval this House in no way assents to any impairment of the existing autonomous authority of the Dominion, but declares that the question of what part, if any, the forces of Canada shall take in any war, actual or threatened, is one to be determined at all times, as occasion may require, by the people of Canada through their representatives in Canada." The amendment was negatived 112-71 but it provides a good indication of the Liberal point of view.

24. *Ibid.*, I, 193-220, 384-387, 540-554, 741-743, esp. Hertzog, p. 197.

25. *Ibid.*, 124-132.

26. *Ibid.*, p. 198.

27. *Ibid.*, pp. 125, 128.

28. *Ibid.*, p. 157. He was echoed by the Leader of the Opposition, Sir Joseph Ward, pp. 161-162.

29. W. K. Hancock, *Survey of British Commonwealth Affairs, I. Problems of Nationality,* 1918-1936 (London, 1937), p. 33, n. 1.

30. Cecil, *op. cit.*, p. 86-7, emphasizes this point.

31. *J.P.E.*, 1920, I, 128 (reported in *J.P.E.* as They).

32. W. M. Hughes, *The Splendid Adventure: A Review of Empire Relations Within and Without the Commonwealth of Britannic Nations* (London, 1929), pp. 108-09.

33. Memorandum of February 17, 1920, on British Representation on the Council of the League of Nations from the unpublished Doherty papers. An earlier memorandum of January 17, 1919, spoke of a proposal made in the Committee on Representation that the selection would be made by the Imperial Cabinet Conference. Glazebrook describes Doherty's indignation at the reduction in function of this Committee from general consideration of the Covenant to discussing the representation of the Dominions and India in the League of Nations. *Op. cit.*, pp. 60-61.

34. Printed in Robert MacGregor Dawson, *The Development of Dominion Status, 1900-1936* (London, 1937), p. 201.

35. Note by Loring C. Christie, February 9, 1920. From the unpublished Rowell papers.

36. Speech by Mr. Rowell to a mass meeting of returned soldiers in the Russell Theatre, Ottawa, on February 15, 1920. Copy in the unpublished Rowell papers. An Associated Press report of the speech was read into the Congressional Record of March 9, 1920, during the debate on the Lenroot resolution. *Congressional Record*, March 9, 1920, Vol. 59, No. 76, p. 4359.

37. N. W. Rowell, "Canada's Position in the League of Nations," *The Canadian Magazine* (Toronto), April, 1920.

38. Arthur D. Howden Smith, *Mr. House of Texas* (New York, London, 1940), pp. 300-01.

39. Henry Cabot Lodge, *The Senate and the League of Nations* (New York, 1925), p. 240. (Speech in the Senate, February 28, 1919.)

40. Miller, *Drafting of the Covenant*, I, 461.

41. *J.P.E.*, 1920, I, 100.

SECTION B. THE DOMINIONS AND THE FIRST ASSEMBLY

1. W. Stewart Wallace, *The Memoirs of Sir George Foster* (Toronto, 1933), p. 209 (Diary entry for November 15, 1920).

2. Cecil, *op. cit.*, p. 101.

3. *Records of the First Assembly*, 1920, Plenary Meetings, pp. 93-99: Fifth Plenary Meeting, Nov. 17, 1920: Cecil declared, ". . . I represent South Africa because the Prime Minister of South Africa . . . was good enough to think that I could, more adequately than anyone else, present to the Assembly the views which he held. In a very real sense I stand before you as a substitute for General Smuts." When Cecil wired to ask Smuts' wishes on special questions, the reply always authorized whatever action Cecil himself felt was best. Cecil, *op. cit.*, p. 110.

4. *See* Henry Borden, ed., *Sir Robert Borden: His Memoirs* (Toronto, 1938, 2 vols.), II, 753 and 1040.

5. Wilson Harris, *What They Did at Geneva* (London, 1921), p. 5.

6. *Cambridge History of the British Empire* (Cambridge, 1930), VI, 734. Newton W. Rowell, "Canada and the Empire, 1884-1921."

7. The Australian Delegation was among those which submitted suggestions for the permanent rules of procedure and many of the points it proposed were adopted. After the rules were approved by the Assembly they were again referred to the Australian Delegation and some of their further suggestions were subsequently made use of. *Report of the Australian delegate on the First Assembly*, 1920, Government paper, No. 72—F. 12210, 1926.

8. *Records of the First Assembly*, 1920, Plenary Meetings, p. 43: Second Plenary Meeting, November 15, 1920. Doherty's protest followed two motions made at the beginning of the second session, the first paying tribute to the memory of Jean Jacques Rousseau and the second extending the thanks of the Assembly to President Wilson for convening the meeting. Being taken by surprise by the first motion with which he was out of sympathy, Doherty, a staunch Roman Catholic, rose after the second motion to protest the lack of notice and to note the Canadian abstention from the Rousseau tribute. His statement caused a mild sensatiön since the translator interpreted the abstention as referring to the thanks being sent to President Wilson. Doherty immediately rose and corrected the mistake but subsequently the story appeared in *The Times* and, alarmed lest the report should cross the Atlantic, Doherty wrote in some indignation to request a formal correction! Doherty to the Editor of *The Times* from the unpublished Doherty papers.

9. *Records of the First Assembly*, 1920, Plenary Meetings, p. 79: Third Plenary Meeting, November 16, 1920. (Sir James Allen.)

10. Cecil, *op. cit.*, p. 112.

11. *Records of the First Assembly*, 1920, Plenary Meetings, pp. 92-3: Fifth Plenary Meeting, November 17, 1920.

12. *Ibid.*, pp. 169 ff. and 174-80: Eighth Plenary Meeting, November 20, 1920. It is worth noting on the other side that Alfred Zimmern writing in 1922 described the Council "as a sort of international House of Lords, or Conference of Elder Statesmen." He believed that the Council was specially fitted for those tasks which were too political to be referred to the Court but were sufficiently detached from popular feelings to provide hope that the decisions of an international authority would be generally accepted. One of his main reasons for anticipating that the Council would always be disappointing as a policy-determining body was the inclusion in its membership of smaller states which meant that instead of being a standing conference of Great Powers, it was an anomalous group lacking any common characteristics of power, interest, or responsibility. Alfred E. Zimmern, *Europe in Convalescence* (London, 1922), p. 144.

13. Rowell to Viviani, November 27, 1920, from the unpublished Rowell papers. The same question had been raised by Balfour at the Council's eighth session at San Sebastian, July 30 to August 5, 1920, and a committee composed of

Balfour, Hymans of Belgium, and Bourgeois of France, had made a report. *Council Minutes*, Eighth Session, Annex 84. The general principle proposed by this report was that neither body should take independent measures in regard to a question in which the other had been or was dealing. Though apparently impartial, this suggestion would in practice have worked to the advantage of the Council because of the greater frequency of its sessions. This report and a memorandum by Sir Eric Drummond, the Secretary-General, had been laid before the First Committee. *Records of the First Assembly*, 1920, Meetings of the Committees, Vol. I, pp. 90-92: First Committee, Annex 4.

14. *Records of the First Assembly*, 1920, Plenary Meetings, p. 290: Fourteenth Plenary Session, December 6, 1920.

15. Cecil, *op. cit.*, p. 113.

16. Cecil in a letter to *The Times*, July 1, 1920, p. 12, and Sir James Allen in a lecture at the Hotel Victoria in London.

17. Cecil, *op. cit.*, p. 112, wrote that Balfour had made "a most unusually perverse attempt . . . to prevent the Assembly discussing Mandates."

18. The Council, which was in session during the meetings of the Assembly, had communicated to the Assembly its decision on the composition of the Mandate Commission taken on November 29th. On the following day, the President of the Council had notified the principal mandatory powers that the Assembly might be expected to interest itself actively in the question of mandates. Within a short time all the "A" and "C" mandates were in the hands of the Council. When the Sixth Committee applied for copies of the drafts, it was refused unless it would agree not to communicate the details of the drafts to the Assembly. This attitude continued despite the fact that the "C" mandates were issued by the Council on December 17th while the Assembly was still in session.

19. The British action may also have been dictated by desire to protect the French, who wished special provisions inserted in their "A" and "B" mandates to permit the recruitment of troops from these areas. Wilson and Lloyd George had finally given in to Clemenceau on this issue at the Peace Conference. It had been raised again at the preliminary British Commonwealth meeting in London before the Assembly, at which time Rowell had registered his objection. Anticipation that the Assembly would object to such a provision was considered by some to be the reason for withholding the draft mandates.

20. Minutes of the subcommittee on "C" mandates, First Meeting, December 9, 1920, from the unpublished Doherty papers, and *Records of the First Assembly*, 1920, Meetings of the Committee, II, 278: Sixth Committee, December 16, 1920. The Report of the Australian delegate to the First Assembly, *op. cit.*, p. 26, emphasized that Cecil in answer to a query regarding the "open door" in "C" mandates declared that he knew from "personal knowledge" of "the promise which was made at Paris by the Supreme Council" and that paragraph 6 had been inserted in Article 22 on the understanding that it gave "complete power to the mandatories except as regards the matters specifically mentioned." None of these affected control over trade or immigration.

21. *Records of the First Assembly*, 1920, Plenary Meetings, p. 169: Eighth Plenary Session, November 20, 1920.

22. *See* René Albrecht-Carrié, *Italy at the Paris Peace Conference* (New York, 1938) for a general consideration of Italian claims and attitudes.

23. Miller, *Drafting of the Covenant*, I, 19.

24. *Ibid.*, II, 16 and 107.

25. By such bodies as the International Miners' Congress, which communicated a resolution to the Governing Body of the International Labour Office asking for "an international office for the distribution of fuel, ores, and other raw materials indispensable for the revival of a normal life" and the International Chamber of Commerce which passed resolutions in 1920 and 1921 recommending the gradual removal of import and export embargoes, particularly on the free movement of raw materials.

26. *Provisional Verbatim Record*, First Annual Conference, International Labour Organization, p. 20.

27. *Records of the First Assembly*, Plenary Meetings, p. 164: Eighth Plenary Session, November 20, 1920.

28. *Ibid.*, p. 169.

29. In the Committee, it was raised by Ador of Switzerland in a resolution to recognize the necessity of instituting a Permanent Economic and Financial Committee whose duties would include "on the basis of the principle set forth in Article 23 of the Covenant, which assures to all States equitable treatment, the examination of measure for preventing monopolies of raw materials and of the means of controlling and distribution of raw materials." *Records of the First Assembly*, 1920, Meetings of the Committees, I, 124: Second Committee, Third Meeting, November 22, 1920. It was the implication in this resolution which was opposed by the Australian, Canadian, and Indian representatives, the latter declaring that Article 23 "in his view no more referred to raw materials or tariff questions than to the injustices of Nature." The Resolution subsequently voted by the Committee was specifically stated to be an "interpretive clause" referring only to the report of the International Financial Conference of experts which had met at Brussels in the autumn and which had led the Council to request the Economic Section of the Economic and Financial Committee to study the difficulties experienced by certain countries in securing raw materials.

30. Newton W. Rowell, "The League of Nations and the Italo-Abyssinia Dispute," *Board of Trade Journal*, November, 1935.

31. For example by Arnold Toynbee during Chatham House discussions, *The Future of the League of Nations* (London, 1936), p. 120. "It seems to me that what really sent the Italians to fight Abyssinia was two things done by North American countries. The first was in 1921 when the Italians raised the point of access to raw materials and the Canadian delegation stamped on it; and the second was the passing of the two American Immigration Acts of 1921 and 1924, which produced this mass of baulked young men in Italy who had to be turned to something, good or bad." *See* also Escott Reid, "Did Canada Cause War?" *Saturday Night* (Toronto), September 28, 1935. Mr. Rowell's speech to the Canadian Club, Toronto, October 15, 1935, reprinted in the *Board of Trade Journal*, was in answer to these contentions.

32. Rowell also noted that the question of raw materials had come before the World Economic Conference in 1927 where recommendations had been made and accepted but could not subsequently be carried out because of growing economic nationalism throughout the world.

33. Rowell, *op. cit.*

34. Millen voiced a reservation on the application of Austria in regard to its attitude on German claims to the former Pacific islands and did not believe that the change of government in Bulgaria was, in the light of the previous thirty years, "evidence of a serious change of heart." In his report to his government, Millen explained his abstention on the ground that he did not know what trade policy Australia was adopting towards these countries and thought it would be "anomalous" to vote for their inclusion if Australia was not resuming full trading relations with them. *Report of the Australian Delegate, op. cit.*, p. 22.

35. *Records of the First Assembly*, 1920, Plenary Meetings, p. 566: Twenty-Fifth Plenary Session, December 15, 1920. Barnes (Great Britain), speaking on behalf of labour, had asked on November 19th for the admission of all ex-enemy states to the League, thereby reiterating the proposal of the Parliamentary Labour party, the Rt. Hon. W. Adamson, Chairman of the Parliamentary Labour party, *J.P.E.*, 1920, I, 227. Cecil, who did not participate directly in the debate since Blankenberg spoke for South Africa, maintained in his autobiography that Germany's exclusion was "a grave error" for which the chief responsibility rested on the French government. He believed its exclusion was not only a grave misfortune for Germany but for the League itself, which in consequence of its absence and that of the United States appeared to be dominated by France and Great Britain and indeed a "mere continuance of their 'War Alliance,'" *op. cit.*, p. 85.

36. Newton W. Rowell, "The League of Nations and the Assembly at Geneva," *The International Review of Missions*, July, 1921, Vol. X, No. 39, p. 413. He had made a veiled reference to Germany in his opening speech to the Assembly when he cited "the necessity of the League consisting of all the great nations of the world . . . so soon as they are in a position to comply with the provisions of the covenant and apply for admission." *Records of the First Assembly*, 1920, Plenary Meetings, p. 169 ff.: Eighth Plenary Session, November 20, 1920.

37. In the plenary session Cecil maintained that the test for admission "Would you be prepared to march to its assistance" was a somewhat doubtful one. "I don't know," he said, "that South Africa would be willing to send a force to protect Bulgaria, or to protect Austria, or to protect Luxembourg, or to protect Costa Rica, yet we have admitted those states." His criterion was "the practical extent of the obligation that we undertake in each case" and he felt that in relation to Georgia the risk was not great. *Records of the First Assembly*, 1920, Plenary Meetings, p. 632: Twenty-Seventh Meeting, December 16, 1920.

38. Letter to his wife from the unpublished Rowell papers.

39. *Records of the First Assembly*, 1920, Meetings of the Committees, II, 190: Fifth Committee, Sixth Meeting, December 4, 1920.

40. *Records of the First Assembly*, 1920, Plenary Meetings, p. 646: Twenty-Eighth Plenary Meeting, December 17, 1920.

41. *Ibid.*, pp. 646-7.

42. *Ibid.*, p. 406: Eighteenth Plenary Session, December 10, 1920.

43. *Records of the First Assembly*, 1920, Meetings of the Committees, II, 202: Fifth Committee, Eighth Meeting, December 10, 1920.

44. Copy of interview given Italian newspaper correspondents on the question of raw materials at Geneva, December 17, 1920. From the unpublished Rowell papers. The interview began by explaining the Canadian point of view regarding raw materials and continued with an exposition of the general attitude towards the functions of international organization.

45. *See* N. W. Rowell's speeches on "The Permanent Court of International Justice" before the Dominion Bar Association, Ottawa, September 8, 1921, and on "Will the Suggested Five Power Treaty take the Place of the Protocol" to the Empire Club of Canada, Toronto, March 26, 1925. Copies in the Rowell papers. *See* also speech by C. J. Doherty to the Empire Club on "The Permanent Court of International Justice," March 31, 1921. *The Mail and Empire*, April 1, 1921, carried an editorial summarizing his speech.

46. *See* above, footnote 29.

47. *Records of the First Assembly*, 1920, Plenary Meetings, 328-9: Sixteenth Plenary Session, December 8, 1920. He continued, "You may say that we should have confidence in European statesmen and leaders. Perhaps we should, but it was European policy, European statesmanship, European ambition, that drenched this world with blood and from which we are still suffering and will suffer for generations. Fifty thousand Canadians under the soil of France and Flanders is what Canada has paid for European statesmanship trying to settle European problems. I place responsibility on the few; I would not distribute it over many; but nevertheless it is European. Therefore, I submit that we should not in this International Assembly part with our control in connection with these matters." Subsequently he apologized if his words should have appeared to constitute an attack upon European statesmanship but pointed out that he had previously brought forward his point of view in the plenary session and in the Committee, apparently without effect. "I thought this morning that there should be no mistake at least as to the views I entertained on the matter, and if I spoke with undue warmth, I wanted to emphasize the points so that they would be clearly understood."

CHAPTER II
NAVAL DEFENCE AND THE FAR EAST

THE war had brought the Commonwealth an acute awareness of the dangers implicit in its far-flung positions. The British Empire had been built upon and held together by sea power. In the nineteenth-century period of British naval dominance throughout the world, supremacy had rested upon control of the narrow seas of Europe—the Channel, the North Sea, and the Mediterranean—through which most of the world's commerce passed, and of various strategic points of global importance, the Cape of Good Hope overlooking the route to India, the Falkland Islands on the alternate route to the Far East, and in the South Pacific the straits between Malaya, the Dutch East Indies, and Australia.[1]   But from 1890 on the British Navy's world-wide influence had been challenged by the rise of the Japanese and American navies which carved out huge areas over which the British Navy could have no practical control.   The growing threat of German naval power in the same period made it necessary to concentrate the British fleet in European waters and left the safety of the outlying parts of the Empire dependent on the good will of the United States and Japan.   Japanese naval aid, invoked through the Anglo-Japanese Alliance,[2] had been needed during the war in clearing the Pacific of a substantial German cruiser squadron, in helping to convoy Australian and New Zealand troops to the European battlefront and in 1917, at the time of crucial danger, in meeting the submarine menace in the Mediterranean.[3]   The American shipbuilding programme and aid in convoying merchant ships had been important, if not one of the decisive factors contributing to eventual victory.   In the light of this experience, the future defence of the British Empire appeared to depend on a continuation of close relations with the United States and Japan and/or an expansion of British naval power to make it possible to protect not only the British Isles and the North Atlantic but also the Far Eastern parts of the Commonwealth and Empire.

The military contributions of the Dominions during the war led naturally to general agreement at the Imperial Conference of 1917 that they should share in future decisions on imperial defence.   The Admiralty hoped to secure from this consultation an agreement that there should be an Imperial Navy centralized in control and flexible in its movements, to which the Dominions would contribute a more proportionate share of expenses.   But its hope of a centrally controlled Imperial

Navy was stillborn. In response to an Admiralty memorandum of May 17, 1918, on the Naval Defence of the British Empire, circulated to the Imperial War Conference, Sir Robert Borden, on behalf of all the Dominion Prime Ministers, presented to Mr. Lloyd George on August 15, 1918, a statement of principles which rejected the conception of having one single navy under central naval control at all times. In support of the Dominion desire for separate navies it pointed out that the Australian Navy had operated effectively as part of the united British Navy during the war. To make separate navies compatible with unified action in wartime it was agreed that there should be common equipment and methods of training through all the navies of the Commonwealth. It was also foreseen that in the future it might be necessary to expand the separate Dominion navies considerably, in which case "some supreme naval authority upon which each of the Dominions would be adequately represented" might become necessary. In the meantime, the Dominion Prime Ministers asked that a high naval authority be sent by the Admiralty to give advice upon their separate defence needs.[4]

In response to this request, Lord Jellicoe, Admiral of the Fleet, visited Australia, New Zealand, and Canada during 1919 and in a series of Reports[5] presented his view of their strategic needs and how they could be met. ". . . experience has shown the necessity," he wrote, ". . . of the Empire possessing much greater naval strength abroad than has been the case during the present century." Modern conditions of naval warfare make it "increasingly necessary" to keep squadrons in different parts of the world "to protect trade and to ensure the early capture or destruction of such enemy vessels as may escape the main blockade." Beyond the general need of maintaining the security of sea communications which was shared by all the Dominions, he pointed out that Australia, "due to the attractions offered by the great potential value of the land, and the very small populations occupying it" was also faced with the danger of invasion. The difficulty of guarding against this was enhanced "by the absence of strategic railways, the immense length of coastline [equal in extent to the distance between Australia and England] and the great distance from the Mother Country with its naval and military support." Hence, he concluded, naval defence was of particular importance for Australia's security.

Jellicoe's specific proposals for a Far Eastern Navy and for convoying between the different parts of the Empire showed how heavy a burden naval defence would place on all parts of the Commonwealth, in particular Great Britain and Australia. He envisaged "a Far Eastern fleet of considerable strength" (including 8 Battleships, 8 Battle-cruisers,

40 Destroyers, and 36 Submarines) made up of ships of the Royal Navy and such Dominion vessels as were furnished by their respective countries. These were to be under the supervision of a high ranking naval officer at Singapore, and generally responsible for the defence of all portions of the Empire from Africa on the west to the Americas on the east. He estimated the cost of this fleet as about a hundred million dollars annually which, he suggested, should be met 75 per cent. by Great Britain, 20 per cent. by Australia, and 5 per cent. by New Zealand.[6] Because of the distance between Australia and the main concentration of the Far Eastern Fleet, he believed that Australia would also need local forces capable of fighting delaying actions until the main fleet could come into action. Each of the Dominions should make provision for potential convoy work, New Zealand and Australia in their own area, Canada through "a small force of light cruisers on her western seaboard" in addition to "a naval force" on the eastern seaboard,[7] and South Africa by providing a squadron stationed at the Cape of Good Hope with "the primary duty of keeping open the trade route round the Cape and protecting the trade on the west coast of Africa." Harbour improvements would also be necessary. The Dominions should make what provisions they considered adequate for docking, repairing and defences, while he assumed that Great Britain would put Singapore, Colombo, and Hong Kong in shape as modern naval bases.

Confronted with this well-considered picture of their defence needs, Dominion statesmen, and particularly the Australians, could not help but be aware of the staggering burden which it would place upon their countries. Australia already possessed a small fleet unit. New Zealand took a step towards assuming more responsibilities by accepting from the British Government the cruiser *Chatham*, whose upkeep would be something more than double its former half-million-dollar annual contribution to the British Navy. The Canadian Unionist Government took the same type of move towards strengthening naval defences by accepting a light cruiser and two torpedo-boat destroyers in place of two obsolete Canadian training ships. There was reluctance, however, to adopt any permanent naval programmes, the more so because of the heavy burden of expenses arising out of the war, and because Britain itself was still undecided upon its long-range naval policy.[8] Moreover, opinion within individual Dominions was divided on the issue. Canadian Liberals, especially French Canadian, actively opposed expenditures upon armaments, particularly in view of the disappearance of Germany as a naval power, and feared any suggestion of centralized naval control. Both in New Zealand[9] and South Africa[10] opposition parties criticized the naval policies being pursued by the Government. Implicit in the discussions on naval affairs in each of the Dominion Parliaments was the hope that the Imperial Conference which was to meet June, 1921, might pave the way towards some measure of disarmament through general agreement, a hope which may have been encouraged by British communications to Dominion Governments.[11]

In fact, steps were being taken in the spring of 1921 to forestall an impending race in naval armaments between the United States and Great Britain, and not before they were needed. The American Naval Act of 1916 had been widely advertised as aiming to produce a navy "second to none." Though the unprecedented building programme had not been carried through when the United States entered the war, the American Navy, though considerably inferior to the British Navy in capital ships, had under construction or authorized in 1918 ships which would give it battle-line superiority in almost every respect. With superior financial and economic resources behind them, the Americans used the threat of naval building as a lever to induce the British to accept the League of Nations at the Paris Peace Conference while the British used the threat of not entering the League as a means of securing a modification of the American building programme. On April 9, 1919, an agreement was reached at Paris whereby the British agreed to support Wilson's plan for a league of nations, including the reservation in the Covenant regarding the validity of the Monroe Doctrine, and in return the American agreed to consider suspending the programme for naval building. Returning to the United States, the President used the same threat of "League or a big navy" in an effort to swing public opinion behind adherence to the Treaty of Versailles, and possibly also to persuade the British to accept naval parity. Though towards the end of Wilson's period in office, Congress repeatedly rejected Administration demands for increased naval appropriations, the attempt to rouse public opinion to a sense of crisis had its effect. Unfortunately, however, instead of securing American entry into the League, the only visible result was an increase in feeling against Great Britain and Japan as the only two powers against which such a programme could be aimed, and against the Anglo-Japanese Alliance which appeared on the surface to range these two countries against the United States.[12] Pointing to Japanese control of the former German islands in the Pacific north of the equator which now flanked American military communications from Hawaii to Guam and thence to the Philippines, American naval experts demanded a navy in the Pacific equal to the combined fleets of Japan and Great Britain, if the Anglo-Japanese Alliance were continued. At this point became apparent the inter-relation of naval rivalry, the Anglo-Japanese Alliance, and the Japanese threat to communications between the United States and its Pacific possessions which was to make it necessary to deal with the whole question of Pacific relations before naval arrangements could be concluded.

In the meantime the stage appeared set for a naval building race between the three countries. Japan, alarmed by American developments, had adopted the Eight Eight programme designed to give it fleet equality with the United States, and by 1921 was devoting half its revenue to its naval and military establishments. Pressure in Great Britain for increased naval building came both from the sense of imperial defence needs and reaction to American competition. A strong group in the United States favoured American naval dominance. But popular feeling against American arms expenditures arose again, Senator Borah reintroduced his resolution of February, 1921, calling for early naval negotiations with Great Britain and Japan, and, through Lord Lee, First Lord of the Admiralty, the British made it known informally "that they were prepared to abandon their traditional policy of a two-power navy and enter into an agreement with the United States for equality."[13]

The message was given to Mr. Adolph S. Ochs, publisher of the *New York Times*, during a visit to London late in April, 1921.[14] Lord Lee, a close friend of his, made it clear that the British were aware of American fears of a possible conflict with Japan and though he thought it was "a needless alarm," felt that public opinion might be quietened by combining Anglo-American naval parity with an arrangement whereby the American fleet could be concentrated in the Pacific and the British in the Atlantic Ocean. Noting that "there also existed a great deal of uneasiness with regard to Japan in British Columbia, Australia, and New Zealand," Lord Lee expressed the hope that Anglo-American negotiations could be undertaken soon "so that all discussion of the navy of the British Empire could be avoided at the forthcoming Dominions Conference in London in June."

The London correspondent of the *New York Times*, Ernest Marshall, acting for Ochs, transmitted this information to the American Secretary of the Navy, Edwin Denby, who regarded it "with favour and as possibly containing the germs of a future arrangement." Denby quickly inter-related the issue of naval policy with the renewal of the Anglo-Japanese Alliance to be considered at the forthcoming Imperial Conference upon which he believed "the attitude of the Australian and Canadian delegates would have an important bearing." He thought their view would be "that the pact should not be renewed unless some modification were introduced specifically excluding the possibility of suspicion that the United States could, under any circumstances, be made the common enemy of the two contracting powers," and emphasized this so strongly as to lead Marshall to think that he had received reports suggesting such a development.

The Anglo-Japanese Alliance

Renewal of the Anglo-Japanese Alliance proved in fact to be the most significant issue considered at the Imperial Conference of Prime Ministers of the Empire, which opened in London on June 20, 1921,[15] and more controversial than naval strength. The necessity of finding means through which some measure of naval disarmament could be reached was stressed both by Hughes of Australia and Massey of New Zealand. The Conference apparently found little difficulty in agreeing that the British Empire should accept naval parity with the United States, indicating their willingness in somewhat negative terms by declaring that "equality with the naval strength of any other Power is a minimum standard" for security.[16] Over the Anglo-Japanese Alliance, however, there was to be sharp division of opinion, particularly between the Australian and Canadian leaders. The latter had made representations to the British Government at least as early as February, 1921,[17] and probably before,[18] against renewal of the Alliance and in favour of a conference of the British Empire, the United States, Japan, and China, on Pacific affairs. This attitude was to be successfully maintained at the Conference against the weight of opinion on the other side.

Though the forthcoming Imperial Conference had been debated in each of the Dominion Parliaments, there had been only suggestions of the official points of view on the Alliance. Meighen, who had succeeded Borden as head of the Unionist Government, emphasized that the importance of the question to Canada arose "in a very great degree, out of the very great interest of the United States in the renewal or the non-renewal thereof,"[19] and hinted that the American point of view might differ from that of Great Britain, Australia, and other parts of the Empire. Rowell, no longer a member of the Government, could afford to be more direct and asked that the Treaty should not be renewed "at least in its present form"[20] in the interests of good relations not only between the British Empire and the United States but also between the United States and Japan. One of the Liberal leaders, Lapointe, asked for assurances that if the Treaty were renewed it should not be binding upon Canada without the consent of Parliament,[21] to which Meighen could only reply, ". . . Canada has the right of assent or non-assent. As to the extent to which we are bound in case war actually takes place, that is another question."[22] In the Pacific Dominions,

Japan loomed larger in considerations, though American apprehensions were recognized. Hughes was convinced that the renewal of the Alliance would be advantageous to Australia as long as there was a proviso that the "White Australia" principle should not be impaired, and sought authority in Parliament to renew it without further reference "in some form acceptable to Great Britain, to Japan, to Australia, and if possible, to America."[23] Particularly in the light of popular feeling against Japan[24] the debate in the Australian House was harmonious and it was generally accepted that the Treaty would make for peace. In New Zealand there was more opposition, the leader of the Labour party attacking it as a war treaty which might bring Britain into conflict with the United States if the latter clashed with Japan, but the Government, citing the advantages of Japanese aid during the war, favoured renewal.[25] The issue appeared most remote in South Africa. Smuts indicated that he favoured renewal if it could be combined with good relations with the United States, and a member of the Dominion party, Merriman, thought it might be a means of protection for the Dutch East Indies because it would restrain Japan, but Hertzog, the Nationalist leader, was against giving advice lest it should mean assuming obligations in the future.[26] Thus the nearest approach to a mandate which the Dominion leaders had in going to the Conference was that if the Alliance were renewed it should be clearly inapplicable against the United States and in a form as acceptable to the latter as possible.

The first few days of the Conference were spent under the impression that action on the Alliance had to be taken before July 13th, since it would then be one year since the two Governments had notified the Secretary-General of the League that they considered the Alliance in its existing form incompatible with the Covenant. The British appear to have planned to renew the Alliance for a year to provide an opportunity to discuss modifications and determine the line of policy to be adopted.[27] In this general approach, they were at one with the Pacific Dominions, and even before the British case for renewal was presented to the Conference by Lord Curzon on June 28th, Hughes and Massey had already proposed renewal. Hughes in his speech declared that the Treaty must specifically exclude any possibility of war with the United States and raised the possibility of meeting with the United States and Japan to determine what would be mutually satisfactory, but emphasized the value of the arrangement with Japan. Curzon was no less emphatic regarding its merits.

On the day following Curzon's speech, Meighen launched his attack against renewal of the Alliance, which was to lead the Conference to attempt to find a new basis of arrangements for the Pacific.[28] Meighen maintained that there was no longer reason for the existence of the Alliance, that such special relations were incompatible with the League conception and that both the United States and China would look on it as tacitly justifying Japanese aggression. Reiterating his belief that good relations between the British Commonwealth and the United States were the cornerstone of British policy and of international peace, he proposed again as in the February before a conference on Pacific affairs between the British Empire, the United States, Japan, and China. Hughes, who seems to have felt that Meighen was mistaking the voice of "a noisy anti-British faction in America for the sentiment of that great Republic,"[29] burst out in opposition to his proposal to terminate the Alliance, declaring that it would have a dangerous effect on Japanese feelings, that the United States could not be depended upon, and that it would seriously unsettle the Pacific situation. At this point Lloyd George intervened dramatically to ease the pressure on Conference discussions by announcing, with suitable corroboration by the Law Officers of the Crown, that the notice of incompatibility sent to the League in July, 1920, had not been a denunciation of the Alliance (the Japanese also did not interpret it as such) and it would therefore continue to run until twelve months after formal termination by either party. The way was open for a more leisurely exploration of possibilities. Meighen, however, took advantage of the new situation to drive his points home. Dominating the meeting of July 1st, he made vivid a new pattern of relations in the Pacific based on three or four-power collaboration in place of the existing two-power arrangements. Hughes' fire of criticism only strengthened Meighen's hand. Suddenly, it became apparent that Meighen had won his case by convincing Lloyd George. The latter took over control of the meeting and asked Curzon to outline plans for a Pacific Conference between the British Empire, the United States, Japan, and China. The meeting gradually swung behind this plan with only Hughes in angry opposition. By the end of the day, the Anglo-Japanese Alliance had been shelved as the basis for discussions.

Meighen's persistence deserves much of the credit for the move. The Conference had also been made directly aware of American opposition to the Alliance and interest in tripartite "co-operation" in the Pacific.[30] Moreover, Lloyd George seems to have become alarmed at the possible effect upon Japan of the leakages from the Conference rooms concerning the dispute over renewal of the Alliance. From this time on, his efforts were bent towards finding an arrangement which would supersede the Alliance, thereby avoiding the awkward situation of mere termination without providing an alternative.

By what means and on what basis could broader arrangements for the Pacific be secured? The Conference appears to have considered a meeting of all those countries "bordering upon or having interests in the Pacific"[31] but the thought of planning political arrangements in the Pacific within an assembly in which they would be so far outnumbered proved unpalatable. Gradually the Conference returned to the conception of a four-power meeting—the British Empire, the United States, Japan, and China—as the best means of securing the *rapprochement* with the United States which was desired, and of permitting China to state its case. Both the political basis for security in the Pacific, and the cessation of the naval armaments race could be considered in such a conference, they believed.[32] If the United States would consent to sponsor the conference, it was felt that its success would be better assured.

At this point British and American plans for an American-sponsored conference practically coincided. Lord Curzon approached Ambassador Harvey on July 5th to suggest that the President "invite powers directly concerned to take part in conference to be held to consider all essential matters bearing upon Far East and Pacific Ocean with a view to arriving at a common understanding designed to assure settlement by peaceful means, the elimination of naval warfare, consequent elimination of arms, etc."[33] At the moment he spoke, Curzon did not consider the matter so pressing but that it could be communicated to the American Government by mail since the Japanese were also being approached. But anxious questions in the British House of Commons on the future of the Anglo-Japanese Alliance led Lloyd George to suggest on the evening of July 7th that some negotiations with the United States, Japan, and China were in progress[34] and to indicate that he would give more specific details on July 11th. In view of this, Curzon pressed that every effort should be made to have a statement by the American Government which the Prime Minister could use in his speech on July 11th. Almost at the same moment that Ambassador Harvey was preparing his telegram describing these developments, the American Government was itself sending telegrams to its diplomatic representatives in Great Britain, France, Italy, and Japan to inquire whether it would be agreeable to the Governments to which they were accredited "to be invited by this Government to participate in a conference on limitation of armament, the conference to be held in Washington at a mutually convenient time."[35] The American Government had planned not to issue an official statement on the conference until after the passage of the naval bill with the Borah resolution, which could not be done before July 12th, but the necessity of responding to the British initiative led it not only to make an announcement through the press by the morning of July 11th but also to widen the purpose of the conference to include the discussion of Pacific and Far Eastern problems by interested powers including China. Thus the interaction of British and American initiatives shaped the character of the forthcoming Washington Conference.

Promising as developments had been, however, they failed to meet the desires of the Imperial Conference for a small conference of the interested parties, including the Dominion leaders, at which "an agreement satisfactory to America, Japan, and the British Empire, which would provide adequate guarantees for China" could be reached. If this could not be secured, Hughes writes, "the majority of representatives of the Empire" held that it would be essential to renew the Anglo-Japanese Alliance.[36] The American Government was asked, therefore, whether a conference on Pacific and Far Eastern problems would not be an essential preliminary to the disarmament conference at Washington. It was suggested that the preliminary meeting should be in London to permit Lloyd George and Curzon to attend and before August 15th when the Dominion Prime Ministers would have to leave for their parliamentary sessions. The plan was strongly endorsed by the Dominion Prime Ministers, and Hughes and Massey were reported to have "implored" American Ambassador Harvey to ask his Government to arrange the programme so that they would be able to attend. Harvey noted their belief that it would be to American advantage "especially as their interests were in all essential respects wholly identical with ours."[37]

Despite numerous attempts, however, it proved impossible to arrange a plan to which the American Government would accede. Secretary of State Hughes felt that a conference in London would not be favourably received by American public opinion in view of the special relations existing between Great Britain and Japan, and feared that an important preliminary meeting would relegate the arms limitation conference to a secondary position.[38] Curzon acknowledged the American problem but frankly did not consider it "as difficult or trying as his own problem, especially respecting the Dominion Premiers, whose presence and participation in considering problems of the Pacific" he felt to be imperative.[39] The next proposal was for "quiet consultation in London"[40] limited perhaps to discussions on the "open door," the territorial integrity of China, Shantung, and leased territory in and around the Pacific. Curzon believed this would pave the way for settlement of all other questions in open conference at Washington, "appease the Dominion Premiers," and make possible consideration of these political questions by Lloyd George, who probably could not get away to Washington for an extended time because of the Irish negotiations. Secretary Hughes seemed less opposed to this idea and, emboldened by this encouragement, the Prime Ministers now produced a third plan, for a rapid trip by Lloyd George, Curzon, Meighen, Hughes, and Massey to Bar Harbour, Maine, for tripartite considerations of the agenda for the larger conference and if possible to reach a "common understanding on wider principles which should underlie future Pacific policy of three Powers."[41] This plan, however, was flatly rejected by Secretary Hughes as having far wider implications than he had envisaged for the London discussions.[42] Thus ended the attempts to have a preliminary conference on political problems of the Pacific at which the Dominion Prime Ministers could be represented. The latter were bitterly disappointed at this outcome and the Summary of the Conference proceedings speaks of the "utmost regret" felt that the opposition of the American Government made the plan impossible.[43]

This regret arose not only from the fact that most of the Dominion Prime Ministers and probably Lloyd George himself would not be able to be present when new arrangements for the Pacific were considered but also because it meant an unsettled situation in regard to the Anglo-Japanese Alliance over which the Dominion Prime Ministers were still unreconciled. In the end, it was decided that the Treaty should not be denounced until the Washington Conference had reached a satisfactory conclusion or a new Treaty had been drawn up to replace the existing one. If the Washington Conference did not arrive at a satisfactory conclusion, the Alliance, adapted to the Covenant, was to stand.[44] Its future was left dependent therefore upon what should be devised at Washington.

Dominion Representation at the Washington Conference

After their strenuous though unsuccessful efforts to arrange a meeting at which Dominion Prime Ministers would be able to participate in consideration of Pacific and Far Eastern questions, the British Government apparently became less alert about the problems which might arise in relation to representation of the Dominions at the Washington Conference. On August 11th, the United States issued formal invitations to Great Britain, France, Japan, and Italy (the former Allied powers with which the United States had been associated in the war) to attend "a Conference on the subject of Limitation of Armament" and to these powers and China, Holland, Portugal, and Belgium to participate in the discussion of Pacific and Far Eastern questions at the Conference.[45] The lack of direct invitations to the Dominions has customarily been interpreted as "a deliberate reminder" that the United States had "not yet recognized the new status which the Dominions believed they had won at the Peace Conference and in the League of Nations."[46] But in the absence of specific notification by the British to the Americans of a desire for a change in the traditional form of invitation, the latter could not have been expected to issue direct invitations to the Dominions.[47] Borden considered the American course of action to be "in full conformity with diplomatic usage."[48] More important at this stage of diplomatic development was the fact that the American Government expected and welcomed Dominion representation on the British delegation. Whatever lack of consideration there was for Dominion "rights" or feelings in this instance seems to have been British rather than American, though American tardiness in making it clear whether discussions on Pacific affairs were to proceed simultaneously with those on disarmament or whether there were to be two separate conferences may well have complicated the situation.

As soon as the British had accepted the invitation to the Washington Conference, Secretary Hughes asked the American Ambassador to ascertain the number of representatives Great Britain wished to have on its commission since "presumably" it would "desire to include Dominion representatives and of course this would be very acceptable to the United States."[49] He thought six would be a good number to "give full opportunity for Dominion representation" but when Ambassador Harvey discussed the matter with Curzon, the latter favoured two or at most three. Harvey had the impression that Curzon and Lloyd George expected to represent the British Empire, a point apparently confirmed by Lloyd George's telegram to Meighen on October 3rd which declared to the latter's surprise that "it was arranged at recent Imperial Conference that His Majesty's Government should represent the whole Empire at Washington."[50] Harvey also felt that Curzon and Lloyd George did not wish to have the Dominions directly represented by delegates "upon same plane of authority as themselves."[51] Several days before this conversation, Meighen had wired Lloyd George to ask information regarding the agenda and scheme of representation proposed for the Conference, and on August 27th he wired again that he was "most anxious" to know how Canada was to be represented on the British Empire delegation.[52] On the same day (August 29th) that Secretary Hughes replied to Harvey that his own preference was for smaller delegations but that he was eager "that idea should not get abroad that we have limited size of delegation and thus made impracticable Dominions' representation,"[53] Lloyd George was answering Meighen that nothing was known yet of the agenda and that "Until we know whether Irish question will require an Autumn Session of Parliament it is impossible to make any nominations here as regards representation."[54]   Not till September 20th, when the British notified the Americans that Lloyd George would be unable to attend the Conference, did the former declare that they would probably wish to send five or six delegates "to give the Dominions representation" and also India, a move immediately acceded to by Secretary Hughes, who declared that he was "particularly glad to know that the Dominions would be represented."[55]

All the troubles regarding the representation of the Dominions at the Conference were not yet over, however, for when the British finally asked for nominations of Dominion representatives to serve on the British delegation, Smuts protested in a wire to Meighen that the United States should send separate invitations to each Dominion, as otherwise Dominion status would suffer.[56]   This message, passed on to Lloyd George, resulted in agreement by the latter that "Dominion representatives should hold same status as at Paris," that is, that the signatures of Dominion delegates would be needed as well as those of the British to bind the British Empire Delegation, and that any Dominion delegate could reserve assent to his Government on any specific point.[57]   Armed with this assurance, Meighen replied to Smuts that there did not seem time enough to secure a change in the form of invitation and accepted on behalf of Canada the procedure suggested by Lloyd George.[58]

To Smuts, under the harrying of the Nationalist party, form assumed a major place: to Meighen, the substance of representation was sufficient.   Those who were reluctant to press for separate invitations foresaw that if the Dominions were not invited to international conferences as members of the British Empire Delegation, they might well not go at all.   What reason could there be for South Africa or indeed for any of the Dominions, to attend a naval conference?   Why should the Dominions be grouped with the great powers and not with Belgium and Holland in a Far Eastern Conference unless they were considered to have some special unity with Great Britain.   Fear of losing the substance in vain pursuit of the form was a restraining influence on many, including Borden, who frankly faced the possible implications of the situation.   But between those who favoured a separate invitation and those who were willing to accept matters as they stood, there was no division regarding the necessity of effective representation at the Conference.   Had the Conference been concerned exclusively with naval disarmament there would have been reason to allow Great Britain to represent the whole Commonwealth, as Lloyd George maintained had been decided at the Imperial Conference. Once it became apparent that Pacific and Far Eastern matters in general would be considered, there was little chance that the Dominions bordering on the Pacific would have been willing to hand over the representation of their interests. Australia and New Zealand had direct concern with any change in power relations in the Pacific and Canada had already assumed some responsibilities for future arrangements in that area, at least in as far as they affected Anglo-American relations.

During the Washington Conference, Sir Robert Borden, Canada's chief delegate, reported, though there were "strong, sometimes vehement, differences of opinion" within the British Empire Delegation, it was accepted that "in matters of vital concern, and especially those involving its political unity, the Commonwealth must speak with one voice."[59] In the twenty-five meetings of the British Empire Delegation of which the New Zealand delegate, Sir John Salmond, speaks in his report,[60] opinions were exchanged in order "to reach in advance conclusions that could be put forward on behalf of the whole Empire."[61] Hence, unlike the practice at the League, Dominion delegates did not express their independent views in the public sessions of the Conference. They were no less effective for this reason in maintaining their special purposes and points of view, as Borden was to point out in a special report to the Prime Minister.[62] Canada's chief aim continued to be good relations between Great Britain and the United States, which Borden sought to implement by supporting new arrangements for the Pacific to take the place of the Anglo-Japanese Alliance and by encouraging the British to accept the naval proposals brought forward by the Americans. The special concern of the Australians and New Zealanders was to see that any alternative to the Anglo-Japanese Alliance safeguarded their position in the South Pacific.

The Washington Conference: Political Arrangements in the Pacific

The Washington Conference was concerned with three great issues: disarmament, political arrangements in the Pacific, and the future of China. Each bore a close relationship to the others, but each was considered more or less separately, partly because of the different groups of powers involved, and partly because an agreement upon disarmament was dependent upon finding a broad substitute for the Anglo-Japanese Alliance. For the sake of clarity, the political discussions between the British, Americans, and Japanese, which resulted in the Four Power Treaty, will be considered first and by themselves though it should be kept in mind that parallel to them deliberations were being held on the startling proposals for naval disarmament which so dramatically opened the Conference.

By the time the Conference convened, both the British and Japanese had made up their minds that new arrangements for the Pacific would have to be sought. The Japanese were the more reluctant to give up the Alliance, though Lord Balfour, the chief British delegate, had been one of the original architects of the agreement and recognized its value for Great Britain not only from the military angle but also as a restraining influence on Japanese policy in the Far East. Already uncertainty about future arrangements had led to a certain hostility in Japan towards the British which made it impossible to have prior discussion on the agenda of the Conference.[63] The Japanese were apparently ready, however, to consider tripartite arrangements with Great Britain and the United States.[64] The Americans had again made clear their desire to have the Alliance terminated[65] and the British decided to enter at once into negotiations.[66]

Borden, who reached Washington before Balfour, Salmond, and Sir George Pearce, the Australian representative, had had conversations with Senator Lodge and Mr. Elihu Root (both members of the American delegation) before the British Empire Delegation met on December 10th for its first comprehensive discussion of the Anglo-Japanese Alliance. He was able to assure the Delegation that Root and Lodge agreed with him that "the greatest success obtainable at this Conference would be an understanding (an alliance being impossible and undesirable) between the British Commonwealth and the American Republic."[67] Root had spoken strongly of the "disastrous effect upon American public opinion of a renewal of the Alliance," and in response to Borden's summary of the opinions expressed by the Australian and New Zealand Prime Ministers at the Imperial Conference had been "disposed to believe that an arrangement as to security in the Pacific could be established which would be much more valuable." Borden explained to Senator Pearce and to Salmond his desire "to obtain from the Americans some guarantee which would be satisfactory to them in case the Anglo-Japanese Alliance should not be renewed" and they seemed to be "a good deal impressed" by what he said. Such preparatory moves to secure agreement were to be among Borden's chief contributions to the success of the conversations which opened next day when Balfour approached Secretary Hughes to discuss the Anglo-Japanese Alliance.

Detailing the disadvantage of the Alliance, American sentiment, and the advantages, "Japanese sense of dignity—Control of Japanese action—Sense of security of Dominions,"[68] Balfour made a personal suggestion that it be replaced by two agreements, one of which was subsequently to form the basis for the Nine Power Treaty pertaining to China, while the other was for a tripartite arrangement between the United States, the British Empire, and Japan for "the preservation of peace and the maintenance of the territorial status quo."[69] This latter arrangement, which Balfour thought of as replacing the existing Anglo-Japanese Alliance, was to include a pledge to respect each other's rights and to consult with each other concerning "the best means of protecting them" whenever they appeared to be "imperilled by the action of another Power." If territorial rights were threatened by any other Power or combination of Powers, any two of the contracting parties were to be at liberty to enter into a military arrangement "provided (a) this arrangement is purely defensive in character and (b) that it is communicated to the other High Contracting Party."[70] The purpose was to maintain "the general peace in the regions of Eastern Asia" and to protect "the existing territorial rights of the High Contracting Parties in the islands of the Pacific Ocean and the territories bordering thereon." It thus covered Australia, New Zealand, and Western Canada as well as other British territories in the Pacific, and American and Japanese territories and possessions in that area.

This proposal was for a very different type of relationship than that provided by the Anglo-Japanese Alliance. The latter had been both a defensive and an offensive alliance pledging aid in case either party became involved in war with more than one country. Balfour's proposal provided for mutual acceptance of territorial arrangements, for *consultation* in case of danger, and for the *possibility* of concluding a defensive military arrangement if territorial rights "in the islands of the Pacific Ocean and the territories bordering thereon" were threatened.[71] In the course of discussions, the latter part of the proposal was to be dropped and also the guarantee of territorial rights in the territories bordering the Pacific Ocean. But two points of Balfour's original suggestion were to appear in considerably modified form in the final agreement, the Four Power Treaty: the mutual pledge of respect for each other's possessions, and the agreement to consult in case these rights were threatened by the aggressive act of any other power.

The final form of the agreement stemmed from suggestions made by each of the main parties, though the American influence was predominant. Balfour had told Hughes at their first meeting that he must see the Japanese delegates, but he apparently delayed some time before broaching the subject to them. The secretary of their delegation maintained that they were "dumbfounded" when they learned "very late in November" of Balfour's memorandum to Hughes.[72] The

Japanese then prepared their own draft of a tripartite arrangement[73] which, though accepted in some measure in the final agreement, contained a recognition of Japan's conquests in Asia which Secretary Hughes naturally refused to accept. The latter's proposals included one entirely new feature, the inclusion of France as a party to the Treaty, an innovation intended in part to mollify that country, which was already incensed over proposed naval ratios but more particularly to disarm criticism of the Treaty in the United States since, as Hughes later put it, the inclusion of France would mean "four votes and not three, and no one could say that England and Japan could combine against us."[74] With this accepted, Hughes then introduced his own draft for a four-power agreement, in which for the first time the pledges were limited to "rights in relation to their insular possessions and dominions in the Pacific Ocean." It also made no provision for action except by consultation through communications to agree on "the most efficient measures to be taken" and in case of disputes between the parties, a joint conference. This, being apparently the maximum on which agreement could be secured, was accepted without opposition and became the Four Power Treaty of which public announcement was made on December 10, 1921.

The limitation in the area covered by the Treaty to "insular possessions and dominions in the Pacific Ocean" was intended by Hughes to "avoid the difficulties connected with the mainland, especially as to China."[75] On the other hand, he maintained that the Treaty covered mandated areas.[76] An amusing question of prestige was raised by the Japanese desire to exclude the mainland of Japan from the pledge of the Treaty since the mainlands of the other major contracting powers were not included (not being islands in the Pacific). Balfour opposed excluding Japan lest it indicate that Australia and New Zealand were in an inferior position and the Japanese finally gave in "to avoid anything which in British eyes would be detrimental to the position of Australia or New Zealand."[77] The decision had ultimately to be reversed, however, due to wholly unjustified suspicions roused by the American press that the Japanese were endeavouring to get a particularly favourable position for themselves by having their homeland guaranteed when the United States was not.[78]

The Four Power Treaty, which was signed December 13, 1921, was the first formal achievement of the Washington Conference. Though it was a less definite agreement than the British had hoped to achieve, it answered their needs in three major respects by terminating the Anglo-Japanese Alliance without precipitating a rupture with Japan, by providing for American participation in Pacific arrangements, and by the pledge covering Australia and New Zealand. Balfour believed that the pledge also covered Vancouver (he probably meant Vancouver Island), though no other part of Canada.[79]

Borden, though feeling that the agreement concerned Australia and New Zealand and the major signatories more directly than it did Canada, believed that it was "of the most vital concern to us that the Powers interested should agree upon some peaceful method of settling their differences in this region."[80] He felt that the "essential and vital" feature of the agreement was that it provided a "definite method" in accordance with which "if relations become strained the issues involved may be adjusted through a joint conference between all the parties to the agreement." By introducing the conference method of settling disputes, public opinion would be able to exert its influence. His own feeling was that the formal restriction of the arrangement to islands in the Pacific would not in fact limit its operation in "any threatened rupture in this region."[81] In asking authority to sign on behalf of Canada, he pointed out to Meighen that the Four Power Treaty was "entirely in line with the proposal and purposes advocated by you at last summer's conference."[82]

The less advantageous aspects of the Treaty were to become more apparent as time went on. In giving up their special relationship with Japan, the British were undoubtedly weakening one of the sources of their influence in the Far East. The new arrangement lacked the personal character and direct binding force of the Anglo-Japanese Alliance. It could not help but be evident, also, that Great Britain had deliberately chosen good relations with the United States in place of a close tie with Japan. Coupled with the realization that the United States and Great Britain were in agreement on disarmament and naval ratios, it served to induce a certain sense of isolation in Japan which was later to be played on cleverly by aggressive military leaders. Moreover, despite Borden's optimism, the provision for consultation in case of a threatened dispute rested only on the voluntary decision of the parties. Borden had pointed out that the agreement imposed "no warlike obligations."[83] Seen from the other aspect, this meant that there was no specific provision for enforcement. Ultimately it rested on the good intentions of the signatories.

In the existing temper of American public opinion, however, no stronger arrangements could have been secured.[84] The Four Power Treaty in resting on self-limiting pledges of non-aggression coupled with provision for consultation in time of danger was in line with traditional American practice. The second reservation to the Treaty stated that "there is no commitment to armed force, no alliance, no obligation to join in defence" and the Senate vote in favour of this was larger than for the Four Power Treaty itself. Even political leaders seemed unaware of the dangers implicit in the exposed position of the Philippines.

The most positive general result of the Four Power Treaty was that it ended the Anglo-Japanese Alliance, a potent cause of antagonism between Great Britain and the United States, and paved the way for an entente between them. Thereby it healed also a potential split in the Commonwealth. In the more immediate situation, the Treaty was an essential preliminary step to an agreement on naval disarmament which was already proving difficult enough to reach.

Naval Disarmament at the Washington Conference

While the discussions which resulted in the Four Power Treaty were being carried on in secret, the Conference was undertaking in public to follow the agenda laid down for it. The five Allied and Associated powers held sessions on disarmament, which centred about naval disarmament, parallel to which nine powers, including China, were engaged in considering Far Eastern issues.

The British had come to the Conference prepared to accept naval parity with the United States but they were completely taken aback by the precise proposals embodied in Hughes' opening speech, which sank "in thirty-five minutes more ships than all the admirals of the world have destroyed in a cycle of centuries," as a British observer wrote.[85] In minute detail, Hughes described not only the ships which the United States was prepared to sacrifice in the interests of disarmament but also those which the British and Japanese should destroy in the same cause. He ended by proposing a ten-year holiday in naval building. Admiral Beatty came forward in his chair like a suddenly startled bulldog, an American reporter observed.[86] Balfour, in consternation, whispered to Borden that he could not possibly agree.[87] But Borden insisted that Balfour had to consent and persuaded him at least not to signify any disagreement with the proposals.

The delegations then retired to consider during the next three days the implications of the proposals which had been made to them. Balfour accepted that they were "bold and statesmanlike"[88] and cabled the Cabinet that as far as the reduction in capital ships was concerned the American plan should be accepted "in principle and without reservations."[89] There were other points, however, to be considered. The far-flung character of the Empire gave cruisers and auxiliary ships special significance for the British. They realized that any agreement should also cover secondary navies which might otherwise become rivals to the reduced British fleet. Also to be taken into account was the situation in regard to submarines, whose menace to the extended shipping lines which linked the overseas Empire to Great Britain had been demonstrated so dangerously during the war. On none of these points was there reason to suppose that there would be serious, if any, disagreement between the British and Americans. Where the naval advisers of the British delegation were least disposed to approve the American plan was in relation to the ten-year holiday in the building of capital ships. They believed that gradual replacements would fit their situation much better both from the point of view of their naval shipyards programme and because the majority of British ships were older than those of the United States. They were not prepared, therefore, to accept the idea of a naval building holiday.

Borden was much disturbed by this attitude. He personally felt that the conception of a naval holiday would appeal strongly to public opinion and should be accepted for this reason if for no other. In a special memorandum prepared for the British Empire Delegation,[90] he strongly urged that they accept in principle the whole American plan and should express willingness to go even farther along the line of disarmament, while avoiding the impression of competing in pacific utterances. He suggested that the British Empire Delegation should not only accept the naval holiday but should propose that a conference would be called three or five years before its termination for the purpose of considering an extension of the holiday in naval building for another ten or even twenty years. If no agreement were reached, the intervening period would provide sufficient time to prepare material and personnel to ensure the Empire's safety. But he felt it was hardly possible that any country would wish to continue competition in arms once it had experienced the benefit of being free from it. In addition, Borden felt that although the American proposals were impressive in conception and courageous in presentation, they embodied a temporary expedient rather than a permanent solution. They included no provision whereby war might be avoided. He hoped, therefore, that it might also be possible to allude to the vital necessity of finding means for the peaceful settlement of disputes.

Pearce, to whom Borden showed this memorandum, added a short one of his own[91] in which he concurred "generally" in the views Borden had set forth. Pearce favoured making an even more definite statement in regard to a reduction in submarines of the type "capable of offensive action at great distances from their home shores" which he believed would be in keeping with the general character of the American proposals "to so reduce naval strength of a character capable of offensive action, as to make such action difficult or impossible."

Borden submitted these memoranda to Balfour the afternoon before the latter was to give the official British reply to the American proposals. Borden pointed out "that naval men naturally attached undue importance to the maintenance of armament plants, while the great mass of the people would prefer to see all such plants demolished." "Especially I urged a wholehearted acceptance of the American proposal," wrote Borden in his diary.[92] Next morning, Borden was again beside Balfour as the Conference session opened. "Before he spoke," wrote Borden, "I had the opportunity of urging upon him the importance of making no reservation. Just as the meeting was called to order, I said to him 'declare that you accept the American proposal in spirit and in principle.' It was with a great deal of satisfaction that I heard him use that exact expression in his speech. . . ."[93]

Borden had succeeded in preventing any official British reservation on the arms proposals but he had not yet carried his point in the British Empire Delegation regarding the naval holiday. Hankey, the secretary of the British Delegation, had received Borden's permission to circulate the memorandum which he regarded as of "great importance," but the naval experts continued to adhere to their view that such a policy would be unwise.[94] Borden strongly maintained his position in subsequent discussions in the Delegation, pointing out how unfortunate it would be to quibble over details in the face of a proposal for parity by a country possessing "financial and material resources which would enable it, beyond question, to outstrip the British Empire in any competition in naval armaments."[95] Fortunately for his point, the British Cabinet also supported the naval holiday though they, too, were under fire of criticism from the Admiralty. In the end, the British accepted the conception of a naval holiday. But by the time it was announced, public ardour was considerably dampened by the recognition that difficulties in reaching agreements on both battleships and cruisers meant that in fact there would be building in both these categories during the ten-year period.

From the first, the Japanese had been reluctant to accept the 5-5-3 ratio for capital ships which formed the basis of Hughes' proposals. A series of negotiations between the Americans and Japanese, in which the British generally stood on the sidelines, culminated in virtual deadlock on November 30th over the Japanese insistence on retaining one of its super battleships which had been built by public subscription. A compromise was eventually secured, however, by allowing Japan to keep its newest battleship, the *Matsu*, even though this entailed subsequent British building to maintain the ratio, and by an agreement to maintain the *status quo* in the fortifications of islands in the Western Pacific. Though Japanese in origin, this arrangement regarding fortifications met with the hearty support of the Pacific Dominions, which felt that it added to their security.

Hughes reacted unfavourably at first to the Japanese proposal on fortifications which was transmitted to him by Balfour on December 1st.[96] He thought that military and naval opinion would be opposed and that the "American people would probably refuse to fetter themselves in regard to their right to fortify their own Possessions." His own counter-suggestion was that if any power did decide to erect fortifications, the others should be notified and would then have the right to terminate the naval agreement. Balfour opposed this as lending an element of instability to the arms arrangement. Hughes was convinced and thereafter turned his attention to using an agreement on fortifications as a means of securing adherence to both the Four Power Treaty and the arms proposals.[97] He insisted, however, that a distinction should be made between fortifications which could be used for offensive purposes and those which clearly contributed to defence. The Japanese delegate, Baron Kato, had included Hawaii among the bases on which no further fortifications were to be erected, but Hughes maintained that it was a defensive base which should be excluded from the agreement. He assumed that the main islands of Japan and the ports of Australia and New Zealand would also be excluded. Finally, after other American delegates had convinced him that, in any case, Congress would never vote the money to fortify the bases adequately, Hughes agreed to pledge the *status quo* in fortifications for Guam and the Philippines if Japan, Great Britain, and France would make the same guarantee for their islands.[98]

Balfour, who agreed that the non-fortification agreement was a logical corollary to arms limitation, had encouraged the Japanese to accept the naval ratio proposed by the Americans and, on December 12th, Kato announced in a private meeting the willingness of his Government to accept the ratio if they received a definite understanding regarding the *status quo* in fortifications on islands in the Pacific. Three days later, public announcement was made that the ratio for capital ships had been accepted.[99] At the same time was made known the agreement that there should be no increase in the fortifications on islands "in the Pacific region, including Hong Kong." This restriction was not to apply, however, to "the Hawaiian Islands, Australia, New Zealand, and the islands composing Japan proper, or, of course, to the coasts of the United States and Canada, as to which the respective Powers retain their entire freedom."

At first sight the arrangement was clear, but almost at once it became apparent that agreement was lacking as to what was implied by such phrases as "the Pacific region," "Japan proper," and "the coasts of the United States and Canada." The American delegation decided to wait for the other parties to take the initiative, which both the Japanese and British did on January 7th at a meeting attended by naval and military experts. The Japanese entered a claim to exclude certain islands from the effect of the non-fortification agreement, especially the Bonins, which they claimed were part of Japan proper, though in fact they lay several hundred miles away from the Japanese mainland. The British claimed exemption for all islands which were outside of a parallelogram bounded by the 180th meridian on the east (the International Date Line), the 30th degree on the north, the 110th meridian on the west and the equator on the south. This parallelogram to which they proposed limiting the non-fortifications agreement included practically all of the Japanese islands, most of the American islands, and very few British islands.[100]

The Japanese proposal came immediately under fire from both sides. The British claimed that the Japanese interpretation infringed the previous understanding. The Americans rejected a Japanese proposal of an informal pledge not to fortify the islands so reserved. The temporary deadlock was broken at a meeting on January 10th at which Kato attempted to make a compromise between the orders of his Government that the Bonin Islands should be excluded from the agreement and the understanding of his colleagues that they should be included, by offering to maintain the *status quo* in the islands of Oshima, Bonin, the Pescadores, and Formosa if, for reasons of domestic policy, they could be referred to by name in a separate declaration and not in the main Treaty.[101]

The British were more fortunate in regard to their proposal to exclude islands outside the suggested parallelogram. The purpose of their proposal, as Balfour disclosed to Kato, was to meet the demand of the Australian delegate, "who desired to reserve the right to fortify Papuan Bay in British New Guinea," though there was no immediate plan to do so.[102] In the final agreement on both British and Japanese proposals, Balfour's proposal of a parallelogram was adopted[103] as the means to designate the islands covered by the agreement. Hughes approved this as fulfilling the purpose of the arrangement which was "to prevent the United States of America and Japan from making bases within reach of one another."[104]

If the effect of the non-fortification agreement was to strengthen Japan's position, it seems equally clear that in any case the American Government would not have been able to convince Congress of the necessity of fortifying Guam and the Philippines. Thus there was little for the Americans to lose and perhaps something to gain by limiting the opportunities for rivalry. From the British side, the agreement not to modernize the fortifications of Hong Kong perhaps weakened their strategic position in China, though there was little reason for the expenditure once the idea of a powerful Far Eastern fleet had been abandoned. Outside of the Japanese, probably the most satisfied with the arrangement were the Australians and New Zealanders. Borden wrote in his official report that "the special interests of Canada, Australia, and New Zealand were . . . taken into account in reaching the formula in the Naval Treaty for preserving the *status quo* in respect of the fortifications of the Pacific islands."[105] Later a New Zealand writer noted that the Pacific Dominions approved particularly of this agreement as indicating that "the so-called 'navalist school' advocating extension of the Japanese Empire southwards had been effectively checked" while at the same time the British Government had not been limited in "its right to construct a major Pacific base at Singapore" or in the "use of the islands adjacent to Australia and New Zealand for naval and air defence."[106]

Though with difficulty the agreement on battleships had been secured, it did not prove possible to arrange a particularly satisfactory limitation on cruisers, auxiliary craft, and submarines. In his opening speech at the second session, Balfour had pointed to the extended communications of the British Empire as necessitating strong forces of the cruiser type. Inability to determine the numbers needed by colonial powers led to an agreement to restrict cruisers to 10,000 tons and eight-inch guns, limits which proved in practice to be high and to which countries began immediately to build. Reduction of submarines capable of offensive action at a far distance from their bases had been suggested by Pearce in his memorandum and was a measure strongly endorsed by the British out of their experience during the war. Unfortunately the consideration of submarines precipitated a sharp altercation between the British and French which intensified feeling already raised by battleship ratios and by an attempt to discuss limitation of land armaments, which despite Borden's intervention,[107] had been virtually blocked by the French delegates.

The British favoured complete abolition of submarines but were advised by Hughes against so radical a move lest it alienate the smaller powers, who looked on the submarine as "the only naval weapon available to a weak power with an extensive coastline," and would feel it "contrary to international policy to abolish it."[108] Hughes believed that among all the non-British powers at the Conference only the United States would support the proposal and that in the long run even American feeling might find it unfair to smaller countries. Lord Lee, First Lord of the Admiralty, still favoured making the proposal in the plenary session but the opposition of Borden, Pearce, and Salmond led Balfour to decide to raise it first in Committee.[109] Even here, however, the proposal resulted in a French outburst due partly to the rather maladroit way in which Lord Lee presented the British case. In the end the British had to accept the unsatisfactory substitute of an American-sponsored code of conduct under which the submarines of adhering parties were supposed henceforth to be operated. Much of the effect of battleship limitation was thus nullified by inability to reach agreement on reductions in other categories.

Consideration of the Future of China

Parallel with these discussions on armaments were being held nine-power considerations of the Eastern issues which centred about the future of China. This was the most obviously controversial subject at issue between the United States and Japan, and much of the latter's hesitation at coming to the Conference had been caused by fear of being arraigned for the encroachments on Chinese territory and economic life which it had made while Great Britain and the United States were distracted by the European war. Beyond this was the growing recognition of the significance of China's development for stability in the Far East. If China itself were to become stable, both internal disorders and external interferences would have to be curbed.[110]

The official Far Eastern sessions at the Conference proceeded cautiously on the basis of proposals made by the Chinese for reducing China's dependence on outside powers, while numerous outside discussions between the Japanese, Americans, and British, and between the Japanese and Chinese sought compromises in knotty issues. Six particular matters were debated with some result. China and Japan engaged on informal discussions on Shantung, which culminated in a promising announcement to the Conference. They also agreed to leave to investigation on the spot a division of opinion regarding the presence of Russian guards and police boxes in China. The consideration of leased territories and spheres of influence in China resulted in the relinquishment by the British of Wei-hai-wei but not of the Kowloon extension of Hong Kong. It was decided that the question of extra-territoriality in China depended on existing Chinese practices and a nine-power Commission was set up to investigate and assist in reforms. The United States, Great Britain, France, and Japan agreed to abandon their separate post offices in China if an efficient Chinese postal service were maintained under the existing administration and French director. Some progress was also made in one of the most difficult of the issues under discussion, that of Chinese revenue and tariffs.   On this subject, Borden acted as British representative and his proposals became the basis of discussion.[111]   They were accepted in principle by all the participating countries except Japan, and finally after innumerable private conversations with the Japanese and American delegates Borden succeeded in reaching an agreement, which combined an increase in the Chinese tariff with safeguards against letting the additional revenue be eaten up by Chinese warlords and military establishments. The attempt was also made to limit internal tariffs in the hope that a freer movement of goods within China might improve its general economic situation.

In the long view, the achievements of the Conference in regard to the future of China were promising rather than permanent.   Steps were taken to facilitate more orderly government within China but Hughes' opposition to any move for international control of internal affairs in China[112] prevented the consideration of external means of curbing its internal disorders.   The Japanese made minor concessions which created a better atmosphere, particularly between the United States and Japan, and might be hoped to mark a new attitude towards China. On the other hand, no definite date was set for the withdrawal of Japanese troops from Chinese soil, nor did the Japanese relinquish their grip on Manchuria.   The discussions culminated, however, in a formal guarantee of China's integrity embodied in the Nine Power Treaty.   Under this agreement, the nine powers—Great Britain, the United States, Japan, China, France, Italy, the Netherlands, Portugal, and Belgium—promised to respect the territorial integrity and sovereignty of China, to allow it full opportunity to develop a stable government, to maintain the "open door," and not to take advantage of disturbed conditions in China to secure special privileges for themselves.   Like the other Treaties concluded at the Washington Conference, there was no provision for guarantees.   The Nine Power Treaty guaranteeing Chinese integrity might be hoped to lessen opportunities for conflict by reducing the causes of rivalry.   Like the other agreements, it rested ultimately on the good faith of all the participants.

In the early days of the Conference, Borden had pointed out in his memorandum that arms limitation was a temporary expedient and that agreement should be sought on some more positive provisions for the pacific settlement of disputes.   When Balfour did not take up the idea in his speech to the Conference as Borden had hoped, the latter proceeded to explore possibilities in conversations with prominent American citizens like W. J. Bryan, who agreed with him on "the necessity of establishing some international tribunal for the investigation and, if possible, the adjustment of international disputes with provision that no hostilities shall be commenced until after the investigation has been concluded."[113]   The deadlock with France over the limitation of land armaments which Briand fiercely refused to consider in France's state of insecurity provided Borden with the opportunity to raise the question with Hughes.   Borden suggested that the establishment of a permanent International Tribunal to which nations agreed to refer their differences before commencing hostilities "would really give to France, though not in the form of an absolute agreement, every security which she could anticipate from a definite treaty such as Mr. Wilson had undertaken in 1919."[114]   "Experience has shown [he wrote later] that public opinion rather than the obligation of treaties, is powerful, under modern conditions, to bring nations to the aid of one another in war."[115] There was ample precedent for such a tribunal, Borden considered, in the thirty treaties with similar provisions into which the United States had entered about 1914 and since the project "would not bind the United States or any other nation to any definite action in the final results" it would avoid the difficulties which "had prevented the United States from accepting the Covenant of the League of Nations."   Hughes showed himself sympathetic to the proposal, saying that "the same idea had been in his own mind," but that he felt the existing situation was not propitious.   He agreed, too, that the security thus offered France "would be equal in its effect to that afforded by a formal guarantee" but had serious doubts as to whether Briand could be convinced.   Three days later Borden again raised the question with Balfour, suggesting that President Harding's endorsement of international agreements on the day before might provide the opportunity to find some means of associating the United States in an arrangement for the pacific settlement of disputes.   ". . . possibly you may agree with me," he concluded, "that, if we cannot have the United States enter the League of Nations, we should spare no effort to bring it into co-operation with us and with other nations, under any effective form of association.   In the end that great country may become a member of the League, under another name perhaps, and with modifications such as the nature of the United States' constitution and the traditions of its Senate may be found to require."[116]   Balfour, however, was "very reluctant" to take steps to duplicate machinery "which already exists" under the Covenant "unless and until" it was clear that "such a step was necessary to bring the

United States into line," and that "the duplication itself would be no more than temporary."[117]

Borden's initiative was to have no direct result either during the Conference or thereafter but it demonstrated the Canadian interest in establishing means for the pacific settlement of disputes and in bringing the United States into as formal arrangements as possible for this purpose. Apparently secure in its North American position, Canada's chief concern in the inter-war period was that international conflicts should be avoided and, more positively, that there should be an *entente* between the United States and Great Britain. Since American membership in the League had not been secured, Canada hoped that at the least there would be good relations between the United States and League powers and favoured any means of strengthening this co-operation.[118]

To all the Dominions, the treaties and agreements concluded at the Washington Conference brought two great advantages: a new basis for cordial relations between Great Britain and the United States, and release from what would have been the crippling burden of an armaments race in which the British Empire would be clearly inferior in resources to the United States. To Australia and New Zealand, with their isolated position in the South Pacific, the Four Power Treaty and the agreement not to fortify further the islands in the western Pacific brought release from the nightmare of Japanese expansion southwards. Canada, under the new Liberal Ministry which acquired office during the Conference, was to seek henceforth to avoid both imperial and general commitments. But the Pacific Dominions, acutely aware of the importance for their security in a time of crisis of British aid,[119] were to continue to support the conception of mutual guarantees within the Commonwealth. They favoured developing Singapore into a strong naval base, a programme begun soon after the conclusion of the Washington Conference and in return for the expectation of British aid if they faced danger were ready to give general, though not unlimited, support to Britain's international policy. To the whole Commonwealth, however, the decisions of the Washington Conference marked a turning point in policies on naval defence and on the Far East. Naval parity with the United States was accepted, and under the naval agreement, the potential weakness of the British Navy in the Far East. Good political relations with the United States were substituted for the special tie with Japan. Henceforth the security of the Empire in the Far East depended on the "omnibus guarantees'" of the Washington Treaties, the Covenant of the League of Nations, the British fleet at the strength decided on at Washington, and such contributions in their own defence as Australia and New Zealand might be able to muster.

REFERENCES FOR CHAPTER II

1. Harold and Margaret Sprout, *Towards a New Order of Sea Power* (Princeton, 1940), ch. 1, gives a vivid picture of the changing position of British sea power.

2. The question has been raised as to whether Japan took advantage of the existence of the Alliance to extend its influence in the Pacific but the burden of opinion is on the other side. The Sprouts say the Alliance was invoked by Britain "and Japan was invited to aid in clearing German naval forces from the Pacific." *Ibid.*, p. 32. Yamato Ichihashi, *The Washington Conference and After* (Stanford, California, 1928), pp. 117-18, cites different views on the subject but is also convinced that the British invoked the Alliance.

3. W. M. Hughes, wartime Prime Minister of Australia, suggests that Japanese aid made the difference between victory and defeat in the war. See *The Splendid Adventure* (London, 1929), pp. 32-34.

4. Cited by Mr. Meighen, *Canada, House of Commons Debates*, April 27, 1921, p. 2640.

5. Admiral Viscount Jellicoe, *Report on Naval Mission to Australia*, 1919; *Report on Naval Mission to New Zealand*, 1919; *Report on Naval Mission to Canada*, 1919, 10 George V, Sessional Paper, No. 61, A, 1920, 52 pp. The wording of the Reports is very similar as regards general topics. *See* also *The Round Table*, 1920, pp. 215-17, 421-27, and 644-51.

6. The percentages were based roughly on the population of Great Britain and each Dominion and on the value of their respective overseas trade with adjustments made for the fact that Australia and New Zealand would bear no part of the expenses of naval defence in the Atlantic. The Reports include fairly elaborate tables showing the data on which the estimates are made.

7. Lord Jellicoe suggested three plans to the Canadian Government. The one indicated was to provide minimum protection of its own trade and the other two were based on the supposition that Canada wished to make some contribution to imperial defence in general.

8. *J.P.E.*, 1920, I, 329 (Ballantyne, Minister of Naval Services, speaking March 25th). The French Canadian press was almost unanimous in opposing Admiral Jellicoe's proposals. *Cf. The Round Table.*

9. *J.P.E.*, 1920, I, 743, 376-7.

10. *Ibid.*, p. 376-7.

11. In discussing naval policy, General Smuts declared on May 20th in the House of Assembly that he did not know if South African defence would be discussed at the Conference and he believed "something far larger and more important would be brought up." *J.P.E.*, 1921, II, 667.

12. When the Anglo-Japanese Alliance was renewed in 1911, a clause was included stating that it would be inoperative in regard to a country with which either of the participants had a treaty of general arbitration. At the time, Great Britain was negotiating such a treaty with the United States, but it was not accepted by the Senate. In September, 1914, a "peace commission" treaty was signed by Great Britain and the United States and this was accepted by Great Britain and Japan as equivalent to a treaty of general arbitration. From this time on, therefore, the Alliance included specific provision that it could not be invoked against the United States. Public opinion in the United States, however, seems not to have been aware of this stipulation.

13. Eugene J. Young, *Powerful America* (New York, 1936), p. 49. Mr. Ochs' memorandum of the conversation with Lord Lee and the report of Mr. Marshall's conversation with Secretary of the Navy Denby are printed verbatim.

66   THE COMMONWEALTH AND INTERNATIONAL SECURITY

14. Lord Lee, who became First-Lord of the Admiralty in February, 1921, with the avowed desire of stopping "the senseless competition in armaments, particularly between the two great English-speaking countries," had responded to the suggestion in President Harding's inaugural address on March 4th that the United States would co-operate in an agreement on naval armaments by making a speech at the Institute of Naval Architects on March 16th putting forward his own point of view.   No official notice of his speech had apparently been taken, however, and Lord Lee, feeling that he could not do anything more in his official position, took the informal approach through Mr. Ochs which is described in the text.   *Ibid.*, pp. 53-4.   For other indications given during the spring of the British desire for an arms limitation agreement with the United States, *see* Sprout, *op. cit.*, pp. 124-25.

15. *Cmd. 1474*, Conference of Prime Ministers and Representatives of the United Kingdom, the Dominions, and India, *Summary* of Proceedings and Documents.

16. *Ibid.*, p. 6.   *See* also N. W. Rowell, *The British Empire and World Peace* (Toronto, 1922), pp. ix-x.

17. J. Bartlett Brebner, "Canada and the Anglo-Japanese Alliance," *Political Science Quarterly*, 1935, vol. 50, p. 53.

18. Sir Robert Borden, *Canada in the Commonwealth* (Oxford, 1929), p. 118, says, "There is good reason for concluding that representations of the Canadian Government during the winter and spring of 1921 had a marked influence upon the determination of this difficult and important question [the renewal of the Anglo-Japanese Alliance]."

19. *Canada, House of Commons Debates*, April 27, 1921, p. 2639.

20. *Ibid.*, p. 2657.

21. *Ibid.*, p. 2639.

22. *Ibid.*

23. *J.P.E.*, 1921, II, 610 (April 13th).

24. These included concern because under the Peace Treaty Japan had secured mandated islands, including the Marshall and Caroline Islands originally surrendered to Australia and other causes of friction arising out of lack of information on official decision.   It seems also to have been generally believed that the request for compulsory military service bore some relation to Japan.   E. L. Piesse, "Japan and Australia," *Foreign Affairs*, April, 1926, pp. 480-86.

25. *J.P.E.*, 1921, II, 659 ff. (March 14th).

26. *Ibid.*

27. *U.S.A. Foreign Relations*, 1921, II, 314.   (Memorandum of a Conversation between Secretary of State Hughes and British Ambassador Geddes, June 23, 1921.)

28. From here on except where noted the description of events follows Brebner's account of the Conference.

29. *J.P.E.*, 1921, II, 93.   He used this phrase during the debate in the Australian House of Representatives, September 30, 1921.   *See* also Hughes, *op. cit.*, p. 125.

30. Curzon repeated to the Conference the substance of the conversation between Hughes and Geddes on June 23, 1921, which is referred to above.   Sprout interprets Hughes' mention of the Congressional resolution on Ireland as an effort to force Great Britain to liquidate the Anglo-Japanese Alliance.   From another point of view, it may be noted that the hostility existing between Ireland and Great Britain which was soon to be eased by the Anglo-Irish Treaty was as serious a cause of Anglo-American friction as was the Anglo-Japanese Alliance.

31. Hughes, *op. cit.*, p. 123.

32. *Ibid.*, p. 124.

33. *U.S.A. Foreign Relations*, 1921, I, 19.

34. *Ibid.*, p. 20. In order not to undermine the impression that the initiative was American, this phrase was omitted from the official record. *Ibid.*, pp. 22-23.

35. *Ibid.*, p. 18.

36. Hughes, *op. cit.*, p. 130. "Reluctantly the representatives of the Empire agreed that the invitation had left our difficulties with the treaty very much where they were." In the Australian House of Representatives Hughes spoke later of his own advocacy of a preliminary conference or meeting. *J.P.E.*, 1921, II, 96 (September 30th).

37. *U.S.A. Foreign Relations*, 1921, I, 26.

38. *Ibid.*, pp. 28-29.

39. *See* statement by Cook (Acting Prime Minister) in the Australian House of Representatives regarding two Conferences and the importance of Australia attending the one on the Pacific. *J.P.E.*, 1921, II, 872-3.

40. *U.S.A. Foreign Relations*, 1921, I, 32. Both Japan and China appeared ready to have a preliminary conference in London. China feared Great Britain might fall back on the Anglo-Japanese Alliance if the disarmament conference failed and wanted a definite termination to the Alliance before the conference met. *Ibid.*, p. 36.

41. Communication from the British Foreign Office to the British Ambassador in Washington, handed to Secretary Hughes July 27th. *Ibid.*, pp. 45-47. This proposal is mentioned in general terms in the *Summary* of Proceedings of the Imperial Conference, p. 5. Bar Harbour was suggested because it was thought the trip there would take less time than to any other American point.

42. *Ibid.*, p. 48 (Secretary of State Hughes to the American Ambassador in Great Britain). He also noted Japanese concern that while British and American representation would be from leading political figures, Japan would be without equivalent personnel.

43. Summary, *op. cit.*, p. 5.

44. Hughes, *op. cit.*, p. 131. *See* also Lloyd George's speech to the House of Commons on July 11th, printed in *Summary*, pp. 3-5. The official life of Lord Balfour declares ". . . on the whole the pull of forces worked for putting an end to the Treaty. This by no means squared with Mr. Lloyd George's inclinations, perhaps even less than Balfour's." Blanche E. C. Dugdale, *Arthur James Balfour* (New York, 1937), p. 317.

45. *U.S.A. Foreign Relations*, 1921, I, 56-58.

46. *See* Hancock, *op. cit.*, I, 88, and also Robert MacGregor Dawson, *The Development of Dominion Status 1900-1936*, p. 48, Arnold Toynbee, *The Conduct of British Empire Foreign Relations*, p. 85, and Robert B. Stewart, *Treaty Relations of the British Commonwealth of Nations* (New York, 1939), pp. 159-60.

47. When the Dominions subsequently received separate invitations to the Genoa Conference, it was because Lloyd George had suggested this procedure during the Cannes Conference.

48. *The Diary of Sir Robert Borden, 1921*, from the unpublished Borden papers, October 20, p. 590.

49. *U.S.A. Foreign Relations*, 1921, I, 60-61.

68   THE COMMONWEALTH AND INTERNATIONAL SECURITY

50. Dawson, *op. cit.*, p. 219. When challenged in the House of Commons on March 13, 1922, by Mr. King, then Prime Minister, Mr. Meighen maintained he had not been party to any arrangement at the Imperial Conference by which Canada should be represented merely by a delegation appointed by the British Government "nor was such an arrangement arrived at while I was a member of the Conference." He pointed out, however, that he was not there to the end of the Conference. *J.P.E.*, April, 1922.

51. *U.S.A. Foreign Relations*, 1921, I, 64.

52. Quoted in Dawson, *op. cit.*, p. 217.

53. *U.S.A. Foreign Relations*, 1921, I, 65. (The Secretary of State to the Ambassador in Great Britain, August 29th.)

54. Dawson, *op. cit.*, p. 217.

55. *U.S.A. Foreign Relations*, 1921, I, 71-72. (Memorandum by the Secretary of State of a conversation with the British Ambassador, September 20, 1921.)

56. Dawson, *op. cit.*, p. 219.

57. R. B. Stewart believes that since the Imperial plenipotentiaries carried general full powers, their signatures bound the whole Empire and that in fact Dominion signatures only bound the Dominions doubly. *Op. cit.*, p. 161. If so, in this as in other places, the form was more important than the fact.

58. Dawson, *op. cit.*, pp. 220-21.

59. Sir Robert Laird Borden, "The British Commonwealth of Nations," *The Yale Review*, July, 1923, p. 787.

60. Report of Sir John Salmond, New Zealand Delegate to the Washington Conference, *New Zealand House of Representatives Journals*, 1922, Appendix, vol. I, A-5, cited in Dawson, *op. cit.*, p. 228.

61. Conference on the Limitation of Armaments held at Washington, November 12, 1921, to February 6, 1922, *Report of the Canadian Delegate*. Sessional Paper No. 47, 12 George V, A. 1922, p. 45.

62. Confidential Memorandum for the Prime Minister and the Leader of the Opposition, January 30, 1923, *Washington Disarmament Conference Correspondence*, from the unpublished Borden papers, pp. 212-15. Borden prepared this memorandum as an answer to the narrow conception of constitutional relations within the British Commonwealth embodied in Sir John Salmond's report to the New Zealand Government upon the Washington Conference. Borden wrote ". . . insistence upon legalistic theories such as those propounded by Sir John Salmond is both undesirable and mischievous. The unity of the Empire is not founded upon doctrinaire legalism, but upon liberty and autonomy, supported and enforced by the conventions of the constitution. Mr. Balfour from first to last treated the Dominion delegates as of equal status with those from the United Kingdom." In his official report, Borden wrote: "so far as the immediate practical aspect is concerned the forms and practices followed at Washington were not affected by the form of the invitation; they developed independently of it . . .," *op. cit.*, p. 46.

63. Dugdale, *op. cit.*, II, 242, quoting letter to Balfour from British Ambassador in Tokyo dated November 10th. See also *U.S.A. Foreign Relations*, 1920, II, 682-84. (Bell to Hughes, June 11, 1920.)

64. The Secretary of the head of the Japanese delegation writes that there was a general expectation in Japan that the Alliance would be superseded. Prince Togoyama of the Japanese delegation indicated his own view to newspapermen as early as November 4, 1921, that it would be "highly beneficial to the maintenance of the world peace, if, for instance, America, Great Britain, and Japan could form an entente cordiale in one form or another." *The New York World*, November 4, 1921, cited in Yamato Ichihashi, *op. cit.*, p. 120.

65. *U.S.A. Foreign Relations*, 1921, I, 73.   (Memorandum by Hughes of conversation with Geddes.)

66. Dugdale, *op. cit.*, II, 235-36.   Before coming to the Conference there had been discussion as to whether Britain "should try to hold the balance, and the power of mediation, by maintaining the neutrality between the United States and Japan enjoined by the Treaty, or whether she should enter at once into some constructive plan for settlement of disputes." Balfour had favoured the latter plan.

67. Sir Robert Borden's *Diary at the Washington Conference on Disarmament—1921-22* (an elaboration of his regular diary dictated to his secretary during the Conference). From the unpublished Borden papers.   November 9th and 10th, pp. 6-8.

68. *U.S.A. Foreign Relations*, 1922, I, 1.   (Hughes' memorandum of conversation with Balfour.)

69. *Ibid.*, p. 3.

70. Memorandum by Balfour handed to Hughes, November 11, 1921.   The word "arrangement" was written in by Balfour at Hughes' suggestion to supersede the word "Treaty" throughout the document, but Hughes noted it "might or might not be treaty." In a marginal note he wrote "The word 'arrangement' as used in this informal and tentative document is deliberately vague." *U.S.A. Foreign Relations*, 1922, I, 2-3.

71. A. W. Griswold in *The Far Eastern Policy of the United States* (New York, 1938), p. 309, declares that the Balfour proposal was that "the United States join the Anglo-Japanese Alliance, with its recognition of Japan's and Britain's imperial stakes in the Far East, and its military obligations still intact." It is difficult to see on what this judgment is based, for the arrangement would not have been binding as an alliance without further action, would have had no relation to other areas than the Pacific or to wars arising out of other causes than a threat to territorial rights. In all fairness, it should also be pointed out that the proposed arrangement gave as much of a guarantee to the American "imperial" stakes in the Far East, e.g. the Philippines, Guam, Hawaii, as to British and Japanese possessions.

72. Dugdale says that members of Balfour's staff "bear witness to his great disinclination to open the subject of the termination of the Alliance with the Japanese in Washington," that he "found the Japanese Delegation as reluctant to discuss matters with him as the Tokyo Foreign Office had been with the Ambassador," and that "it took him some time to overcome the feeling." *Op. cit.*, pp. 236 and 242. Ichihashi maintains that no action was taken by the Japanese delegation until "very late in November." Two members of the delegation called on Balfour and only then learned of the memorandum for a tripartite agreement. He comments that they "had little dreamed of such treatment at the hand of the British delegate." *Op. cit.*, pp. 120-121. This would seem to indicate that Griswold is not correct in stating that Hughes "faced a solid Anglo-Japanese front." *Op. cit.*, p. 309.

73. The Japanese draft was presented November 26th.   On November 20th, Senator Lodge, Mr. Root, and Mr. Chandler P. Anderson of the American legal staff had discussed a possible alternative to the Anglo-Japanese Alliance. Two days later, Lodge and Anderson prepared the draft of a non-aggression treaty covering island possessions in the Pacific, which was revised on the 26th, and apparently formed the basis for Hughes' proposals. Diary of Chandler P. Anderson, cited in Sprout, *op. cit.*, p. 169.

74. Sprout, *op. cit.*, p. 170.   Balfour in a letter to Sir Charles Eliot thought it was to soothe the "somewhat ruffled pride" of the French. Dugdale, *op. cit.*, p. 243. Hughes' initiative in regard to the inclusion of France is referred to in a letter he wrote to Mr. Frank Simonds, December 29, 1921, *U.S.A. Foreign Relations*, 1922, I, 40.

70 THE COMMONWEALTH AND INTERNATIONAL SECURITY

75. *U.S.A. Foreign Relations*, 1922, I, 13-14. (Memorandum by Sir Maurice Hankey, Secretary of the British Empire Delegation, of a conversation at Hughes' home, December 8, 1921, at which the four delegations were present.)

76. Final agreement had not yet been reached as to American rights in the mandated areas in the Pacific. Hughes made the acceptance of the Four Power Treaty dependent upon reaching an arrangement safeguarding American interests in the mandated territories. An account of a conversation between the American and British delegations earlier in the afternoon of December 8th, in which Hughes claimed similar rights in the islands mandated to Australia and New Zealand as in those mandated by Japan is given in *ibid.*, 1922, I, 10-12. The Covenant provided that mandated territories should not be fortified.

77. *Ibid.*, 1922, I, 15-23. (Meeting of December 8th.)

78. Mark Sullivan, *The Great Adventure at Washington* (New York, 1922), pp. 216-228, gives an account of how the newspapers raised public feeling through this story. Certain Senators were also reported to object to the guarantee of the main islands of Japan. This was used as a basis for reopening the issue and an amendment to the Four Power Treaty was signed February 6, 1922, *U.S.A. Foreign Relations*, 1922, I, 37-38, 42-44, 46-47.

79. *U.S.A. Foreign Relations*, 1922, I, 18.

80. Borden to Meighen, *Washington Conference Correspondence*, December 8, 1921, pp. 80-2.

81. In a press statement on the Four Power Treaty made December 11, 1921, Borden said that although the Treaty related only to the Pacific he trusted that as with the convention of 1817 which applied only to the Great Lakes but extended in practice to the whole Canadian-American boundary, the spirit of this agreement would govern all controversies between the four powers. He considered it to be a "notable step towards the assurance of peace." *Ibid.*, p. 230.

82. Borden to Meighen, December 10, 1921 (Telegram), *ibid.*, p. 85.

83. Borden to Meighen, December 8, 1921, *ibid.*, pp. 80-2.

84. For indications of American opposition to the Anglo-Japanese Alliance and approval of the Four Power Treaty, *see* E. Tupper and G. E. McReynolds, *Japan in American Public Opinion* (New York, 1937), pp. 157-161.

85. Colonel A. a C. Repington, *After the War* (New York, Boston, 1922), p. 432.

86. Sullivan, *op. cit.*, p. 27.

87. Wilson Harris who was at the Conference wrote that Balfour was not capable of the kind of acceptance of the American proposals with which Lloyd George would have brought the roof down. "He moreover was handicapped by knowledge. He could see certain points where reservations were needed." "Washington Impressions," *The Contemporary Review*, January, 1922, p. 12.

88. Lord Riddell's *Intimate Diary* (New York, 1934), p. 337.

89. Dugdale, *op. cit.*, II, 236.

90. *Notes*, 1921. From the unpublished Borden papers. "Memorandum for the British Empire Delegation," November 14, 1921, p. 333 ff.

91. *Ibid.*, p. 339.

92. Borden *Diary* at the Washington Conference, November 14, 1921, p. 14.

93. *Ibid.*, November 15th, p. 16.

94. Borden wrote in his Diary, "An English cynic and wit told me in 1915, that his wife was so much interested in a hospital which he had established in France that she regarded the war as merely a convenient means of supplying it with patients. Somewhat the same idea gets into the minds of sailors, who are inclined to believe that nations exist for the sake of the navy and not the navy for the advantage of the nation."

95. Borden to Balfour, November 26, 1921, *Washington Conference Correspondence*, p. 67. Borden was endorsing a message sent by Balfour to the British Cabinet.

96. *U.S.A. Foreign Relations*, 1922, I, 74. (Conversation between Hughes and Balfour.)

97. *Ibid.*, p. 80. (Conversation between Hughes, Balfour, and Kato at the State Department, December 2, 1921.)

98. *Ibid.*, p. 86 (Hughes to Warren, Ambassador in Japan, December 3, 1921), and p. 92. *See* also Sprout, *op. cit.*, p. 171.

99. *U.S.A. Foreign Relations*, 1922, I, 127-30.

100. Colonel Roosevelt's diary, cited in Sprout, *op. cit.*, pp. 239-40.

101. *U.S.A. Foreign Relations*, 1922, I, 150.

102. Ichihashi, *op. cit.*, p. 86. *See* also Borden *Diary* at the Washington Conference, January 9, 1922, for account of British Empire Delegation meeting at which Pearce raised his objection.

103. Ichihashi declares that Balfour and Kato entered into a verbal agreement whereby the latter would support the British claim if the parallelogram scheme were dropped. He claimed Balfour violated the agreement by reintroducing the map on which the parallelogram was marked following Hughes' endorsement of this means of defining the arrangement. *Op. cit.*, p. 88.

104. *U.S.A. Foreign Relations*, 1922, I, 155-56.

105. Report of Canadian Delegate, *op. cit.*, p. 45.

106. Ian F. G. Milner, *New Zealand's Interests and Policies in the Far East* (New York, 1939), p. 21.

107. Borden, *Diary* at Washington Conference, November 23, 1921, p. 34. Borden spoke on Hughes' suggestion. He wrote "Declaring in the first place that no one would think of imposing upon France conditions which her Government might regard as inconsistent with the national safety I expressed the hope that conditions might develop which would enable Mr. Briand to take a more hopeful view of the situation; and that I strongly urged that the situation which confronted the Conference and which was undoubtedly both difficult and delicate might be considered by the heads of the five delegations. In leading up to this I emphasized the fact that the members of the Conference would find themselves in a most unfortunate position, and the people of the world would be left almost without hope if we were precluded from discussing the limitation of land armament. After another eloquent and vehement discourse from Mr. Briand it was finally agreed on a motion of Senator Lodge that the subject should be taken into consideration by the Chief Delegates with power to deal with the question of aerial attack, the use of poisonous gases, and other methods of war, and the re-enunciation of more definite principles of International law governing the conduct of war."

108. *Ibid.*, December 19, 1921 (pages not numbered). Report by Balfour on his conversation with Hughes regarding an open discussion of the submarine question.

109. *Ibid.*, December 20, 1921. Report of British Empire Delegation meeting.

110. Milner, *op. cit.*, pp. 110-11, cites a New Zealand newspaper comment of much later date which suggested that the Dominions have been more conscious than Great Britain of the relation between the problem of China and naval power in the Pacific.

111. Borden to Meighen, *Washington Conference Correspondence*, p. 120 ff. This information was given as part of a summary of the results of the Conference up to late in December. Borden gave a "short but comprehensive speech [on January 20, 1922] which frankly exposed the present condition of political demoralization in China, the domination of the military governors and the astonishing expenditure for civil war" but in addition pointed out the Chinese contributions in art, literature, etc. Balfour approved the speech and the Chinese delegate expressed his appreciation. The speech was printed in the *Washington Post*, and according to Borden was well received in Canada. It seems to have been generally felt that the speech was useful in aiding an agreement on Chinese affairs. Borden *Diary* at the Washington Conference, January 20, 1922.

112. Borden *Diary* at the Washington Conference, December 7, 1921, p. 69. Balfour "suggested that the proposed resolution might be made somewhat stronger by imposing conditions upon China if the provincial armies were not disbanded and the military expenditure decreased to a reasonable amount. I informed him of my impression that Mr. Hughes could hardly be induced to assent to this as he seemed entirely opposed to any proposal for international control of internal affairs in China; he considered that China must work out her own political salvation."

113. *Ibid.*, November 18, 1921, p. 23.

114. *Ibid.*, November 23, 1921, pp. 34-5.

115. Borden to Balfour, November 26, 1921, *Washington Conference Correspondence*, pp. 58-60.

116. *Ibid.*

117. Balfour to Borden, November 29, 1921, *ibid.*, pp. 68-9.

118. At a subsequent private discussion on the relation of the Washington Conference to the League of Nations, Borden was to maintain strongly that the American people were "as earnest and as far advanced" as those of any nation in supporting the settlement of international disputes by peaceful means. Though he felt that the United States could not be expected to adhere to the Covenant "for many years," he believed, in opposition to Balfour, that it should be encouraged "to adhere to and co-operate in action by the League of Nations wherever possible." He opposed bringing the League into discussion in a plenary session or committee, however, feeling that it would have only the contrary effect to that desired. Borden *Diary* at the Washington Conference, December 17, 1921.

119. In commenting on the Four Power Treaty in the Australian House of Representatives, Prime Minister Hughes declared that it "had cleared away all those difficulties that made for war in the Pacific; it had, so far as human effort could achieve such things, brought about peace where there had been war, and it had given them for, at any rate, ten years' assurance of peace. If they required assurance to be doubly sure, if they were not satisfied with that, as, indeed, some of them might not be, then there was only one sure and certain defence for Australia, and that lay in a virile and sufficiently numerous population. Their present safeguard lay wholly where it had always been—in the fact that they were a partner in the British Empire. That was the beginning and end of their safety." *J.P.E.*, 1922, III, 829.

CHAPTER III

REACTIONS TO BRITISH POLICIES IN EUROPE AND THE NEAR EAST

By 1922, Great Britain had given up or modified three out of four of the policies which had been most characteristic of it in the period before the war. Membership in the League of Nations had been officially substituted for the balance of power. Naval supremacy had been replaced through the Washington agreements by parity, at least in battleships, with the United States. Special relations with Japan had been superseded by a generalized arrangement, the Four Power Treaty, which acknowledged the predominant position of the three major parties in their own areas in the Pacific: Japan in the north-west sector; the United States in the eastern Pacific to Hawaii and north to the Arctic; and the British Empire in the south-west. The fourth policy had been partnership with France, the ultimate safeguard of the balance of power in Europe once imperial Germany threatened to dominate the continent. But the similarity of aims induced by danger failed to carry over into the period of peace. Differences as to policy towards Germany and in their conceptions of the function of international organization as well as rivalry in the Near East placed strain on Anglo-French friendship after the war. Though it remained axiomatic to seek agreement with France, there was no longer the same compulsion to do so after the disappearance of Germany as a military threat.

The stabilization of Europe rather than Anglo-French partnership was the predominant aim of Great Britain's European policies during the twenties. In this primary aim Britain was at one with the Dominions. But Britain's closeness to the continent forced it to consider in detail the means whereby such stability could be assured, and with detailed arrangements the Dominions had little desire to be associated.

During the Peace Conference and immediately after, the recognition of the importance of European stability for all members of the Commonwealth helped to induce a more or less common front on European policies. But the Dominion hope that Britain would concentrate less on Europe and more on the areas with which they were directly concerned proved ephemeral. Nor did they find much more than lip service to the lofty conceptions of consultation on which the post-war Commonwealth was supposed to rest. Confronted by this fact, Australia and, to a much lesser extent, New Zealand strove for prior notifications of British intentions, particularly in the Near East area so vital to the supply lines through which they were linked to Britain, and, if possible, for influence on British decisions. Their exposed positions made them so sensitive to any events affecting Britain that their dominant aim was for a unified British policy sponsoring stability in all areas. In return they were willing to pledge the full support to Britain which they expected from it. But those Dominions whose geographical position made for security rather than insecurity—Canada, South Africa, and the new Dominion, the Irish Free State—reacted against involvement in policies affecting areas with which they had little direct concern. Rather than seeking to modify imperial policies, as Australia attempted to do, they began to withdraw themselves, at least in form, from the implications of developments they had not influenced. This withdrawal began over Near Eastern affairs, but its effects were to become apparent also in European policies by the time of Locarno, though without indicating in the latter situation the divergence in interest which promoted it in Near East affairs. In fact, though it has often been suggested that there was a basic divergence in the British and Dominion attitudes towards European security, the conflict in points of view on this issue was rather between that held by British countries and that of France.

British and Dominion statesmen shared the same aim at the Peace Conference of making a territorial settlement in Europe which would attain its stability out of the justice of its arrangements.[1] In contrast, the French looked on the Treaty of Versailles as the means whereby they could prevent Germany from again acquiring the position of political dominance in Europe which threatened to result from its natural superiority of resources and manpower. French plans for security centred about control of the Rhineland or, at a minimum, of the bridges crossing the Rhine, which they felt would give them a defensible front at which to check future attempts at invasion. But British and Dominion representatives, backed by President Wilson, rejected the idea of separating the Rhineland from Germany and opposed a permanent occupation of German territory.

In their reactions to French proposals, Dominion statesmen made a clear distinction between forcing Germany to disarm which was a measure necessary for general security and interfering in its internal affairs which they refused to do. During discussion on March 11 and 12, 1919, of the French plan for an advanced military frontier, Philip Kerr told Tardieu that Dominion representatives had said that they stood behind the Treaty provisions reducing the German army "to numbers which could not be a menace to its neighbours" and keeping it behind the Rhine.[2] "If Germany refused to abide by these military terms and began once more to rear its head," they would be able "to call upon their people to help to force Germany to fulfil its undertakings." But for what they called "purely European questions such as the future of the Rhenish provinces," they had declared that "they were not going to leave a man in Europe or to bind themselves to interfere in any way." In recounting this, Kerr added to Tardieu that since the Dominions had sent a million men to the war, "their opinions could not be ignored by any British Government." There was, however, no difference of approach between the British and Dominion representatives on the general issue. Both felt that German disarmament coupled with Allied military strength were sufficient in themselves to provide French security, while forcible separation of Rhineland territory would only lead to agitation by its inhabitants for which there would be much sympathy within their own countries.

Despite their unwillingness to permit French domination of the Rhineland, the British and Americans were anxious to find a means of satisfying the French insistence that they be safeguarded against another German attack. It was as a compromise to provide French security and avoid annexations that the Anglo-American Treaties of Guarantee were offered to France. The initiative for the guarantee was taken by Lloyd George, who told Colonel House that "he would . . . be willing to say that, in the event of an invasion, the British would come at once to the rescue."[3] Wilson agreed quickly to make a similar offer, and the proposal was made to Clemenceau on March 14, 1919.[4] With it was combined the provision that there should be only a short occupation of the Rhineland, which was to be a guarantee for payment of reparations not a measure of security.

The French fought this limitation on the period and purpose of the Rhineland occupation, which they wished to turn into a territorial guarantee to supplement the political one. But the Americans would go no farther than endorsing "the original British proposition" for settling the Rhineland issue, the establishment of a demilitarized zone on the left bank of the Rhine. In an American Note of March 28th, whose first paragraphs were ultimately incorporated in the Treaty, the "maintenance or assembling" of German armed forces in this demilitarized zone was declared to be a hostile act. Clemenceau finally agreed on April 14th to accept the demilitarized zone plus the Treaties of Guarantee as adequate provision of security if the Rhineland occupation period were extended to fifteen years, with evacuation of certain areas every five years if Treaty provisions had been fulfilled. Lloyd George, who did not learn of this additional proviso until his return from addressing the House of Commons on the settlement, probably agreed only because the German delegation had already been invited to Versailles. The provision came under severe criticism, however, when it became known by British Ministers and by the Dominion Prime Ministers. After a series of meetings, they authorized Lloyd George on June 1st to hold out for a period of occupation not exceeding two years and also for a smaller occupation army.[5] Unless these changes were made, they opposed using the British army and navy to enforce the peace terms. But despite Lloyd George's efforts, he was not successful in regard to either point. He did, however, secure a joint Declaration signed June 16th, that as soon as Germany had given satisfactory guarantees for the fulfilment of its obligations, the Allied and Associated Powers would seek an agreement among themselves to end the occupation.

Despite, or perhaps because of this long-drawn-out inter-Allied struggle over the purpose and character of the occupation, the final provisions embodied what has been called an "intentional misunderstanding."[6] The British and Americans looked on the occupation as a guarantee for the fulfilment of the provisions of the Treaty: the French continued to regard it as an "essential rampart." They counted that German non-fulfilment of Treaty provisions would enable them to retain their forces in the Rhineland area and used every means to strengthen their control in this area. This antagonized British and Dominion opinion, which felt the French were misusing their position in the Rhineland to create conditions which could only lead to trouble. Thus the original division between the French view that the peace settlement should be a means of weakening Germany and the British view that it should provide a stable basis for European reconstruction became reflected in their attitudes towards the Rhineland occupation and gave rise to continued friction. Not until the Locarno Treaties was there to be a reconciliation of the French and British views on the Rhineland issue.

The French had held out so strongly for the occupation provisions of the Treaty because they were sceptical of ratification by the United States of its Treaty of Guarantee. So, too, were the President's advisers.[7] But Wilson used the offer of the guarantee as a lever to persuade the French to accept the provision in the Covenant maintaining the validity of the Monroe Doctrine and hoped that the Senate would see the guarantee was "only of temporary duration to bridge the gap between war and the firm functioning of the League of Nations." In fact, however, it was never reported out of the Senate Committee on Foreign Relations, though paradoxically Senator Lodge favoured it.[8]

From their side, the British had no difficulty in securing Parliamentary approval, and on November 20, 1919, they exchanged ratifications with the French. The British and American Treaties of Guarantee, however, were each contingent upon the ratification of both. American inaction on their Treaty left the British Treaty of Guarantee "pending," and the British Government decided against extending the pledge by itself.

At Sir Robert Borden's request, the British Treaty of Guarantee had included an article declaring that it would "impose no obligations upon any of the Dominions of the British Empire unless and until it is approved by the Parliament of the Dominion concerned,"[9] though Clemenceau had specifically asked that the Dominions would join the guarantee.[9a] It has sometimes been thought that it was Dominion reluctance to participate in the guarantee which led the British to take advantage of American non-ratification not to extend the guarantee themselves. But this can hardly be substantiated. Though Dominion plenipotentiaries did not sign this Treaty at the Peace Conference, both Australia and New Zealand adhered to it. In the Australian Senate, the Government representative interpreted Australia's adherence as approving of the fact "that Great Britain, America, and France had entered into a certain agreement" though not as putting upon Australia "the moral responsibility of actually participating in war" to uphold the guarantee. He saw it "as a clear indication to Germany that she would not be allowed to break the Peace Treaty to which she had subscribed."[10] Borden intended to recommend the Treaty to the Canadian Parliament but ultimately decided to follow Botha's example in South Africa and not to introduce it at the August session.[11] Had it been presented it would doubtless have passed, for strangely enough in view of their later policies the Liberals pressed for action on the Treaty of Mutual Guarantee. W. S. Fielding questioned why the Canadian Parliament had not been asked to give its assent and showed himself unsatisfied by the answer that the United States had not yet approved and that it would be "time enough for us to take action when it appears that there is some prospect of the Treaty going into effect."[12] He queried disapprovingly in reply, "We must wait for guidance from Washington?" There is little, therefore, to indicate Dominion opposition which might have affected British governmental opinion.

Why, then, it may be asked, did the British not give the guarantee to France, even if the United States refused to do so? "It is commonly recognized," writes an authority on Anglo-French relations, "that the failure to maintain the Anglo-French Treaty was a blunder of the first magnitude."[13] The French could and did feel that the British, having acquired their substantial benefits through the sinking of the German fleet and the transfer of the German colonies,[14] now left France alone on the continent to police the settlement. This sense of isolation led the French to intensify their insistence that Germany must adhere strictly to the clauses of the Treaty of Versailles. This French reaction in turn coincided with a popular outburst in Great Britain against the Treaty, both on the grounds that it was not a settlement of justice, and that the provisions for reparations would handicap economic reconstruction. This divergence of views between France and Great Britain may well have been the reason for the latter's short-sighted action in not making effective the Treaty of Guarantee lest it appear to constitute an endorsement of the French view of the Treaty of Versailles. The tragedy was that by not giving the guarantee, the British intensified those very reactions of the French towards the Treaty to which they were most opposed.

In the Dominions there were many who echoed the objections to the Treaty of Versailles which pervaded British opinion. Smuts had put his signature to it, not because he considered it "a satisfactory document but because it is imperatively necessary to close the war."[15] He called for a "new spirit of generosity and humanity," and believed that the reparations demanded could not be "exacted without grave injury to the industrial revival of Europe." An experienced British observer believed that many of the British and American signatories agreed with him.[16] In the South African House, Merriman of the South African party expressed fears that the "Treaty might be sowing the dragon's teeth."[17] The New Zealand Labour party refused to vote for ratifying the Peace Treaty, objecting particularly to the occupation clauses as "a glaring injustice."[18] The hope in the Dominions as in Great Britain was for the restoration of normal conditions in Europe as soon as possible so that economic revival would be facilitated, and it was feared that the Treaty would retard this development.

The British and Dominion reactions to the Treaty did not mean that France would not have received their support if it had again been the object of German aggression. Smuts, in his declaration on the Treaty, offered to meet the Germans "half-way" if they made a "real, honest effort to fulfil their obligations . . . to the extent of their ability," but warned that "any resort to subterfuges or underhand means" to break or evade the terms of the Treaty would "only revive old suspicions and arouse anger and prove fatal to a good understanding." Ultimately French security was a vital interest of the British Commonwealth. The French were aware of this aspect of the situation, for in 1922 Poincare declared that a British pledge to defend French territory against aggression would be "a mystification without any real value" since Britain would have to do as much in its own interest whether or not there was a commitment.[19]   But ultimate readiness to come to the aid of France was something different from giving support in any issue which arose between France and Germany.   Particularly in view of the condition of Germany after the settlement, the British felt that rigid interpretation of the Treaty was unreasonable and, in its unfortunate effect on economic reconstruction, perhaps dangerous.

This irritation over the carrying out of the peace settlement helped to drive the British and French farther apart.   Moreover, the clash of French and British policies in the Near East, and the disagreement over submarines at the Washington Conference acerbated feelings. So serious did the situation appear that in December, 1921, while the Washington Conference was in session, negotiations on behalf of better Anglo-French relations and a possible defensive alliance were initiated by the French Ambassador in London.   These were succeeded by a discussion between Lloyd George and Briand (whose immediate purpose was to formulate policy in response to a German notification of inability to meet the next reparation payment) and culminated at the Cannes Conference on January 20, 1922.

The French, who had by this time established alliances with Poland and the Little Entente countries, sought a much broader agreement with Great Britain than the original unilateral guarantee of France against invasion which was considered humiliating and even perhaps restrictive of French freedom of action.   The British, though concerned to satisfy the French demand for security, refused to incur obligations in Central and Eastern Europe and to establish a defensive and offensive alliance which would bind them rigidly to France.   Instead, they proposed once more a guarantee against aggression which they believed a united Commonwealth might support.[20]

"With regard to the safety of France against invasion," they wrote in a Memorandum dated January 4th and submitted at Cannes before the official sessions opened, "Great Britain will regard this as an interest of her own and is therefore prepared to undertake that, in the event of unprovoked German aggression against French soil, the British people will place their forces at her side."[21]   Such an undertaking, they declared, "was discussed at the Imperial Conference last summer, and it is probable that the opinion of the Empire would support that of Great Britain in giving such a guarantee to France."   For this reason it would be far better than an offensive and defensive alliance, "for it would, the British Government believes, carry with it the wholehearted opinion, not of Great Britain alone, but of the Dominions."   The

British draft of Treaty submitted January 12, 1922, imposed no obligations on the Dominions, unless and until it was approved by the Dominion concerned. This was to be expected from the precedent with the Treaty of Mutual Guarantee, but Imperial Conference discussions appear to have led the British Government to believe that the Dominion Governments would have accepted the obligation in the interests of European stabilization.

From the British side, however, the guarantee against aggression was looked on as only one part of a general settlement. Preliminary to its entering into force, they wished all outstanding difficulties between themselves and the French to be settled. These apparently included renunciation of the submarine, cessation of support for the Turks who were opposing British policy in the Near East, a truly international régime for Tangiers, and "participation in the right spirit" at the Economic Conference to be held at Genoa.[22] Before a start could be made to find a compromise between the British and French views, popular clamour in France suggesting Briand was subservient to British policy led to his overthrow. Poincare, who succeeded him, made a counter-proposal on January 26th of a treaty to last thirty years which included a reciprocal guarantee, close co-operation between the General Staffs of the two countries, and a provision that violation of the disarmament clauses of the Treaty of Versailles would constitute an aggression against France. This latter provision which the French felt to be particularly important was categorically rejected by the British Government as tantamount in the view of British public opinion to "embarking upon a policy of military adventure and potential danger."[23] Implicit in the French proposals, the British believed, was responsibility in Eastern Europe as well as for France's safety. Nor was there any effort by the French to come to an agreement on any of the issues the British believed to be outstanding between them. The negotiations therefore gradually petered out, leaving Anglo-French relations in a worse state than before they began.

Subsequent developments served but to intensify the division between the two countries. Great Britain attributed to France the failure of the Genoa Conference from which it had hoped for improvement of economic conditions in Europe. An even more serious cause of disagreement was France's invasion of the Ruhr in January, 1923, ostensibly to collect reparations, against which the British protested though without effect. Not until the policy demonstrated its unfortunate effects upon the French as well as the German economy were the French ready to turn to another line, first to seek assurance through broader League commitments and upon the failure of that policy to accept in 1925 the British guarantee of the Franco-German frontier embodied in the Locarno Treaty.

In the meantime, French policy had been as severely criticized in the Dominions as in Great Britain. Smuts declared that "statesmen in Europe seem to have lost all sense of proportion, and are prepared to sacrifice even the future of the world to their ideas of security and reparation."[24] The leader of the New Zealand Labour party believed that bad as was the Treaty of Versailles, France's violation of it was making matters worse not only for the Germans but for Britain and the rest of the world.[25] S. M. Bruce, who became Prime Minister of Australia in 1922, felt that if the French occupation of the Ruhr continued "another Alsace-Lorraine would be established in Europe, one of the greatest tragedies they could contemplate."[26]

Great Britain and the Dominions were of one mind as to the overriding importance of economic reconstruction. Their dependence upon world trade made a freeing of its channels through a solution of the reparations problem a matter of vital interest. On the other hand, to answer France's equal concern with political stability, Great Britain was unwilling to go further than to guarantee the support against actual aggression, to which in any case its interests and those of the Dominions would be likely in a time of crisis to lead them. As Sir Austen Chamberlain later pointed out, "only in the case where her interests are immediately at stake and where her own safety must be directly affected by the result of any change has Great Britain ever consented to bind herself beforehand to specific engagements on the Continent of Europe."[27] The same might be said of the Dominions, that only when they were convinced that British interests or safety required a European commitment were they ready to accept it with equanimity. The guarantee of the French frontier which they might well have been ready to underwrite in 1919 and even in 1921 they also endorsed at the time of Locarno. They were not, however, to put their signatures to the guarantee in 1925 because in the meantime British imperial policies and Dominion nationalist sentiment had accelerated the movement towards separate agreements for the individual parts of the Commonwealth.

Though the Dominions were well aware of the importance to themselves of British security and thereby of security in Western Europe, they all shared reluctance to be involved in the political affairs of Europe. In regard to imperial policies, on the other hand, the difference in the geographical positions of the Pacific Dominions and the others tended to be reflected in their reactions. To Australia and New Zealand the route through the Mediterranean and Suez Canal which cut off a week in the distance by ship from Great Britain to the former was in fact a "life-line" as long as they looked to British support in a time of crisis. Hence they concerned themselves to a degree almost incomprehensible to Canadians, with the issues of Egypt, the régime at the Straits, and the Near East in general. Thus it was over imperial rather than European policies that divergence in interests became evident within the Commonwealth and then between Great Britain, Australia, and New Zealand, on the one hand, and Canada, South Africa, and the Irish Free State, on the other.

Despite the greater concern of Australia and New Zealand with imperial issues, it does not appear that in the early post-war period they were more successful than the other Dominions in securing the opportunity for consultation before British *fait accomplis* were produced. The classic example of confronting the Dominions with a dangerous situation before they had been informed of the policies which led to it is the crisis over the Turkish advance on Chanak in 1922. Before this had happened, however, the Australian Government had been startled by indirect word of a "radical change in policy"[28] by the British towards Egypt, whose strategic position flanking the Suez Canal route made its future of vital import to the Dominions at the far end of that line of imperial communications.

At the beginning of the war, the British had unilaterally declared a termination of Turkish suzerainty over Egypt and proclaimed a protectorate. Aspirations of independence, encouraged by the declarations which had been made to the Arab states, including one by Lord Robert Cecil, coupled with the absence of a clear-cut British programme for Egypt, led to disturbances at the end of the war calculated to force Great Britain's hand. Lord Milner, having investigated the situation for the British Government, proposed a settlement to the Egyptian Nationalist leader, Zaghlul, under which Egypt should be recognized as independent, under a constitutional monarch, and a treaty of alliance signed with Great Britain under which the latter's interests in imperial communications would be safeguarded through stationing British troops in the Canal Zone. Before this suggestion had been considered officially, Zaghlul published it, thereby forcing the British Government to give it cognizance. Word through the press of the probable intention of the British Government of adopting the Milner Report was the first notice received by the Australian Government of the developments. Hughes felt strongly that it was unwise to make such wide concessions when ultimate independence could not be granted to Egypt without endangering imperial interests, but he was to have little opportunity to affect the ultimate decision.

It was concern over the situation in Egypt which led the Australian Government to suggest that an Imperial Conference should be called in 1921.[29] But when it met and the Dominion representatives were brought abreast of the situation, Hughes found to his regret that "though the British Government had made no formal declaration, the situation had developed to such a point that the Government was committed, and nothing remained for the representatives of the Empire but to register their formal acquiescence."[30] Yet he signified his disapproval in no uncertain terms. "A position of vital importance has been abandoned, not as a result of long and careful deliberation . . . but because by blunders and treachery we have been led into an *impasse*. Egypt is the gateway to the East: the safety of the Canal is vital to the safety of Australia . . . here is a remedy, which, while disastrous to us, is going to be unacceptable to the great bulk of the Egyptian people. . . . We shall always have to give a little more . . . in order that we may placate the implacable. How can we safeguard our interests? . . . Speaking as a civilian, I think it impossible to hold the Canal with the hinterland held by a people bitterly hostile."

It was with no satisfaction that the Dominion delegates heard the British Prime Minister declare that he, too, had been without knowledge of Lord Robert Cecil's declaration, which helped to stimulate the disturbances and without responsibility for the tentative treaty agreed upon by Milner and Zaghlul and published prematurely by the latter. If anything, it disturbed them more that the British Government should have allowed itself to be forced into such an unwanted and tense situation. Both by its lack of repudiation of the Milner proposals and by the "vacillating" policy of Lord Allenby, the Special High Commissioner in Egypt, who had readmitted Zaghlul to his country, Hughes believed that the British Government had committed itself beyond recall. Under the circumstances, he declares, there was nothing to be done except to lay down "in clear and definite terms" the limits beyond which concessions should not be allowed to go. These involved the reservation of four points: the security of the Suez Canal as an essential link in imperial communications, the defence of Egypt against foreign aggression or interference, the protection of foreign interests and of minorities, and the status of the Sudan.[31] These were declared reserved to the British Government in a declaration of February, 1922, issued jointly with an Egyptian Constitution providing for a king and parliament responsible for all domestic affairs. In contrast to the original Milner-Zaghlul proposal for the stationing of British troops in Egypt, they were not confined to the Canal Zone under the 1922 arrangements.

Events were to prove that Hughes was right in believing that this combination of apparent independence with protection of British interests in the Canal would not satisfy the Egyptian Nationalists. In 1924, Sir Lee Stack, the British Governor-General of the Sudan, was murdered in the streets of Cairo. Twice subsequently, in 1927-1928 and 1929-1930, the British attempted to make the appearance of Egyptian independence more realistic by incorporating the reservations of British vital interests in a treaty which, at least in form, was between two equal parties. In 1927, the treaty was submitted to the Dominion Governments before being approved by the British and was to have been subject to ratification by the individual Dominions. But the Egyptian Prime Minister who accepted it was overthrown by the Nationalist party. The later negotiations ended in a similar fiasco. Not until the Italo-Ethiopian conflict brought both sides into a mood for compromise was a comparatively satisfactory settlement to be achieved.

Whether, on the other hand, Hughes was right in thinking that the British could have offered less to the Egyptians is open to question. But a more clear-cut policy from the beginning might well have saved many of the difficulties.

Where there could be no question was that Hughes was right in feeling that the Dominions, of which at least Australia and New Zealand were vitally concerned, should have been given prior information regarding the situation in Egypt and consulted as to their views. To the Imperial Conference in 1921, Hughes expressed the hope "that we shall learn wisdom from what has happened, and devise some means to prevent its recurrence which might lead to still more disastrous consequences."[32] Yet despite British assurances that such a development would not take place again,[33] and Conference resolutions supporting improved methods of communication, the Dominions were confronted a little more than a year later with what might have been a still more serious situation in the Chanak incident.

The background of the Chanak crisis lay in Turkish Nationalist repudiation of the Treaty of Sèvres, which had only been signed in August, 1920, after successful military action against Nationalist forces by the Greeks under Venizelos. Subsequently the Greeks not only continued their advance into Asia Minor but repudiated Venizelos, under whom they had made their contribution to the Allied cause during the war, thereby alienating most Allied statesmen except Lloyd George. In September, 1921, the Greeks suffered a defeat and a month later the French Government secretly negotiated a separate peace with the Turkish Government, one of the causes of Anglo-French friction which had led to the abortive efforts to conclude an alliance between the two countries. Italy also concluded an agreement with the Turks. By September, 1922, the Greeks were in headlong retreat before the Nationalist forces of Kemal Pasha. Only the Allied troops in the neutral zone guarding the approaches to the Straits at Chanak and across the Ismid Peninsula stood between Kemal's army and its crossing into Europe. The French and Italian Governments ordered the withdrawal of their forces, which were evacuated on September 21, 1922. If the British were to oppose Kemal's forcible entry into Europe, they faced the prospect of defending the Straits alone. Just before midnight on September 15th, Lloyd George sent messages to the Dominions regarding the situation and asked whether, if war resulted with Turkey, they wished to be represented by a contingent. At approximately the same time, the press was given a similar message which mentioned the communications to the Dominions, "inviting them to be represented by contingents in defence of interests for which they have already made enormous sacrifices."[34]

Once again the Dominions had been confronted with a situation beyond their powers to influence. This time the situation had reached crisis dimensions before it was called to their attention. Moreover, two aspects of the matter were particularly disturbing: the unprecedented request to send troops, and the release of the appeal to the press at the same moment it was sent to the Dominion Governments. Because of the delay involved in decoding the official message, the press reports provided in fact the first notification both of the issue and of the appeal to the Dominions which either the Canadian or the Australian Prime Minister received.

It has been customary to say that the Australian and New Zealand replies automatically pledged support to Great Britain over the Chanak crisis while Canada and South Africa played for time.[35] Though true in essence, it makes too precise a differentiation between the attitude of the Pacific Dominions and of the others, and too complete an identity between the Australian and New Zealand reactions. The latter countries both felt themselves intimately affected by any change in the régime of the Straits because of its relations to imperial communications. But there was considerable difference between the wholehearted tenor of "Government of New Zealand desire to associate themselves with action being taken, and will send a contingent,"[36] and Hughes' more restrained answer that the Australian Government wished to associate itself with the British Government "in whatever action is deemed necessary to insure the freedom of the Straits and the sanctity of the Gallipoli Peninsula, and would be prepared, if circumstances required, to send a contingent of Australian troops."[37]

In his speech to the Australian House, Hughes drew a distinction between "the'vital interests of the Empire" in which he felt that they must act in association with Great Britain and the rest of the Empire, and a "filibustering expedition" in which they "did not want to take part." In the immediate situation, he distinguished between maintaining the *status quo* in Constantinople and the inviolability of the Gallipoli Peninsula and being dragged into war to support the ambitions of Greece. Australia's objective, he declared, was "limited to the preservation of the Empire." From Great Britain, he had asked explicit information regarding its objective. In the meantime, the Australian Government had appealed to the League, which was in session, an act with which all the Dominion representatives associated themselves.[38] While the Australians, Hughes declared, were prepared to accept Lloyd George's judgment that "demonstration of their intention was the surest way to prevent war," and, if all efforts failed, were ready to range themselves beside Great Britain "with all the resources at their disposal," the aim of their policy was to prepare the way for settlement either by a conference or by the League of Nations.

Behind this restrained and reasonable statement lay a great deal of indignation. Hughes was later to write that the British action had placed the Dominions in a position which was "not only embarrassing but deeply humiliating."[39] Once more a press despatch had brought him word of a crisis in British policy in an area in which Australia was vitally concerned and once more there had been no previous notification of the events leading up to the crisis. "Had the position been communicated through confidential channels," wrote Hughes, "we should at least have been able to express our feelings freely, and possibly even to insist that the situation should be handled by the representatives of the Dominions acting with those of Britain." But he considered that "the world-wide publicity precluded this course." He was prepared even to consider that the notification to the press "savoured of sharp practice" and "appeared to be a dodge to manœuvre the Dominions into a position from which there was no retreat."

To the Canadian House of Commons, Mackenzie King told a similar story of not only hearing through the press that "several Dominions had been invited to send contingents to the Near East" but even, before his own notification from the British Government had been decoded, that New Zealand had volunteered a contingent.[40] Even more serious was what he called "the vital part of the despatch"; the "enquiry" whether the Dominions wished to be associated with the action the British Government had taken and to be represented by a contingent. This was, he emphasized, "the first and only intimation" from the British Government "of a situation in the Near East which had reached a critical stage."

It was not in the reaction but in official responses that Hughes and King differed. Where Hughes felt himself forced to pledge aid immediately, King made it clear that action was dependent upon due consideration of the situation. He asked the fullest information, offered to have daily Cabinet sessions, and, if necessary, to call Parliament. ". . . it is neither right nor proper for any individual, or for any group of individuals, to take any step which might limit the rights of Parliament," declared the Canadian Prime Minister in his official explanation of his action to the Commons, "in a matter which is of such concern to all the people of our country."

The difference in response rested on the differing emphasis given to the two major points raised by a situation which threatened to involve war. The first was that conflict might be staved off through the appearance of solidarity. Following this line, Hughes believed that in such a crisis "when we were pushed willy nilly to the very edge of the arena of war . . . there was nothing that we could have done except what we did."[41] Stanley M. Bruce, who had succeeded Hughes as Prime Minister by the time of this later consideration of the incident, agreed that "It was a proper action and probably the promptness with which it was taken prevented war occurring."[42] This was a different attitude from that expressed in New Zealand by both the Government and the official Opposition, and by Sir Earle Page, leader of the Country party in Australia,[43] or represented by Meighen's statement in Canada at the time of the incident, "When Britain's message came, then Canada should have said: 'Ready, aye, ready; we stand by you.' "[44] The latter represented an unquestioning support and one wonders whether in fact Meighen would have expressed himself so definitely had he been in office. The former was a solidarity expressed in a moment of crisis, limited to "vital interests of the Empire" and intended to pave the way for a settlement.

The second point involved in the official responses to Lloyd George's "enquiry" was the need for Parliamentary decision in situations which might involve war. Not only King was to put forward this principle. Smuts declared that the South African Government could not commit itself until it consulted Parliament.[45] Senator Gardener, Leader of the Opposition in the Australian Senate at the time of the incident, thought that the most serious aspect of the Prime Minister's attitude was that "off his own bat, and off the Government's own bat, Australia stood pledged to war. While Parliament existed no such condition of things should obtain."[46]   The New Zealand Labour party moved disapproval of the Government's action and declared itself "of opinion that preliminary to discussion and decision on any proposal to engage this country in further war all information in possession of the Government should be placed before Parliament and the country."[47]   The Leader of the Canadian National Progressive party and J. S. Woodsworth of the Labour party endorsed King's insistence upon consulting Parliament.[48] In Great Britain itself the action helped materially to topple the Lloyd George Government a few days later.   If the Dominions were to have any real claim to independent decisions in foreign affairs, it was essential that they should have both the information on which to judge the situation and the opportunity to consult public opinion through parliament.   In the broad view, it may be said that King's and Smuts' reaction was the one necessary both for implementing Dominion status and for warning the British Government against such action in the future. Hughes' response was the one most valuable in the particular situation.

The Chanak incident assumed such an importance both for constitutional developments within the Commonwealth and in moulding the attitudes of certain leaders and parties in the Dominions, particularly King and the Canadian Liberal party, that it is worth considering how such a blunder could have been made.   For the lack of earlier information, the British Foreign and Colonial Offices must take their share of blame.   The actual messages to the Dominions and the notification to the press, however, appear to have been the work of two men, Churchill and Lloyd George.   Curzon declared that neither he nor the Foreign Office had been informed.   The British Government later stated that the message to the press was intended "for the official guidance of the official spokesman" and not for publication.[49]   Others have believed that the statement was drawn up by Churchill and was supposed to be given by Lloyd George's secretary to the press in general terms.   The latter found it difficult to paraphrase the statement and finally received Lloyd George's permission to issue it as it stood.   As for the messages to the Dominions, a subsequent communication from the British declared that "It was intended mostly for the two Dominions which had fought so bravely in the Dardanelles—that is, Australia and New Zealand." To the others, said Smuts, who made this information public, it had been addressed "*pro forma.*"[50]   If so, it was a pity that this was not made clear when the messages were first sent out.

Whether the expression of support by Australia and New Zealand influenced the course of events at Chanak, as Bruce was to say, is difficult to judge.   In any case, Kemal decided not to attack the neutral zone which was defended after September 21st only by British soldiers.

Agreement was reached on a Conference which served as a preliminary to drafting the Treaty of Lausanne. The British stand had had good effect as far as the international situation was concerned.

As far as the Dominions were concerned, the results were mixed. Bruce used the Chanak incident to illustrate the need for better imperial communications. In 1924, a Liaison Officer was sent to London "as a personal representative of the Prime Minister of Australia." He was given access to the confidential files of the British Foreign Office and served as a special link between the two Governments.[51] By this and other means the Australian Government attempted subsequently to maintain close confidential touch with British policy and to exert influence on it behind the scenes rather than through public declarations. The effect on King and on a considerable portion of Canadian public opinion was very different. Here the incident provided a rude shock through evidencing the potential dangers in the British connection. Far from inducing a desire to share more closely in the formulation of Britain's imperial policies, the reaction was to avoid, as far as possible, their implications. There might be legal responsibilities in the existing state of constitutional relations: if possible there should not also be moral responsibilities. The Chanak incident helped to mould the temporizing policy which was to mark King's reactions to imperial affairs thereafter. At the same time it encouraged the Liberal party in Canada to renounce the rather timid colonialism it had shown at the time of the peace settlement and to embark upon the movement towards Commonwealth decentralization and Dominion nationalism which was to be characteristic of the succeeding period of constitutional development.

In the end, however, the divergence between future Australian and Canadian attitudes towards imperial affairs was less a matter of party than of geography. Australia's isolation was from Great Britain. Its proximity to the great masses of Oriental peoples, of which the Japanese at least had shown aggressive inclinations, made it doubly conscious of the necessity of keeping as close to Great Britain as distance would permit. Both Pacific Dominions were keenly interested in the progress of the Singapore base begun in 1922, which would make it possible to bring the largest battleships to the Pacific area. Incidents like Chanak only made the Australian Government increasingly concerned to forge more strongly links of consultation as well as of communications.

In contrast, Canada's isolation was from the storm centres of the world. This gave it the opportunity to pursue a separate policy untroubled by thought that it might need in the future to call for aid from Great Britain. Its closest relations outside of the Commonwealth were inevitably with the United States. Wisdom, inclination, and tradition moulded the Canadian desire to conduct its relations with the United States in its own manner.   Borden's plans to have a Canadian Minister in Washington, announced May 10, 1920,[52] but not carried through till 1926, Rowell's[53] and Meighen's[54] claims that Canada should be allowed to handle its affairs with the United States by itself were forerunners of King's insistence in 1923 that the new Halibut Fisheries agreement with the United States should be between "the United States and Canada," not between "the United States and Britain" as previously, and that the Canadian representative alone should sign, not the British Ambassador[55] also.   This conception of separate responsibility where there was separate interest was to be carried still farther by the Canadian Government under the stimulus of British action in regard to the Treaty of Lausanne and to become the constitutional practice of the Commonwealth.

The Treaty of Lausanne provided the final settlement of the relations of Turkey and the Allied countries.   In view of the fact that Anglo-Turkish relations had provoked the Chanak appeal to the Dominions, it may be considered the more surprising that the British Government made no effort to have Dominion representation at the Conference which drafted this Treaty.   The Canadian Government did not demur at this exclusion, as Meighen subsequently declared it should have done in order to preserve the position established at Versailles and Washington.[56]   Instead it maintained that because Canadian plenipotentiaries had had no share in negotiating the Treaty, the Canadian Government would not ratify it.   It did not object to the British plenipotentiaries ratifying on behalf of the whole Empire but King maintained that though this created a legal obligation, it did not lay a moral obligation upon Canada.   In regard to any situation arising out of a breach of the Treaty of Lausanne, the Canadian Government reserved the right to take whatever action seemed justified under the circumstances.

The Canadian emphasis was, in fact, being put upon form rather than substance.   It was an outgrowth, however, of the position assumed at Chanak, and in the Halibut Treaty.   By the time the Treaty of Lausanne had been signed, the Imperial Conference of 1923 had agreed that each part of the Commonwealth should conclude its own international agreements, though all parts were to be kept informed of negotiations and to be permitted to express views or participate if so desired.   Nonetheless the Canadian position led to the expression of considerable concern in the British House of Commons,[57] probably because it was realized that it implied that in this situation Canada divorced itself from the implications of British imperial policy, at least as far as prior commitments were concerned.

More surprising than the Canadian attitude is the fact that Australia apparently made no effort to be represented in the drafting of the Lausanne Treaty. The explanation of this may lie in the Australian acceptance of the fact that its interests in regard to the Straits were precisely those of Great Britain and the belief that in the face of French objection to Dominion representation,[58] Australian insistence upon being represented would only have made Great Britain's task at the Conference more difficult. In any case, the demilitarization of the Dardanelles which the Straits Convention provided fitted Australian purposes exactly. There can be little doubt that Australia's acceptance that the British Government should ratify on behalf of the Empire had no hint in it that Australia was relieving itself of any "moral obligation" to support the settlement.

When the final discussions on the positions of the Dominions in relation to the Treaty of Lausanne took place in the British House of Commons, a new Labour Government was in office. This Government was to be responsible in the succeeding months of its term of office for two unfortunate breaches of customary unity with the Dominions: the first when it extended formal recognition to the Soviet Government in Russia without giving prior notification to the Dominions, and the second by agreeing without consultation with the Dominions to have only three representatives at the Inter-Allied Conference on the Dawes Report on reparation. Because of this agreement it was not possible to have full representation of the Dominions as at Washington, but a compromise was reached with Canadian concurrence that the third member of the British Empire Delegation should be chosen by rotation from a panel representative of all the Dominions. The British Labour Government agreed that neither of these cases should be considered a precedent and in regard to negotiations for the Geneva Protocol, which will be considered in the next chapter, made its utmost effort to keep in close touch with the Dominion Governments. Even more serious from the point of view of the Dominions, however, had been the Labour Government's reversal of the economic policies agreed upon at the 1923 Imperial Conference. Although the Canadian and South African Governments in particular were always careful to make clear that the decisions of Imperial Conferences were not binding unless ratified by home Parliaments, all the Dominion Governments reacted critically against this British change of an agreed policy.

The Labour Government fell later in 1924 and the Geneva Protocol went with it. A Conservative Ministry came into power in Great

Britain pledged to provide other means to safeguard peace.   In place of the general guarantee of the League plan, the Conservatives favoured a regional arrangement limited as far as the British were concerned to the old European danger point in the west, the frontier between Germany and France.   In the Locarno Treaty, this guarantee was finally made in a manner satisfactory both to Great Britain and to France.

The Locarno arrangement is justly famous.   It placed upon Great Britain little more responsibility than had the 1919 Treaty of Guarantee and it had the great advantage from the point of view of public opinion that it was not aimed specifically against a particular state but against any aggression in a given area.   Though the French regretted the unwillingness of the British to extend a similar guarantee in the east, the arrangements entered into at this time covered Germany's eastern borders as well as its western frontier.   The Locarno Treaty was in fact a series of documents including arbitration treaties between Germany and its eastern and western neighbours, and French treaties of mutual assistance with Poland and Czechoslovakia applicable in case of aggression by Germany.   By combining in this manner the French and British approaches to the organization of European security,⁵⁹ the Locarno Treaty ended the long period of friction between the two countries.   It also led to a new era of co-operation with Germany from which had come the proposal for guaranteeing the Rhineland frontier, and paved the way for German entry into the League of Nations.

Like the earlier proposals for guaranteeing the French frontier, the Locarno Treaty included a provision that it should not be binding upon the Dominions without their consent.   Moreover, unlike the practice adopted at Lausanne, the British plenipotentiaries specifically represented Great Britain at Locarno, not the Empire.   The British Government had attempted to hold a conference with the Dominions before the Locarno Conference, but without success.⁶⁰   It kept the Dominions informed of developments during the negotiations but did not consult them about the form of the arrangement.⁶¹   There could be little reason for surprise, therefore, if the Dominions availed themselves of the obvious opportunity not to sign the Treaty.

In fact, none of the Dominions did adhere to the Locarno Treaty but the customary inference drawn from this that they had no desire to "accept obligations in a matter which affected them so remotely and was charged with such potentially dangerous consequences"⁶² is oversimplified.   A British guarantee of the Franco-German frontier was far from being a "remote" issue to the overseas Dominions.   However much they wished to avoid being implicated in minor European disputes, they recognized that the safety of Great Britain rested upon control by a friendly power of that part of the Continent which bordered the Channel. In the Australian House, Bruce declared that the question of Australia's participation in the Treaty demanded their serious consideration.[63] Later he declared, "While we may not have anything to do with the Treaty by express declaration, we cannot escape from its consequences should the malice of circumstances bring it into operation, otherwise than by leaving the Empire. . . . I think that silence on this matter cannot conceivably, in the final analysis, diminish our obligation . . ."[64] The Prime Minister of New Zealand, J. G. Coates, declared on November 17, 1925, "As far as this Dominion is concerned the Pact will be submitted in due course for ratification by our Parliament."[65] At the express request of the British Government,[66] however, Dominion action on the Treaty was postponed until after there had been an opportunity at the Imperial Conference of 1926 for a full examination of the effect of the Locarno Treaty on the whole field of foreign affairs and defence.

No material on the course of these discussions at the Conference is available. It is necessary, therefore, to guess at the implications of the two statements in the Summary of Proceedings[67] which may bear upon them. The first specifically notes the "satisfaction" of the Conference at the Foreign Secretary's report on the efforts to ensure peace in Europe, "culminating in the agreements of Locarno" and "congratulates" the British Government "on its share in this successful contribution towards the promotion of the peace of the world." The second part of the report which may or may not bear relationship to the Locarno Treaty is that concerned with establishing a form of treaty which would indicate precisely which parts of the Empire were signatories. This was a natural culmination of the arrangement endorsed by the 1923 Imperial Conference. It accepted as permanent practice the form adopted at Locarno whereby Great Britain entered into agreements only on its own behalf. Thereby it became unnecessary in future to insert clauses in British treaties excluding the Dominions from their effect.

The conjunction of these two sections of the Summary together with earlier statements from Australia and New Zealand suggest that the general endorsement of the Locarno Treaty was the means taken of avoiding any obvious division in the Commonwealth in regard to Dominion ratifications. The attitude of the Australian and New Zealand Prime Ministers had made it obvious that it was their intention to recommend the Treaty to their Parliaments for ratification. On the other hand, it seemed equally clear that Canada,[68] South Africa and the

Irish Free State did not desire to adhere to the Treaty. The compromise appears to have been secured through a declaration general enough for all to accept.

Speaking in the Canadian House on March 30, 1927, Ernest Lapointe, Minister of Justice, declared that Canada had taken the position that it was not bound by the Locarno Treaty.[69] In regard to foreign affairs in general, he held that the developments of the 1926 Conference meant "the definite recognition that neither Great Britain nor the Dominions are committed to any active obligations except with the assent of their own governments or parliaments." The crux of both statements appeared to lie in the words "active obligations."

Long before the Dominions entered World War I at the side of Great Britain, it had been accepted that they and they alone should determine the extent of aid which they would provide in a given circumstance. In the period before 1914, the Dominions had made no claim to share in, though occasionally to influence the form of British political agreements. At the Peace Conference, however, Dominion statesmen had put forward their well-justified claim to separate signatures of the Treaty of Versailles. But by so doing they introduced a new problem in Commonwealth relations of which they appear to have been hardly conscious. Henceforth the alternative for the Commonwealth was either that all its parts should sign every important agreement with which any part was concerned, or that the Commonwealth should cease to act as a unity. If the former, then the Dominions became directly obligated by every agreement into which Great Britain's world-wide interests might draw it, or alternatively Great Britain would be prevented from entering any agreement which did not fit the purposes of every part of the Commonwealth. This would mean placing upon the Dominions direct responsibilities far wider than any small states might reasonably be expected to carry, or else hamstringing British policy. But if the latter line of separate arrangements should be chosen, as Canada insisted over the Halibut Treaty, and as was done at Locarno, could the special Commonwealth relation continue to exist? This was the question which disturbed statesmen like Smuts, who prized the unity of the Commonwealth above any special agreement,[70] or Bruce to whom the Commonwealth relation was essentially "an unwritten treaty of mutual guarantee,"[71] upon which Australia's security largely depended. The reconciliation of the two most sharply defined Dominion points of view—the Canadian, seeking security through the avoidance of active responsibilities, and the Australian, supporting a "mutual guarantee with Great Britain"—was found by advancing far enough constitutionally to revive the old distinction between British responsibility and Dominion obligations. General Commonwealth unity was retained since no part of the Commonwealth desired secession, as even such ardent nationalists as General Hertzog,[72] by then Prime Minister of South Africa, and Henri Bourassa,[73] veteran French Canadian parliamentarian, were ready to assert. But differentiation in interests and responsibilities was acknowledged by asserting that only a treaty approved by the Government of a particular part of the Commonwealth involved "active obligations" upon that part. Thereby the problem was resolved as far as it could ever be. What would happen in practice if Great Britain or a Dominion became involved in war under a treaty not signed by other parts of the Commonwealth was left judiciously to events to determine.

Involved in much of the discussions which directed this constitutional evolution is an emphasis on form which may appear academic. Yet form is the expression of desire and as such significant in indicating preferred lines of policy. The Commonwealth was working out through trial and error a means of expressing the new self-consciousness of the Dominions and the old distinction between the world-wide interests of Great Britain and the more limited concerns of the Dominions. What made it difficult to draw the line too sharply was that individual Dominions differed widely from one another in the character and extent of their interests. Imperial communications through the Mediterranean and Suez were of immediate and vital concern to Australia and New Zealand, far less to the other Dominions. It is little wonder, therefore, that the constitutional crises which centred around Near East affairs found the Dominions divided in their responses if not always in their attitudes. A compromise could be more easily secured in relation to a British agreement regarding western Europe. Here, despite the difference between the reactions of the Pacific Dominions and the others, there was less real division of opinion. None of the overseas Dominions desired to be involved in European politics, yet all realized the importance of western Europe to the safety of Great Britain. Like Great Britain itself, they were reluctant for commitments but approved those like Locarno which appeared to strengthen security rather than add danger.

In the course of this period, as the Dominions felt their way in international affairs, Great Britain, too, was working out the implications of its new lines of policy. By 1926 it had accepted the implications of post-war Dominion status and the next five years were to see the harmonious evolution of constitutional forms culminating in the Statute of Westminster, 1931.[74] Its consultation of the Dominions in 1927 regarding new arrangements with Egypt indicates more conformity with their demands to be given the opportunity to express their opinions on political issues. Naval affairs and the Far East provided difficult times but no essential change in policy. In European policies, Great Britain swung back to a closer relation with France after Locarno, but at least for the next five years attempted to maintain the good tripartite relations which Locarno's inclusion of Germany induced. Side by side with these developments throughout the decade but more particularly before Locarno were the efforts to evolve a satisfactory League policy which would strengthen Great Britain's position without placing upon it too heavy demands.

At Geneva, there was less, though some, restraint on the public expression of Dominion opinions. On the whole, the Commonwealth presented a united front on important League issues but discussions of League projects for general security and of the one American-sponsored plan, the Kellogg Pact, provided opportunity for the Dominions to put forward their particular points of view. Taken together with their reactions to Great Britain's European and imperial policies, they afford a broad view of how the different Dominions approached the issue of security in the decade of the comparatively peaceful twenties.

REFERENCES FOR CHAPTER III

1. W. M. Jordan, Great Britain, France and the German Problem, 1918-1939 (New York, 1943). See Chapter I for a general consideration of the difference between the British and French concepts of peace. For the discussions regarding the Treaty of Versailles, see p. 174 ff.

2. Paper respecting Negotiations for an Anglo-French Pact (Cmd. 2169, France No. H.M.S.O., 1924), p. 62. Cited hereafter as Anglo-French Negotiations.

3. Charles Seymour, The Intimate Papers of Colonel House (London, 1926-28), IV, 370-71.

4. Anglo-French Negotiations, p. 69.

5. Ibid., pp. 106-07 and 92. The latter is a statement to the Dominion Prime Ministers on April 11th regarding the British proposal for demilitarization of the west bank of the Rhine.

6. Jordan, op. cit., p. 188.

7. J. Paul Selsam, The Attempts to form an Anglo-French Alliance, 1919-1924 (Philadelphia, 1936), p. 10 ff.

8. Jordan, op. cit., p. 39.

9. H. W. J. Temperley, A History of the Peace Conference, III, 337-40.

9a. Anglo-French Negotiations, p. 103.

10. J.P.E., 1920, I, 132 (September 10, 1920).

11. Sir Robert Borden's *Diary*, 1919, pp. 442-45, Aug. 8, 11, 12, 22, 23, 25. From the unpublished Borden papers.

12. *J.P.E.*, 1920, I, 468-9 (April 8, 1920). Fielding called it "the Treaty between Great Britain, France, and the United States."

13. Jordan, *op. cit.*, p. 39.

14. *See* memorandum by Clemenceau to Lloyd George, March 31, 1919, *Anglo-French Negotiations*, pp. 89-90.

15. Wilson Harris, *The Peace in the Making* (New York, 1920), Appendix IV. Smuts was much impressed by the German comments on the Treaty. Sir George Foster wrote in his Diary that Smuts "was positive that their case was perfect on the fourteen points as basis—legal and agreed—for Treaty, and that any excess over these was indefensible and implied bad faith. He was emphatic for a recast of the whole Treaty on these lines." Foster adds, "He got little support on this" in the British Empire delegation. W. Stewart Wallace, *The Memoirs of the Rt. Hon. Sir George Foster*, pp. 200-01. Diary entry for May 30, 1919.

16. *Ibid.*, pp. 188-89.

17. *J.P.E.*, 1920, I, 206-07 (September 10, 1920).

18. *Ibid.*, 165 (September 2, 1919).

19. *Anglo-French Negotiations*, p. 166. *See* also p. 170.

20. *Ibid.* Part II contains the documents. Selsam, *op. cit.*, 20 ff., gives a full account of the negotiations.

21. *Ibid.*, pp. 116-17. *See* also *Canada, House of Commons Debates*, April 11, 1922, p. 867. The Memorandum on Anglo-French relations, Lloyd George's proposed Treaty with France and a copy of the Cannes resolutions were brought to the House on April 11th and incorporated in Hansard but there was no discussion upon them.

22. Selsam, *op. cit.*, pp. 30 and 56, citing Viscount D'Abernon, British Ambassador to Germany, *An Ambassador of Peace—Pages from the Diary of Viscount D'Abernon* (London, 1929-30), I, 247, and *Anglo-French Negotiations*, No. 47, p. 165.

23. *Anglo-French Negotiations*, p. 153.

24. *J.P.E.*, 1923, IV, 383 (January 24, 1923).

25. *Ibid.*, pp. 870-71 (June 20, 1923).

26. *Ibid.*, p. 853 (August 1, 1923).

27. Sir Austen Chamberlain, "The Permanent Basis of British Foreign Policy," *Foreign Affairs* (New York), July, 1931, pp. 535-546.

28. Hughes, *The Splendid Adventure*, p. 181. Hughes not only gives a long review of the Egyptian situation but a verbatim account of much of what he said on the subject at the Imperial Conference, 1921.

29. *Ibid.*, p. 117.

30. *Ibid.*, p. 181—quoting from his speech at the Imperial Conference.

31. Lloyd George in subsequently addressing the Commons on the foreign relations of the Empire declared, "At the last Imperial Conference, they (the Dominions) were there discussing our policy in Germany, our policy in Egypt, our policy in America, our policy all over the world, and we are now acting upon the mature, general decisions arrived at with the common consent of the whole Empire." *British House of Commons Debates*, December 14, 1921, pp. 28-30. Reprinted in Dawson, *Development of Dominion Status*, pp. 210-11.

32. Hughes, *op. cit.*, p. 182.

33. *Ibid.*, p. 241.

34. *The Times* (London), September 18, 1922. Reprinted in Dawson, *op. cit.*, p. 234.

35. E.g., Dafoe in the *Winnipeg Free Press.* Reprinted in Dawson, *op. cit.*, p. 244.

36. *J.P.E.*, 1923, IV, 138-39 (September 19, 1922).

37. *Ibid.*, pp. 95-7 (September 19, 1922).

38. Cecil had drawn the Assembly's attention to the hostilities between Greece and Turkey on September 6th. (*Records of the Third Assembly,* 1922. Plenary Meetings, I, 47-8: Fifth Plenary Session.) Balfour, answering two days later for the Council, considered that to expect results from the moral action "of the League" in the face of Kemalist action was "surely a rather forlorn hope," *ibid.*, p. 69. Cook (Australia) and Cecil both urged League consideration of the Chanak crisis, *ibid.*, 1922, Sixth Committee, pp. 45-6: Ninth Meeting, September 22, 1922.

39. Hughes, *op. cit.*, pp. 242-43.

40. *Canada, House of Commons Debates,* February 1, 1923, pp. 30-3. Considerable portions of the speech are reprinted in Dawson, *op. cit.*, pp. 239-44. According to King's account, the British indicated the French and Italians were supporting their stand.

41. *Australia, Parliamentary Debates* (House of Representatives), July 30, 1923, pp. 1775-78. Reprinted in Dawson, *op. cit.*, pp. 249-51.

42. *Ibid.*, July 24, 1923, pp. 1481-84. Reprinted in Dawson, *op. cit.*, pp. 246-49.

43. *J.P.E.*, 1923, IV, 98-9. "If Great Britain thought it necessary to go to war, they believed that Australia, as a part of the great British Empire, should always be ready to come to her assistance."

44. Dawson, *op. cit.*, p. 237. Meighen spoke before the Toronto Business Men's Conservative Club, September 23, 1922.

45. *J.P.E.*, 1923, IV, 588 (May 21, 1923). He was answering Hertzog's challenge that Lloyd George had made "his appeal to the Dominion over the heads of the nation." *Ibid.*, 586.

46. *Ibid.*, 102 (September 20, 1922).

47. *Ibid.*, 140-41 (September 19, 1922).

48. Dawson, *op. cit.*, p. 61.

49. *J.P.E.*, 1923, IV, 592-93. Cited by Smuts.

50. *Ibid.*, pp. 591-93.

51. The Liaison Officer is in charge of a branch of the Australian Department of External Affairs which is attached to the High Commissioner's Office in London.

52. Announcement was made simultaneously in the British and Canadian Houses of Commons. The British statement is reprinted in Dawson, *op. cit.*, p. 202. The original plan was that the Canadian Minister should be the ordinary channel of communication between Canada and the United States and that in the absence of the British Ambassador, he should take charge of the Embassy and of the representation of Imperial as well as Canadian interests. When Canadian representation in Washington was finally established, the latter provision was dropped. See *ibid.*, pp. 96-7.

53. *Canada, House of Commons Debates,* April 27, 1921, p. 2653.

54. At the Imperial Conference, 1921.   *See* Dawson, *op. cit.*, p. 210.

55. *Ibid.*, pp. 67-72 and 254-57.

56. *Canada, House of Commons Debates*, June 9, 1924, pp. 3059-61.   Meighen thought the policy involved in the Lausanne Treaty and especially in the Straits Convention was a mistake and that it would have been Canada's responsibility to endeavour to restrain the British from it.   *Ibid.*, pp. 2937-52.

57. *J.P.E.*, 1924, V, 228-40, 405-15 (April 1, 1924).   The debate was on a motion to postpone second reading of the Treaty of Peace (Turkey) bill until there had been assurance that the Dominions were fully informed of their liabilities under the settlement and were prepared to ratify the Treaty with the Straits Convention included.

58. Dawson, *op. cit.*, p. 73.

59. For the negotiations leading to Locarno, *see* Jordan, *op. cit.*, pp. 96-7.

60. *J.P.E.*, 1926, VII, 7 (November 18, 1925, the British Foreign Secretary, Austen Chamberlain).

61. Prime Minister King in the Canadian House of Commons, *J.P.E.*, 1925, VI, 519 and 723 (June 10 and 26, 1925), and Prime Minister Coates in the New Zealand House of Representatives, *ibid.*, 1926, VII, 151 (September 28, 1925).   The British Government refused permission to make the correspondence on Locarno public.   King in the House of Commons, *ibid.*, p. 305 (March 15, 1926).

62. Dawson, *op. cit.*, pp. 101-02.

63. *J.P.E.*, 1926, VII, 328 (January 14, 1926).

64. *Ibid.*, p. 826 (August 3, 1926).

65. Quoted in *The Round Table*, XVI, 443, cited by A. Gorden Dewey, *The Dominions and Diplomacy: The Canadian Contribution* (New York, 1929), II, 271-72.

66. *J.P.E.*, 1926, VII, 530-49 (June 21, 1926).

67. *Summary of Proceedings of the Imperial Conference, 1926*, Cmd. 2768.

68. On June 21, 1926, Prime Minister King officially moved the Resolution of the 1923 Imperial Conference regarding separate signatures of treaties and made it clear that he had in mind the Locarno Treaty to be considered at the 1926 Conference.   *J.P.E.*, 1926, VII, 530-34.   Dandurand said in the Canadian Senate "that the Locarno Treaty was an accomplishment that could not be sufficiently loudly hailed by the world at large."   *Ibid.*, p. 525 (May 17, 1926). It is interesting to note that N. W. Rowell felt that the Locarno Treaty contributed so much to European peace and stability that "even if Canada did join the mother country in the execution of the Pact of Guarantee her obligation would prove less onerous than her obligation would be if there were no Locarno agreements."   Address on "Recent Developments in International Relations" to the Toronto Bankers' Educational Association, December 2, 1925.   From the Rowell papers.

69. *Canada, House of Commons Debates*, March 30, 1927, pp. 1705-07.   Reprinted in Dawson, *op. cit.*, pp. 350-51.

70. Dewey, *op. cit.*, II, 250.

71. *J.P.E.*, 1926, VII, 826 (August 3, 1926).

72. *Ibid.*, 1925, VI, 622 (April 28, 1925).

73. *Ibid.*, 1926, VII, 788 (March 22, 1926).

74. For this development *see* Dawson, *op. cit.*, p. 103 ff.

CHAPTER IV

ATTITUDES TOWARDS PLANS FOR GENERAL SECURITY

AMONG smaller states the Dominions were unique in their membership in two world-wide groupings, the British Commonwealth and the League of Nations. The League provided them with international recognition and a platform for the public expression of their views. The codes of conduct embodied in the Covenant were as appealing to them as the idealism of its aims. But when it came to a question of security for themselves, none of the Dominions could feel that the League of Nations was an adequate substitute for the Commonwealth connection. They looked on the League far less as a means of protection than as a restraint on the imperial adventures of the Great Powers, including Great Britain, as their desire for League consideration of the Anglo-Turkish situation at Chanak had shown.[1] Thus, in contrast to continental and Near Eastern states, the Dominions tended to interpret the League's function in security negatively rather than positively, security *against* war rather than *in* war. Its primary purpose from their point of view was not to provide support in time of crisis but, as Rowell had said, "to prevent war and to preserve the world's peace by substituting some other method of settling international disputes."[2] Hence their stress was laid upon conciliation, disarmament, and judicial procedures in the hope that more stringent measures might never become necessary.

This emphasis on prevention rather than protection, on conciliation rather than force, became characteristic of all members of the Commonwealth during the decade following the First Assembly. It marked a shift in the British attitude towards the functions of the League, which curiously enough coincided with a shift in the opposite direction by the French, leading to a divergence in their aims in this field which was no less obvious than in their concepts of a satisfactory peace settlement. At the Peace Conference it had been American and British statesmen who strove to make "a league to enforce peace," through Article 10 guaranteeing the territorial integrity and political independence of states, and Article 16 imposing penalties for violation of the Covenant. The French were sceptical of the value of the League in this regard. But as other means through which they hoped to maintain their predominant position in Europe became less secure, the French fell

100

back on the League as a support for the territorial settlement of Versailles and a safeguard of their own position and that of their allies in the east of Europe. They developed the thesis that if League guarantees were sufficiently comprehensive and automatic because of previous military arrangements, no aggressor would dare to break the peace. In the meantime, however, the abstention of the United States from the League had changed the British view of its functions. Strongly supported by the Dominions, the British Government and people came to look on the League as a means of encouraging good relations between nations rather than as a bulwark against aggression. They feared that too rigid commitments might encourage states to embark on provocative policies and, at the same time, would limit their own freedom of action to exercise restraint. Moreover, they dreaded the heavy responsibilities which any general policy of guarantees would inevitably lay upon Great Britain. The attempt to limit the obligations of the Covenant by deleting Article 10 was a Canadian one. But Commonwealth countries in general favoured efforts to clarify commitments and to emphasize the ultimate right of member states to make their own decisions in matters involving the use of force.

At no time were the British willing to enter into specific military arrangements to underwrite League commitments. They were not unaware, however, of the importance of attempting to reconcile their approach to the security functions of the League with that of France. The two major attempts to bolster the guarantees of the Covenant, the draft Treaty of Mutual Assistance and the Geneva Protocol, were both proposed by British statesmen. The Protocol, the result of official British initiative, embodied in fact the most far-reaching proposals of the inter-war period for bridging the gulf between the negative and positive views of international security—security *from* and security *in* war.

It came to the fore, however, at a time when awareness of the need for a general agreement was not strong enough to outweigh causes of difference. The means of establishing international stability had become a party issue in Britain. British election returns, the traditional American approach to the freedom of the seas, and confusion about the implications of the Protocol all contributed to its rejection. So, too, did the lack of understanding on each side of the motives which underlay the negative and positive approaches to security. Logical as each appeared to its own supporters since it arose out of strategic position and interests, it could not help but be alarming to the adherents of the other. French policies towards Germany reinforced British and Dominion desires to clarify their commitments and to be able to determine their action in the light of given circumstances.   No less was it true that the confidence in the League of its more dangerously situated members was shaken at an early date by moves, such as that sponsored by Canada, to make the use of force in relation to League commitments dependent upon the judgment of individual countries.

The Covenant represented both the negative and positive approaches to international security with its dual emphasis on means of conciliation and on guarantees and punitive measures.   But usage and interpretation were to be as important as initial form in shaping its effect.   Almost immediately, the provisions for guarantees and for sanctions came under criticism as being too broad, too indefinite, or too uniform for so varied a group.   The effort to make them more precise and yet differentiated according to the particular position of individual countries was to weaken in fact if not in form the protection they offered to League members in time of need.   At the same time such adjustments as were made were far from meeting the original Canadian contentions on Article 10.

Already at the Peace Conference, Canadian representatives, in particular, Doherty, had voiced opposition to Article 10 as making the League "a mutual guarantee society of unlimited liability" in which "though the risks be unequal . . . the same premium is to be paid by all the members."   This struck at the heart of the conception of limited responsibility evolved in the pre-war British Empire.   "Let the mighty, if they will, guarantee the security of the weak," wrote Doherty in his Peace Conference memorandum which the Canadian Government placed officially before the Assembly in 1921,[3] "the respective positions will be more nearly equalized if no reciprocal guarantee is exacted. The burden of that reciprocal guarantee will be in many instances to the young and undeveloped States quite out of proportion to its value to the States benefiting by it and to any benefit resulting to the burdened States from the guarantee in its favour."   Moreover, he argued, distinction ought to be made between guaranteeing states created by the peace settlement, which should be done only by those countries responsible for the settlement, and endorsing "actually existing territorial possessions," which he opposed altogether unless full opportunity were given for consideration of their justice and stability.   Doherty thus favoured differentiating obligations according to the stage of growth, the proximity to danger and the degree of responsibility for the peace settlement of individual countries while he also wished to extend immediate protection only to states created by the settlement and to others only after review of their situation, and if necessary change.

Article 10 was singled out for opposition both on the ground that its purpose was too broad and that the obligation it involved differed materially from that of other Articles of the Covenant. The obligation under Article 10 he believed to be "direct and absolute" while that of the others was "extremely remote," unconditional whereas theirs were subject to conditions which rendered their operation "extremely improbable," and most serious of all, binding to military action which the others did not demand. Moreover, the latter had "as justifying it" the fact that it was "the sanction of the very Covenants into which all the parties are now entering." Also cases involving violation of procedures prescribed by the Covenant would be considered by the Assembly, not the Council, and since Canada would be represented and a unanimous verdict necessary to apply force "it will be her own decision for which she will be called upon to ensure respect." In contrast, under Article 10, the Council was to advise the means to be taken to protect the guarantee, and Doherty believed "the obligation—subject to such advice—is absolute." This vesting in the Council of the right to recommend action necessary to uphold the guarantee of Article 10 was looked on as challenging long cherished rights of individual decision.

At the Peace Conference, the Canadian opposition to Article 10 could receive little publicity and when the Canadian representatives returned to Canada they were forced to uphold the Covenant, including the guarantee of Article 10, in the debates in Parliament on the Treaty of Versailles. On his own initiative, Doherty introduced a motion at the First Assembly to eliminate Article 10 but there was no time to give it consideration. By the next Assembly, the Canadian Government had decided officially to endorse the argument presented in Doherty's memorandum which they submitted for publication in League records. On discussion it became apparent that there was wide divergence as to the legal and political effect of the Article as well as to its merits.[4] It was decided therefore to postpone consideration until the Assembly meeting of 1922.

At that gathering the representatives of the new Liberal ministry in Canada, having become convinced by conversations at Geneva that it would be impossible to secure the deletion of Article 10,[5] dropped the request for elimination of the Article and asked instead for clarification of its exact meaning and effect.[6] In particular they asked whether it was within the power of the Council "to set the nations at war by their decisions?"[7] It was a reiteration, as Fielding pointed out, of the motion which had been made in the Canadian Parliament during discussions of the Treaty of Versailles, and it marked an interesting shift in emphasis from the Doherty memorandum, though apparently one which had been made perforce. To secure clarification, two amendments were proposed by the Canadian delegation. The first was that the Council's advice on means to fulfil the obligations of the Article should take into account "the political and geographical circumstances of each State." The second embodied a clause to be added to Article 10 asserting that "the opinion given by the Council" should be looked on "as a matter of highest importance" and taken into consideration by all League Members which should use their "utmost endeavours" to conform to its conclusions, but ending with the statement that "no Member shall be under the obligation to engage in any active war, without the consent of its parliament, legislature, or other representative body."[8] The amendments thus sought to ensure that Council requests should be conditioned by the circumstances of individual states and to safeguard Canada's right of ultimate decision in case of a request for military aid.

Since it became apparent in discussions of the new Canadian proposal that there was still considerable division of opinion, it was decided that the Council should seek further information on the attitude of states towards the amendments. When the Fourth Assembly met in 1923, the replies of twenty-five governments had been received, though none from the Commonwealth countries. Most of the answers opposed an amendment lest it weaken the force of the Article. In the face of this opposition, the Canadian delegates realized that the attempt to secure an amendment would evoke wide division in the Assembly though they believed that the necessary majority could have been secured. Somewhat reluctantly they agreed that the points which they had hoped to embody in their amendments should be incorporated in an interpretative resolution, explanatory of the "spirit" of Article 10.[9]

In introducing this resolution, whose final form was shaped by a British representative, the Rapporteur, M. Rolin of Belgium, pointed out that it would not have much legal force but great moral influence.[10] Along with others, including the British, he maintained in addition that the resolution in no way weakened the effect of Article 10. At no time, he believed, had Article 10 implied that the advice of the Council was mandatory or presupposed "immediate military interventions." The League must rest on the strength and will of the peoples of every Member State, he concluded, theirs must be the ultimate responsibility for its success. The representative of France, swayed by the appeal of Sir Lomer Gouin to judge Canada's sincerity by the sacrifices it had been willing to make in the war, appealed for unanimity on the resolution. But the Persian delegate, unconvinced that the resolution did not weaken the force of Article 10, cast a vote against it,[11] thereby preventing it, under the unanimity rule, from having binding force. Even more symptomatic of the feeling against the resolution was the fact that while twenty-nine delegations voted in favour of it, twenty-two were absent or abstained.

From the Canadian point of view, it is significant to notice that Senator Gouin agreed with the Rapporteur that the resolution "in no way affects Article 10." All he had asked was that Canada be given "a clear interpretation of Article 10 in order that we may know what obligations we have undertaken by signing the Covenant which has united us."[12]

Although the interpretative resolution differed markedly from the original proposal to delete Article 10, two major points had been secured. The recognition that political and geographical position should be a determining factor in making recommendations for action answered by indirection the original point of differentiation of status and risk. In the second place, the agreement that constitutional authorities should make the ultimate decision in regard to specific means for meeting obligations protected Canada's jealously-guarded autonomy. But between the original attempt and the final result, there was the difference between avoiding the obligations of a collective guarantee and securing an assurance that, in particular situations, the position of countries would be taken into consideration in proposing measures to be taken, and that individual rights of decision on action were safe-guarded.

In seeking to evaluate the Canadian attitude in regard to Article 10 in relation to its general conception of how peace should be preserved, it is worth noting that the Doherty memorandum had accepted Canada's general obligation under the other Articles of the Covenant which it acknowledged "may subject her to becoming engaged in wars entered upon for the enforcement of the obligations of the nations Members of the League." This endorses the conclusion that, from the beginning, the Canadian action was motivated by the desire to safeguard Canada's ultimate right of decision in particular instances, by a belief in differentiation of function, and by reluctance to guarantee all existing territorial arrangements, not by unwillingness to assume some risks to support the procedures of the Covenant for the maintenance of peace. Even the Doherty memorandum had accepted that the use of force might at some time be inevitable. In 1923 the Canadian Government explicitly accepted the obligations of Article 10, reserving only its right not to enter into war without the decision of the Canadian legislature.

Over and over again, Canadian statesmen informed their League audiences that Canada looked for no individual advantage from the

League, except as Doherty put it "the great benefit and advantage of living in the better world that we believe the League is destined to bring about." Secure in its British connection (which was accepted comfortably as a means of support however it might be eyed askance as a source of potential trouble through unwelcome commitments) and in its good relations with its southern neighbour, Canada could well afford in the early twenties to emphasize its blessings. Looked on from this perspective, and analyzed with understanding of the motives, its stand was not uncommendable. At the moment when Canada was asserting, within the Commonwealth, its right of ultimate decision, it was not likely to do less within the League of Nations. Similarly, Canada's emphasis on differentiation of function was an obvious outgrowth of its position within the Commonwealth. In addition, it had a justification which is generally recognized today.

Seen from the angle of building a strong League, Canadian policy had less to commend it. The attack on Article 10 weakened the faith of dangerously situated countries in the League's protective power. What sympathy was shown for the Canadian action came largely out of the hope that it might lead to American entry into the League, though the Canadian delegations were always careful to insist that this was not their motive.[13] Taken as a whole, the Canadian stand tended to weaken faith that the League would provide security in time of danger and thereby to make more difficult subsequent efforts to re-establish confidence in the possibility of achieving international security through the League of Nations.

None of the other Commonwealth countries actively supported Canada's stand on Article 10 but all endorsed its final move clarifying the commitments involved in the guarantee and asserting, with due respect for the Council's advice, the ultimate right of decision in cases of war of the constitutional authorities of each country.

In both these respects, the resolution on Article 10 bore resemblance to the ones which had been passed in 1921 concerning the obligations arising out of Article 16 of the Covenant which indicated the sanctions to be applied against a Covenant-breaking state. These resolutions concerning Article 16 stemmed from proposals made by the Scandinavian countries in March, 1919, that the military and geographical situations of states should be taken into consideration when military aid was required, and that states which did not vote for sanctions should not be expected to apply them.[14] These suggestions were eventually referred to an International Blockade Committee, established by the First Assembly, which also sought other information regarding effective means of enforcing sanctions. The Committee's report served as the basis for nineteen Assembly resolutions on "The Economic Weapon" intended to constitute "rules for guidance" of the Council and League Members and unanimously recommended as a provisional measure on October 4, 1921.[15] These resolutions declared among other things that the unilateral action of a defaulting state did not create a state of war but merely entitled other Members of the League to resort to war, that it was the "duty" of each Member State to decide for itself whether a breach of the Covenant had been committed, and that "the effective application of the economic sanctions" outlined in Article 16 should only be postponed if desirable for the success of the general plan of action or if it "reduces to a minimum the losses and embarrassments" entailed by certain Members through the application of the sanctions.

The similarity of the Scandinavian and Canadian proposals and of the resolutions on Articles 10 and 16 show both the trend in this early period and that it was directed by states which expected little in the way of protection from the League and were concerned at the demands which might be put upon them. They placed their stamp on the form of League action for the resolutions on Article 16 formed part of the procedural rules for the application of economic sanctions in the Italo-Ethiopian conflict. Incidentally it may be noted that in relation to the analysis of means to enforce "The Economic Weapon" the Canadian delegation pointed out that the potentially injurious effects on League States of barring the offending state from their financial facilities while other similar facilities remained open to them in non-Member states applied equally to commercial dealings. "If, for example," they wrote, "the export of food to a defaulting State were stopped by the countries of the League, this action could only be injurious to those countries themselves if the defaulting State were able to obtain its supplies from some country not a Member of the League."[16]   It was a point of which they were to be particularly conscious at the time of the Italo-Ethiopian conflict because of similarities in the Canadian and American exports of primary products.

Despite the similarity in form and purpose of the resolutions on Article 16 and Article 10, the difference in the time of acceptance made the latter more disturbing to those states which sought protection from the League. In 1921 when the resolutions on Article 16 were passed, the general emphasis was upon clarifying the meaning of the Covenant and getting the League into smooth running order; by 1923, when the Canadian delegation accepted an interpretative resolution on Article 10 in place of the original proposal for its deletion, the unsettled state of European politics had led to a renewed emphasis upon the need for collective security. Since neither alliances nor a punitive policy towards Germany had yielded France the results it desired, the effort was to be made to stabilize the European situation through further League commitments. The first line of policy, endorsed by Commonwealth countries, of emphasizing the ultimate right of decision of individual states, was giving place to the second, supported by the continental states under the leadership of France of increasing commitments to the point where there would be no "gap" in the Covenant of which an aggressor might take advantage. Symptomatic was the French delegate's advice to those countries which felt that the interpretative resolution weakened the force of Article 10: "Adhere to the Treaty of Mutual Guarantee which is in course of preparation. . . . This Treaty will set at rest all your doubts."17   More binding military commitments to supplement the general guarantees of the Covenant was the new emphasis stimulated by the desire for security in case of attack.

The Draft Treaty of Mutual Assistance was, however, not only a means of establishing more complete security arrangements but more particularly the first comprehensive effort to inter-relate security and disarmament. The original considerations out of which it arose were of disarmament, particularly in land armaments since reductions in naval armaments had been secured at the Washington Conference. The person to whom the Treaty owed most was Lord Robert Cecil, who continued to serve as the representative of South Africa at the Second and Third Assembly meetings. In its emphasis on disarmament, the Draft Treaty of Mutual Assistance, and its forerunner, Resolution XIV, appealed strongly to the Dominions, among which Australia in particular had stood out as an advocate of arms limitation. But to those parts of the proposed Treaty which particularly interested France and other continental countries, the provision of guarantees, the Dominions and Great Britain were to be unwilling to agree.

When the Permanent Advisory Armaments Commission, set up by the Council to implement the provisions of Article 9 of the Covenant, declared itself against reduction of armaments, the First Assembly had recommended the appointment of a Temporary Mixed Commission which should include specialists in political, social, and economic as well as military fields. This Commission of which Cecil was a member was asked by the Second Assembly in 1921 to make general proposals for reduction of national armaments. Cecil soon felt that there was no use recommending plans for disarmament unless they were combined with special measures of protection for those countries which were willing to accept reduction of armaments. He persuaded the Technical Mixed Commission to his point of view and in 1922 presented the Third

Assembly with a plan for general disarmament coupled with defensive agreements organized on a continental basis. The Permanent Commission brought forward at the same time technical arrangements for pre-arranged military co-operation. On the basis of a French-proposed compromise between the two plans, Resolution XIV was formulated, a basic step towards the Draft Treaty of Mutual Assistance.

These plans for inter-relating security and disarmament followed closely the breakdown of the Anglo-French negotiations for an alliance. They appealed to French representatives as a wider arrangement than an Anglo-French treaty, and as making the League, as they had proposed before, "a sort of international military insurance company against the risks of aggression." The British did not commit themselves though Fisher thought that if continental powers accepted an arrangement of this kind in good faith Great Britain might be willing to do so also. He pointed out, however, the difficulties of the position of the Commonwealth in relation to a system of regional guarantees "since the mere fact that one member of the British Empire was a party to a regional agreement would automatically involve the Empire as a whole." Later he questioned "Was Great Britain to be regarded as a European state . . . Under these circumstances what should be the attitude of New Zealand, for instance, if the eastern frontiers of Poland were threatened?"[18]

Dominion representatives were less articulate on this problem. The best argued opposition to the proposal came from Scandinavian delegates who maintained that disarmament of itself would ensure security. The Australian representative merely reiterated his support of disarmament[19] and Fielding expressed regret that submarines had not been abolished at the Washington Conference.[20] On the issue of security, Fielding, "while heartily sympathizing with the general purpose and spirit" of the resolutions, expressed himself as "somewhat alarmed" at the phrase "binding them to provide immediate and effective assistance."[21] He feared that this challenged the right of Parliament to determine whether the country should enter war and Cecil's answer that no state would adhere to the Treaty without the consent of its Parliament hardly met his point.

Despite these varied responses, the Assembly unanimously voted for Resolution XIV which outlined four general principles regarding disarmament and security. These were that reduction of armaments could not be "fully successful unless it is general"; that many Governments could not seriously reduce their armaments unless they "received in exchange a satisfactory guarantee of the safety of their country"; that such a guarantee could be found in "a defensive agreement . . .

open to all countries, binding them to provide immediate and effective assistance in accordance with a prearranged plan" to a state which was being attacked, the obligation being limited "in principle" to countries situated "in the same part of the globe" (detailed provisions were to be made on behalf of countries in special danger of attack); and that previous consent to reduction of armaments was necessary before adherence to the Treaty should be permitted.[22]   The Council was asked to secure the comments of Governments upon these principles and the Temporary Mixed Commission to prepare a Draft Treaty based upon them.

Among Commonwealth Governments, only the Canadian replied to the request of the Council for its observations on the principles of Resolution XIV.   It expressed itself in favour of "a general policy of reduction of armaments" and as willing to consider "any proposal tending to the achievement of such an aim."[23]   But a Treaty of Mutual Guarantee "binding the parties to it to render assistance to a country which is attacked" raised serious questions which would make it difficult for Canada to accede "without much consideration and reservation." One special feature of its situation was emphasized, the fact that its dual position in North America and as "a nation forming part of the British Empire" made it difficult to limit its obligations to a single part of the globe.   Beyond this, however, stated the comments, it seemed "very unlikely" that, under existing circumstances, the Canadian people would be willing to accept "any agreement binding Canada to give assistance as proposed to other nations."   For this reason the Government did not see its way to participate in the Treaty of Mutual Guarantee.   The answer was not surprising in view of the fact that the Canadian Government was just preparing its final move for the resolution on Article 10 aimed to safeguard the right of Parliament in any case involving war—but it was hardly encouraging.

In the meantime, the Temporary Mixed Commission had been at work on the draft treaty.   After ironing out initial differences of opinion between Cecil and the French members of the Commission,[24] agreement was reached on a draft Treaty of Mutual Assistance which was transmitted to the Assembly.   It began by stigmatizing "aggressive action as an international crime" and went on to declare that parties to the Treaty would provide assistance to any other signatory on their continent provided that it had conformed to the disarmament provisions of the Treaty.   Indications were given as to how the assistance was to be made effective and the Council was empowered to use the same measures to meet a threat of aggression as to cope with aggression itself. "Complementary" defensive arrangements were permitted.   Proposals were made as to how disarmament should be undertaken though without going into details.   Cecil made it clear in the Assembly that the Council was to determine when a state had disarmed sufficiently to be eligible for the protection of Treaty signatories.[25]

The draft Treaty was considered at length in the Third Committee of the Fourth Assembly but with little new brought forward on either side.   The Scandinavian countries had maintained their opposition to the guarantee provisions in their replies to the Council.   The French and Belgians had emphasized on the other hand that the Treaty was hardly specific enough to enable them to disarm.   It was apparent even before the Treaty was submitted to home Governments for their consideration that there was a sharp division between those countries which might reluctantly accept the guarantee provisions in the hope that they would make disarmament possible and those countries which were interested only in further protection and looked on disarmament with the same reluctance the others looked on guarantees.   Even without the complications caused by the overthrow of the British Conservative Government, there seems little likelihood that the League countries could have come to an agreement over the Treaty.   But the accession to power in Great Britain of Ramsay MacDonald's Labour Government probably sealed its fate, since Labour had long supported conciliation and disarmament as international aims.

The inclusion of military alliances and the potential increase in British responsibilities were the basis of the Labour Government's objections to the draft Treaty.   In its official rejection, the new British Government focussed its opposition on five main points: that difficulty in defining the "aggressor" and in marshalling military support from a number of countries for protection in case of attack made the guarantee "so precarious" that it would not give the assurance necessary to persuade countries to disarm; that because air and naval armaments would be most easily marshalled to extend protection, the obligations involved by the Treaty would "involve an increase rather than a decrease in British armaments"; that the attempt to continue partial treaties alongside of the general treaty might well lead to conflict between them; that some countries, notably Canada, did not feel able to assume the obligations of the Treaty; and that it involved an "undesirable" extension of the authority of the Council.[26]   At the same time, the Labour Government expressed itself ready for an international conference which would have disarmament as its major purpose and would include non-member as well as Member states of the League.   In so doing, it committed itself to a "pledge" to do everything possible to bring about agreements whose "immediate effect would be a substantial reduction in armaments." On the day before the British answer was sent, the Australian Government signified its rejection of the draft Treaty,[27] and four days after the Canadian Government did the same.[28] New Zealand and South Africa signified their dissent to the British Government.[29] The Commonwealth thus stood united in its opposition to the draft Treaty of Mutual Assistance which, despite the adherence of France and other continental states, was never to come into operation.

Cecil charged in the House of Lords that the new British Government by its unwillingness to undertake commitments was jeopardizing the best chance yet offered of combining disarmament and security. Lord Parmoor, he writes, "thought that peace could always be preserved without the use of force—an opinion which he found unsustainable as soon as he got to the Assembly the following September."[30] Beyond this, Cecil accused the British Government of having persuaded the Dominions to follow its lead. In reply, Parmoor asserted that Dominion opposition had played a rôle in the British decision, and questioned "Is it possible to conceive the idea of separate Dominion opinion from that of the Mother Country on a matter of this kind?"[31] Balfour supported him in maintaining that the continental character of the guarantees of the draft Treaty cut across "the lines of a much better and more powerful arrangement and one more conducive to peace," the Commonwealth.

Cecil was probably correct in feeling that the British Labour Government made its decision on the draft Treaty out of its own reasons and not because of opposition by Dominion Governments. The general increase in British responsibilities which the Treaty would probably have involved would have been enough to make any British Government hesitate though Cecil may also have been right in thinking the gain would have been worth the cost. But it may be doubted whether the attitude of the British Government was decisive for the Dominions. Though New Zealand and Australia might well have concurred in such an agreement to preserve Commonwealth unity, they feared that an expansion of British responsibilities in Europe weakened the potential aid which might be extended to themselves in a moment of crisis. As for Canada, its opposition to the proposed Treaty had been expressed a year before the formal rejections were sent.

In its final communication of July 9, 1924, the Canadian Government agreed "generally" with the conclusions in the British answer. It noted that the Treaty would not come into effect for North America unless ratified by the United States (which had already refused adherence because of its "constitutional organization" and non-membership in the League[32]) but felt that Canada's position in the British Empire "affects the protection afforded her by the continental limitation." In any case, this limitation appeared to the Canadian Government to be of doubtful usefulness since it questioned whether hostile action could ever be undertaken "upon the principle of limited liability." The Treaty involved an obligation "wider in its extent and more precise in its implications" than Article 10 in regard to which Canada had already indicated disapproval of any interpretation implying the obligation to "intervene actively." It considered therefore that in as far as the Treaty "purports to impose a future obligation to take specific action in circumstances incapable of present definition" the Canadian people would not consider accepting it.

Cecil felt that in fact the Dominions would not have been much affected by the Treaty since they would not have been bound to action outside their continents.[33] The peculiar situation of Australia occupying a continent of its own formed in fact the burden of the Australian reply. "There is neither obligation to assist nor guarantee of receiving assistance so far as Australia is concerned," its Government pointed out. But actually such an interpretation, like Cecil's, foundered on the special relations existing between the Commonwealth countries. No regional arrangement could fit the purposes of the Commonwealth unless the advantages in avoiding war appeared to outweigh any additional dangers it involved of becoming engaged in conflicts. The comments of the Canadian Government were evidence of a sense of ultimate Commonwealth unity in time of crisis which makes an interesting corollary to its reaction to the Lausanne Treaty.

An arrangement of the type of the draft Treaty of Mutual Assistance failed to meet the needs and desires of the Dominions in two important ways. In the first place their geographical position made the regionally organized guarantees of little value. Even had the United States adhered, which was never a serious possibility, the Treaty would not have afforded more protection to Canada than did the Monroe Doctrine. In the second place, the position of the Dominions within the Commonwealth might involve them all in war if it should result from the use of British forces in a conflict into which the Treaty had drawn Great Britain. Far from furthering the hope of disarmament, their major reason for supporting it, the plan appeared to extend the necessity for British armaments. The Dominions might well fear that it would also extend the necessity for using them.

The draft Treaty of Mutual Assistance had been rejected but the British Labour Government as a major factor in this rejection felt the responsibility of proposing an alternative means of securing disarmament. At the Fifth Assembly, encouraged by a prior agreement with the

French on the necessity of seeking a solution to the problems of disarmament and security, it sponsored the most elaborate proposals for the maintenance of peace to be introduced in the inter-war period. These capped the twin pillars of the draft Treaty, disarmament and security, with a means both for settling disputes and for determining the aggressor, compulsory arbitration. Refusal to arbitrate was to be the touchstone of aggression. This three-fold structure embodied through the efforts of Politis and Beněs in the Geneva Protocol focussed the attention of the most distinguished representatives an Assembly had ever known, and appeared, at least during the lifetime of the Fifth Assembly, to offer a reconciliation of the positive and negative views of international security.

The Geneva Protocol placed its primary emphasis upon compulsory arbitration of non-justiciable disputes and submission to the Permanent Court of International Justice of all justiciable disputes. For this latter purpose it proposed that all states adhering to the Protocol should accept the optional clause of the Statute of the Permanent Court providing for its compulsory jurisdiction in legal issues. By these means, it provided an answer to the two major "gaps" in the Covenant, the lack of a definition of aggression, and the possibility of undertaking war legitimately if the conciliation and investigation procedures of Article 15 should fail. But with the exception of these provisions, the Protocol was the Covenant made more explicit. The main difference as far as security provisions were concerned was that since there was a test of aggression in the willingness to arbitrate, the Council could immediately determine the aggressor against which all states were bound to institute sanctions.[34] While the procedure for penalties did not differ in any essential from that provided under the Covenant, it would be much speedier, surer, and therefore in practice a much better protection. An international conference to be called the following year was to provide for disarmament. Upon its success was to depend the coming into force of the Protocol.

In the course of discussing the provisions of the Protocol, two matters proved to be of special concern to Commonwealth countries. The British Government desired to make sure before it signed the optional clause that action which it might undertake at sea for the enforcement of the Protocol could not be considered by the Permanent Court under non-British standards of maritime law.[35] This was argued out during five sessions of the Legal Committee and the British Government's point was accepted. The second issue, which was to cause much more trouble both inside and outside the Assembly meetings, concerned the matter of domestic jurisdiction. Where the Covenant (Article 15, section 8) made the Council responsible for deciding what subjects fell within domestic jurisdiction, Article 5 of the Protocol transferred this function to the Permanent Court and reserved from compulsory arbitration issues which the Court decided to be within domestic jurisdiction. On September 25th, at the seventh meeting of the First Committee, the Japanese delegate, Adatci, suggested adding to Article 5 the words "Without prejudice to the Council's duty of endeavouring to conciliate the parties so as to assure the maintenance of peace and of good understanding between nations." This proposal "raised serious doubts in the minds of several delegations as to whether it would not have the effect of setting up the Council as an appellate tribunal from decisions of the Court," the Australian delegation later wrote,[36] "and thereby make possible interference in domestic affairs."

The First Committee to which the Japanese proposal had been brought was presided over by Sir Littleton Groom, head of the Australian delegation, and he lost no time in discussing the issue with other members of Commonwealth delegations. In a letter written at the time to Bruce, the Australian Prime Minister, Groom described the efforts made inside and outside the committee to find a solution satisfactory both to the Japanese and to Dominion delegates.[37] In the meeting with Commonwealth delegates, only Arthur Henderson approved the Japanese amendment, and Sir Cecil Hurst, legal adviser to the British Government, was asked to prepare a substitute clause. Next day, Hurst proposed as an alternative a general reservation to be placed at the end of the Protocol stating that it in no way interfered with all the rights provided by the Covenant and in particular the right of conciliation of the Council. This Adatci flatly refused to accept. According to Groom's account, Adatci then formally made his amendment, which was supported by the French representative. Hurst did not move and Groom, fearing that the amendment might go by default, vacated the chair to oppose it and urge Hurst's compromise. Other speakers supported Groom and Adatci finally withdrew his amendment, making, however, "every possible express reservation as to the whole system which the Committee proposed to establish."[38] He also indicated that he would introduce another amendment which would omit the presumption of "aggressor" in the event of hostilities regarding an issue which the Court had decided was under domestic jurisdiction. The situation had become extremely tense and it looked as if the future of the Protocol was in danger.

Before the second amendment was introduced, negotiations were carried on with other delegations in the hope of securing a satisfactory compromise. Also the Japanese representative on the Council, Ishii, came to see Groom "confidentially." Declaring that the Japanese were anxious for a peaceful settlement, Ishii stressed their desire to be sure that under the Protocol they would remain in "the position that matters were now under the Covenant."[39]   Groom made no promise but they had a friendly conversation and later Ishii saw Parmoor and others. That evening, however, the second Japanese amendment was moved by Adatci.   For a moment Groom thought that the plans which had been made were going to fall through and that he would have to speak against the amendment after all.   The French delegate, however, who was privy to the plan to have the reply to the Japanese made by a delegate from a country outside the Commonwealth, came to the rescue by proposing that the matter be referred to a sub-committee, to which Groom was appointed.

The following day Groom met with the Council at their invitation and heard Ishii support both Japanese amendments to the Protocol. A Drafting Committee made up of British, French, and Italian representatives was set up and agreed upon an alternative that afternoon. This was to replace the original Japanese amendment to Article 5 of the Protocol with a sentence declaring that if an issue were held to be solely within the domestic jurisdiction of a state, the decision should not prevent consideration by the Council or Assembly under Article 11 which allowed them to take cognizance of any situation endangering the peace of the world.   The British delegates tried to get Groom to accept this alternative clause the same evening but he refused to be rushed. The next morning in the meeting of Commonwealth delegates, Groom said there was "some very straight speaking."   The Canadian and Indian delegates supported the British on acceptance of the new clause and it became clear that the representatives of other countries in the Assembly were prepared to accept it.   The South African and New Zealand delegates shared Groom's reluctance to accept the clause, but in a private conversation in Groom's apartment admitted that "we had practically to accept the amendment or our action of opposition might wreck the situation."   The Australian delegation agreed that it could not take the responsibility of injuring the plan and decided to allow the situation to stand.   The sub-committee of which Groom was a member, brought in the proposal devised by the Drafting Committee with some slight amendments, and it was passed unanimously as an addition to Article 5 of the Protocol.   A similar provision was added to Article 6 in place of the second Japanese amendment.   The Report of the Rapporteurs "expressly" stated that the Protocol "in no way derogates" from the Covenant provision which "protects national sovereignty," and cited Hurst's exposition of this fact to the First Committee.   Hofmeyr of South Africa declared in the Committee that he would have preferred a different solution but that he accepted it and would recommend the Protocol to his Government.[40] Groom made it clear that he had no authority from the Australian Government or Parliament to accept on their behalf but wrote Bruce that he thought "on the whole" the Protocol was "satisfactory" and the amendment as accepted "quite satisfactory."[41]

On October 2nd, the Geneva Protocol was accepted unanimously by the Assembly for transmission to the home Governments of the representatives who had worked so earnestly and rapidly to formulate the plan.   On that day, Senator Dandurand, head of the Canadian delegation, put forward in the plenary session the Canadian point of view on the "three chief pillars upon which this structure has been erected—arbitration, security, and disarmament."[42]   He pointed to Canada's long history of experience with all three resulting, he declared, not only in "a hundred years of peace on our borders, but we think in terms of peace, while Europe, an armed camp, thinks in terms of war." To those fearful of challenge to the rights of domestic jurisdiction, he offered the experience of the International Joint Commission as an "intimation that the exercise of a right may be tempered by equity and conciliation."   In the light of this experience he believed that Canada "faithful to her past," would be prepared to accept compulsory arbitration and the compulsory jurisdiction of the Permanent Court.   He believed, too, that it would be ready "to accept all the sanctions that might be imposed in case she refused to accept the decisions of the court of the arbitrators."   In disarmament, Canada had already attained the goal towards which the Assembly was striving.   That left but one point, the crucial one of the sanctions.   Here, Dandurand skilfully sketched the conflicting pulls on Canadian policy.   "We will be loyal," he declared, to the Covenant signed at Versailles, but when we signed it, "Canada was then far from thinking that she would have the whole burden of representing North America when appeals would come to our continent for assistance in maintaining peace in Europe."   The absence of the United States had increased "in our eyes, the risks assumed, and the history of Europe in the past five years has not been such as to lessen that apprehension."   And then in words often quoted and somewhat resented by his European listeners, Dandurand picked up the French simile for the League to illustrate Canada's position. ". . . in this Association of Mutual Insurance against fire, the risks assumed by the different States are not equal.   We live in a fire-proof house, far from inflammable materials.   A vast ocean separates us from Europe."   Canada had already shown in its attitude to Article 10 its desire for precise interpretation of its obligations, for differentiation of responsibilities because of position, and for ultimate Parliamentary decision in case of war. "We hope," he added, "that it will be possible to find in the Protocol which is presented to us, the policy expressed in last year's resolution interpreting Article 10." In voting to recommend the Protocol to the Governments of Member states, he pledged his country at least to consider "with the fullest sympathy" how far the Protocol would meet the needs of Canada and whether "it can undertake to subscribe to its obligations."

The Protocol had passed its first great hurdle of Assembly approval. Within a few days seventeen states had signed and, before the end of October, Czechoslovakia had ratified the Protocol. But even while the Assembly was in session, opposition had been rising in Great Britain and in the Dominions, stirred by exaggerated press accounts of the implications of its provisions. Led by *The Times*, rumours began to circulate that the British Navy was being handed over to the League of Nations as an instrument of enforcement for the Protocol. On September 17th, *The Times* began its first editorial with the words, "The future control of the British Navy is now being discussed at Geneva."[43] Public concern reached such a point in Great Britain that Henderson felt it necessary to make a formal denial at Geneva on September 22nd, stating categorically that there "is no idea and never has been any idea of placing troops or ships at the free disposal of the Council to use as they see fit."[44] The issue on which the rumour was hung was the one already mentioned concerning the jurisdiction of the Permanent Court over belligerent naval operations undertaken for enforcement of the Protocol. Agreement had been reached by the time of Henderson's announcement that the British Fleet under those circumstances would not be subject to any but British maritime law. Despite this fact, *The Times* still continued to hint editorially that "our precious possession, the Navy, is somehow to be brought into this sphere of unknown contingencies over which the British people will have no direct control."[45]

Equally effective in stirring feeling against the Protocol were reports in *The Times* that the Japanese amendments were intended to cover the questions of immigration and tariffs.[46] An editorial on September 30th declared that Japan's objective "affects the whole question of immigration in the British Empire." Even after the speech by Hurst declaring that the Protocol made no change in the authority of the Council or Assembly,[47] *The Times* correspondent wrote in a despatch printed on the day the Assembly unanimously recommended the Protocol to the home Governments, "Japan is now at liberty to bring the immigration issue before the League Council."[48]

These misleading reports filtering through to the Dominions led to concern in both Australia and New Zealand. "Australia is feeling a little mystified and more than a little uneasy over the somewhat cryptic messages which have been received from Geneva about the Arbitration Protocol," wired *The Times* correspondent in Sydney, citing four Australian papers all of which feared the "White Australia" policy might be in danger.[49]   In answer to anxious questions from the Leader of the Opposition, the Prime Minister of New Zealand declared that he had cabled their delegate at the Assembly meetings to watch the issue carefully. Regardless of the outcome, he maintained, New Zealanders would not have the question of whether people could enter their country submitted to arbitration.[50]   Later, in official comments to the British Government, the New Zealand Government suggested that the Permanent Court might have held that its system of immigration restrictions was contrary to the comity of nations and therefore not merely domestic jurisdiction.[51]   This possibility it declared to be "negligible," however, compared with allowing the Court to determine Great Britain's belligerent rights at sea, a point which showed that the basis of its information had been the alarmist newspaper reports, not the decisions of the Assembly.

While the press prejudiced the public against the Protocol,[52] the political situation in Great Britain gave the MacDonald Government no opportunity for explanations. Six days after the Protocol had been recommended to Governments by the Assembly, the British Labour Government was defeated. An election held at the end of October returned the Conservative party to office. The Geneva Protocol was even less to its liking than the draft Treaty of Mutual Assistance had been to the Labour Government. Though it made all possible efforts to confer with the Dominions,[53] it is clear that it made its own decision to reject the Protocol. But on March 12, 1925, when Sir Austen Chamberlain, now Foreign Secretary, announced to the Council of the League the British rejection of the proposal, he could also state that all the Commonwealth Governments were in agreement in their refusal to accept the Protocol.

It is often said that the opposition of the overseas Dominions was the main reason for the rejection of the Protocol by the British Government,[54] but the evidence hardly bears this out. Chamberlain declared in the House that amendment was considered but that it was decided that to make it acceptable to Britain and the Empire, it would have to be changed so radically as to make a new arrangement.[55]   Cecil wrote that the majority of the Committee of Imperial Defence "had no doubt" that the Protocol should be rejected. Despite his own feeling that the Protocol was too complicated, he "urged amendment rather than rejection, with no support."⁵⁶   The British Conservative Government was to refuse consistently to accept even the Optional Clause, lest, it is said, the situation with Egypt should be brought before the Permanent Court.   Nor did it believe in general guarantees but in the type of limited regional arrangements which took form in 1925 in the Locarno Treaty.

On the other hand, the opposition of the Dominions to the Protocol was in general much less strong than to the draft Treaty, and with a few changes some, at least, of the Dominions would probably have been willing to accept it.   The most outright opposition was that of New Zealand, but it declared not only that it would be guided largely by the British decision but also that "If, as has been contended, the Protocol really defined no greater obligations than are already undertaken by the Nations in the Covenant itself, it might well be the case that, even in the short space of time allowed, Great Britain and the Dominions might have assented."⁵⁶ᵃ   The immediate reaction of the Australian Government was that "it would be unwise to reject the Protocol without cogent reasons or without endeavouring to formulate some alternative positive policy."⁵⁷   At the same time, it reserved its rights in regard to immigration and thought whatever policy was decided should be acceptable to the United States.   Subsequently, after the British Government had decided to reject the Protocol, the Australian Government maintained that the existing procedure of inquiry by the Council was more flexible than the principle of compulsory arbitration and suggested that the latter was dangerous as long as powerful states remained outside the League.   It also found the amendment in regard to domestic jurisdiction unacceptable.   It seems most likely, however, that Australia's ultimate rejection of the Covenant was due, at least in part, to influence from the British Government.⁵⁸

The Canadian response regarding the Protocol was also not given until after the British Government had made its decision, notification of which was made to the Dominions on March 3, 1925.   There is a well-substantiated story that when Dandurand returned to Canada after the Assembly, he was "court-martialled" at midnight by a number of Liberal leaders for his stand on the Protocol.   He justified it so successfully that he turned the tables and persuaded them to accept the principles "*a bas de protocol,*" arbitration, disarmament, and security. Though the official Canadian answer maintained that it was not considered "in the interests of Canada, of the British Empire, or of the League itself" to recommend adherence to the Protocol and "particularly" to its "rigid provisions for application of economic and military sanctions in every future war," it avowed positive support of the League's work of "conciliation, co-operation, and publicity," offered to take part at any time in a general conference on disarmament, and favoured a variety of methods for peaceful settlement of disputes.[59] Under this heading, the Government declared its willingness to consider acceptance of the Optional Clause, with certain reservations, and "methods of supplementing the provisions of the Covenant for settlement of non-justiciable issues, including the method of joint investigation." Regarding the latter it reserved "ultimate decision in domestic issues" and the right not to undertake "further obligations to enforce decisions in case of other States."

The last member of the Commonwealth to make its attitude known was the Irish Free State, which did not join in the Commonwealth exchange of opinions but publicized its rejection through a statement in the *Dail* which was subsequently transmitted to the Colonial Secretary and thence to the other Dominions.[60] Its Government echoed the fears of the South Africans that the sanctions provisions of the Protocol might lead the League to take on more of the character of a military alliance. Such sanctions, moreover, might be effective against a small power, it believed, but would be powerless "to prevent either the oppression by a larger power of small states or the occurrence of a war of world magnitude." On the other hand, the Irish Free State strongly supported the principle of arbitration.

All the Dominion Governments had expressed some opposition to features of the Protocol. Nonetheless, from their varied answers and from comments inside and outside of their Parliaments, it appears that the difficulties in the way of their acceptance of the Protocol were not insuperable. The sanctions were the most adversely criticized feature of the plan but it does not seem that, in fact, there would have been a greater though probably a speedier obligation to apply these than under the Covenant. The Conservative and Labour parties in Canada endorsed the rejection of the Protocol, the former on the ground that it would have been tantamount to advising "Great Britain to underwrite the security of the world."[61] In contrast, the New Zealand Government criticized the Protocol because it had no provision "enabling or entitling a nation which is not itself attacked by aggression to come at once to the assistance of a friendly nation which is so attacked." In Australia, the Labour Opposition, headed by Charlton who had been a delegate to the Fifth Assembly and sat through the Commonwealth discussions on the Japanese amendment, supported the Protocol and objected to the way in which the Government had rejected it without Parliamentary discussion.[62] The Federal Council of the League of

Nations Union in Australia concluded after a searching inquiry into the provisions of the Protocol that not only would the sanctions have been a far lighter burden than under the draft Treaty of Mutual Assistance, but that the "White Australia" policy would be safer under the Protocol than under the Covenant.[63] It is difficult to avoid the conclusion that much of the opposition was based on misconceptions. Further discussion and consideration of the Protocol and some encouragement from the British Government might well have brought the Dominions to accept it with only minor amendments.

While Dominion reactions can hardly be considered, therefore, to have been influential on the British Government's decision to reject the Protocol, the attitude of the United States may well have been a significant factor. Both Great Britain and the Dominions were concerned to know how the United States would view the Protocol. In rejecting its provisions for sanctions, the Canadian Government had drawn attention to the effect of the non-participation of the United States particularly in the case of contiguous countries like Canada. The South African Government in its reply suggested that the Protocol might make it more difficult for countries still outside the League, notably the United States, to accept membership, and consequently would increase the tendency of the League to become a limited political alliance, instead of a universal organization.[64] The Australian Government had also raised questions as to American reactions. The British Ambassador, in fact, did discuss the Protocol with the American Secretary of State on January 5, 1925,[65] making it clear that "It was a cardinal point in British policy to maintain friendly relations with the United States and to co-operate with this Government wherever possible." This was the time when the British Government was considering amendments to the Protocol as it feared that if it were thrown out altogether, there might be a continuation of competitive armaments in Europe with all their "possible consequences." In considering modifications, the British wished to know the American attitude in case blockade operations by the British Government under the Protocol conflicted with American interests. The answer of the Secretary of State was not encouraging. He felt that the American Government would continue to insist upon its traditional stand on neutral rights, and subsequently declared that "there could be no hope of applying the sanctions successfully in opposition to the views of the United States as they might be entertained by its people when a contingency arose." This view, the Secretary thought, should be communicated to other League Members but without mentioning the American statement.

It seems likely that it was this American stand rather than Dominion reactions which confirmed the British Government's opposition to the Protocol.

The Geneva Protocol was the last great attempt to strengthen the general system of collective security through the League of Nations. It was succeeded by the regional guarantee of Locarno which made a final reconciliation between the French and British views of Rhineland security.   But had the Protocol been accepted, it might well have done the more valuable service of reconciling the positive and negative views of international security: security *in* as well as *against* war.   The emphasis on judicial process appealed to those states like the Dominions which sought to avoid war by providing peaceful means of settling disputes.   The speedy means of determining the aggressor and thereby bringing sanctions into operation appealed to those states to whom protection was the greatest need.[66]   Out of the combination of arbitration and security might well have come disarmament.   At least it is sure that no combination less than the three was to be capable of providing the conditions needed for peace.

With the failure of the Protocol, the efforts to bolster security through providing guarantees ceased to be made inside the League. Instead they were undertaken between the Great Powers, notably at Locarno, though in co-ordination with the League structure.   The efforts to secure reduction of land armaments continued within the League though without noticeable success.   In addition, there was a marked increase in arrangements whereby countries agreed to limit their own action when disputes arose.   Some of these took the negative form of renunciation of war; others the positive form of accepting the compulsory jurisdiction of the Permanent Court in justiciable disputes, and conciliation and arbitration for non-justiciable questions.   Thus efforts to maintain peace followed the three lines of the Geneva Protocol but, because they were piecemeal, they failed to do what the Protocol might have done, that is, to institute a comprehensive and generally binding scheme which would answer any emergency.[67]

Yet in the period from 1925 to 1930 there seemed the possibility of achieving a European settlement which would act as a centre of world peace and pave the way for a truly universal League.   In 1926, after a preliminary fiasco, the League moved one step nearer universality with the admission of Germany in an atmosphere to which the "Locarno spirit" extended.   In 1928, the United States took its first general initiative in international affairs since the Washington Conference by sponsoring the Kellogg-Briand Pact, or Pact of Paris.   In this most all-inclusive self-limiting agreement of the inter-war period, nearly fifty states pledged themselves to outlaw war as an instrument of national policy. In 1929, Great Britain and all the Dominions accepted the Optional Clause of the Permanent Court, and in 1931, except for South Africa, the General Act for the Pacific Settlement of International Disputes. On the surface, it looked as if the Dominions had come close to their goal of an international situation in which there were peaceful methods of settling disputes without automatic commitments. It was a pleasant prospect but unfortunately deceptive!

To the Dominions, one of the most encouraging signs for the future during the late twenties was the American initiative in regard to the Kellogg-Briand Pact for the outlawry of war. The original suggestion appears to have been that of Professor James T. Shotwell, an American citizen though Canadian by birth, who proposed to Briand that the tenth anniversary of the entry of the United States into the war might be marked by a treaty between their two countries renouncing war. Briand made the proposal through the press on April 6, 1927, and followed it up by sending a draft treaty in June to Kellogg, Secretary of State. Not until December did the American Government reply to the French initiative but at that time Kellogg proposed both a bilateral treaty of arbitration with France, and a multilateral renunciation of war signed by all the principal powers. Though France made some reservations to broadening the arrangement, the United States, on April 13, 1928, transmitted a draft treaty to Great Britain, Germany, Italy, and Japan, couched in much the same terms as Briand's original proposal. About two weeks later Kellogg in an address to the American Society of International Law gave his official interpretation of the Treaty. Two days before, the German Government had signified its acceptance, and on May 19th, the British Government also approved though with rather vague reservations. It suggested that direct invitations be extended to the Dominions and to India and this was done almost at once. On June 23, 1928, the final stages began with the despatch of an American note containing the Treaty with a revised preamble, and Kellogg's address, to fourteen Governments including the Dominions, Belgium, Poland, and Czechoslovakia, in addition to those originally approached. The British, Dominion, and European Governments decided to accept subject to individual "interpretative" notes and on August 27, 1928, the Kellogg-Briand Pact was signed in Paris. Next day, the United States extended the invitation to forty-eight other governments and through the French an invitation was extended to the Soviet Union. By 1930, practically all the self-governing states of the world had accepted the Pact.

The Kellogg-Briand Pact incorporated a self-denying pledge on the part of the signatories that, condemning "recourse to war for the solution of international controversies," they renounced it "as an instrument of national policy in their relations with one another." In his interpretation of its meaning, Kellogg declared it was compatible with war undertaken in self-defence or in execution of responsibilities under the Covenant, the Locarno Treaty, or treaties guaranteeing neutrality (presumably including the French alliances), or against a state which resorted to war in violation of its pledge under the Pact. These modifications were mainly in response to French proposals and were taken as official explanations of the Pact.

Less widely accepted were the British Government's interpretations of its obligations under the Pact. In what was generally called the British "Monroe Doctrine," declaration was made that "there are certain regions of the world the welfare and integrity of which constitute a special and vital interest for our peace and safety. . . . Their protection against attack is to the British Empire a measure of self-defence."[68] The Pact was thus accepted by the British Government "upon the distinct understanding that it does not prejudice their freedom of action in this respect."

The British reservation was commonly thought to refer particularly to Egypt and it was suggestive that Egypt, Persia, and Turkey in their adherences to the Pact attempted to free themselves from the implications of any special reservations made by other countries. From the point of view of the Commonwealth, it is interesting to note that both the Canadian Prime Minister and the Irish Minister for External Affairs declared in Parliament that the terms of the British note were binding only upon Great Britain.[69] On the other hand, Great Britain did not deposit its adherence to the Pact until after receiving the approval of the Dominions. None of them, however, officially endorsed in any way the British reservation.

From their side, each of the Dominions signified its independent acceptance of the Pact:[70] Australia and New Zealand sent general expressions of gratification through the British Government. The Irish Free State accepted "unreservedly." South Africa noted it would "take it for granted" that self-defence or violation by another party of the provisions of the proposed Pact would relieve it from the pledge and that its adherence in no way would preclude it "from fulfilling, as a member of the League of Nations, its obligations towards the other members thereof under the provisions of the Covenant of the League." The most carefully considered answer from a Dominion was that of Canada which, in giving the reasons why it felt the Pact was compatible with the Covenant, presented a reasoned picture of its attitude towards the League.

The Canadian Government, the note declared, looks on the League "with its limitations, as an indispensable and continuing agency of international understanding, and would not desire to enter upon any course which would prejudice its effectiveness." Its "pre-eminent value," the note continued, "lies in its positive and preventive action." By bringing together into periodic conference the representatives of fifty states, it "builds up barriers against war by developing a spirit of conciliation, an acceptance of publicity in international affairs, a habit of co-operation in common ends, and a permanently available machinery for the adjustment of differences." In regard to sanctions, the Canadian Government noted its opposition to any interpretation which would involve their application "automatically or by the decisions of other states." For "the full realization of the ideal of joint economic or military pressure upon an outlaw Power" which some of the founders of the League had supported, it would be necessary, Canada believed, to have "either an approach to the universality of the League contemplated when the Covenant was being drawn, or an adjustment of the old rules of neutrality to meet the new conditions of co-operative defence."

It is difficult to avoid the conclusion that the Canadian Government was taking this opportunity of presenting directly to the United States its view of the values and obligations of the Covenant. The emphasis was the one which had been made consistently by the Canadian Government but for the first time since the Peace Conference it could be presented directly to the American Government. Whether there was implicit in the statement an appeal for universality is difficult to maintain or to refute.

From 1927 to 1930, Canada held a seat on the Council as one of the nine non-permanent members created in the reorganization of 1926 when Germany received a permanent seat. In that year, the Irish Free State had sought a place on the Council, though not as one of the Dominions. The following year, election was accorded to Canada, thereby beginning the precedent of having one Dominion represented on the Council. The period of Canada's Council responsibilities proved, however, to be singularly uneventful. Its new position provided Canada with a place on the Preparatory Committee for the Disarmament Conference where its influence was invariably thrown on the side of large-scale reduction of armaments and of abolishing such means of attack as chemical warfare. Otherwise, it was not confronted with any important issues bearing on security.

Some important developments took place, however, in these years. In the matter of compulsory jurisdiction of the Permanent Court, a long-cherished Canadian hope was realized in 1929 when all Commonwealth countries accepted it for justiciable disputes with non-Commonwealth countries. It was a move which the Canadian representatives at the First Assembly had supported though they were prepared not to accept for Canada, until Great Britain was ready to agree. In its answer to the Geneva Protocol, the Canadian Government had officially endorsed the principle of compulsory jurisdiction. So had the Irish Free State Government.[71] At the Imperial Conference in 1926, however, the British Government secured "a general understanding" that no Commonwealth Government would take action in the matter until there had been further discussion.[72] The Kellogg-Briand Pact brought the issue to the fore again. The Australian Government declared early in 1928 that it had come to a decision regarding the Optional Clause and hoped soon to enter into communication with other parts of the Commonwealth.[73] Apparently no further action was taken by the Australian Government, but in February, 1929, the Canadian Government began to take the initiative again by instituting discussion with the other members of the Commonwealth.[74] On May 7, 1929, King announced in the House of Commons, the Canadian Government's willingness to sign the Optional Clause, but not until after conferring with other members of the Commonwealth as had been pledged in 1926.[75] A month later, a Labour Government, pledged to accept the compulsory jurisdiction of the Permanent Court, came into power again in Great Britain. Informing the Dominions, on August 1st, of its intention to adhere to the Optional Clause,[76] it began correspondence seeking to secure a general acceptance by Commonwealth countries at the 1929 Assembly. As late as a few days before the Assembly convened, MacDonald despaired of signature because of "certain difficulties" being made by one of the Dominions.[77] Henderson exerted pressure, however, to maintain the British Government's stand and conversations among Commonwealth delegates, during the early part of the Assembly, resulted in acceptance of the Optional Clause by all the Commonwealth countries.

There was general agreement, except by the Irish Free State, that intra-Commonwealth disputes should not be submitted to the Permanent Court, though South Africa and Canada both declared that they believed such matters were justiciable by the Court, but that they preferred to settle them in other ways. The Canadian delegation would have preferred to make a separate declaration of policy on this point, rather than an express reservation, but consented when "a strong desire was expressed" that it should join with the others.[78]   The Australian, New Zealand, and South African delegations believed it necessary to make reservations covering not only *inter se* disputes but also issues which, according to international law, were under domestic jurisdiction. A reservation covering the latter issue was drafted during the Assembly meetings and was believed by the countries concerned to cover immigration.[79]   On September 14th, before this reservation had been completed, the Irish Free State had signed without any reservations, accepting for twenty years on the sole condition of reciprocity.   Five days later, a declaration of acceptance was made on behalf of Great Britain, New Zealand, South Africa, and India.   On September 21st, Australia and Canada made their declarations.[80]   The Commonwealth had taken the step of pledging itself to submit all justiciable disputes, not reserved, to the Permanent Court of International Justice.   So effective was its example, that fifteen other states undertook the same move within a short time.

To the agreement of Commonwealth countries to submit justiciable disputes to the Permanent Court, was to be added in less than two years formal acceptance by all, except South Africa, of the General Act for the Pacific Settlement of International Disputes whose object was to cover non-justiciable disputes.   The result of the work of the Committee on Arbitration and Security of which Canada was a member, the General Act combined three model multilateral treaties providing for conciliation and arbitration.   Already when announcing at the 1929 Assembly the intention of the Irish Free State to sign the Optional clause, its delegate had declared his intention of seeking authority to sign the General Act.[81]   At the 1930 Assembly, Henderson made known the favourable disposition of the British Labour Government,[82] though it preferred not to sign until after discussion with other Commonwealth countries at the forthcoming Imperial Conference.   The ultimate result of these deliberations was the adhesion to the General Act of all Commonwealth countries except South Africa[83] in the summer of 1931. So far as guaranteeing their own conduct was concerned, the nations of the Commonwealth had gone almost as far as they could go.   But time was to prove that unfortunately it is not enough to guarantee one's own standards of behaviour.

The decade following the First Assembly had been a time of questioning and of experimentation.   Speaking on his experience at Geneva heading the Canadian delegation to the Eleventh Assembly, Sir Robert Borden answered those who were disappointed in the achievements of the League by declaring that in the light of the "storm in which it was born," the marvel was that "it survived at all."[84]   He believed that its supreme service had been "in the intimate association of the member states, in the broadening of their outlook, in their training in the habit and practice of peaceful arbitrament and generous co-operation." From the point of view, at least of the Dominions, these were the major functions it could have fulfilled.   One after another at different times in the last years of this decade, representatives of the Dominions had affirmed their faith in a League which was characterized not by force but by its encouragement of the habits of peaceful living together. Their fears of being called upon to fulfil with force the obligations of the Covenant had been calmed by the general acceptance of the Kellogg-Briand Pact.[85]   The British move to amend the Covenant to bring it more in line with the declaration to outlaw war[86] met with their endorsement.   They had never denied the obligation to use force if the Covenant were broken though they maintained their ultimate right to decide for themselves in the light of given circumstances.   But the developments after Locarno and particularly the greater interest in international peace shown by the United States, encouraged them to hope that the nations were acquiring the habit of peaceful settlement of differences. In particular the British Government's signature of the Optional Clause and the General Act relieved them of concern lest they be drawn into a British imperial quarrel.   For the unanimity which the Commonwealth exhibited over plans for the organization of general security through the League was a measure of its own ultimate solidarity.

Viewed more broadly, the history of the efforts of the twenties to build an international structure of general security was less encouraging. The failure to bridge the gap between the negative and positive approaches to security resulted in a weakening of the Covenant which was to be all too obvious when it was put to the test.   Behind this weakness was more than inability to agree theoretically upon the attitude to be adopted to situations yet unknown.   Basic to it was the too great stress laid by both the proponents of the negative and the positive approach upon their individual needs and interests.   There was too little awareness, on the one side, of the overriding need to stop aggression wherever it might take place and, on the other, of the necessity of making constructive concessions out of which a stable situation might arise.

It is one of the great tragedies of the League that the most serious issue it had yet faced should have occurred at a time when most of the nations of the world were battling with economic depression and in an area where the customary difficulties of securing information and exerting influence were intensified by remoteness.   The only hopeful sign when the Sino-Japanese dispute flared up on September 18, 1931, was that the traditional interest of the United States in the Far East meant a greater possibility of securing its co-operation while the Kellogg-Briand Pact and Nine Power Treaty offered instruments through which it could work with League powers. But the chance that the League could deal only with the prevention of war and avoid the issues involved in a large-scale state of war vanished with the first shots fired on the South Manchurian railway at Mukden. The period of plans was over. The Members of the League of Nations were confronted with the first of the practical tests of collective security.

REFERENCES FOR CHAPTER IV

1. *See* above. Chapter 3, p. 86.

2. *See* above. Chapter 1, p. 22.

3. League of Nations, Committee on Amendments to the Covenant, *Memorandum submitted by the Canadian delegation* (C. 215, M. 154, 1921). Reprinted in G. P. deT. Glazebrook, *Canada at the Paris Peace Conference*, Appendix C.

4. *League of Nations Official Journal*, 1921, Spec. Sup. No. 6, p. 12.

5. *Records of the Third Assembly*, 1922, First Committee, p. 23: Fifth Meeting, September 14, 1922. Lapointe.

6. *Ibid.*, Plenary Meetings, I, 215-16: Fifteenth Plenary Session, September 23, 1922.

7. *Ibid.*, pp. 216-17.

8. Quoted in *O.J.*, 1923, Spec. Sup. No. 13, pp. 75-76: Fourth Assembly, Twelfth Plenary Session, September 24, 1923.

9. The resolution read as follows: "The Assembly, desirous of defining the scope of the obligations contained in Article 10 of the Covenant so far as regard the points raised by the Canadian delegation, adopts the following resolution:
    "It is in conformity with the spirit of Article 10 that, in the event of the Council considering it to be its duty to recommend the application of military measures in consequence of an aggression or danger or threat of aggression, the Council shall be bound to take account, more particularly, of the geographical situation and of the special conditions of each State.
    "It is for the constitutional authorities of each Member to decide, in reference to the obligation of preserving the independence and the integrity of the territory of Members, in what degree the Member is bound to assure the execution of this obligation by employment of its military forces.
    "The recommendation made by the Council shall be regarded as being of the highest importance, and shall be taken into consideration by all Members of the League with the desire to execute their engagements in good faith." *Ibid.*, p. 75.

10. *Ibid.*

11. *Ibid.*, p. 81. He requested time in order to ask his government to agree to the interpretative resolution in view of the pending Treaty of Guarantee but the Canadian delegate refused to accord it.

12. *Ibid.*, pp. 80-1.

13. *Records of the Third Assembly*, 1922, Plenary Meetings, I, 216-17: Fifteenth Plenary Session, Sept. 23, 1922 (Fielding). The French delegate, Barthelemy, had declared, "The Canadian proposal was no doubt suggested by the hope that the seat which remains vacant in this Assembly would soon be filled. . . . We feel that the United States would bring us such strength that we could well consent to some sacrifices; but that if Article 10 is to be modified, it must be modified when the United States joins us and in agreement with the United States." *Ibid.*, pp. 213-14. Fielding was answering him.

14. Miller, *Drafting of the Covenant*, II, 592. The Scandinavian States also proposed that countries which were to be asked to co-operate in economic and military sanctions should have a voice in reaching the decision on their imposition, and that states should be allowed to declare permanent neutrality.

15. *O.J.*, 1921, Spec. Sup., No. 6, pp. 24-6: Resolutions and Recommendations adopted by the Second Assembly.

16. *Memorandum by the Canadian Delegation on a Portion of the Report of the International Blockade Committee.* Second Assembly, 1921, Meetings of the Committees, I, 15-6 (verbatim record): Third Committee, Fourth Meeting, September 16, 1921, Annex II.

17. *Records of the Third Assembly*, 1922, Third Committee, p. 12: Second Meeting, September 11, 1922 (de Jouvenal).

18. *Ibid.*, pp. 35-37: Sixth and Seventh Meetings, September 16 and 19, 1922.

19. *Ibid.*, Plenary Meetings, I, 276: Nineteenth Plenary Session, September 23, 1922 (Cook).

20. *Ibid.*, Third Committee, p. 14: Second Meeting, September 11, 1922.

21. *Ibid.*, p. 17: Third Meeting, September 12, 1922.

22. *O.J.*, 1922, Spec. Sup., No. 9, pp. 26-7: Resolutions and Recommendations adopted by the Third Assembly.

23. *O.J.*, 1923, Spec. Sup., No. 16, p. 129: *Fourth Assembly*, Third Committee, Annex I, Part I (Dated June 19, 1923).

24. Cecil, *A Great Experiment*, p. 151.

25. *O.J.*, 1923, Spec. Sup., No. 16, p. 54: *Fourth Assembly*, Third Committee, Eleventh Meeting, September 20, 1923.

26. *O.J.*, 1924, Spec. Sup., No. 26, pp. 143-45: *Fifth Assembly*, Third Committee, Annex III, Treaty of Mutual Assistance, British Reply, July 5, 1924.

27. *Ibid.*, pp. 142-43. (Reply dated July 4, 1924.) *See* also speech by Sir Littleton Groom in *ibid.*, p. 27: Fourth Meeting, September 12, 1924.

28. *Ibid.*, p. 146: Annex III (Reply, July 9, 1924).

29. *Great Britain, House of Lords Debates*, July 24, 1924, Cols. 70-72 (Parmoor).

30. Cecil, *op. cit.*, p. 158.

31. *Great Britain, House of Lords Debates*, July 24, 1924, Col. 71 and Balfour, Cols. 1001-02.

32. *O.J.*, 1924, Spec. Sup., No. 26, pp. 141-42: *Fifth Assembly*, Third Committee, Annex III (Reply of the United States, June 16, 1924).

33. Cecil, *op. cit.*, p. 158.

34. In Committee discussions of the Protocol, Sir James Allen declared that he had always interpreted the obligation under paragraph 2 of Article 16 as "a moral obligation" which left it to the states to decide whether they should accept the recommendations of the Council for military sanctions. He opposed extending it into a legal obligation through the Protocol if that was the intention, both because he thought the people of New Zealand would resent a legal but not a moral obligation, and he feared it would make it "practically impossible for America ever to enter the League." *O.J.*, 1924, Spec. Sup., No. 26, p. 61: *Fifth Assembly*, Third Committee, Eighth Meeting, September 24, 1924.

35. *See* speeches by Sir Cecil Hurst, *O.J.*, 1924, Spec. Sup., No. 24, p. 18: *Fifth Assembly*, First Committee, Third Meeting, September 11, 1924, and Arthur Henderson, Foreign Secretary, *O.J.*, 1924, Spec. Sup., No. 26, pp. 41-3: *Fifth Assembly*, Third Committee, Sixth Meeting, September 22, 1929.

36. *Report of the Australian Delegation to the Fifth Assembly, 1924*, p. 13.

37. *Nation Building in Australia: The Life and Work of Sir Littleton Ernest Groom* (London, 1941), pp. 178-79.   The letter is printed in full and was taken from the Groom Papers, League of Nations, October 2, 1924.

38. *O.J.*, 1924, Spec. Sup. No. 24, p. 57: *Fifth Assembly*, First Committee, Ninth Meeting, September 26, 1924.

39. Groom Papers, *op. cit.*

40. *O.J.*, 1924, Spec. Sup. No. 24, p. 89: *Fifth Assembly*, First Committee, Thirteenth Meeting, September 30, 1924.

41. Groom Papers, *op. cit.*

42. *O.J.*, 1924, Spec. Sup. No. 23, pp. 221-22: *Fifth Assembly*, Twenty-eighth Plenary Session, October 2, 1924.

43. *The Times* (London), September 17, 1924.   Its special correspondent had written, on September 13th, that Lord Parmoor was "understood to have suggested in private conversation that the British Fleet might be employed for the purpose of enforcing or supporting economic penalties against aggressors."

44. *O.J.*, 1924, Spec. Sup. No. 26, pp. 42-3: *Fifth Assembly*, Third Committee, Sixth Meeting, September 22, 1924.

45. *The Times*, September 25, 1924.

46. *Ibid.*, September 29th and 30th.

47. The author was told by a member of the British delegation, who believed that the attitude of *The Times* was intentionally obstructionist, that Hurst's speech was given to *The Times* correspondent with the express request to see it was in both English and Dominion newspapers the morning after it was delivered. In this way it was hoped to prevent any agitation from arising on this point. Instead of printing Hurst's speech, the report of *The Times* correspondent suggested that the Protocol did in fact threaten interference with the domestic jurisdiction of states.

48. *The Times*, October 2, 1924.   The following day the Geneva correspondent commented, "The hasty concession to Japan in allowing matters of 'domestic jurisdiction' to come in certain circumstances before the Council of the League is considered a short-sighted expedient, which may ultimately prove a disastrous obstacle to universality." *Ibid.*, October 3, 1924.

49. *Ibid.*, October 3, 1924.   *See* also report of hostility aroused in Australia which appeared in *The Round Table*, XV, 378.

50. *J.P.E.*, 1924, V, 140-42.   Repeated by the Leader of the Liberal Opposition. G. W. Forbes in a later debate on the issue, September 28, 1925. *Ibid.*, 1925, VI, 145.

51. *Protocol for the Pacific Settlement of International Disputes: Correspondence relating to the Position of the Dominions*, Cmd. 2458 of 1925, No. 8.

52. Arnold Toynbee, *Survey of International Affairs*, 1925, p. 2, attributes the unfavourable reception of the Protocol in the Dominions in large measure to the fact that "exaggerated and even absurdly distorted accounts of obligations to which Great Britain was alleged to have committed herself found their way into the Press of the Dominions." Cecil calls the story on the British fleet "a singularly unscrupulous proceeding on the part of the British critics of the Protocol" though he personally did not approve the policy of the Protocol, *op. cit.*, p. 159, and *Nation Building in Australia*, p. 180, speaks of the misrepresentation of the Protocol in both the English and Australian Press. *The Times* reports also suggested there was division between British and Dominion delegates at the Assembly though, in fact, such close contact was kept between them that Groom speaks of "the British Empire delegation."

53. *Cmd. 2458.* The attempt was made to call an Imperial Conference in May, 1925, to reach a collective decision on the Protocol. This proving unsuccessful recourse was had to consultation by correspondence.

54. *E.g.,* G. M. Gathorne-Hardy, *A Short History of International Affairs, 1920 to 1939* (3rd ed.; New York, 1942), p. 62.

55. *Great Britain, House of Commons Debates,* November 24, 1927, Cols. 2101-02.

56. Cecil, *op. cit.,* p. 166. For the British Government's case against the Protocol see Sir Charles Petrie, *Life and Letters of the Rt. Hon. Sir Austen Chamberlain,* II, 250 ff., and for the official rejection, *Cmd. 2368.*

56a. F. L. W. Wood, *New Zealand in Crisis: May 1938-August 1939* (Auckland, 1939), p. 1, declares that the New Zealand Government "plainly disliked the principles of the Geneva Protocol at a time when that 'mischievous' document was endorsed by Mr. MacDonald's Government in Britain: but her objections were expressed publicly only when it was known that they were shared by the Conservative Cabinet which had in the meantime displaced MacDonald."

57. *Cmd. 2458,* No. 5. Its later comments are in No. 12.

58. This is suggested in the *Cambridge History of the British Empire,* VII, I, 544; and by Ramsay MacDonald in *Great Britain, House of Commons Debates,* November 24, 1927, Col. 2098. Chamberlain replied equivocally. *Ibid.,* Cols. 2110-11.

59. *Cmd. 2458,* No. 11 (March 4, 1925), and telegram to the Secretary-General of the League in substantially the same words, summarized in *Canada, House of Commons Debates,* 1925, II, 1049, and *O.J.,* 1925, Spec. Sup. No. 33, pp. 88-9: *Sixth Assembly,* Twelfth Plenary Session, September 16, 1925 (Hewitt Bostock).

60. *Cmd. 2458,* No. 16.

61. *J.P.E.,* 1925, VI, 305 (Meighen). Woodsworth spoke on behalf of Labour, pp. 722-23.

62. *Ibid.,* pp. 781-92. The debate was on the report of the Australian delegates to the Assembly and began August 14, 1925. *See* also pp. 583-87.

63. H. Duncan Hall in the *Manchester Guardian Weekly,* March 6, 1925, reported the findings. Cited in Dewey, *The Dominions and Diplomacy,* II, 230. David Hunter Miller felt that the right "to determine and control" domestic matters was "more unquestioned" under the Protocol than under the Covenant since it could not be questioned by the League, the Court, arbitrators or war. All that was possible was "friendly discussion and consideration" under Article 11 of the Covenant and that that was always possible for Members of the League. *The Geneva Protocol* (New York, 1925), p. 71. Latham, the Australian Attorney-General, argued in *The British Yearbook of International Law,* 1926, p. 185, that Australia would be better off under the Protocol since it would have the help of the League if attacked in a dispute over domestic jurisdiction even after the three months' delay enjoined by the Covenant.

64. *Cmd. 2458,* No. 7.

65. *U.S.A. Foreign Relations,* 1925, I, 17-8.

66. It has been questioned whether the Protocol would have satisfied the French conception of security. *See* Jordan, *Great Britain, France and the German Problem,* p. 208. But Cecil speaks of Briand's "great disappointment when the British rejected it." *Op. cit.,* p. 167.

67. In 1927, most League countries were anxious to revive the Protocol but Great Britain was, according to Cecil, "the one formidable opponent," *op. cit.,* p. 190.

68. For text of Sir Austen Chamberlain's note to the American Ambassador, May 19, 1928, *see* J. W. Wheeler-Bennett, *Information on the Renunciation of War (1927-1928)* (London, 1928), pp. 115-19. The British statement was repeated when the British Government signified its final adherence. The term "British Monroe Doctrine" arose from the succeeding sentence. "The Government of the United States have comparable interests any disregard of which by a foreign Power they have declared that they would regard as an unfriendly act."

134   THE COMMONWEALTH AND INTERNATIONAL SECURITY

69. *Ibid.*, p. 38.

70. *Ibid.*, pp. 126-134.

71. At the Sixth Assembly, the delegate of the Irish Free State objected to the implication that the British delegate's explanation of the hesitancy of the British Government in signing the Optional Clause covered the other members of the Commonwealth also. He declared then that the Free State Government, while sympathetic to the idea, wished to go more fully into the practical aspects of the application of the Optional Clause before making a decision. *O.J.*, 1925, Spec. Sup. No. 34, p. 24: *Sixth Assembly*, First Committee, Sixth Meeting, September 23, 1925.

72. *Cmd. 2768*, p. 28.

73. *J.P.E.*, 1928, IX, 701. (J. G. Latham, Attorney-General, April 26, 1928.) On August 31st, however, Bruce was reluctant to commit himself to any definite course of action. *Ibid.*, 974-75. The Labour party had come into office by the time the Optional Clause was signed.

74. *Canada, Senate Debates*, April 4, 1930, pp. 342-43 (Dandurand). Repeated by King in the House of Commons, April 9th, *Debates*, p. 350.

75. *Canada, House of Commons Debates*, May 7, 1929, p. 2299.

76. *O.J.*, 1929, Spec. Sup. No. 75, p. 43: *Tenth Assembly*, Fifth Plenary Session, September 4, 1929 (Dandurand).

77. Cecil, *op. cit.*, p. 202.

78. *Canada, Senate Debates*, April 4, 1930, pp. 342-43.

79. *J.P.E.*, 1930, XI, 968-69 (J. G. Latham, July 4, 1930), and p. 449 (Prime Minister Hertzog, January 27, 1930).

80. *Journal of the Tenth Assembly, 1929*, No. 18, pp. 313-14: Verbatim Records, September 21, 1929.

81. *O.J.*, 1929, Spec. Sup. No. 75, p. 110: *Tenth Assembly*, Thirteenth Plenary Session, September 11, 1929 (McGilligan).

82. *O.J.*, 1930, Spec. Sup. No. 84, pp. 40-1: *Eleventh Assembly*, Fourth Plenary Session, September 11, 1930.

83. South Africa refused to sign the General Act for fear it might be forced to concede its "Asiatic legislation" to arbitration. Even the possibility of reservation of domestic affairs was not felt to be sufficiently sure to make adherence advisable. The Prime Minister, in a discussion on the General Act in the House of Assembly on April 23, 1931, col. 2791 ff., declared: ". . . the Minister of Finance and I said: ' No, we cannot do it: as far as we are concerned, it looks very dangerous.'"

84. "In the Kindergarten of Peace," Address delivered by the Rt. Hon. Sir Robert Laird Borden, Ottawa, November 17, 1930. Reprinted from *Interdependence* (League of Nations Society in Canada, Ottawa), January, 1931.

85. *E.g.* Hertzog in the South African House of Representatives, April 10, 1930. *J.P.E.*, 1930, XI, 1036.

86. Introduced by Arthur Henderson. *O.J.*, 1929, Spec. Sup. No. 75, pp. 59-60: *Tenth Assembly*, Seventh Plenary Session, September 6, 1929. Printed together with the draft resolution of Committee in *ibid.*, p. 510, Annex 32.

CHAPTER V

PARTICIPATION IN COLLECTIVE ACTION: THE SINO-JAPANESE DISPUTE

In the years succeeding the Washington Conference, the Pacific area had attracted comparatively little attention. The Washington agreements had temporarily put an end to the three most potent causes of divisions between Great Britain, the United States, and Japan: naval rivalry, expanding territorial influence in the Pacific Ocean, and encroachments in China. The growing power of Japan had scarcely been noticed in the absence of specific causes of friction. In the twenties the danger point appeared to be Europe, and attention was concentrated on its political and economic projects. Even the developing strength of the Soviet Union was largely ignored as the problems of central and western Europe absorbed attention. In 1930 and 1931, Briand's plans for European Union were holding the centre of the political stage, though closely rivalled by the ill-fated Austro-German Customs Union. When the Mukden incident occurred, the statesmen assembled at Geneva for the Council and Assembly meetings had little conception of how serious the situation in the Far East might become. In fact, few seemed to have realized at any time during the first Sino-Japanese dispute that what was taking place was not only a shattering blow to the peace structure which had been set up after the war, but also a dangerous undermining of the basis of peace in the Pacific which rested on all three aspects of the Washington arrangements.

The complexity of the general situation in Manchuria to which Chinese disorders had contributed as unfortunately as Japanese encroachments, in which there were disputed treaty rights,[1] and unusual difficulties in securing accurate information, contributed to the difficulty of recognizing what was involved in the Mukden incident and the events which followed it. So, too, did the general political scene in both China and Japan. In China, rival régimes were vying for power and military rebellion in the north was threatening to plunge the country back into anarchy. In Japan, the division though less obvious was hardly less dangerous. There, the civil administration found itself incapable of controlling the army, a fact which was to result in stultifying the normal means of exerting external pressure on a country's action.

Putting further difficulties in the way of organizing collective pressure in this highly complicated situation was the concentration

135

upon their own domestic affairs of the countries which should have been most concerned with trouble in the Far East.   Their energies were chiefly directed towards releasing themselves from the morass of economic depression which became intensified throughout Europe[2] and in the United States during the summer of 1931.   On August 24th, the British Labour Government split on an issue of financial retrenchment and gave place to Ramsay MacDonald's Coalition Government.   Within forty-eight hours of the first Japanese action in Manchuria, Great Britain had suspended the gold standard.

The overseas Dominions, dependent to a high degree upon their exports of primary products, had taken the full shock of the 1929 depression, and were still caught in its grip.   In Canada, the hope of securing more favourable trade opportunities within the British Empire which led to the Ottawa Agreements was a powerful factor in the policy of R. B. Bennett's Conservative Government which had come into power in 1930.   In New Zealand, economic distress led to a coalition of the United and Reform parties to save the country from further disasters, a move announced on the day of the Mukden incident.   Australia's Labour Government was soon to be replaced by a coalition under J. Lyons, which included the Country party whose chief interests were in securing markets for Australian wool and wheat.   At few points in the inter-war period were economic motives so greatly to the fore as late in 1931 and during 1932.   Their general effect, not only in the Dominions but also elsewhere, was to make countries cautious about adopting new policies, to place particular weight on well-assured trading opportunities of which those with Japan bulked large, particularly with Australia[3] and to induce a general sense of self-centredness which complicated efforts to rouse public opinion to an awareness of the significance of rather remote political developments.

Beyond the influence of economic considerations, however, was the fear evident in both Australian and British official circles that aggressive impulses or the curbing of its purposes might lead Japan to attack British territories in the Far East.   They were well aware that the division of the Pacific into spheres of influence under the Four Power Treaty and the agreement respecting bases had left the British portion far less adequately protected than either of the others because of the much wider responsibilities of the British fleet.   It had been planned that the South Pacific would be guarded by the great base at Singapore but not only were its fortifications proceeding slowly (the more so because building had been suspended during the periods of office of the two Labour Governments in Great Britain) but its strategic position was such that it could better defend British interests in India than in

China or even the Pacific Dominions. The direct line between Japan and Australia lay three thousand miles off from Singapore, the reason why Jellicoe had felt Australia needed a small battle fleet of its own to protect it until the main battle force at Singapore could be brought into position. When the British gave up the plan of a Far Eastern Fleet due to the arrangements of the Washington Conference, it became apparent that there could never be a substantial number of first-class British fighting ships in the South Pacific. In 1931 and thereafter, the situation in Europe was too tense to spare to the Far East even a small portion of the British Navy. It was realized that in the event of serious trouble in the Far East, British territories had few means of defence available. The underlying fear of Japan which never quite vanished from Australian minds after the unexpected conclusion of the Russo-Japanese war near the beginning of the century was heightened by recognition of the blatancy of the "White Australia" slogan.[4] Taken together with knowledge of the insecurity of the British position in the Far East, it acted to induce a strong degree of caution in Australian policy in regard to any action undertaken by or against Japan, a reaction which seemed to have been very similar to that felt in British official circles.

Counter pulls on Commonwealth policies in the year and a half between the outbreak of the Sino-Japanese dispute and Japan's final condemnation by the League were fear of involvement in action which might precipitate conflict and the desire to uphold the Geneva peace structure, and to maintain solidarity with the United States. Though sympathies with China were more strongly evident in the United States than in Commonwealth countries, it became less easy as time went on for any group to condone Japan's behaviour in terms of the undoubted provocations China had given in earlier times. But there was little change in interpretations of interest. Out of conflicting views of whether it was more important to uphold the principles underlying collective security or to avoid division with Japan were to come some of the more obvious differences of opinion between Commonwealth members and within Commonwealth countries that had yet occurred. In general, the division tended to follow geographical position, those parts of the Commonwealth with Far Eastern interests, Great Britain, Australia, and New Zealand, pursuing a cautious policy, the Irish Free State and South Africa supporting a strong stand by the League of Nations while Canada balanced between them. It must be said, however, that the junior members of the Commonwealth, like the smaller powers in the League, were always aware that the brunt of any action against Japan would be borne by the Great Powers, and tempered their words accordingly. From their side, the Great Powers, including the United States, were to be concerned not to precipitate a serious rupture with Japan. None the less, as the gravity of the situation became more apparent, they were to attempt to restrain Japan through a graduated series of pressures.

In the first sessions of the Council to which the dispute was immediately referred by the Chinese delegate[5] under Article 11, comparatively little was done. Cecil, who was the representative of the British Government on the Council at the time, felt that he was "particularly awkwardly placed, without instructions, and not even in close political alliance with the actual British Government."[6] He suggested that the American Government should be kept informed of developments and the Council received from Hugh Gibson, the American representative at Berne, "a promise of diplomatic support." But in view of the Japanese pledge to withdraw troops to the railway zone, Cecil gathered that it was only "a minor incident which would be settled by the time we moved again," and the Council did no more than pass "the usual resolution" as had been done in other cases,[7] calling on the parties to cease hostilities so the dispute could be settled. This was officially endorsed by Stimson, American Secretary of State, who assured the Council that the United States was "in wholehearted sympathy" with its attitude. The Chinese were understood to be requesting a commission of inquiry but it was reported that the United States was doubtful of the wisdom of pressing for such action at this stage.[8] The Assembly which was in session was restive lest the Council should be too conservative in its attitude but was persuaded to accept two short communications on the subject in lieu of a debate. Since the Assembly adjourned on September 29th, there was no further opportunity for expression of views by its members till it was reconvened in special session the following spring for the express purpose of considering the dispute.

At the second meeting of the Council on October 13th, there was more recognition that the situation was serious. Japanese aeroplanes had bombed Chinchow, and the Japanese Government was shifting its emphasis to the "fundamental" basis of normal relations with China. Prentiss Gilbert, the American Consul-General in Switzerland, was welcomed to the Council table as an observer, too warmly, Cecil believed, as the practice was not repeated though not entirely due to isolationist pressure in the United States, as he suggests. Gilbert's presence was intended as official recognition that the United States believed that the Kellogg-Briand Pact was applicable, at least Article 2, as there was not yet an official state of war. In closed session of the Council, it was decided to invoke the Pact formally. On October 27th, identical notes were sent by six of the larger countries represented on the Council, including Great Britain, to both Japan and China drawing their attention to the Pact, while three days later similar notes were sent by the United States. There was no consideration of action but no country, including the United States, seems to have been ready for such a development. While editorial opinion in the United States appeared to be gradually consolidating behind the Administration policy of co-operation with the League of Nations,[9] Stimson himself writes that the American Government "in its efforts at co-operation with the League under Article XI had gone to the limit of its legal authority and at least to the limit of its popular support."[10]

Lord Reading had replaced Cecil as official British delegate but Cecil was present at the sessions and with Reading's permission got together an unofficial committee of four members to see what could be done if Japan proved to be obdurate, and action were desired under Articles 15 and 16. The group felt that Japan would be very vulnerable to economic sanctions but that no action would be effective unless the United States participated. Such considerations proved disturbing to Reading, who "begged" Cecil "to take no further action of that kind."[11] Cecil gathered his anxiety was due largely to the financial crisis, which was acute. He also felt that there was not much concern over what happened in Manchuria "where Britain had no territorial interests and very little trade." Reading, however, devised a resolution with the Secretariat calling on Japan to withdraw its troops within a stated period of time. Cecil felt rightly that this was somewhat rash if no action was to be taken to enforce it, as proved to be the case. The only obvious result was that the Japanese had to take a public stand in opposition to the resolution, which therefore had force only as an expression of opinion, since action under Article 11 had to be unanimous.

In the interval before the next meetings of the Council in November, no progress was made towards getting the Japanese to define the "fundamental" grounds of their dispute with China. In the meantime, the British election of October 6th had returned an overwhelming majority for MacDonald's coalition government, the Labour Opposition having only 56 seats compared to 558 for the administration. Reading was replaced as Foreign Secretary by Sir John Simon. The American press continued in general to approve the co-operation between the United States and the League. Many English newspapers were modifying, however, the sharp tone taken at the beginning of the dispute and, while maintaining the necessity for upholding the League, were tending to emphasize the difficulties of the procedure for securing a settlement. The possibility that the Soviet Union might take a hand in the dispute was causing increasing concern in both English and European newspapers. Though liberal and radical editors were supporting Briand's efforts to find a solution, much of the French press was gradually adopting the pro-Japanese attitude which became so evident during the next Council session in Paris with unfortunate effects on Briand's leadership. It is commonly accepted that the Japanese were spending huge sums of money to influence French newspapers and that until well on in 1932, French public opinion was more concerned about the future of Indo-China than the future of the League. Editorials in Scandinavian countries and other small European powers were arguing on the other hand that failure to deal effectively with the dispute would be a moral defeat for the League, and cripple efforts for disarmament.[12] In the Dominions, there seems to have been little appreciation as yet of the critical character of the situation.

In contrast to the earlier session, the third part of the Council meetings which began in Paris on November 16, 1931, were almost entirely in private. General Dawes acted as American observer during the latter part of the session but felt nothing would be gained by joining in any of the public meetings which were held merely to announce decisions reached in private. Dawes had already had confidential talks on the situation not only with Sir John Simon but also with the Japanese Ambassador in London, and followed these up with conversations with Briand and the Chinese representative on the League Council.[13] The American feeling was that the time limit for withdrawal of Japanese troops was unfortunate, and with this Simon and Briand agreed. The latter raised the question of the American attitude in case the Council considered possible sanctions under Article 15 or 16 but Dawes made clear that he "had been informed that the United States would not join in the consideration of the question of sanctions or in the enforcing of them if hereafter imposed by the League."[14] But though it was thus obvious that American co-operation would not extend to forcible action against Japan, Dawes was to play a significant rôle during this period by effectively exerting influence to keep the Japanese and Chinese from taking a stand which would cause the breakdown of negotiations.

The Council discussions sought to reconcile the Chinese and Japanese attitudes towards arrangements existing between them, the Chinese objecting to those concluded under duress but offering to refer them to the Permanent Court, while the Japanese insisted on all existing rights, apparently including those of the 1905 secret agreement and the "Twenty-One Points." The breadth of the Japanese contentions startled the Great Powers which began to feel concerned for their own position in China, and General Dawes let it be known that the United States stood behind the established principles of the "open door" in commerce, and respect for the administrative and territorial integrity of China.[15] At the same time, it was recognized that there were large-scale disorders in Manchuria and that at least to some extent these justified Japanese troop movements. Anxious to continue the process of mediation, the Council, under threat of a Chinese appeal to the Assembly under Article 15, now adopted a Japanese proposal for a Commission of Enquiry to investigate the situation on the spot. This procedure usually followed the cessation of hostilities but since no progress could be made in the latter direction, it was generally agreed that the customary arrangements should be reversed.[16] Attention was turned, therefore, to plans for the Commission and to formulating a resolution which both China and Japan could be persuaded to accept.

At this juncture, the smaller powers on the Council, led by the representatives of Spain, Norway, Yugoslavia, and the Irish Free State, began to play more of a rôle. Generally satisfied by the handling of the first two meetings of the Council, and recognizing the more direct interests and responsibilities of the Great Powers, they had previously been content to remain in the background. But as Sean Lester, the representative of the Irish Free State, writes, the smaller countries had constantly in mind that they might some day stand in need of the protection of the Covenant and were anxious that no precedents should be given which would weaken their position.[17]

The Irish Free State had succeeded Canada on the Council in 1930, probably because Australia was not interested at that time in assuming the responsibility.[18] Both under the Cosgrave Administration and that of de Valera, who came into office in February, 1932, steady support was given to a strong League policy partly as a counterbalance to the Commonwealth relation.[19] Sean Lester was allowed considerable discretion of action and appears to have made good use of the particular opportunities of his position as representative of a small European country having no stake in the dispute, with access at times to the special information of the British representative and more understanding of British and American reactions than was possessed by the delegates of some other minor powers. Though, like the delegates of other small countries, he was careful not to try to place upon the Great Powers more responsibility than they felt willing to assume, Lester's influence was consistently thrown on the side of maintaining the authority of the League to the fullest extent that seemed possible.

On three points, the representatives of the small powers attempted with varying success to influence decisions during these sessions of the

Council.   In regard to the Commission of Enquiry, they tried to make the sending of the Commission conditional upon withdrawal of Japanese troops, and to have at least one small League state represented on the fact-finding body.[20]   On both points, they were overruled by the permanent members of the Council, which decided that the Commission should be composed of only five members, representing Great Britain, France, Germany, Italy, and the United States, and that it should be sent regardless of developments in hostilities.   To this the smaller states finally acceded but with reservations that it should not be a precedent for the future.[21]   On the third point, the formulation of the draft resolution on the situation, the smaller countries had more success though even here they could not persuade the Great Powers to go as far as they would have liked.   The resolution did, however, include reference to the undertaking made by the Japanese Government on September 30th to withdraw Japanese troops within the railway zone. As for the Commission, though its functions were to be purely advisory, its mandate was wide since it was declared that "In principle no question which it feels called upon to study will be excluded," if it affected international relations or "good understanding" between China and Japan.[22]

The acceptance of this resolution by both China and Japan was considered by Dawes to be imperative "not simply because it would bind them to an agreement for peaceful settlement of the present difficulties, but because it would constitute a formula for the relationship of these two nations in the future, behind which might be mobilized the moral sentiment of the world."[23]   Even in the light of subsequent developments he felt that it "at least brought about the prevention of a general war between China and Japan at this time," preserved the prestige of the League of Nations and avoided the danger of proceeding under articles of the Covenant or under the Nine Power Treaty which might have led "either to war or some form of sanctions."   Cecil had much the same point of view, and late in December felt justified in speaking optimistically at a League of Nations Union meeting in London on the progress which had been made.   He believed that the resolution of December 10th to which the Japanese had acceded "would have saved something from the wreck"[24] if it had been carried out, and that nothing more could have been done unless the League powers and the United States were ready for sanctions, which it was apparent they were not.   But it was soon apparent that even this view was too favourable and that the military party in Tokyo was supreme.   By the beginning of 1932, Japan had compelled the Chinese to retire within the Great Wall, leaving all of Manchuria under the control of officials belonging to or subservient to Japan.

In the face of this situation, Stimson decided upon a move which he had been considering as early as November and which he hoped might serve as a rallying point for opposition to Japan and as a "substitute for sanctions."[25] This was to enunciate the doctrine of "non-recognition" which he believed was directly supported by the pledges of the Nine Power Treaty. On January 4th the note on non-recognition was approved by the President. The following day, though Stimson considered that the character of the note precluded prior consultation on its wording, he saw the British Ambassador, read him the draft and suggested that it would be more effective if Great Britain and France took similar steps. The same procedure was followed with the French Ambassador. On January 7th, the Note on "non-recognition" was sent to Japan, China, and the six other original signatories of the Nine Power Treaty. The Dominion Governments did not receive the note probably because the United States did not consider them original signatories of the Nine Power Treaty. The Note declared that the American Government would not recognize any impairment of American rights including those relating to the integrity of China and the "open door" policy and concluded that "it does not intend to recognize any situation, treaty, or agreement which may be brought about by means contrary to the covenants and obligations of the Pact of Paris of August 27, 1928, to which treaty both China and Japan as well as the United States are parties."[26]

Stimson looked for at least a sympathetic endorsement of his stand by the British Government and was correspondingly discomfited by a Foreign Office communique of January 11th declaring that it was not considered necessary for the British Government to send a similar Note since the Japanese representative at the League had declared Japan to be "the champion in Manchuria of the principle of equal opportunity and the 'open door' for the economic activities of all nations."[27] The French and Italian governments also decided to take no formal stand. The Japanese took advantage of the opportunity to act as if the United States had been rebuffed by the League powers and acknowledged the American statement as if the Japanese programme for Manchuria had been supported.

The inopportuneness of the British statement has often been commented upon as an indication of British unwillingness to follow American leadership in action against Japan. It has also been held against Canada that in this situation, unlike that concerning the Anglo-

Japanese Alliance, it was not alert to forestall potential Anglo-American friction. But there seems little parallel between the cases nor do the facts substantiate the view that Great Britain diverged sharply from the line of American policy except momentarily and then in appearance rather than fact. The story behind the Foreign Office communique has been made public by a former official, Sir John Pratt, who declared that its tone was the result of carelessness, not intention. Approved in haste, officials did not appreciate that it might sound like a rebuff until it had actually appeared in print.[28] In addition, the Foreign Office apparently did not recognize the general purpose of the American Note, which they thought was intended only as a reservation of American interests in China similar to that made in 1915 at the time of Japan's "Twenty-One Demands." Moreover, since Great Britain was engaged as a League power in endeavouring to conciliate China and Japan, it was felt that the British Government could not take the same stand as could Stimson, who had already made up his mind that all hope of moderation on the part of Japan had vanished. Beyond this, however, it is apparent that British reactions were affected throughout the conflict by questions as to how far Stimson had the support of his own Government and how far the United States was prepared to go. Clearly the British did not wish to become involved in a policy whose success demanded more action on the part of the United States than it was prepared to take. In the immediate situation, the British reaction may be interpreted as being partly the result of slowness in grasping the full implications of the American Note, partly carelessness, and partly the result of Britain's position as a League Power. It was unfortunate, however, that care was not taken to make this clear in the United States for the British lack of response rankled long in the American public mind.

Sir John Pratt maintains that in any case the British Government did its utmost to associate the League of Nations with the American statement of "non-recognition." On January 29th, four days after the next session of the Council opened, a declaration of "non-recognition" of arrangements inconsistent with international obligations, including Article 10 of the Covenant, was read by its President. This was followed by an "urgent appeal" by the neutral members of the Council addressed for the first time to Japan alone, "to recognize the very special responsibilities for forbearance and restraint which devolve upon it in the present crisis."[29] Moral pressure was being brought to bear as far as possible but moral pressure was not enough.

Speaking of this period during which the Council had been dealing with the dispute under Article 11, which meant that action could be undertaken only with the unanimous agreement of all its members, including the two parties, Sean Lester declared that no one who had not participated in the secret discussions "could fully realize" the difficulties which any proposal for "more energetic measures" encountered.[30] He spoke also of the "many assurances which unfortunately proved to be unreliable." The smaller powers on the Council had no uncertainty by this time, however, about the implications of Japan's action. ". . . it was no longer a question between China and Japan," Lester declared, "but also a question between Japan alone and the League of Nations."

Whatever hesitation the Great Powers might have had in intervening against Japan in a dispute over Manchuria vanished with the outbreak in January, 1932, of Japanese naval action against Shanghai, the centre of the boycott which was threatening Japanese trade in China. As the international port at the entry of the Yangtze Valley and chief centre of communication with central China, the fate of Shanghai was of direct interest to all powers concerned in Far Eastern commerce, and because of the presence of their nationals in the city and of military and naval forces in the vicinity, there could be no question about what was taking place. The powers with direct interests in Shanghai began to negotiate directly. This time Stimson waited for the British to take the initiative. Consultations resulted in a common course of action being adopted. On February 2nd, in a meeting at Geneva which forced an hour's postponement of the opening of the Disarmament Conference, the British representative, J. H. Thomas, announced that the British and Americans had presented a formal request to both China and Japan to end hostilities, to withdraw their troops in the Shanghai area where a neutral zone could be arranged, and to begin negotiations at once "to settle the outstanding differences in the spirit of the Pact of Paris and the Council Resolutions of December 10th."[31] The French, Italian, and German delegates associated themselves with this request.

Seeking further means of pressure upon Japan, Stimson now considered a joint invocation of the Nine Power Treaty. This he proposed to Sir John Simon by telephone, talking to him on four separate occasions between February 11th and 15th. Stimson declares that he became convinced "that the British Government were reluctant to join in such a démarche"[32] and he therefore dropped the plan. Sir John Pratt takes exception to this statement, declaring that in answer to a draft of Stimson's proposed joint invocation the Foreign Office telephoned to Geneva a paragraph containing the "non-recognition" doctrine which was embodied in the declaration of the neutral members of the Council on February 16th, and also sent a written message to Stimson "stating that the British Government was most anxious to co-operate with America in this matter" and that it hoped the League Powers which had participated in the resolution and were also signatories of the Nine Power Treaty "might also associate themselves with the proposed joint invocation."[33] Pratt believes that the lengthy process involved in getting several Governments to agree to the draft of the joint invoking of the Treaty caused Stimson to drop the idea and to substitute a personal declaration. What seems a likely reconciliation of the two accounts is that the British, not wishing to be placed in a position demanding forcible action which American public opinion was very unlikely to support, preferred to broaden any invocation of the Nine Power Treaty to include all signatories with seats on the Council. Stimson, feeling that haste was more important, preferred to make his position known by other means. This was through a letter of February 24, 1932, to Senator Borah, Chairman of the Committee on Foreign Relations, which stressed the interdependence of the treaties signed during the Washington Conference and indicated that naval ratios and the truce on fortifications, particularly for such places as the Philippines and Guam, might be considered dependent upon respect for the Nine Power Treaty.[34]

Spurred by this move, the Council under the leadership of Sir John Simon made a last effort to bring about cessation of hostilities at Shanghai by calling a conference of the powers having special interests in the foreign settlement, including China and Japan. A move by the smaller powers to secure representation at the conference for all interested countries, and to have it held under League auspices and directly related to the Assembly deliberations which were about to begin, was rejected on the ground that it might affect the American co-operation which had been pledged. The original plan was accepted by the Japanese representative the day before the Extraordinary Assembly opened on March 3, 1932, and the conference proved ultimately successful in securing the withdrawal of Japanese military forces.

The results achieved by this more vigorous action over Shanghai in which the direct interests of the Great Powers were involved is inevitably compared with the dilatory progress of developments regarding Manchuria. It must be admitted that the presence of foreign military and naval forces at Shanghai meant not only that there were outside witnesses of the Japanese aggression but also means of bringing immediate pressure. It seems also clear, however, that there was more support in both British and American governmental and public opinion for action in this area where there were direct interests, than in Manchuria though in the latter the aggression had long before this become equally obvious.

Despairing of effective action in Manchuria through the conciliation procedure of the Council, China at last decided in February, 1932, to appeal under Articles 10 and 15, a move which led to the calling of a special session of the Assembly, which opened March 3rd. The effort to mobilize world opinion through public discussion of the issues was to be substituted for the Council's attempts to find a basis for settlement in its secret sessions. In the Assembly meetings, many countries were to have their first opportunities to express their opinion on the situation which Japan had precipitated, and among them the overseas Dominions.

Comparatively little consideration had yet been given to the Sino-Japanese dispute in Dominion parliaments or press. Questions in the Australian House as early as October, 1931, had indicated uneasiness lest Australia be involved in a conflict in the Pacific.[35] When the Shanghai crisis developed, Labour Senators from New South Wales moved in the Federal chamber that Australian naval and military forces should not be permitted to engage in active service outside the shores of the Commonwealth and maintained that they would never consent to Australian participation "in what is nothing more than a sordid trade war."[36] Other members declared that economic sanctions against Japan including cutting off the supply of wool from Australia would be "so costly and complex" as to be "impossible of application." Government spokesmen were cautious in reply and particularly at the time of the Shanghai negotiations appeared anxious not to have a general discussion lest it complicate an already serious situation. Latham declared Australia was ready "to lend any aid of which it is capable in co-operation to bring about a peaceful solution of the problem which had arisen,"[37] and the Prime Minister assured the House, the Government would do "everything in its power to avoid the Commonwealth becoming involved in war."[38] Constant consultation was going on between the Australian and British Governments, it was made clear, and the British Government had been assured of the full support of Australia in its efforts to find a solution. Implicit in certain more general comments was tenseness lest the path of Japanese aggression turn too far south. In London on February 22nd, Major Horsfall speaking as an Australian urged that the inevitable Japanese expansion should be directed west towards Asia "instead of south towards the Australian Commonwealth."[39] Fear and reluctance to antagonize a valuable customer were to be conditioning factors of Australian policy during the Sino-Japanese dispute.

In no other Dominion did there appear to be much direct concern with the dispute. The New Zealand press carried adequate news and comment on the situation,[40] but the general attitude appeared to be one of unquestioning support for whatever policy the British Government should adopt. Though there were definite apprehensions in British Columbia regarding Japan's policy, there seemed little interest in Eastern Canada. Some feeling for Japan's campaign on behalf of "law and order" in China was evident in business journals.[41] Fear of Chinese communism may have alienated certain groups, particularly in Quebec, but on the whole sympathies were with China. Mackenzie King, now Leader of the Opposition, made the sole comment on the situation in the House of Commons in declaring optimistically on February 8, 1932, that they were about to witness what "the force of international public opinion" might mean in a given situation.[42] He attributed to the League, and to public opinion on the question of international peace, the fact that there had been only "isolated encounters here and there" during the past weeks, instead of "the most unparalleled butchery that mankind has ever known." In South Africa there was not even this amount of comment. With the exception of the Australians, therefore, Dominion delegates went to the Assembly meetings without having been given any indication of public feeling on the dispute.

When the Assembly met, fighting was dying down in Shanghai, and the Commission of Enquiry had sailed for Manchuria. Japan had already decided on February 19th to establish the puppet state of Manchukuo which was to be inaugurated March 9th, less than a week from the opening of the Assembly. Though the Japanese delegate maintained that the Assembly was concerned only with the situation at Shanghai, the Assembly itself refused to be circumscribed and both individual delegates and the final resolution regarded the conflict as a whole. It was a late stage in the situation, however, to attempt to exert influence by the pressure of public opinion.

The Assembly's first resolution called upon Japan and China to take "immediately" the necessary measures to ensure cessation of hostilities and requested the powers with special interests at Shanghai to report to the Assembly on their response. Though fighting in the city did not cease entirely until the end of April, there were no further large-scale actions. This was the result of earlier Chinese resistance and the negotiations of the Great Powers rather than of the Assembly's resolution but the development brought the latter a certain prestige which encouraged it as it turned to wider issues. For the first time the smaller powers had the opportunity to make public comment on the situation and they proceeded to outline their general view of League obligations and of the implications of the Sino-Japanese dispute in a manner which appeared designed to give a lead to the Great Powers.[43]

Among the smaller countries which pointed out the implications of the issue for the future of the League system were the Irish Free State, Canada, and South Africa. ". . . the duty of the Assembly is not only to settle the dispute between two Members of the League, but also and above all to uphold the sanctity of the Covenant," declared Sean Lester.[44] The first step was not only the cessation of hostilities but also "the restoration of the *status quo ante*." The final settlement must be on the basis of all the international agreements involved. "We must not only settle this dispute; we must settle it right," he added, "It is a hard task, the hardest and most responsible which the League has ever been called upon to undertake. But it is a task that is a direct expression of the League's fundamental purpose."

Sir George Perley, speaking on behalf of Canada, pointed out that far more "than the solution of a single problem is at stake in our deliberations."[45] For twelve years, "the world has been endeavouring to build up, through the League, a system of outlawing war and settling disputes by reason rather than by force." The action taken by the Assembly "will go far," he declared, "to show how successful we have been in this effort." The Canadian view was that the Assembly should strive to "bring about a real and effective armistice," and to distinguish between "the rights of a case and the manner in which those rights are realized and enforced." Beyond this, he maintained, "We should affirm as solemnly as possible the fundamental truth that no infringement of the territorial integrity, and no change in the political independence, of any Member of the League of Nations which is brought about by force, in disregard of the undertakings of Article 10 of the Covenant, can be recognized as valid and effective by the other Members of the League." It was a formal restatement of Stimson's non-recognition doctrine, to which Sir John Simon had also given voice the day before, a doctrine which fitted perfectly the Canadian conception of the means whereby peace should be retained. As early as the Peace Conference, Sir Robert Borden had brought forward a similar suggestion as a possible means of closing the "gap" in the Covenant.[46]

The most forceful of the three Dominion speakers and one of the most dynamic within the whole Assembly was te Water, High Commissioner in London for the Union of South Africa, who began, with typical forthrightness, "We have no other name for the state of affairs in China today than that of war."[47] Tracing developments step by step, he declared his country to be convinced that "Japan has acted in contradiction to what we believe to be the obligations to which equally with all of us, she is bound." Then turning to the "grave responsibilities and duties which a crisis such as this places upon every State Member of the League," he acknowledged it was "just and seemly" that the strength of the advocacy of a policy should be in proportion to the sacrifices "s ch policy may entail." In this situation the Great Powers must bear the burden and the smaller powers wait for them to lead. ". . . at this great crisis in our affairs," they looked for wise, and above all, strong leadership from the Great Powers, "leadership which can be interpreted in terms of action and not in terms of words." And he ended by challenging, "Are the Great Powers satisfied that they have pointed the way?" No other Assembly delegate had put the issue in more realistic or less compromising terms.

On March 11th, after the conclusion of the debate which had evidenced the strength of the feeling against Japan's action and on behalf of the principles of the Covenant, the Assembly formally approved the principle of non-recognition, declaring, "it is incumbent upon the Members of the League of Nations not to recognize any situation, treaty, or agreement which may be brought about by means contrary to the Covenant of the League of Nations." It was the immediate result of proposals made by Great Britain and a number of other states, but in a broader sense it was an almost world-wide endorsement of the principle which Stimson had formulated on January 7th. Stimson himself later declared, ". . . when the entire group of civilized nations took their stand beside the position of the American Government, the situation was revealed in its true sense. Moral disapproval, when it becomes the disapproval of the whole world, takes on a significance hitherto unknown in international law."[48] Yet moral disapproval was to have all too little effect on the course of events.

Under the Assembly resolution, a Committee of Nineteen was set up consisting of the members of the Council and six elected members, none of which were from the Dominions.[49] This Committee acted subsequently as an Assembly organ to consider the dispute while the latter reassembled only rarely and for important decisions. In the succeeding weeks, an armistice was arranged at Shanghai. The smaller countries were to attempt to fix also a date by which Japanese troops were to be withdrawn from Chinese territory but met persistent resistance by the Great Powers which feared that to do so might complicate the task of the Commission of Enquiry. The preliminary report of the Commission on April 30th had drawn attention to the great preponderance of Japanese and "Manchukuo" troops in Manchuria.[50] Signs that Japan planned to recognize "Manchukuo" led to a private meeting of the Committee of Nineteen on June 24th to debate an appeal to Japan not to make such a move but the smaller countries were unable to convince the Great Powers of its value. The Committee did, however, address an "urgent appeal" to the Japanese Government to observe its obligations under the resolutions of September and December, 1931. In July, after receiving rather reluctantly from the Assembly an extension of time for its Report, the Lytton Commission which had returned to China to collate and supplement its Manchurian information, made a special visit to Japan to attempt to persuade its Government not to recognize "Manchukuo" or at least not before the Lytton Report had been presented to the Assembly. On September 4th, the Commission formally adopted its Report at Peiping. Ten days later, even before the Council could consider the request of the Japanese Government for six weeks' delay before the official publication of the Report, Japan signed a defensive alliance with "Manchukuo," thereby according it official recognition. This *fait accompli* and the recommendations of the Lytton Report were to form the basis for the considerations of the Assembly when it met once more in December, 1932, in special session to deliberate its course under Article 15 of the Covenant.

In the meantime, public opinion in the Dominions was showing more signs of awareness of the implications of the general situation, though without evidencing any support for forcible action. On April 18th and 19th, during a debate in the South African House of Assembly on the estimates for External Affairs, a good deal of faith was expressed in the ultimate value of the League as a moral, but not as a coercive force. General Smuts, now Leader of the Opposition, maintained that the League "should not become a super-authority and endowed with armies and navies and other forces. The League is simply a great organ of public opinion."[51] Though he agreed that results of League action in the dispute had been disappointing, he considered the doctrine of non-recognition to have been of great importance. Prime Minister Hertzog echoed Smuts' emphasis. What had happened was no reason to condemn the League. "When all is said and done, we cannot forget that the League of Nations has no force behind its authority." To which he added, "one thing is very certain, viz., that I would be the last person ever to advocate that the League of Nations should, along with its authority, have an armed force at its disposal."[52] Hertzog appeared somewhat confused in his attitude towards sanctions, suggesting first that the League could have exerted a stronger moral influence if there had been no sanctions in the Covenant to give the nations pause in expressing themselves. Later, he declared that there might be sanctions "but they must only be applied in certain given cases where a moral expression of the League is not sufficient to produce the desired effect, and where we have to do with circumstances where the sanctions can actually be applied." Though challenged as inconsistent,[53] there was in fact a certain truth in Hertzog's view, that in cases such as the Sino-Japanese in which there was only the intention of exerting moral pressure, the very presence of provisions for sanctions tended to restrain utterances. Though Hertzog admitted that there might be situations in which it would be desirable and feasible to apply sanctions, it is clear that neither he nor Smuts was prepared to consider them in relation to the Sino-Japanese dispute.

This emphasis on the force of world opinion as *a* sanction, or even *the* sanction of League action was also evident in the speeches of the new Prime Minister of the Irish Free State, Eamon de Valera, whose country had acquired at this time by the ordinary rules of rotation the position of Presidency of the Council. In this rôle, de Valera was to establish a considerable "Geneva reputation" for himself through his quiet practical approach. One of his first responsibilities was to recommend accepting the Japanese request for delay in the opening of discussion on the Lytton Report. At the same time he forcefully expressed regret that Japan in recognizing "Manchukuo" had "taken steps which cannot but be regarded as calculated to prejudice the settlement of the dispute."[54] In opening the Thirteenth Ordinary Assembly, September 26th, he expressed the hope that the Lytton Report, which would be considered subsequently by a Special Assembly, would be "conducive towards a just and final settlement" and that "the methods and principles of the Covenant will find a justification in their triumph over all the difficulties with which this problem was surrounded."[55] Lest there be complacency, he warned that outside criticism placed the League in the position of "defendants at the bar of public opinion with a burden of justification upon us which is almost overwhelming." To silence criticism, to bring the critical millions to its support, to provide an alternative to competitive armaments demanded "the security for national rights which an uncompromising adherence to the principles of the Covenant will afford." No state, he concluded, should be allowed "to jeopardize the common interest" by action against the Covenant, and "no State is powerful enough to stand for long against the League if the Governments in the League and their people are determined that the Covenant shall be upheld." The moral effect of the speech was to be obvious from the number of references made to it in the course of the discussions. An Australian representative, speaking for the first time since the dispute had arisen, endorsed de Valera's point that "the League is on trial." Though the scope of its activities was wide, "to the average man its chief function is to banish war from the world," he declared, ". . . by its success or failure to achieve this great end mankind at large will judge it."[56]

Though there was no evidence of intention to use forcible action against Japan, opinion was gradually hardening, aided by another declaration of policy by Stimson on August 8th. In a speech to the Council on Foreign Relations in New York, the Secretary of State maintained that the doctrine of neutrality had become obsolete through the Covenant and the Pact of Paris and had been replaced by the doctrine of consultation based on the belief that "an act of war in any part of the world is an act which injures the interests of my country."[57] Three days later President Hoover declared that in the future threat of aggression would automatically bring about consultation about how to meet it. This statement met enthusiastic response from leading English newspapers,[58] though the French press seemed more doubtful of its significance. The most effective instrument for marshalling public opinion was, however, the Lytton Report, a masterpiece of historical and analytical writing which was made public on October 1, 1932, simultaneously in Geneva, Washington, Nanking, and Tokyo.

Taking a broad view of Sino-Japanese relations and of the points at issue between China and Japan in the past as well as the present, the Lytton Report proposed a large measure of autonomy for Manchuria within the sovereignty and administrative integrity of China, order to be maintained by a local gendarmerie while foreign troops on both sides were withdrawn. This was the compromise between retaining the existing régime in Manchuria which, it declared, had not been called into existence by a genuine and spontaneous independence movement, and restoring the original *status quo* which the Commission did not consider would be any more satisfactory. For the wider issue of general Sino-Japanese relations, the Commission recommended the encouragement of economic *rapprochement* between the two countries, a treaty of non-aggression, and a restatement of mutual rights and responsibilities embodied in new treaties. The stability of China, an essential element for a satisfactory future, should be furthered by international co-operation in Chinese internal reconstruction. The Report also outlined the practical steps[59] which might be taken under the auspices of the League to bring about the proposed solution for Sino-Japanese relations.

The Japanese Government, however, refused to accept either the points of fact embodied in the Report or the recommendations for a solution.[60] In six meetings between November 21st and 28th, the Council formally received the Lytton Report, listened to statements by the Japanese and Chinese delegates, heard Lord Lytton declare that the Commission had nothing to add to its Report after seeing the Japanese comments on it,[61] and turned the case over to the Assembly for settlement under Article 15. In so doing, de Valera as President of the

Council expressed the hope that "no solution will be rejected which offers the possibility of a just and permanent settlement of this tragic dispute."[62] "It would be an intolerable defiance of public opinion," he added, "if in a dispute such as this" the machinery to settle disputes "were not availed of to the full" or if its working "were impeded by any want of the necessary co-operation on the part of one of the States concerned."

The Report had received wide comment in the press of most countries with recognition of its great thoroughness and impartiality. American newspapers generally stressed its fairness and considered that it supported the Chinese case. The majority of English papers reacted similarly, though the Conservative organ, *The Morning Post*, emphasized the Commission's criticism of China's lack of central government.[63] The French press was divided between admiration for the Report and the feeling that its proposals would have little effect.[64]

In the Dominions, comments were varied but little indication was given of clear-cut lines of policy. The Canadian press divided, though not on party or regional lines, between those newspapers which believed the Report created a definite issue between the League and Japan, and those which criticized it as unrealistic and considered that the only thing to do was to patch up any settlement possible.[65] Rare was the comment of the *Winnipeg Free Press*, a consistently strong supporter of the League, which recognized that the Manchurian situation had made obvious the League's lack of power to bring correspondence between its principles and the "establishment and maintenance of conditions in keeping with those principles."

An attempt by Woodsworth in the House of Commons on November 18, 1932, to elicit information on the Bennett Government's policy in regard to the Far East and the Lytton Report had little result except in indicating some of the difficulties faced by countries remote from the seat of the League. Bennett refused to make any declaration of policy on the ground that the matter was *sub judice*, that is, under consideration by "a body charged with authority," the Assembly.[66] Lapointe, deputy leader of the Liberal party, while accepting that parliament should not take a definite stand, challenged the Prime Minister's refusal to have a general discussion which might be enlightening for the Canadian delegate to the Special Assembly. Bennett, however, maintained his point that it would be inexpedient to make declarations even of opinion, when policy at Geneva would need to be governed by developments during the meetings themselves. In a comment of some significance in view of the concern subsequently to be aroused by the speech of the Canadian delegate to the Special Assembly, Bennett declared that "Like all other problems of this kind which are dealt with by tribunals other than the parliament of Canada, the representatives of the countries affected always must accept great responsibilities where they cannot get the fullest possible instructions from their governments." All he considered possible under the circumstances of distance from Geneva, was that the representative would have "from the government of the day a clear appreciation of their understanding of the problem" and such modifications as arise to influence it. The view was allowed to pass uncriticized in parliament though not in periodicals,[67] but it had elements both of truth and of danger in it. On the one hand, too rigid instructions would run the danger of making policy inflexible, and as Bennett said, thereby rendering the influence of the country negligible. It was to prove equally possible that too little indication of prevailing sentiment could lead to unrepresentative utterances by a delegate.

In neither South Africa nor the Irish Free State were there discussions indicative of policy and even in the Pacific Dominions comparatively little was said which bore upon the important decisions to be taken at the Special Assembly. The New Zealand press generally showed concern at the difficult task confronting the League, recognizing that its prestige was at stake and possibly both the effectiveness of the Covenant and the Kellogg-Briand Pact.[68] Japan's breach of its obligations and its unwillingness to allow the mediation of the League were condemned though there was also realization of the weakness of China's case due to its internal instability. Surprisingly enough, the one comment in the House of Representatives voiced a trenchant criticism of British policy for not following American leadership quickly enough. The speaker foresaw eventual conflict between the United States and Japan in which Great Britain would be implicated and demanded, "Are we as a Dominion also to be dragged at the heels of Britain as a consequence of the blunders of British statesmen without making our emphatic protest . . .?"[69] The view met with no response but it may have represented something of the growing independence of judgment and increasing concern with Pacific affairs which were to mark New Zealand policy in subsequent years.

In contrast to the "tepidity" of opinion in the other Dominions,[70] there had been no abatement of Australian anxiety during the year. Rumours that Japan was attempting to gain a foothold in the Malay Archipelago, though denied, increased agitation, and the "vulnerability of our empty north" was brought again into the debates of the House.[71] Though Senator Dunn of the New South Wales Labour party declared that Australia was in no danger of attack while Japan had its hands full "because of the responsibilities that it has assumed in Manchuria,"[72] others emphasized Australia's "virtually unprotected" position, "except for the strength of the British Empire,"[73] a point with which Sir George Pearce, the Minister of Defence, tacitly agreed. On the other hand, complete disillusionment with the League of Nations was expressed. Hughes, Australian representative to the Thirteenth Ordinary Assembly, was quoted in the House as saying the League was "useless,"[74] while Senator Dunn declared that "He realizes as so many others, that the League, which was established for the purpose of preventing and settling international warfare is impotent."[75] Even Prime Minister Lyons went so far as to say that "admittedly, the advantage we gain from our representation is not commensurate with the amount that we contribute."[76] On the eve of the meeting of the Special Assembly to consider the Lytton Report, Australia was still the only Dominion with a clear-cut point of view on Far Eastern affairs, and official opinion there was convinced of the impotence of the League of Nations in the situation in which it found itself.

Once more the Assembly was to attempt through marshalling world opinion to influence the course of events in the Sino-Japanese dispute, or at the least, to make its own stand clear. Speaking on behalf of the Irish Free State, Senator Connolly opened the general discussion with an unreserved acceptance of the Lytton Report and of the doctrine of "non-recognition."[77] He approved the Report's proposal of a "local gendarmerie force" to provide the "basis of ultimate order and settlement" in Manchuria. "The creation of such a force and the withdrawal of all armed forces other than it, might be carried out under the guidance and direction of the League," he declared, thereby ultimately making possible the creation of conditions in which the opinion of the inhabitants could be ascertained. "Let there be no mistake," he added, "if the moral force of the League is broken on this issue, then the League as at present constituted cannot survive, and the worst cynicism of the League's critics will have been justified." An American observer spoke of Connolly's address as an "outspoken speech" which "furnished the key-note to remarks of the other representatives who followed him,"[78] including those of smaller European countries like Norway and Sweden. An initial impetus had been given to an uncompromising stand based on the Lytton Report and the Covenant. A resolution circulated the following day, December 7th, of which the Irish Free State was one of the sponsors, sought to transform this into a general declaration.

On that day, however, the tone of the debate changed sharply with Sir John Simon's speech which placed its emphasis on the fact that the Lytton Report brought out the "really complicated character of the Manchurian conflict."[79] He favoured continuation of conciliation with which he felt the United States and Soviet Russia should be associated. The Italian and German delegates also emphasized the necessity for continued mediation and perhaps further investigation. The next morning they were followed by C. H. Cahan, the representative of Canada, who "in a curious oration spoke strongly on both sides," as a commentator aptly observed.[80]

Cahan's speech, which was to be the object of so much unfavourable comment both in Geneva and in Canada, appears to have been a combination of what he acknowledged to be "more or less personal" opinions, which stressed the unusual character of the situation in the Far East because of China's lack of order, and of "my Government's" orthodox, if cautious, view that if compromise and conciliation were ineffective, the League should stand upon its principles.[81] "It is doubtful to my mind," he declared in the first part of his speech, "whether the National Government of China has yet been in a position to comply fully" with the prescribed conditions of membership in the League. He criticized the boycott in China as "a grave infringement . . . of the existing rights of other States and manifestly provocative of emergency action by such other States for the purpose of protecting such rights," and compared Japanese action in 1931 with British protests against China in 1927. From the point of view of the League, he stressed the difficulties in "defining and construing the underlying principles" of an institution under a written constitution like the League of Nations, and declared that "exaggerated ideas" should not be entertained concerning the effect on its authority of any decisions taken by the Assembly. The second part of his speech, in which the words "my Government" appear in nearly every paragraph, contained a cautious proviso against establishing a precedent regarding the use of Article 10 which might "be deemed to exceed the terms of this article as already construed by competent authorities" and a recommendation that the "possibilities of conciliatory settlement" should be explored to the fullest. "Any discussion of sanctions or action against a party unwilling to accept settlement would be out of place at this stage of our proceedings," it was declared. The Lytton Report can "probably" be accepted by the Assembly, as the premise of its future action even if it is not based entirely upon "the particular recommendations made by the Commission." In regard to machinery for the amicable adjustment of future differences, the Canadian Government, through Cahan, respectfully suggested the establishment of a Permanent Joint Commission similar to that of Canada and the United States.[82] Finally after cautions against "precipitate action," the speech, after endorsing an invitation to the United States and Soviet Russia to participate in any machinery for conciliation, declared that after all available means for reconciliation of the parties had been exhausted, further delay in making the League's position clear "might prove most unfortunate."

The latter part of the speech presented a fairly typical Canadian stand in favour of conciliation, as long as it offered any possibility of success. If mediation finally failed, the League should then take its stand, though there was clear implication that forcible means should not be taken to implement it. What caused the adverse comment at Geneva and in Canada was the first part of the speech which emphasized the disorderly condition of China in a distinctly unsympathetic manner.[83] Some delegates believed that "Cahan had been persuaded by the British delegation to the Assembly to make his remarks conform with those that had been expressed by Sir John Simon."[84] Later interpretations have accepted the views that as an "elderly man of conservative views," Cahan would have felt it was "something like impiety" to diverge from the line of policy of the British Government.[85] There is another possible explanation, however, of both Cahan's and Simon's emphasis which is connected with the resolution circulated under the auspices of the Irish Free State and three other countries on December 7th. This was the day on which the British speech was made, and the day before Cahan addressed the Assembly.

This resolution, based on the Lytton Report, provided an uncompromising statement of the situation between China and Japan which it described as "disguised war."[86] The Japanese operations could not be considered as "measures of legitimate defence," it observed, or the existing régime in Manchuria as the outcome of "a sincere and spontaneous movement of independence." The resolution observed therefore that recognition of the régime was "not compatible with international obligations." In conclusion, it authorized the Committee of Nineteen "to solicit the co-operation" of the United States and Soviet Russia "for the purpose of getting into touch with the parties with a view to ensuring a settlement of the dispute on the basis of the above-mentioned findings."

The Japanese delegate, at least, found the resolution too strong for, on December 8th, the day of Cahan's speech, Matsuoka asked its authors to withdraw it on the ground that it "condemns Japan and is one-sided," the very thing, he added, against which Sir John Simon and other delegates "wisely counselled" the Assembly.[87] If it were not withdrawn, he asked that it be put to the vote "so that we may know the sense of the Assembly." And in a veiled warning he concluded, "I am afraid, let me add, that the handling of this resolution may, I even think will, entail consequences perhaps not intended or anticipated by the authors of the resolution." In view of subsequent developments, Matsuoka may have been hinting that such a resolution would precipitate Japan's withdrawal from the Assembly, or even an open clash with League powers.

Both Sir John Simon's and Cahan's speeches may well have been intended to lead opinion against a resolution which they feared would make it impossible to continue negotiations with Japan. If so, their emphasis on the complexity of the situation and the faults on China's side are more understandable. The British Commonwealth meetings during the Assembly are said to have been the scene of violent disagreements and these may have occurred over the Irish Free State's sponsorship of the resolution. Even though the Irish representatives did not feel obligated in any way to bow to the opinion of other members of the British Commonwealth group, they were punctilious about exchanging information. Failing to dissuade the Irish delegate from his course, Sir John Simon may well have felt that the next best thing was indirectly to lead opposition to the resolution. That it was, in fact, a serious cause of concern to Commonwealth representatives was evidenced by a short speech by Bruce, the Australian delegate, who, after subtly stressing the complexities of the situation in China, warned that if the Assembly passed any resolution "with either an open or implied censure in it," a step would be taken which would make it "very difficult, if not impossible" to carry out the task of "bringing about a reconciliation and settlement within the principles of the Covenant."[88] Cahan himself declared that his speech was made "after consultation with the other dominion members."

In his subsequent explanation to the House of Commons, Cahan implied that there might have been an even more serious source of division within the Assembly, between those who wished to confine action to "reasonable efforts towards effecting conciliation and cooperation of these two countries, Japan and China, in Manchuria, under the nominal sovereignty of China," and those "who were insistent that the League should proceed to sanction more extreme measures."[89] These latter measures, Cahan suggested, might have meant involving Canada in war in the Far East. In 1936 he declared that from information he had received at the time of the Sino-Japanese dispute, he had become convinced that "conditions on the Pacific were such that the imposition of sanctions against Japan might and probably would have led to a naval conflict in the northern Pacific in which, for a time at least, the British flag might have been driven from the north Pacific Ocean."[90] And to this he added, "That, at least, was the possibility that Great Britain and the British dominions were face to face with at that time." It appears also that in response to a direct question by Sir John Simon, Stimson had made it clear that the United States could not be counted on for any armed support in case League action against Japan should precipitate a clash. In such a situation, it is hardly surprising that the British opposed a step which might have had such results.

Cahan's original explanation to the House included a confusing statement to the effect that the Lytton Report had proposed "the formation of an international army of police" to maintain peace and good order in Manchuria, and that the question had arisen as to who would supply and maintain them. The Japanese, he declared, said they were ready to withdraw if such an international force were organized. And Cahan was asked, "How many thousands of troops, ten, twenty, or twenty-five, would Canada be prepared to put into the far east as part of a joint international force?" To this he had replied "in private, not in public" that under existing conditions he did not believe the Canadian parliament "would appropriate a single dollar towards maintaining a single company of troops in the far east for that purpose." The Governments of Great Britain, France, and other important European countries had taken the same position in private. "They were unwilling," he concluded, "to sacrifice millions of money for the sake of preserving, through an international organization of their military forces, continued peace in Manchuria."

Presumably, the "international army of police," of which Cahan spoke, was the "effective local gendarmerie force" of the Lytton Report. Whether it was ever seriously proposed to make this an international force seems impossible to prove, or whether the Japanese could have been serious in what Cahan declared to be their willingness to withdraw from Manchuria if such a force were organized. The proposal has not been mentioned in other official quarters. But at least it seems fairly sure that sanctions, at least of an economic type, were being considered at Geneva during the meeting of the Assembly. A resolution denouncing Japanese aggression would have been the first step towards them. In this light there is nothing surprising in a British attempt to keep the road open to mediation as long as possible, and to postpone a rupture between the Assembly and Japan. In such a situation, it would only be expected that Sir John Simon would receive the support of Australia and New Zealand, and particularly under the circumstances of Cahan's personal views, that of Canada. The rather surprising silence of South Africa at these meetings of the Assembly may well have resulted from the unwillingness to take a stand on either side.

Whatever the circumstances surrounding it, the resolution was never brought to a vote although there is no evidence that it was withdrawn.[91] It was replaced, however, by a non-controversial resolution proposed by Switzerland and Czechoslovakia. Since the latter country was one of the sponsors of the original resolution and Beneš, its representative, in one of the greatest speeches of his career, had strongly maintained during this Assembly the necessity of upholding the Covenant, there seems reason to believe that opposition to the first resolution was based on good grounds. The second resolution merely noted the receipt of the Lytton Report and requested the Committee of Nineteen to draw up proposals in view of the sentiment of the Assembly and to submit them at the earliest possible moment.[92] This resolution was unanimously adopted without discussion at the Fifteenth Plenary Session on December 9th.

In pursuance of this resolution, the Committee of Nineteen attempted to formulate proposals to assist conciliation between Japan and China. Two guiding directives for its mediation procedure were laid down in draft resolutions prepared by Great Britain and four other countries; that the doctrine of non-recognition of situations in defiance of the Covenant, the Kellogg-Briand Pact, and the Nine Power Treaty should be maintained, and that the United States and the Soviet Union should be invited to join the Committee of Nineteen to make a new body to conduct negotiations with the parties with a view to a settlement. It soon became apparent, however, that there was a fundamental difference of opinion between the Committee and Japan on both these points. By January 16, 1933, it was clear that conciliation no longer held any hope of success. Sir John Simon then took the lead in urging the Committee of Nineteen to prepare its final statement which, he proposed, should include complete acceptance of the Lytton Report. Assurance that the incoming Roosevelt Administration in the United States had no intention of altering American policy[93] strengthened the determination of the Committee to proceed to the final steps. In order, however, that the break should come on a question of principle rather than procedure, the Committee waited until the Japanese declared formally that they would not give up the control of "Manchukuo."[94] With this before them, the Committee proceeded to adopt its report and to convene the Assembly on February 21, 1933.

After a short preliminary meeting, the Assembly came together on February 24th for final action on the Committee's report, which reiterated the judgments of the Lytton Report, and reaffirmed the doctrine of "non-recognition." "They will continue not to recognize this régime [in Manchuria] either *de jure* or *de facto*," the report concluded. "They intend to abstain from taking any isolated action with regard to the situation in Manchuria and to continue to concert their action among themselves as well as with the interested States not members of the League."[95]   That there was no chance that Japan would accept such a report was made clear at once by its delegate, who declared that to the nation of Japan, the Manchurian problem was "a question of life and death" on which no concession or compromise was possible.

Only three delegates made statements, one of them Dr. Riddell, who on behalf of the Canadian Government gave a reasoned explanation of its acceptance of the report.   In its recommendations were to be found "a solid basis for peaceful development in the Far East," and it hoped the parties would eventually accept a régime based upon them.[96] For the perseverance of the Committee of Nineteen in its "anxious task," it expressed appreciation.   "The public opinion of the world, in which the Canadian Government believes lies the final and effective sanction for the maintenance of the integrity of international agreements," had seen the careful exploration of every possibility by the Committee and "recognized reluctantly" that there had been no response to its efforts.   The gravity of the decision to be taken was acknowledged; the shock to "the faith of the world in the possibility of peaceful settlement" was pointed out, along with the possibly disastrous effects on the structure of security, the limitation of armaments, and international economic co-operation if this faith were destroyed.   For these reasons, the Canadian Government affirmed its intention of voting for the report.

Of forty-four countries voting, forty-two approved the report. Japan rejected it and Siam abstained.   The President declared, "I have not abandoned the hope that a day will come when our offer will be accepted by both parties."[97]   The Japanese answer was to announce the withdrawal of the delegation from the Assembly.   The final stand taken by the Assembly had precipitated the breach with Japan to avoid which such prolonged efforts had been undertaken.

Though there could no longer be hope of conciliation, the Assembly voted to continue following the dispute though, despite the wishes of a number of smaller states, not under its own direct jurisdiction but through a new consultative committee.   This was to be composed of the members of the Committee of Nineteen with the addition of Canada and Holland among League powers and the United States and the Soviet Union.[98]   The United States agreed to join the Far Eastern Advisory Committee but the Soviet Union refused.[99]   When the Committee met for the first time on February 25th, it discussed a possible embargo on arms to the Far East but without taking an immediate decision. Two days later the British Government placed an embargo on arms to both Japan and China[100] but it met with severe criticism[101] and revoked its decision about two weeks later. No other country except Canada[102] made any effort to declare an arms embargo and the Advisory Committee was unable to accomplish anything in this regard. Its main achievement was to circulate a report on "non-recognition" to ensure uniform action by all governments.

Japan's resignation from the League of Nations was cabled to the Secretary-General on March 27, 1933. Coupled with the Japanese conquest of the province of Jehol and the continuation of an active military policy, the announcement made it difficult to remember that as far as declarations were concerned, the League had upheld its principles in the end. It was more obvious that the long process of conciliation and moral pressure had placed little restraint on Japanese aggression.

The consideration of the Sino-Japanese dispute by the League of Nations was the first great test of the post-war collective security system. The dispute had arisen and in part been provoked by the most severe economic crisis of recent times. It had occurred in a region where complex treaty provisions were in force, where it was difficult to get accurate information, and above all, where the aggressive party had military and naval supremacy. During its progress, the serious economic situation had placed an unremitting strain upon the resources of all concerned, and had led to a breach between the two most important powers concerned, the United States and Great Britain, over the repudiation of war debts. While the shadow of repudiation hung over the Assembly which considered the Lytton Report, the shadow of Hitler and Nazi domination in Germany hung over the meetings in which Japan's condemnation was voted. On the positive side had been the constant moral support of the United States and its willingness for co-operation, and, at times, leadership. One of the major factors handicapping League efforts in earlier periods had been redressed in this situation.

In the light of American co-operation, British policy during the Sino-Japanese dispute appears somewhat ineffective except over Shanghai, but popular criticisms of Sir John Simon's handling of the situation are exaggerated, if not misleading. There was no hiatus between American "leadership"[103] and British response. The unfortunate British *communiqué* issued after Stimson's Note on "non-recognition," and the British desire in March, 1932, to broaden the basis of protest over the Nine Power Treaty to all signatories which were members of the Council, provide little basis for the popular contention. It is this fact which makes inapplicable any criticism of Canadian policy on the ground that it failed to keep American and British policies moving in parallel lines for the burden of evidence is that in fact the two countries pursued very similar courses of action out of very similar motives. It has to be remembered that the United States was, in some regards, in an easier position because it was not responsible as was Great Britain, for marshalling the opinion of League members, nor had it behind it the uncertain ultimate responsibilities of the Covenant.[104]   At the same time the American State Department was as unwilling as the British Foreign Office to take even the step of an arms embargo at the time when moral pressure was being exerted to the full.[105]   None the less, if, as seems sure, the Committee on Imperial Defence and the British Cabinet vetoed from the beginning any thought of military sanctions against Japan,[106] it seems unfortunate that the British did not take the initiative in exerting moral pressure.   The only chance of such pressure being effective would seem to have been in the first weeks of the controversy when it might have strengthened the hand of the Japanese civilian administration, instead of, as later, further antagonized the dominant military group.   Even in the spring of 1932, determined pressure by the Great Powers over Shanghai coupled with effective Chinese resistance curbed, if it did not stop, Japanese aggression.   The key-note of British policy over Manchuria seems to have been to continue mediation to the very last possible moment while a less conciliatory attitude might have had more effect.

In considering the attitudes of all members of the Commonwealth, there is a marked difference between those of Great Britain, Australia, and New Zealand, whose strategic interests were involved in an area in which they felt incapable of defending them, and whose economic ties with Japan were strong, and those of the Irish Free State and South Africa, neither of which were influenced by these considerations. Canada stood midway between the two groups, more concerned in fact as a Pacific country than it was prepared to recognize. The Irish Free State and South Africa were the strongest supporters of League action, but even the efforts of the South African representative to marshal opinion behind a maintenance of League principles lacked the backing of a willingness for sanctions.

If any of the Dominions were particularly influential on British policy during the dispute it was Australia. Mainly this was because of the similarity of concern over a potential Japanese attack on British possessions in the Far East. In this regard, the Australian reaction probably strengthened the British resolve to avoid any action which might lead to a breach, though had Australia been eager for positive action, it is very doubtful whether it would have changed British policy in any way. In one other respect, British and Australian views were parallel and that was in considering that the League system did not really apply to the Pacific. They felt that the League obligations and security provisions were intended for fully organized and responsible states,[107] within which category they did not include China, and might well not have included Japan, whose civil administration had proved incapable of restraining its military elements. Moreover, there was some feeling in Great Britain that Japan had been forced into the League at the time of the Peace Conference purely on grounds of prestige and expediency and therefore should not be held too strictly to account. In general, official opinion in Australia tended to feel that it was unrealistic to attempt to apply the League system to the Pacific area and that the sooner this was realized and changes made in the League structure to accord with reality, the better for the League itself as well as for its members in that area. For behind Australian and British anxiety lurked the fear that the League might take active measures against Japan which would leave Great Britain and Australia with the responsibility of carrying them out. A similar anxiety probably lay behind Cahan's speech at the December Assembly.

To modify these reactions based on strategic considerations, economic interest and a general view of international realities would have demanded an alert and informed public opinion which was aware that a dangerous blow to the structure of peace might be more serious than any of these other considerations. Neither in Britain, nor in any of the Dominions, did even a small portion of the public react in the manner which would have been necessary. Nor may it be said did any substantial portion of the American public. All that can be said is that the course of the dispute led to a gradual awakening of public opinion within the Commonwealth to the seriousness of the fact that Japan could defy the League with impunity.

In Canada, there was noticeable quickening of concern in the press when the Assembly found it impossible to persuade Japan to accept the Lytton Report and had to take the final step of condemning its attitude. Beyond the editorial criticism of Japan's stand was widespread questioning regarding its ultimate effect on international life. Many papers believed that a turning of the way was ahead, either towards international solidarity or international anarchy.[108] Continuing criticism of Cahan's Assembly speech led to a half-hearted endorsement of it by the Prime Minister as not being contrary to instructions, though Bennett admitted that "isolated sections . . . might leave the impression that he was endeavouring to support one particular phase of the situation rather than another."[109]   It seems also to have led to the statement by Riddell at the last meeting of the Assembly which was approved by both Liberals and Labour when it was read in Parliament.[110] Moreover, official explanation was demanded from Cahan himself, evidencing a degree of public concern which marked a wide advance over the earlier apathy.[111]

Expressions of disappointment marked the brief considerations in the New Zealand Parliament of the outcome of League actions towards Japan.   The leader of the Labour Opposition asked for a motion approving the attitude of the League and asking Japan to accept its decision, but the Prime Minister felt it would serve no useful purpose and expressed an earnest, if fruitless, hope that "a peaceful solution can still be found."[112]   When the annual contribution to League expenses was challenged on the ground that "hopes of some benefits arising from Geneva had hardly been realized," Forbes answered that "although results were sometimes disappointing," the most important of all causes, world peace, should have "the strongest support."   The general impression was of regret but not of despair.

Somewhat surprisingly much the same response was present in Australia.   A comment on Australian attitudes during the dispute, probably written by Sir William Harrison Moore, declared that public opinion had been "extraordinarily confused and not very vocal."[113] The Government's policy, as he noted, had been to support the British Government's efforts for conciliation and to restrain public utterances as far as possible but not to consider the possibilities of action under the post-war "system of international engagements" or to discuss the interest of the Australian people in "the maintenance of a stable international order in the Pacific."   Hughes, reporting to the House as Australian representative to the Thirteenth Ordinary Assembly, reiterated the view that the League could never be "for the world, and particularly for Australia, an effective substitute for the British Empire."[114]   But at the same time he declared that if the League had been unable to "banish wars or settle disputes between warlike nations," the fault lay not in itself but in the nations which composed it.   Believing that "it has fully justified its existence, and is today an integral part of world government," he proposed that far from separating itself from the League, Australia should use every effort to make its situation better known to other League members.   "The day may come when it will have to hear our case," he added.   In conclusion, he suggested that Australia might seek a seat on the Council of the League, advice which was to be followed at the next Assembly when Australia succeeded the Irish Free State on the Council.

There was recognition, therefore, even in Australia, of the value of the League in maintaining a stable world order. In all the Dominions there was a unanimous desire for its continuation as a moral factor in the preservation of peace. In both Great Britain and the Dominions the recognition was also growing among certain groups that more than moral pressure might be necessary in case of another serious breach of the peace. The next great test of the League's collective security system was to find a sharper appreciation in the Dominions of the importance of effective League action, and a more clearly formulated conception of the part which they were willing to play.

REFERENCES FOR CHAPTER V

1. By the Treaty of Portsmouth, after the Russo-Japanese War of 1904-05, the Japanese had acquired former Russian leaseholds in the Liaotung Peninsula and the right to station troops along the South Manchurian Railway. By the "Twenty-One Demands" of 1915, the Japanese secured ninety-nine-year possession of these rights and the right for Japanese subjects, including Koreans, to live and work in South Manchuria. The Chinese persistently disputed the validity of this treaty as being concluded under duress but the Japanese did not abandon these parts of the "Twenty-One Demands" at the time of the Washington Conference. On the contrary, they encouraged financial and economic penetration of Manchuria and, less successfully, settlement by their subjects in this area which they looked on as a buffer between themselves and Russia, and as of particular significance as a secure market in a time when opportunities for trade were becoming more limited. This penetration resulted in numerous incidents particularly in relation to Korean settlement and the Japanese had used their armed forces in Manchuria on several previous occasions to prevent discrimination or violence against their subjects.

2. In May, 1931, the threatened insolvency of the Austrian Credit-Anstalt shook the credit structure of Europe, and the Hoover proposal for a moratorium on inter-governmental debts was accepted too late to save the Darmstadter Bank which closed July 13th.

3. In a period of sharply contracting markets, the Japanese demand for Dominion products had remained fairly constant and, in the case of Australia, increased. While Australia itself was reducing imports in response to a curtailment of the borrowing facilities on the London market by which it customarily met its adverse balance of trade, Japan was expanding its exports, and drawing the raw materials for its manufactured goods increasingly from Australia. From 1929 to 1933, Japan doubled its imports of raw wool, taking 96 per cent. of the increase from Australia. In 1931-32, Japan was buying practically one-quarter of the Australian raw wool supply as compared with 29 per cent. taken by Great Britain and only 7 per cent. by Japan a decade earlier. Forty per cent. of Australian wheat was going to China and Japan in 1931-32, a vast increase from the 7.5 per cent. averaged in the years 1926-27 to 1929-30, and approximately the same amount as exported to Great Britain. On the average, Australia was exporting about three and a half times as much to Japan at the beginning of the 1930's as it bought from Japan. Not only was the Japanese trade of great immediate significance in the depression period but there was widespread optimism in Australia that a long-cherished hope of substantial

trade with Far Eastern countries was about to be realized.   G. E. Hubbard, *Eastern Industrialization and Its Effect on the West* (London, 1935), pp. 350 ff. *See* also Jack Shepherd, *Australian Interests and Policies in the Far East* (New York, 1939), pp. 24-30; and Bank of New South Wales, *Monthly Circular*, March, 1934.

Trade between Japan and the other overseas Dominions was much less extensive than between Japan and Australia but like the latter provided reciprocally advantageous commercial intercourse. Japan was a useful outlet for New Zealand wool though exports to Japan (including specie) were only about 0.3 of New Zealand's total external trade. Japan also bought wool from South Africa, partly as a matter of trade policy and somewhat to the concern of Australians. Australia, *Parliamentary Debates* (House of Representatives), September 16, 1931, 132: 5 (Dr. Earle Page), and September 24, 1931, p. 271 (Mr. Killen).

Canada, too, benefited substantially in its exchange of goods with Japan to which it sold about twice as much as it bought.   Harold G. Moulton, *Japan, An Economic and Financial Appraisal* (Washington, 1931), pp. 473-74. There were also numerous financial contacts between Japan and Canada and commercial relations such as those involved in the Canadian Pacific Railway which had led to the opening of a Canadian legation in Tokyo in 1928.

4. Some 11,000 Japanese immigrants were received in Australia from 1902 to 1924 but restrictions were tightened in 1925 and emigration increased. In 1930 only 75 entered the country to join the 3,952 settled there. There was a slow rise in immigration of Japanese into Canada following the "Gentleman's Agreement" of 1908 but the number began to fall again after 1919. The number of Japanese in Canada was 23,342 in 1931, of whom 22,205 were in British Columbia. The immigration policy of South Africa was aimed at precluding Asiatics from permanent settlement and in 1930 there were only 21 Japanese residents in the Union. *Cf.* respective Year Books, 1932 and 1933.

Discrimination existed in New Zealand and Canadian law concerning the immigration of Chinese. Discrimination also existed against Asiatics resident in or even born in the Dominions. In South Africa, Asiatics were restricted in movement to the province in which they were domiciled. Except for Japanese who served in the Great War, Asiatics in British Columbia were debarred from the provincial and federal franchise and Chinese were not permitted to vote in Saskatchewan. People of Asiatic race, even though British subjects, were debarred from the professions of law and pharmacy. In New Zealand, Asiatics were excluded from the provisions of the Old Age Pensions Act and the Family Allowance Act as well as discriminated against in other legislation. *Cf.* J. B. Condliffe, *New Zealand in the Making* (London, 1930), p. 435.

5. China had just taken its place as a member of the Council on the special endorsement of Japan and with the first unanimous vote with which a state had ever been elected.

6. Cecil, *A Great Experiment,*; p. 223.

7. League action in previous disputes, e.g. over Corfu and between Greece and Bulgaria, has not been described because it took place only within the Council on which no Dominion was represented at the time. For details *see* T. P. Conwell-Evans, *The League Council in Action* (London, 1929). It may be noted that China refrained from appealing under Article 10 because its delegate had been assured that if he appealed under this Article, a unanimous vote, including that of Japan, would be required. W. W. Willoughby, *The Sino-Japanese Controversy and the League of Nations* (Baltimore, 1935), p. 37. Mr. Willoughby was with the Chinese delegation at the Twelfth Assembly in 1931.

8. *The League and Manchuria, The First Phase, September 18-30;* Geneva Special Studies, II, 10, 7, October, 1931. A day-by-day account of events, written at the time and with access to first-hand information. There is a series of these studies, covering the whole dispute. *See* also Henry L. Stimson, *The Far Eastern Crisis* (New York, 1936), p. 36.

9. *The League and Manchuria, Second Phase,* pp. 40, 42, 43, 46, 54, 59.

10. Stimson, *op. cit.,* p. 82.

11. Cecil, *op. cit.,* p. 226.

12. Summary of newspaper opinion in *The League and Manchuria, Third Phase,* pp. 4, 14, 17, and 25. In the middle of October despatches from Washington held that unless Japanese policy in Manchuria was modified, there would be no hope of a truce in naval armaments. *Ibid., Second Phase,* p. 16.

13. Charles G. Dawes, *Journal as Ambassador to Great Britain* (New York, 1939), p. 411.

14. *Ibid.,* p. 416.

15. *The League and Manchuria, Second Phase,* p. 37.

16. Stimson believed that his conference with the Japanese Ambassador on November 19th had an influence in deciding the Japanese to put forward the proposal for a neutral commission of inquiry. *Op. cit.,* p. 78.

17. Sean Lester, "The Far Eastern Dispute from the Point of View of the Small States," *Problems of Peace,* Eighth Series (London, 1933), p. 120. Lester subsequently became an influential League official and ultimately Secretary-General.

18. *Australia, Parliamentary Debates* (House of Representatives), October 23, 1931, 132: 1195 ff. (Coleman). He thought it was because Australia had no permanent representation at Geneva.

19. A sign of the independent attitude of the Irish Free State was the registration of the Anglo-Irish Treaty with the League of Nations Secretariat, on July 11, 1924, under Article 18 of the Covenant. The British Government protested on the ground that neither the Covenant nor any convention concluded under the League auspices was considered to govern the relations *inter se* of the various parts of the British Commonwealth. *League of Nations Treaty Series,* 27, p. 449. The Free State refused to accept this interpretation, maintaining that Great Britain and the Irish Free State were separate members of the League of Nations and therefore bound by its stipulations as were all other members. The *inter se* doctrine has been consistently repudiated by Irish Free State Governments as witness the attitude over the Optional Clause. All other parts of the Commonwealth have accepted the *inter se* doctrine.

20. *The League and Manchuria, Third Phase,* pp. 60 and 64: cf. also *C. 55, M. 30, 1932,* VII, January 12, 1932, Letter from the Polish Government to the Secretary-General regretting that one or more of the elected Members of the Council had not been represented on the Commission. It was said that Japan would not have agreed to a Commission comprising representatives of countries not possessing considerable special interests in China. Cf. *The League and Manchuria, Fourth Phase,* p. 7.

21. M. Zaleski of Poland, Meeting of the Council on November 21st, and repeated by Matos of Guatemala, Gonzales-Prada of Peru, and Garay of Panama, in the meeting of December 10, 1931. Sze in replying for China said: "Reference has been made to the special character of the question before us. I should like to say that China cannot be expected to admit that the operation of treaties, covenants, and accepted principles of international law stops at the border of Manchuria."

22. For resolution and explanation *see O.J.,* 1931, No. 12: 65th Session of the Council, Nineteenth Meeting, December 9, 1931.

23. Dawes, *op. cit.,* p. 426.

24. Cecil, *op. cit.,* pp. 227-28.

25. Stimson, *op. cit.,* pp. 93-5.

26. The latter part of the American Note read as follows: "The American Government deems it to be its duty to notify both the Government of the Chinese Republic and the Imperial Japanese Government that it cannot admit the legality of any situation *de facto* nor does it intend to recognize any treaty or agreement entered into between those Governments or agents thereof which may impair the treaty rights of the United States or its citizens in China, including those which relate to the sovereignty, the independence or the territorial and administrative integrity of the Republic of China or to the international policy relative to China, commonly known as the 'open door' policy; and that it does not intend to recognize any situation, treaty, or agreement which may be brought about by means contrary to the covenants and obligations of the Pact of Paris of August 27, 1928, to which treaty both China and Japan as well as the United States, are parties." It was transmitted to the British Foreign Office from Washington on January 5th.

27. The British communique declared: "His Majesty's Government stand by the policy of the 'open door' for international trade in Manchuria, which was guaranteed by the Nine-Power Treaty at Washington.

"Since the recent events in Manchuria, the Japanese representatives at the Council of the League of Nations at Geneva stated on October 13, that Japan was the champion in Manchuria of the principle of equal opportunity and the 'open door' policy, and would welcome participation and co-operation in Manchurian enterprise.

"In view of these statements, His Majesty's Government have not considered it necessary to address any formal Note to the Japanese Government on the lines of the American Government's Note, but the Japanese Ambassador in London has been requested to obtain confirmation of these assurances from His Government."

28. Letter from Sir John Pratt, published in *The Times*, November 30, 1938. Reprinted in *British Far Eastern Policy*, prepared by the Information Department of the Royal Institute of International Affairs (London, 1939), pp. 50-1.

29. *League and Manchuria, Fourth Phase*, p. 51, quoted in full.

30. Lester, *op. cit.*, pp. 128-29.

31. Willoughby, W. W., *The Sino-Japanese Controversy*, p. 237.

32. Stimson, *op. cit.*, p. 164.

33. Letter from Sir John Pratt in *The Times*, November 10, 1938. Reprinted in *British Far Eastern Policy*, pp. 48-9. Pratt attributes Stimson's statement to a slip in memory.

34. Dept. of State, *Press Release*, February 27, 1932.

35. *Australia, Parliamentary Debates* (House of Representatives), 1931, 132: 709. Ward asked that "in no circumstances will Australian lives be sacrificed in the event of a war for Chinese markets," and repeated the question on February 25, 1932, *ibid.*, 133: 276.

36. *Ibid.* (Senate), March 3, 1932, 133: 560-61.

37. *Ibid.* (House of Representatives), February 24, 1932, 133: 205.

38. *Ibid.*, February 25, 1932, p. 276.

39. *International Affairs*, March, 1932, pp. 177-78.

40. A. D. McKinlay, "The New Zealand Metropolitan Press," *Pacific Affairs*, January, 1933, p. 12.

41. *E.g., Journal of Canadian Bankers Association*, "The March of Events," January, 1932, pp. 146-47.

42. *Canada, House of Commons Debates*, February, 1932, I, 30.

43. Stimson, visiting Geneva in April, noted that the small powers had a livelier sense of the ethical significance of the controversy than the Great Powers and that the latter had not manifested much leadership; *op. cit.*, p. 201.

44. *O.J.*, 1932, Spec. Sup. No. 101, p. 70: *Special Assembly*, General Commission, Fifth Meeting, March 8, 1932. The three Dominion speeches were made in this session. The General Commission had been set up as a Committee of the Whole at the beginning of the Assembly.

45. *Ibid.*, p. 74.

46. *See* above, Chapter I, p. 8.

47. *O.J.*, 1932, Spec. Sup. No. 101, p. 75: *Special Assembly*, General Commission, Fifth Meeting, March 8, 1932.

48. Stimson, *op. cit.*, p. 204, in his speech on August 8, 1932, to the Council of Foreign Relations. An official message from the American Government sent at the time of the resolution declared that the agreement " not to recognize the validity of results attained in violation of the treaties in question" was "a distinct contribution to international law and offers a constructive basis for peace." *League and Manchuria, Fourth Phase*, p. 96. Message printed in full.

49. According to Vigilantes, *Inquest on Peace* (London, 1935), p. 20, the British Government cast its vote for Portugal instead of South Africa thereby defeating the latter which it feared in view of te Water's speech in the Assembly might seek to institute severe measures against Japan. Whether or not the story is well founded, subsequent discussions in South Africa do not encourage the view that its Government would have been ready to sponsor a programme of action against Japan.

50. *C. 407, M. 225, 1932, VII* (L.O.N. Doc.). Preliminary Report from the Commission of Enquiry.

51. *South Africa, House of Assembly Debates*, 19, 3342 ff.

52. *Ibid.*, col. 3314 ff.

53. In reply to a challenge that there was a contradiction in his attitude towards sanctions:
    "Prime Minister: I do not know. It may be so.
    "Roper: The Prime Minister cannot have it both ways. If he considers the provision of sanctions prevents the League carrying out its functions properly, surely you must abolish the provision of sanctions altogether. You cannot have sanctions for undefined eventualities. I should like to know the Prime Minister's policy.
    "Prime Minister: It is not a question of policy."
    Ibid., col. 3355 ff.

54. *O.J.*, 1932, No. 11, p. 1731: 68th Session of the Council, Second Meeting, September 24, 1932.

55. *O.J.*, 1932, Spec. Sup. No. 104, p. 24: *Thirteenth Assembly*, First Plenary Session, September 26, 1932.

56. *Ibid.*, p. 3388: Third Plenary Session, September 27, 1932 (W. M. Hughes).

57. Stimson, *op. cit.*, p. 204.

58. *The Times*, August 9, 1932, declared it would be a real guarantee of peace "far more effective than any formal engagements" and *The Daily Herald* on the following day hailed it as a deliberate attempt to support the small powers which had championed "non-recognition" in March. The Japanese were irate and apparently strengthened in their resolve to recognize "Manchukuo." *League and the Lytton Report*, p. 12.

59. The practical steps which the Commission proposed were that the Council invite China and Japan to discuss a solution of their dispute: that an advisory conference, composed of representatives of the two governments, of delegations representing the local inhabitants of Manchuria and neutral observers if the parties agreed, should meet to discuss detailed proposals for a special régime for the administration of the three Eastern Provinces: that the Council should be called upon in case of any disputed points and would then attempt to find a

settlement: and that another Conference with the help of neutral observers should consider matters pertaining to the respective rights and interests of Japan. It was suggested that the broad outlines of the form of administration for Manchuria should be agreed upon between the parties with the assistance of the Council before the Advisory Conference met, and various definite suggestions as to the allocation of powers were included in the Report. *C. 663, M. 320, 1932,* VII (L.O.N. Doc.). Report of the Commission of Enquiry.

60. The Japanese observations on the Lytton Report were transmitted on November 19, 1932. *C. 775, M. 366, 1932, VII* (L.O.N. Doc.).

61. The Japanese representative strongly opposed giving Lord Lytton an opportunity to say whether the Commission desired to add anything to its report, but de Valera, supported by Sir John Simon and other representatives, upheld the right of the Council to invite Lord Lytton to speak if he desired to do so.

62. *O.J.,* 1932, No. 12, Part I, p. 1911: 69th Session of the Council, Ninth Meeting, November 25, 1932.

63. *The Daily Mail* commented on November 12, 1932: "The Japanese reply to the Lytton Report *re* Manchuria was issued last evening. It is an exceedingly able document, which will convince all reasonable people that Japan has right on her side. The essential passage in Japan's reply is that she has treaty rights and vast economic interests in Manchuria, and that having a large number of her people settled there, she is vitally interested in the country.

"As everyone knows she won those rights by prolonged struggle with the Russian Empire in 1904-05, and will never tamely surrender them.

"It would be an outrage on humanity to bring about such a solution in order to save the face of the League of Nations. But the misguided idealists who have so openly taken side with the Chinese war lords and communists mean to make strenuous efforts to force Great Britain into some wild scheme of economic and financial boycott of Japan which they hope would drive Japan from Manchuria."

64. For survey of newspaper comments between October 3rd and 6th, *see The League and the Lytton Report,* p. 26.

65. Survey of newspaper comments in *Interdependence,* December, 1932. *The Toronto Star, The Vancouver Province, The Border Cities Star, The Saint John Telegraph Journal,* saw the Report as making a definite issue between the League and Japan. *The Toronto Mail and Empire* and *The Calgary Albertan* considered it fair and courageous. *The Victoria Times* felt the League must take a stronger stand if it wished to encourage states such as the United States or Russia to join it. *The Montreal Star, The Montreal Gazette, The Toronto Globe, The Montreal Standard,* and *The Victoria Colonist* criticized the Report and the League as unrealistic.

66. *Canada, House of Commons Debates,* November 21, 1932, cols. 1367-70.

67. It was criticized by W. L. Grant, Principal of Upper Canada College, Toronto, and President of the Toronto Branch of the League of Nations Society, in an article "Is Canada Treating the League of Nations Seriously?" which appeared in *Saturday Night,* December 31, 1932. "The League is no more a quasi-judicial body than is the House of Commons, indeed rather less so. While our delegates should obviously be free to watch changing conditions they should also be given very positive instructions about some such matters as the Lytton Report. . . . Above all they should be appointed far enough ahead for full debate in parliament on the questions likely to come up."

68. A. D. McKinlay, "The New Zealand Metropolitan Press," *Pacific Affairs,* January, 1933, p. 13.

69. *New Zealand, Parliamentary Debates* (House of Representatives), October 4, 1932, 233: 230-1 (McKeen).

70. W. L. Grant, *op. cit., Saturday Night,* December 31, 1932.

71. *Australia, Parliamentary Debates* (House of Representatives), October 12, 1932, 133: 1086. Casey asked about the reputed ambitions of Japan in connection with the Island of Timor. *Ibid.*, October 14, 1932, 136: 1292-3. McNicoll raised the point.

72. *Ibid* (Senate), November 3, 1932, 136: 1823.

73. *Ibid.*, p. 1811 (Senator Hardy), and p. 1818 (Senator Sir George Pearce).

74. *Ibid.* (House of Representatives), October 20, 1932, 136: 1516 (Beasley).

75. *Ibid.* (Senate), November 3, 1943, 136: 1824-25.

76. *Ibid.* (House of Representatives), October 20, 1932, 136: 1517.

77. *O.J.*, 1932, Spec. Sup. No. 111, p. 32 ff.: *Special Assembly*, Tenth Plenary Session, December 6, 1932.

78. Willoughby, *op. cit.*, p. 444.

79. *O.J.*, 1932, Spec. Sup. No. 111, p. 50: *Special Assembly*, Twelfth Plenary Session, December 7, 1932.

80. Freda White, "Manchuria and Peace," *Headway*, January, 1933.

81. *O.J.*, 1932, Spec. Sup. No. 111, p. 57 ff.: *Special Assembly*, Thirteenth Plenary Session, December 8th, 1932.

82. Mr. Mackenzie King on February 8, 1932, in his reply to the Address, *Canada, House of Commons Debates*, 1932, I, 30, had declared: "I venture to say that if the Orient had as we have on this continent something in the nature of an international joint tribunal which would deal with questions of international difference, we would certainly not be witnessing today what we are forced to witness."

83. The Chinese representative made clear that he found them so in answering observations made during the debate, "particularly by the delegate of Canada who spoke this morning with such animation and tried to paint a rather sorry picture of China." *O.J.*, 1932, Spec. Sup. No. 111, p. 65: *Special Assembly*, 1932, Fourteenth Plenary Meeting, December 7, 1932.

84. Willoughby, *op. cit.*, p. 456.

85. A. R. M. Lower, *Canada and the Far East—1940* (New York, 1940), p. 21.

86. *Doc. A.* (*Extr.*), *162, 1932, VII. O.J.*, Spec. Sup. No. 111, Annex 10.

87. *O.J.*, 1932, Spec. Sup. No. 111, p. 56: *Special Assembly*, Thirteenth Plenary Session, December 8, 1932.

88. *Ibid.*, pp. 61-2.

89. *Canada, House of Commons Debates*, May 16, 1933, p. 5066 ff. Reprinted in part in MacKay and Rogers, *op. cit.*, p. 342.

90. *Ibid.*, March 2, 1936, p. 638.

91. Willoughby, *op. cit.*, p. 464, n., says as far as he knows it was never withdrawn.

92. *Doc. A.* (*Extr.*), *163, 1932, VII. O.J.*, 1932, Spec. Sup. No. 111, Annex XI.

93. Stimson, *op. cit.*, p. 222. On January 9th, Stimson had had a conference on foreign policy with Roosevelt, president-elect, and learned that there would be no change in American policy under the new Administration. On January 17th Roosevelt made a press statement to this effect.

94. In a letter of February 14, 1933, from the Japanese Government, *O.J.*, 1933, Spec. Sup. No. 112, Annex V, p. 82.

95. *O.J.*, 1933, Spec. Sup. No. 112, p. 24: Eighteenth Plenary Meeting, February 24, 1933.

96. *Ibid.*, p. 21, Seventeenth Plenary Meeting, February 24. 1933.

97 *Ibid.*, p. 22.

98. Cahan in his speech to the House of Commons maintained that his address at Geneva influenced the Assembly's decision to give Canada a seat on the Committee. It seems more likely, however, that it was the final statement read by Riddell. It may be noted that Australia was added to the Far Eastern Advisory Committee during the 1937 Assembly.

99. On March 11th, the United States accepted the invitation to consult with the Advisory Committee. *Doc. A. (Extr.)*, *39*. The Soviet Union refused the invitation on March 7th, *Doc. A. (Extr.)*, *38*.

100. *The China Review*, July-September, 1932, p. 5, noted that the export of arms and ammunition to China and Japan from Great Britain, August, 1931-April, 1932, inclusive, amounted to £204,144 to Japan and £54,967 to China.

101. Even Sir Austen Chamberlain opposed the double embargo and the Opposition took a determined stand against it. *Great Britain, House of Commons Debates*, February 27, 1933, 275 (debate in Committee on Supply).

102. Toynbee, *Survey of International Affairs*, 1933, p. 513.

103. *See* B. B. Wallace, "How the United States Led the League in 1931" in *The American Political Science Review*, February, 1945, pp. 101-16, for a salutary analysis of the limitations on American "leadership" in the Sino-Japanese dispute.

104. When the final Assembly report was being drafted by the Committee of Nineteen, there was still uncertainty as to whether the exhaustion of the resources of Article 15 would not automatically bring the sanctions of Article 16 into play. The Secretary-General and his legal advisers decided that it would not and the Committee adopted this view.

105. In February, 1932, the United States State Department let it be known that it had been in communication with the British and French Governments and that all three powers had agreed to discourage and, if possible, stop parliamentary debate on this subject. *Baltimore Sun*, February 20, 1932. Following this the State Department asked the House Committee on Foreign Affairs not to agree to hearings on a resolution by Representative Fish authorizing the President to prohibit sale of munitions to countries where a state of war existed.

106. *See* for example E. H. Carr, who accepts this fact in his review of Norman Hillson, *Geneva Scene*, in *International Affairs*, July, 1937, pp. 618-19.

107. *E.g.* Norman Hillson, *Geneva Scene* (London, 1936), p. 55.

108. For a survey of comments in Canadian newspapers on the Assembly report, *see Interdependence*, March, 1933.

109. *Canada, House of Commons Debates*, January 30, 1933, II, 1664.

110. *Ibid.*, February 24, 1933, III, 2430-31. Reprinted in MacKay and Rogers, *op. cit.*, pp. 340-41.

111. *Ibid.*, May 16, 1933, V, 5059 ff. Reprinted in part in MacKay and Rogers, *op. cit.*, pp. 342 and 344.

112. *New Zealand, Parliamentary Debates* (House of Representatives), February 28, 1933, 235: 770.

113. *The Round Table*, June, 1933, p. 684 (dated March 29, 1933).

114. *Australia, Parliamentary Debates* (House of Representatives), May 23, 1933, 139: 1627 ff.

CHAPTER VI

RESPONSE TO GERMAN REARMAMENT AND THE ORGANIZATION OF SANCTIONS AGAINST ITALY

THE first large-scale violation of the treaties on which the inter-war security system rested occurred in the Far East. It was followed in rapid succession by the Chaco War, by Hitler's repudiation of the limitation on armaments imposed on Germany through the Treaty of Versailles, by Italy's aggression against Ethiopia, and by German violation of the Locarno Treaty through reoccupation of the Rhineland. South America might appear remote to Commonwealth statesmen and there could be little chance that a war between Paraguay and Bolivia would have far-reaching effects. But developments affecting the balance of power in Central Europe and the Suez Canal route to the Far East involved direct issues of security as well as basic challenges to the collective system. The overriding question in the months following the announcement of German rearmament in March, 1935, and the Italian attack on Ethiopia in October was whether these dangers would force a new alignment between national and international interests and thereby lead to effective action in support of collective security.

The question had a particular pertinence for the countries of the Commonwealth. The League system of collective security had seemed to offer a means whereby their divergent interests could be harmonized and given common direction through allegiance to principle rather than to a particular power. It had received a rude shock through Japan's action in Manchuria. If no action were taken in the case of open disregard of the Treaty under which the League itself had been set up or even more in the case of an open attack on a member of the League, the system would have proved itself so ineffective as to be virtually useless. What would disappear from the realm of practical politics would be the stabilizing influence in international affairs through which the Commonwealth had hoped to resolve its own greatest problem, the issue of war.

But if these long-range views dictated a policy of full support of League action, the immediate dangers which such a policy might involve suggested lines of action arising out of national rather than international considerations. In the Sino-Japanese dispute, both British and Australians had been held back by the fear that international action might lead to reprisals. In issues closer to hand, the fear of being involved in local or general war acted as a powerful deterrent. Paradoxically, the dread of war was to be the most serious handicap to securing support for a system which might in the end have been able to banish war.

Behind this latter view also lay scepticism regarding the purity of the principles under which the League had acted in practice. Much of this feeling in Commonwealth countries arose from a deep disappointment at the failure of one great hope long maintained within the Dominions and in substantial groups in Great Britain: that security might be achieved through general disarmament. Canadians and Australians had asserted their faith in disarmament from the first days of the League. Few sessions of Dominion parliaments passed without mention of the hope that through disarmament a new international atmosphere would be achieved. At the Disarmament Conference itself, Dominion representatives had found themselves in a somewhat awkward position. Since their countries had comparatively few armaments, they had little to offer in the way of reductions. Nor did they wish to embarrass Great Britain or to propose a lessening of British naval strength which in its already reduced form was little enough protection to the more exposed Dominions.

Among the Dominions, Australia had the most specific proposals for reduction of armaments including the abolition of submarines, the prohibition of gas and chemical warfare and of large land guns, reduction in the size of warships and naval armaments, and limitation of conscription by agreement.[1] In an effort to get around the reluctance of countries to make public their existing armaments lest they be disadvantaged thereby, its representative, Mr. Latham, had proposed using estimates of needs for limited periods as standards from which to work. But these and other proposals from smaller countries had comparatively little effect. For the most part Dominion representatives had to content themselves with supporting British proposals when they were progressive and remaining silent when they were not. In the complicated negotiations and final series of counter-proposals between Great Britain, France, Germany, and Italy, through which a formula was sought satisfying to all parties, they had little or no share. The ultimate failure of the Conference with Germany's withdrawal crushed their hopes, like those of many others, of this means of improving international relations.

Not only disillusionment but also fear resulted from the developments of 1934. Germany resigned from the League following its withdrawal from the Disarmament Conference, thereby giving notice that it recognized no restrictions on its own freedom of action and at the same time further weakening the League as a possible safeguard against aggressive action. Some compensation for its withdrawal resulted from the entry of the Soviet Union into the League in 1934. But this new member was greeted with less than enthusiasm by most of the Dominions and with undisguised dislike by the representatives of the Irish Free State.

Equally serious from the point of view of collective action was increasing isolationism in the United States, which gave rise to the Neutrality Act which prevented the Executive from discriminating officially between belligerents. This was demonstrated all too clearly in 1935 when the President found himself incapable of sharing in collective pressure to force mediation in the Chaco War. In the spring of 1935, League powers finally agreed to impose an arms embargo on both Bolivia and Paraguay with the understanding that it would be lifted in favour of whichever country first agreed to meet League demands. General American pressure supported League efforts to secure a settlement but despite the greater concern of the United States than of most League powers with peace in South America, it was unable to follow their example of raising the arms embargo against Bolivia when it acceded to League demands and so creating a differentiated pressure on the country least willing to seek peace. Though President Roosevelt's own desires were clearly for collective measures against an aggressor, the Neutrality Act imposed a strait jacket which strictly limited the action which could be taken to co-operate with League powers in subsequent attempts to curb aggression. This not only served as a deterrent to League action but by its very example supported the isolationist groups in other countries. Where the United States had provided leadership during the Sino-Japanese dispute, at least to the extent of graduated moral pressure, it now became tacitly the leader in the movement of withdrawal from collective responsibilities.

This unfortunate example coincided with the increase in tension throughout Europe. The Nazi Government's ruthless measures within Germany and its belligerent attitude in external affairs had roused again the fears which had been but dormant since the Allied victory in 1918. Though aggression in 1935 was to be the result of action by Italy and not Germany, the growing power of the latter was the dominant factor in the international scene. It gave rise to two distinct types of response which reflected once more the different approaches of Great Britain and France to the problem of peace on the continent. France wished to organize overwhelming strength against Germany and crush its military power before it became dangerous.

Great Britain, supported by the Dominions, believed that through extending the equality which Hitler was demanding, a basis for agreement might be secured.

This divergence between French and British reactions was to be obvious not only in regard to Germany but also to Italy's aggression against Ethiopia.   In a surprising reversal of rôles, the British Government was to be the chief organizer of collective action against Italy while the French did almost everything to sabotage League sanctions. Indirectly, however, these new policies were conditioned by the growing power of Germany.   France's chief response to this development was to strengthen its alliances in eastern Europe and to establish new ties with Italy and the Soviet Union.   In January, 1935, a Franco-Italian Pact and military agreement freed French and Italian soldiers from the task of guarding their adjoining African colonies so they could be used in Europe in the face of a possible German threat.   On May 2, 1935, the culmination of the French system of alliances was reached with the announcement of a treaty with the Soviet Union.   A year later the Franco-Soviet Treaty was ratified.   Germany was to claim it to be a threat to its safety and use it as justification for remilitarizing the Rhineland.   But temporarily at least the French Government put its greatest reliance on the new relationship with Italy as a counterpoise to Germany.   For this Laval was to be willing to sacrifice the possibility of effective League action in the Italo-Ethiopian conflict.   Paradoxically, the greatest upholder of collective security was to let it down at the one moment in the inter-war period in which a large part of British public opinion had become convinced of the merits of forcible collective action.

This attitude was not held by most of the members of the British National Government under Mr. Baldwin.   Its views were reflected more accurately by the negotiations during 1935[2] for a European Pact aiming at a four power agreement between Great Britain, France, Germany, and Italy.   The British Government still hoped in the early part of 1935 to stabilize Europe through arrangements of this or a more limited kind.   German rearmament, particularly in the air, tended to reinforce this trend in official policy as was indicated by the Stresa Conference with Italy and France and subsequently by the Anglo-German Naval Agreement in June.   But its effect on British public opinion was to shatter any illusions of isolation from the continent and to reinforce belief in the necessity of an effective collective security system.   This sentiment became known dramatically through the Peace Ballot, a nation-wide manifestation of a surprising degree of willingness for economic, and if necessary, military sanctions.   This demonstration of feeling was to influence the British Government in its decision to support economic measures against Italy when the latter invaded Ethiopia in October, 1935. The British Government seems also to have argued at that time that though forcible measures against Germany were unwise, it might have a salutary effect on its future actions if it were given a demonstration of effective League pressure against an open aggressor.

This British policy, induced in part by the pressure of public opinion, and in part by shrewd evaluation of the general situation, did not find immediate response in the Dominions. Their Governments had been watching with some uneasiness the British manœuvring in continental politics. Their traditional dislike of seeing Great Britain engaged in European affairs was intensified by their fears that it might be drawn into war thereby. The question which confronted them was how best to prevent such an eventuality. Was it by attempting to restrain Great Britain from being involved further in European affairs? Was it by demonstrating their solidarity with Great Britain? Or was it by encouraging the British Government to take a strong stand behind the general principles of collective security? Between these courses of action, there was in fact division not only between individual Dominions, but also within them, which complicated the process of developing common lines of policy and ultimately of maintaining a common League front in support of the principles of collective security.

In no other Commonwealth country was public sentiment in support of the collective system as strong in 1935 as in Great Britain. In each of the Dominions, however, with the probable exception of Australia, there were groups which were internationalist in view, and eager to support the League as a counterpoise or a complement to the British connection. In Australia, such influences had little effect. Governmental policy aimed at keeping close touch with Great Britain and, if possible, restraining it from risking danger. The Labour Opposition, split between State and Federal groups since a division over financial policies while in office in 1931, was generally isolationist in feeling and suspicious of the League as an instrument of "imperialism." This sentiment was to increase rather than diminish during 1935 and to lead to a union of the party under Mr. Curtin, officially, though by no means unanimously, opposed to the imposition of sanctions in the Italo-Ethiopian conflict.

In its neighbour, New Zealand, governmental policy was similarly motivated by the desire to maintain a virtual identity of policy with Great Britain though without the urge to restrain Britain from any policy it felt advantageous to follow. Speaking of the proposed European pact in the House of Representatives on February 19, 1935, Mr. Forbes, the Prime Minister, declared that "if Great Britain became involved in war, New Zealand would also be involved,"[3] though the Dominions would not be parties to the Pact any more than to Locarno. The "welfare of the Old Country" sentiment and the legal position as New Zealand accepted it made this inevitable, he felt. Forbes was to reiterate his conclusions to the press in Ottawa in April on his way to the King's Jubilee in London, going so far as to say that if war broke out there would be no need to call Parliament except to make necessary arrangements.[4] But this was challenged by Mr. Savage, leader of the Labour Opposition, who maintained that any policy of co-operation in war abroad must be based on "discussion, negotiation, and agreement."[5] Though in no way denying the common interests of New Zealand and Great Britain, Savage's attitude was representative of the traditional stand of the New Zealand Labour party in favour of Parliamentary decisions and also of the growing independence of attitude to be evidenced with the coming into power of the party late in the year. Strongly internationalist in sentiment from a Christian Socialist point of view the New Zealand Labour party was to provide a striking contrast both in attitude and policy to the Labour party in Australia.

In Canada an internationalist view was less a matter of party than of particular groups in the community, notably in the universities. The Conservative Government under Bennett which had taken office during the depression was still in power, its ties to Great Britain strengthened by the successful conclusion of the Ottawa Agreements for inter-Empire preference concluded in 1932. There were already signs, however, that a Liberal ministry would be returned to office at the next election, destined to take place in October, 1935. Traditionally less "imperialist" in sentiment than the Conservatives, the Liberal party seemed unlikely to support a strong international policy because of its inclusion of practically all the French Canadian members in the House, the most strongly isolationist group in Canada. In fact, the Liberals and Conservatives were to vie with each other during pre-election speeches in September, 1935, in pledges against participation in a war in which, in Bennett's words, "the rights of Canadians are not involved."[6]

In the two other Commonwealth countries, the Irish Free State and South Africa, Prime Ministers were in office who might be expected to look on a League policy as a counterpoise to dependence upon Britain. de Valera, who had come into power in 1932, was a convinced internationalist who had supported a strong League policy during the Sino-Japanese dispute when the Irish Free State held a seat on the Council. This he was to continue during the sanctions period of the Italo-Ethiopian campaign in the face of considerable opposition from public opinion. "If your worst enemy happens to be going to heaven by the same road you are, you don't for that reason turn around and go the other direction," he asserted trenchantly to those who accused him of following the British lead at Geneva.[7] He might well have pointed also to his speeches and such actions as the termination of land annuities payments to the British Government as evidence that whatever policy he was following was independently conceived.

The most interesting alignment of parties within the Commonwealth existed in South Africa where economic difficulties in the Union had led to a coalition and, in 1934, to fusion between Smuts' South African party and Hertzog's Nationalist party. This union was based on a programme of "South Africa first" combined with the maintenance of the existing relationship between the Union and the British Commonwealth and of co-operation with the other members of the Commonwealth. It was a heroic effort to bridge the division between British and Afrikaans within the country through recognition of the distinctive cultural heritage of each and of their joint national aspirations. It was also an attempt, largely successful, to find a common denominator between Smuts' view of the Commonwealth as an essential nucleus of an international order, and Hertzog's growing conviction (first induced by the Balfour Report of the 1926 Imperial Conference) that South Africa could find its fullest freedom and development in close friendship with Great Britain.

South African extremists on both sides found the platform of the new Fusion Party unsatisfactory. Fearful that in fact Hertzog's statements regarding the relation with Britain meant secession, Colonel Stallard, formerly of the South African Party, organized the Dominion party, which stressed South Africa's position as an integral part of the British Commonwealth. On the other wing, Malan led part of the old Nationalist party, largely drawn from Cape Province, into a separate party which stressed independence and neutrality, and commanded considerable public support. Hertzog, his old leader, though he made some concessions to those members of his own party who cherished the ideal of neutrality and asserted the forms of independence in the Status of the Union Act of 1934,[8] recognized that in fact the issue of neutrality was somewhat academic. To refuse to participate in a war in which Great Britain was engaged would split the United party from top to bottom and break a bond with Britain which he was well aware was important for South Africa's defence. Yet in the nature of things, South Africa's support of British policy could never be as wholehearted as that of Dominions as British in race as Australia and New Zealand.[9] An active international policy offered in some measure the middle way between neutrality on one side and a strong pro-British policy on the other, neither of which would have commanded the support of the country as a whole.

Public opinion in most of the Dominions seems at least to have been more alert to international developments on the eve of the crisis precipitated by the announcement of German rearmament, than at the time of the Sino-Japanese dispute. The economic situation had improved in all the Dominions with the exception of the Irish Free State, which was suffering from the effect of the trade war with Great Britain which had followed its repudiation of the obligation to pay the land annuities. In the overseas Dominions attention could be focussed once more on political issues. This is not to suggest that there was much clearly thought-through conviction either on behalf of or against collective security measures except among limited groups. Readiness to follow a British lead was a more common sentiment. Most predominant of all was the desire to avoid war. The clashes were to come over how best this could be achieved, both in the face of German rearmament and of Italian aggression against Ethiopia.

DISCLOSURE OF GERMAN REARMAMENT

The unilateral repudiation of the disarmament provisions of the Treaty of Versailles by Hitler on March 16, 1935, followed by the disclosure of German land, sea, and air armaments precipitated what was potentially the most serious situation faced on the continent since the conclusion of World War I. Was it a reason for drastic action to prevent further rearmament? Or was it a manifestation of the natural urge for equality which, if satisfied, might provide a stable basis for future relations? The French thought the former: the British tended to the latter interpretation. Though they worked together, the French and British failed to find a common policy, as has been said, thereby making it more difficult subsequently to secure unified action in the Italo-Ethiopian conflict.

Within a short time, British, French, and Italian leaders, meeting at Stresa, Italy, had established the so-called "Stresa Front" of unity and mutual support against a possible threat of aggression by Germany. The French were eager to plan also for sanctions against Germany so that it would be unable to complete its rearmament programme. The British were reluctant for immediate action. With Italian support they secured agreement on a compromise proposal for setting up a League Committee to consider means of enforcing the Covenant. This was done at the next meeting of the Council in the middle of

April,[10] at which Germany's action was condemned. It was apparent that the British were using this means to stave off French proposals for immediate action and to substitute for them more general discussions under League auspices looking towards ultimate means of restraining Germany in case its policy became more openly aggressive.

This League body, known as the Committee of Thirteen on Collective Security, was destined to play a significant rôle in preparing the way for the organization of sanctions against Italy. Such a development was not foreseen, obviously, when it was established. The general mandate of the Committee was to devise proposals for rendering "the Covenant more effective in the organization of collective security," and it was asked in particular to define "the economic and financial measures which might be applied, should in the future a State, whether a Member of the League of Nations or not, endanger peace by the unilateral repudiation of its international obligations." Meetings were held from the end of April until the middle of August and the Committee also set up two sub-committees, one on legal issues which met from June 24th to 28th, and the other on economic and financial measures which met from July 1st to 13th. By the time the reports were ready, it had become apparent that its investigations would probably serve as the basis for sanctions not against Germany but against Italy, a member of the "Stresa Front." But the plans of the Committee were originally worked out with Germany in view.

In addition to setting up this Committee, the Council, on the request of the French Government, also condemned Germany's unilateral action at its April meeting and declared that its repudiation of the disarmament clauses of the Treaty of Versailles "confers upon itself no right." Bruce, representing Australia and asking for unanimous support of the resolution, declared that Germany's action had "crystallized" the doubts and fears induced by the failure of the Disarmament Conference and the apparent weakness of the League.[11] "That action has forced an issue and compelled us all to face the situation," he pointed out. "Either the League of Nations must be an effective instrument for the maintenance of the world's peace or we must recognize that it has failed." If it failed, then nations would take steps to ensure their own security like those planned at Stresa. "Would such a result be in the interests of world peace," he asked, "of the comity of nations and particularly of Germany?" The action proposed by the resolution, the establishment of the Committee to consider means of strengthening the Covenant, was "no more than is essential if the League of Nations is to become an effective instrument for deterring the aggressor and maintaining the peace of the world." Out of their unanimity in support of this stand, he hoped the way would be paved "for the co-operation within the League of all European nations in the framing of agreements, freely negotiated in an atmosphere of complete equality, which will ensure to the world a new régime of peace and security." It was an indication of the fear that Europe was drawing once more into armed camps and of the hope for ultimate agreement.

The Canadian Government was no less concerned that the recent developments should not precipitate a more far-reaching crisis. In a guarded statement it noted "with anxiety" the announcement of German rearmament and regretted that this unilateral action had taken place on the eve of "promising efforts to deal with the whole European arms questions" including revision by agreement of the treaty restrictions on German rearmament. The Government would continue "to follow the situation with care . . ." it was declared.[12]   In the meantime, Canada had been offered a seat on the Committee of Thirteen on Collective Security set up as the result of the Stresa deliberations and Council resolution. This invitation was not surprising since only Canada and South Africa among the Dominions had permanent representation at Geneva which was needed to follow those out-of-session deliberations, and the effort was being made to have all the major "groups" in the League represented on the Committee. In accepting a place the Canadian Government was careful to make it clear that by so doing it was not accepting the view that repudiation of international obligations "without recourse to war calls for the adoption of sanctions by League Members. . . . Any proposals for the applicability of sanctions in such a case should be considered in the Committee on their merits," it concluded.[13]   It was a not surprising comment from a country which had consistently sought to safeguard its ultimate freedom of decision in both Commonwealth and League but it is worth noting that among all the countries accepting membership on the Committee, only Canada made such a proviso.

The deliberations of the Committee on Collective Security can best be considered in connection with the organization of sanctions against Italy. As far as Germany was concerned, though the plans and ideas of the Committee were turned in that direction throughout its course, British influence had been effective in preventing drastic action against that country, such as France would have liked to undertake. Recognizing this fact, General Smuts, speaking at an Imperial Press Conference dinner at Capetown as early as March 21st, paid tribute to the British Government's unceasing efforts to preserve peace. What had happened, he declared, "could have and has been foreseen" but was no reason "to make us slacken our efforts, or make us turn back on the great experiment of organizing peace."[14] And he continued, "I am deeply grateful to the British Government for remaining calm, in spite of what has happened in Berlin and for going straight ahead with the task of building the bridge of peace between the nations." That it was late, he recognized, but perhaps "not too late to bring peace and sanity back to Europe and set the wheels of general recovery in motion again."

Explicit in General Smuts' comments was the belief that in this situation mediation and not force was the right policy. Implicit in Bruce's statement to the Council and the Canadian comment was the hope that European conflict would be forestalled by a judicious combination of firmness and conciliation. Faced with Germany's unilateral denunciation of the Versailles disarmament provisions, the reaction of all the Commonwealth countries appears to have been largely similar. There was some sympathy for its claims to equality; considerable hope that the achievement of equality in arms might even make easier the task of finding an ultimate agreement with Germany; perhaps an equal amount of fear, particularly in the light of revelations on the strength of German air power that drastic measures at this time would cause conflict. If conciliation could avoid the necessity for force, the Commonwealth stood united behind it.

The King's Jubilee in May, 1935, brought to London the Prime Ministers of the overseas Dominions and made possible a quasi-Imperial Conference at which both the international situation and imperial defence were discussed.[15] It seems probable that during these meetings Dominion statesmen continued to advocate a policy of conciliation towards Germany. General Hertzog is said to have been particularly outspoken on Germany's behalf, comparing its position of inequality with that which had kept South Africa dissatisfied until the Imperial Conference of 1926. None the less there was recognition that the situation was potentially dangerous and that it would be unwise to ignore this. In the most revealing of the brief communiqués issued after these informal discussions, it was declared that the Dominion representatives "are wholly in favour of a system of collective security for maintaining the peace of Europe. At the same time, they held it to be of paramount importance that the door should be kept open for her full and frank co-operation."[16] If Germany was to be treated as an equal, however, it was essential that it should be demonstrated that "full faith and confidence" could be placed in its future actions. Subsequent meetings extending throughout the month[17] considered imperial defence partly in the light of preliminary conversations held in certain Dominions during the visit of Sir Maurice Hankey, secretary of the

Committee of Imperial Defence, early in the year,[18] partly of the British Government's White Paper on Imperial Defence issued March, 1935,[19] but perhaps even more with reference to the situation created by German rearmament.   Bennett, returning to Canada at the end of May, declared that the British Government "had frankly communicated the facts of the situation to the Dominion Prime Ministers" and that the latter "had approved measures taken by the British Government for strengthening national defences."[20]   It would seem very unlikely that the Anglo-German Naval Agreement formally concluded in June, 1935, providing the German Navy should not exceed thirty-five per cent. of British naval strength, was not also given their stamp of approval.

That Commonwealth Governments were aware of the threat to peace involved in German rearmament appears both from the approval of plans to strengthen the Covenant and from the considerations on imperial defence.   Yet there was a wide difference between the comments of the Canadian and the South African Prime Ministers after the Jubilee meetings.   Bennett felt it necessary to affirm that "no decision had been taken and no commitments asked for or given."[21]   Nor, he declared, had the British Government "tried to influence the foreign policy of the Dominions in any direction."   The old fear of appearing to be bound to take action in some future situation still outweighed the advantages of solidarity, particularly in the light of the apparent security of Canada's position in the world.   Moreover, it is only fair to say that Bennett realized that his position in Canada was uncertain and that he was unwilling to provide ammunition for an election attack by those sections of Canadian opinion which feared involvement in British wars. Bennett's caution, however, contrasted sharply with Hertzog's outspoken affirmation of solidarity with Britain.   If the Union wanted friends in the world, he said at a civic banquet reception in Capetown on June 10th, then it must stand by Great Britain and the Commonwealth. "Don't let these go," he added amid loud cheers, "because who are the others?"[22]   Partly it was satisfaction because the British Government had agreed to transfer the native territories to the Union in due course,[23] a development originally provided for under the South African Act of Union, delayed because of British dissatisfaction with South African native policy, but long sought for by South Africa to ensure the consolidation of its territory.   But his statement was probably more influenced by recognition of the dangers in the international situation.   Though he declared, "I am an optimist concerning the European situation, I believe that no nation would dare to defy the others and be responsible as the creator of war,"[24] the isolation of South Africa's position underlined its need for British friendship.   Nor, though Hertzog was sympathetic to Germany's claim for equality and hopeful that its acceptance might ease the path of international relations, could he be unaware of the potential dangers of Nazi intrigue in Southwest Africa on the borders of the Union.[25]

The general response of Commonwealth countries to German rearmament thus followed two lines. It was formally accepted in the hope that the achievement of arms equality would satisfy Hitler's demands. The Anglo-German Naval Agreement of June, 1935, was a tangible sign that British policy was directed towards securing good relations with Germany on the basis of arms equality. But in addition to this, attention was given to increasing defences at least in Great Britain and strengthening the League of Nations, both of which might be hoped to act as deterrents to more aggressive German moves. Hence the discussions on defence at the Jubilee meetings, the Committee of Thirteen on Collective Security, and the opposition to Italy's moves against Ethiopia in as far as they threatened to precipitate conflict. Though most members of the British Government appear to have had little of the intellectual conviction on behalf of collective security which animated more than ten million British citizens who voted in the Peace Ballot, they seem to have been convinced ultimately of the value of effective League action against Italy as a deterrent against future German action. Unfortunately for the success of this move, the French Government was to prove almost as reluctant for drastic measures against a fellow member of the Stresa Front as Great Britain had been against Germany.

ITALO-ETHIOPIAN DISPUTES

During the spring of 1935, the situation between Italy and Ethiopia had been assuming increasingly threatening aspects which were only overshadowed by the crisis over Germany's repudiation of the Versailles disarmament provisions. Friction between Italy and Ethiopia was of long standing, particularly over frontier incidents arising frequently from the undefined boundaries between Ethiopia and the adjoining Italian colonies of Eritrea and Somaliland. It had, too, an historical basis, for late in the nineteenth century Ethiopia had only maintained its independence through the defeat of invading Italian armies. In 1906, Great Britain, France, and Italy had recognized each other's interests in this last independent native kingdom of Africa. After World War I, however, Italy apparently constituted itself Ethiopia's sponsor for a time. It pressed with French support for Ethiopia's admission to membership in the League in 1923 despite British and Australian[26] reluctance because of the still backward condition of the country, and signed a Treaty of Arbitration and Conciliation with Ethiopia in 1928. This seeming faith in Ethiopia's potentialities for development appeared justified after 1930 as Emperor Haile Selassie worked shrewdly though necessarily slowly to modernize and centralize his country. Yet there were many elements of barbarism and disorder in Ethiopia which could be and were used by Mussolini as pretexts for the policy of interference on which he embarked in 1935.

The immediate incident out of which trouble arose occurred in December, 1934, at Walwal, which lay in territory whose ownership had long been disputed between Ethiopia and Italy.[27] Italian soldiers in occupation of the waterholes at that spot were forced to retire temporarily in the face of stronger Ethiopian forces. Both sides brought up reinforcements and subsequently fighting broke out in which a number of Italians were killed. The incident was not unlike others which had occurred in the past and had been settled amicably. In this case, however, Haile Selassie would neither accept full responsibility nor renounce his claim to the disputed territory. Mussolini took advantage of this to begin moving troops into Italian East Africa on the excuse of defending the colonies against further Ethiopian aggressions. These moves only served to intensify tension in this area and increasing incidents and fear of a large-scale attack led Ethiopia to appeal to the League.

Alert to potential trouble in the neighbourhood of the Suez Canal, the British Government, where possible in conjunction with the French, used its influence to encourage a settlement through direct negotiations between the disputing parties under their conciliation agreement. At various times during the spring assurances were given on both sides of willingness to seek a settlement. Italy proved generally obstructionist, however, attempting to veto Ethiopia's choice of foreign members for its representatives on the Arbitration Commission and subsequently so to limit its jurisdiction as to cause virtual cessation of its activities. Italian troops continued to move through the Suez Canal to Italian East Africa. In the light of Italian assurance and faced with the threat of German rearmament, the British were hesitant to exert stronger pressure. At Stresa, though the issue appears to have been discussed informally, no official effort was made to persuade Italy to settle its difference with Ethiopia. Italian solidarity with Great Britain and France evidenced by a reaffirmation of the Locarno pledge was at that time looked on as the most important need in the situation.

More blatant pronouncements regarding Italian aims in Africa and obstructionism in the work of arbitration led Eden to take a firm stand, however, at the May meeting of the Council and to demand that the conciliation procedure be concluded by August 25th. In June Sir John Simon was replaced at the Foreign Office by Sir Samuel Hoare, a move generally considered to indicate a firmer tone in British policy, induced in part by the Peace Ballot. Violent anti-British utterances in the Italian press were countered by a British attempt to achieve a settlement through cession of a strip of British territory to Ethiopia to provide it with a corridor to the sea at the port of Zeila in return for which Ethiopia was to give Italy territorial and economic concessions. Not only was this offer rejected by Italy, however, but it also caused French indignation since there had been no prior consultation and French interests in trade through the port of Djibouti might well have been affected. Taken together with the Anglo-German Naval Agreement announced a few days before, it acted to widen the breach between Britain and France and unfortunately did nothing to ease the Italo-Ethiopian situation. Official statements recognizing Italy's need for expansion but emphasizing Britain's intention to uphold the Covenant were no more successful in stopping the movement of troops to Africa. At the end of July, the British Government imposed an arms embargo on both disputants and in company with the French undertook intense diplomatic activity, but again without noticeable effect on Mussolini's preparations for war. Failure of further efforts in August to achieve a settlement either through the Conciliation Commission or through Anglo-French proposals confronted the Council and the Assembly in September with the necessity of taking their stand in the issue, and the British Government with the responsibility of assuming leadership in their deliberations. If action were to be taken, it would only be in response to British initiatives.

By this time it was fairly clear that Mussolini had made up his mind to invade Ethiopia when a favourable opportunity occurred. When this decision had been made is difficult to determine but it seems clear that it was some time between Hitler's repudiation of the disarmament clauses of the Treaty of Versailles on March 16, 1935, and Eden's visit to Rome on June 23rd to propose the cession of Zeila. The date could probably be gauged more exactly if access were had to the records of the Committee of Thirteen on Collective Security, for it is known that in the early period of its work the Italian representative was co-operative in planning for possible sanctions but suddenly became obstructionist thereafter. The change in attitude probably coincided with Mussolini's decision. It seems likely, therefore, that it was reached some time in May. Mussolini could be sure that for the next few months both Britain and France would be deeply concerned with the problems arising out of German rearmament. He may well have felt also that this period offered the best opportunity to conclude his African adventures and return in full force to Europe before Hitler undertook any aggressive move against Austria. These hypotheses suggest that Mussolini could only have been restrained by diplomatic pressure early in the spring and that the firmer tone in British policy which developed in June was too late to influence developments. From that time on, measures as well as influence were necessary to stop Mussolini's plans.

The British had taken the lead both in diplomatic pressure and at League meetings up to that time, however, and it is unfortunate that on the continent, in certain quarters in the Dominions, and even within Britain itself, this leadership was attributed more to imperial interests in the area than to concern for the future of the League. It is worth comparing these comments with those of some right wing Conservatives like Sir Henry Page-Croft, who took the opposite point of view, asserting that there was not enough imperial interest involved to warrant taking such risks against Italy.[28] Editorials by traditionally imperialist papers like the *Daily Mail*[29] and the *Morning Post*[30] opposed any British action. An interdepartmental fact-finding committee set up early in 1935 to estimate the extent of British interests in Ethiopia found no important ones except Lake Tsana, the waters of the Blue Nile, and certain tribal grazing rights.[31] But unfortunately, suspicions, fear of involvement, isolationism, and different interpretations of interest were to hamper efforts to make League action effective. So, too, was the sincere and probably justified belief of many that economic sanctions must lead inevitably to military measures if they were to achieve their purpose.

In the Dominions, there was considerable uneasiness over the situation. In a campaign speech in London, Ontario, King declared on August 15th that the Liberals if elected would not send an expeditionary force overseas without parliamentary approval. Bennett replied that "Canadian troops cannot be despatched overseas to participate in any conflict arising out of the present Ethiopian dispute."[32] A Cabinet minister expressed his opposition to Canadian participation in the Ethiopian trouble and declared that not the life of "one Canadian boy" should be sacrificed. Early in September, before the Assembly opened, Bennett reasserted that Canada should be "kept out of trouble" and should "not be embroiled in any foreign quarrel where the rights of Canadians are not involved."[33] King answered that this assurance was not enough. The Bennett Government's term of office had expired and it had no right "directly or indirectly" to commit Canada "to a stand with respect to what may be done abroad in relation to the possibility of war."[34] He feared that conflict might arise out of economic interests in the Near East and challenged the Prime Minister to say what he would reply to a request from London for action which might lead to war. What his own answer would be was suggested by his reference to the Chanak crisis concerning which he maintained that there was no doubt that "the action of Canada in refusing to plunge into a conflict of which we knew nothing averted action which might have resulted in a perilous war." Lapointe at the same meeting in Quebec City seconded King's views and declared that no interest in Abyssinia was worth the sacrifice of a single Canadian life.[35] Even allowing for the circumstances under which these statements were made, they indicated no enthusiasm on the part of either party for League action. Mr. King had even shown some suspicion that Britain might precipitate an issue over its interests in the Near East and thereby draw Canada into war. Among newspapers only a few like the *Toronto Daily Star*[36] were outspoken in support of British leadership in the League.

In Australia, the Government ranged itself solidly behind the British Government but made no reference to the collective security system. Lyons declared on August 25th that he had pledged Australia "to the hilt" to support British efforts to maintain peace.[37] Hughes, wartime Prime Minister and Vice-President of the Commonwealth Executive Council under Lyons, warned the following day that there was no surer way of "unleashing the dogs of war for another more terrible world conflict than a single-handed attempt by Great Britain to intervene between the Italians and Ethiopians."[38] To attempt to enforce an economic boycott against Italy would be to imperil the existence of the Empire, he maintained, since in the light of Great Britain's naval and air strength in the Mediterranean it was not certain that it would emerge victorious from the struggle. Even if it did win, Britain would be weakened so seriously as to leave it a prey to more powerful nations. These apprehensions indicated that in this situation the Australian Government was concerned with Great Britain's position rather than that of the League. It seems also to have felt that conflict with Italy would offer more threat to the vital Suez Canal route than would any change in Italy's position in East Africa which resulted from its present policy.

Where the Government counselled caution, the Labour party was consolidating in active opposition to any action by Australia. The New South Wales group in a resolution at an anti-war meeting on September 4th declared that it viewed with concern the "cynical disregard of League principles by Great Powers" and expressed its "unflinching determination not to allow Australia to become involved."[39] Its leader, Mr. Lang, subsequently told the press that if the League took action against Italy a general war would start and that Australia should keep out and concentrate upon its interests in the Pacific Ocean.[40]

In contrast, the New Zealand and South African Governments strongly supported British efforts through the League. Endorsing Great Britain's attempt to secure a peaceful settlement, Forbes pointed out that they had undertaken certain responsibilities in signing the Covenant.[41] "I do not think New Zealanders would like us not to stand up to the undertaking," he declared. "We feel that the League of Nations is the hope of the future and that its testing time has come. . . . We are not going to shirk our obligations."   Smuts in an early statement on August 12th appealed for loyal support of the League and felt that if Great Britain and France stood together and took a strong line with Italy, the latter might be persuaded to take a more moderate view.[42]   As to sanctions in case of a conflict between Italy and Ethiopia, Smuts felt sceptical about their application unless all the Great Powers outside as well as inside the League would enforce them.[43] Even if an outbreak occurred, he felt it would not end the League which mankind needed to prevent another world war. In regard to Ethiopia, he indicated his belief that while Italy might overwhelm it "at first go off with aeroplanes and poison gas . . . it is one thing to overwhelm a country and another to occupy it . . . she may find she has bitten off more than she can chew."

In South Africa there was more popular reaction to the situation than in other overseas Dominions. Excitement among the natives of South Africa and popular demonstrations against Italy by white labour groups evidenced widespread sympathy for Ethiopia. On August 12th, the general secretary of the South African Trades and Labour Council protested to the Prime Minister the Union subsidy of meat being exported to Italian troops in East Africa.[44] On August 31st, Capetown dockworkers, supported by the Cape Federation of Trades, refused to load frozen beef for this destination on to an Italian vessel, the *Sabbia*.[45] The move met with divided reactions by the farmers, some of whom opposed supplying meat to the Italian forces while others regarded it as a great opportunity to strengthen local markets by clearing the country of thousands of otherwise unmarketable cattle. The Government, at first cautious in its reaction, finally acted to discourage such unofficial "sanctions" after the General Council of the Cape Federation of Trades decided to make "an appeal to the conscience of South Africa." This attitude of opposition to private boycotts was maintained throughout the conflict, the Government regarding it as the corollary to an equally scrupulous imposition of all officially proposed sanctions.[46]

As the Assembly meetings approached, Hertzog indicated that the Government was prepared for a firm stand. "The League should do its duty and adopt all measures at its disposal," he declared in a formal statement on September 8th, "to secure on the part of the parties to the dispute compliance with the obligation undertaken by them as members of the League and abstention from all hostile acts in conformity with the rules, they, as such members, have undertaken to observe."[47] To this he added a warning at a Free State United Party Congress at Bloemfontaine on September 10th that if South Africa forsook its friends or sent them away it would have to look to its own defences. Smuts endorsed the necessity of adhering to the friendship of the British Commonwealth.[48] A week later at another party congress he declared that he did not believe that economic sanctions would lead to war. If they did so, however, it would not be a British war but one under the Covenant to which South Africa was a signatory.[49] And he warned that, if the League should fail, the world would go "back to the law of the jungle."

This variety of reactions was somewhat reflected in the speeches at the Assembly which opened in Geneva on September 9th. The dispute was before the Council under Article 15 but a Committee of Five, representing Great Britain, France, Poland, Spain, and Turkey, was still attempting mediation. It was with this knowledge that Assembly speeches were made, and also in the hope of providing restraint on Italy through a demonstration of international public opinion.

Beginning the general discussion on September 11th, Sir Samuel Hoare provided the key-note by endorsing the principles of collective security as assuming "a scrupulous respect for all treaty obligations" and particularly no resort to war for the settlement of disputes in violation of the Covenant.[50] In words often quoted,[51] he declared that Great Britain stood for the "collective maintenance of the Covenant in its entirety, and particularly for steady and collective resistance to all acts of unprovoked aggression." This was a principle of international action to which the British people and their Government held "with firm, enduring, and universal persistence." True, he pointed out the difficulties faced by the League through its lack of universality and declared, "There are too many empty chairs at our table. We want no more," a suggestion that Italy should be kept within the League. True, too, he emphasized that "if the burden is to be borne, it must be borne collectively. If risks for peace are to be run, they must be run by all. The security of the many cannot be ensured solely by the efforts of a few, however powerful they may be." In these latter respects the speech conformed to the traditional League attitude of

British Conservatism. But the uncompromising stand expressed in those parts of the speech first quoted appeared to, and in some measure did, herald a new day in British support of the League. The question was how far that support extended.

Conditioning the answer to this question was the fact that the day before Hoare had wrung a reluctant consent from Laval to the imposition of certain economic sanctions only by agreeing, as the latter subsequently made known to the Chamber of Deputies, "upon ruling out military sanctions, not adopting any measure of naval blockade, never contemplating the closure of the Suez Canal—in a word, ruling out everything that might lead to war."[52] Behind this stand by Laval was the fear of a German-Italian *rapprochement* if the latter country were thwarted by force from achieving its objective. Despite the definiteness with which Laval outlined this assurance, it was not a formal pledge restricting British freedom of action. But particularly in relation to Hoare's emphasis on common action, it indicated the unlikelihood that more forcible measures would be taken if economic sanctions were ineffective. Behind Hoare's brave words, therefore, was the fact that if Italy went to war, there was Anglo-French agreement that restraint through League action should be exercised on a basis of limited liability. To succeed, economic sanctions would have to be effective without provoking Mussolini to regard them as an act of war. Thus from the beginning, the attempt was made, at least in private conversations, to draw a line between measures which would handicap Italy in its struggle with Ethiopia and those which might provoke it to hostilities against League states. In Canada and Australia, it had already been suggested that no such line could be drawn.

In their Assembly speeches, the representatives of these two Dominions attempted to preserve a balance between support of the collective system and the heartfelt hope that collective action would not become necessary. Bruce noted that the Assembly was meeting "under the shadow of a great political issue," involving "the whole structure which has been erected since the great war for the maintenance of peace by collective action."[53] The external policies of countries must be based on the principles of renunciation of war and of collective action for the maintenance of peace. But in illustrating the expression of these principles he added to the Covenant, the Kellogg Pact and Locarno, the agreements concluded at Stresa, thereby shrewdly pointing out the complex division of interests which complicated the situation. The Hon. G. Howard Ferguson, High Commissioner in London under Bennett's Government, "devoutly . . . hoped that a peaceful solution" might be found by the Council which was "based upon principles of equity and justice."[54]   On behalf of his Government, however, he declared that if such a solution could not be reached "Canada will join with the other Members of the League in considering how by unanimous action, peace can be maintained." Both speeches were cautious, but the Canadian indicated that if the break came, his country would support whatever action was agreed upon.

As might have been expected from earlier declarations, the speeches by the representatives of New Zealand, the Irish Free State, and South Africa were far less reserved. Sir James Parr supported Hoare's declaration "without reservation" and recognized that the responsibility under the Covenant was "not for one but for all of us."[55] Speaking for "a small nation," he pointed out that "It is the small nations that will lose most if the principle of collective security breaks down." And he added, "The League of Nations has failed greatly to keep the peace on other occasions; I pray that it will not fail now, for it cannot afford to fail again." Both the Irish and South African speeches echoed this belief that the League was facing its last chance. "Make no mistake," declared de Valera, "if on any pretext whatever we were to permit the sovereignty of even the weakest State amongst us to be unjustly taken away, the whole foundation of the League would crumble into dust. . . . If the Covenant is not observed as a whole for all and by all, then there is no Covenant."[56]

For both the Irish Free State and South Africa, this particular issue of a threatened Italian attack upon an African state raised special problems.   To the Irish Free State, most Catholic of countries, it was a hard test, as de Valera made clear, to take a stand against the homeland of the Holy See. ". . . to oppose those whom we admire and would welcome an occasion to serve—what more heart-rending alternative can there be to the abandonment of duty and the betrayal of our deepest convictions and of our word solemnly given?" he asked. But he gave his own answer in declaring, "It is a hard price, but harder still and more terrible is the future in store for us if we should fail to be ready to pay it. . . ."

From the other side, te Water, speaking as the representative of "the one permanent and indigenous white civilization in Africa," focussed the danger of a new partition of Africa, "danger to the adventuring nations themselves, danger to the black peoples of Africa, and menace to our own white civilization."[57] The "fundamental concept" of South Africa was that the native had "no concern in the white man's madnesses and wars."   It lay in danger of being shattered by "the slow and apparently relentless march of the disease of war into our continent. Let it never be forgotten:" he urged, "the long memory of Black Africa never forgets and never forgives an injury or an injustice." Then turning to the Great Powers, he appealed to Italy to "pause and consider even at this eleventh hour" and voiced the hope that the protestations of Great Britain and France to the Assembly could be depended upon.

It was noteworthy that among the Dominion delegates the most outspoken speeches had been by representatives of countries most directly affected by the controversy, South Africa and the Irish Free State: the one because the threatened dispute was in his own continent, the other because of the bonds of religion existing between his state and that which lay in danger of being stamped as an aggressor. New Zealand had echoed the words of the British Foreign Secretary though those which gave the greatest indication of support for collective security. Canada had reiterated its hope of peaceful settlement but noted its readiness to assume obligations should events make it necessary. Australia had gone no further than to endorse the principles of the League but without committing itself to action. Despite the apparent similarity of general support of collective security, the speeches probably indicated in fact as wide a divergence on the issue of how security could best be maintained as had yet appeared within the Commonwealth.

In comparison with the speeches of representatives of other small states, those of Canada and Australia were matched in restraint only by that of Belgium.[58] The Scandinavian countries also asserted that no possibilities should be overlooked which might lead to a pacific settlement of the dispute.[59] None the less, they stated clearly that support of the Covenant was the fundamental issue at stake. The spokesman of the Little Entente defined their attitude as unswerving allegiance to and dependence on the League of Nations.[60] Closer to the note struck by Australia was the speech by Laval which combined a declaration of loyalty to the Covenant and solidarity with Great Britain with an assertion of the value of France's new-found friendship with Italy. Conciliation still remained the hope of the French Prime Minister, and at all stages of the dispute was to continue to do so.

On September 28th, the Assembly adjourned, having completed its ordinary business. Ten days earlier, the Council's Committee of Five had proposed a plan for international assistance to Ethiopia and certain economic and territorial concessions to Italy by Great Britain and France. This was rejected as brusquely by Mussolini as earlier Anglo-French proposals had been. The Committee of Five announced its failure on September 24th and the Committee of Thirteen (comprising all Council members except Italy) undertook its task of drafting a report under Article 15, paragraph 4. Before it was completed Italian forces crossed the Ethiopian border and on October 3rd a battle was in progress.

Mediation and attempted restraint through declarations had failed. The members of the League were confronted with the necessity of taking action if they were to uphold the principles to which they had pledged themselves.

The Organization of League Action

On October 7th the thirteen neutral members of the Council adopted unanimously a report that "the Italian Government has resorted to war in disregard of its covenants under Article 12," and also the report drafted under Article 15, paragraph 4. Thereby these countries pledged themselves to action under Article 16. On October 9th, the Assembly resumed its work and for two days listened to speeches on the momentous decision before the League, none of which were by representatives of the Dominions. Italy opened the debate by justifying its action as self-defence and the expression of its "new spirit." It stressed the fact that there had been no talk of sanctions in either the Sino-Japanese or the Paraguay-Bolivian conflicts.[61] Austria, Hungary, and Albania refused to take part in the application of sanctions against Italy, and Switzerland made a reservation. But the rest of the states of the League followed the British lead that "Action must now be taken."[62] Before the close of the general debate, it had been decided to set up a committee "to consider and facilitate the co-ordination" of the measures contemplated under the obligations of Article 16.[63]

The Co-ordination Committee composed of one delegate from each participating Member of the League and declared to be "a Conference of States Members meeting to consult together with a view to the application of the provisions of Article 16"[64] began sessions on October 11th. It set up in turn a Committee of Eighteen which was to guide the work of the larger body. This Committee of Eighteen included in its membership nine of the states which had been represented on the Committee of Thirteen on Collective Security: Great Britain, Canada, France, the Netherlands, Poland, Spain, Turkey, the Soviet Union, and Yugoslavia. South Africa also became a member of the Committee of Eighteen. The centre for the organization of sanctions, it soon became apparent that the Committee of Eighteen would build substantially upon the work of the earlier Committee.[65]

During its deliberations between April and August, the Committee of Thirteen had considered all types of sanctions both direct and indirect.[66] Its original emphasis had been upon means of preventing an aggressor country from securing commodities essential for war. The first proposal for this purpose was that the aggressor should be cut off from certain raw materials such as zinc and nickel. This would have placed the main burden of sacrifice on raw material producing countries like Canada, and Riddell, its delegate on the Committee, had worked consistently to broaden the basis of sanctions so that their impact would fall more equally. This involved suggesting additional materials such as oil and also other types of sanctions such as financial restrictions and exclusion of imports. Despite the obstructionism of the Italian member, who attempted in the later meetings of the Committee to limit its proposals for sanctions to a small number of articles, the view that sanctions should be comprehensive and broadly based was generally adopted in the Committee.

For the speedy devising of the sanctions programme by the Committee of Eighteen, it was of the utmost importance that such careful consideration had already been given to the types of pressures which could be imposed.[67] In some measure because of the similarity of membership between the Committee of Thirteen and the Committee of Eighteen, the meetings of the latter could be looked on as a continuation of the former, the more so as both bodies functioned in private. That some of its members such as Riddell so considered it is evidenced by the informal citing in the Committee of Eighteen of earlier discussions in the other body. Not only did these considerations form a general background to the work of organizing sanctions against Italy but the stand which Riddell had taken in the earlier Committee in favour of broadening the basis of sanctions and equalizing sacrifices was to form the key-note of his attitude in subsequent discussions.

With impressive rapidity, the Committee of Eighteen proceeded to organize the programme of sanctions against Italy. In the first meeting on the afternoon of October 11th, Canada was brought into some prominence through a vigorous speech by Ferguson in favour of immediate action.[68] In response to a statement by the Argentine delegate which he interpreted as suggesting delay on technicalities, Ferguson declared that "a stage has been reached at which, if the League was to be taken seriously by the world, it was absolutely essential that it should take some definite progressive action. . . . Let them show the world that the League would no longer be scoffed or laughed at, but that it meant business. . . ." He proposed the imposition of an arms embargo and the suggestion was quickly endorsed by Eden. It was agreed to adopt the list of arms issued by President Roosevelt under the Neutrality Act with the addition of powder and explosives. The proposal to lift arms embargoes from Ethiopia and impose a general embargo on export of arms to Italy was referred to the Co-ordination

Committee at once and adopted unanimously that evening. A definite step had been taken through the initiative of the Canadian and British delegates on the first day of the consideration of sanctions.

The following day, te Water proposed adding "moral sanctions" and breaking diplomatic relations with Italy.[69] There was reluctance for this among the other delegates, however, in particular Madariaga of Spain whose country's fear of antagonizing Italy was reflected frequently in the discussions. Subsequently when Hertzog was asked if te Water acted under instructions in making this proposal, he replied that "Mr. te Water spoke as a member of the Committee of Eighteen; Members of this committee do not in their discussions speak on behalf of their Governments."[70] Later the Prime Minister declared that Italy had said it would regard severing of relations as an act of war.[71] The measure was, in fact, never given serious consideration as a sanction, perhaps for this reason.

Discussion was speedily undertaken, however, on the other major types of sanctions which were to be imposed against Italy. Eden proposed barring Italian imports and estimated that this would cut off about seventy per cent. of Italy's export trade.[72] He was strongly supported by Riddell, who pointed out that the Committee of Thirteen had had little or no difficulty in dealing with this question.[73] The French delegate asked for a sub-committee to consider measures whereby the Covenant-breaking state could be deprived directly of "the material means for carrying on the war."[74] He suggested that these would include "the key products of war manufactures; metals, minerals, chemical products, machine tools, to which should be added means of transport, such as ships, and everything utilizable for means of transport, such as fuel oil, coal, lubricating oil, etc." Te Water urged a parallel examination of both plans which were referred to the Sub-Committee on Economic Measures and subsequently formed the basis for Proposals III and IV.[75] Te Water also endorsed the principle of compensation for loss of trade through imposition of sanctions[76] but though mutual assistance formed Proposal V, it never became very effective. These three proposals were adopted by the Co-ordination Committee on October 19th. The other of the five sanctions measures which were presented to Governments in the course of the month provided for a ban on credits to Italy and was voted October 14th as Proposal II. In the remarkably short time of nine days, a fairly comprehensive programme of sanctions had been drawn up and approved by a committee representing 52 states members of the League. The wheels were turning to bring pressure to bear upon Italy.

None the less, from the beginning hesitations and reservations were noticeable. These had led to another vigorous statement by Ferguson at the opening of the fourth meeting of the Committee of Eighteen on October 14th.[77] Pointing to the substantial sacrifices the sanctions programme would impose on Canada as a raw material producing country, he declared that he had hoped that other nations "would share the burden with Canada." If, however, "by a process of disintegration, one country after another was going to discover difficulties so great that they thought they could not face them, then let the delegations go home . . . if public confidence in the League was to be maintained, and if the delegates were to have the support of the world behind them, they must stand together."

The speech was not particularly important in its effect upon proceedings but it is significant both in relation to the reputation which Canada was suddenly acquiring for forceful action and as an indication of the problems which the attempt to organize sanctions was encountering. The British Government seems to have had to exert a good deal of pressure on certain other countries (not within the Commonwealth) "in order to induce them to act up to their assumed part in the common undertaking."[78] The effort to establish a comprehensive sanctions programme had to proceed from the very beginning against the handicap of technical objections and the citing of special circumstances by some of those pledged to organize it. In the light of these reservations, the attitude assumed by the Canadian representative was the more noticeable. It meant that subsequent Canadian suggestions would be treated with particular interest. These circumstances also point up the difficulties encountered by British leadership and indicate the force of the drive which Eden put behind the sanctions programme.

REACTIONS WITHIN THE COMMONWEALTH

In the meantime, feeling was consolidating in Commonwealth countries, behind or against sanctions. All accepted and enforced the five sanctions proposals forwarded to them from Geneva in October. But there was considerable variety of opinion within each member of the Commonwealth as to what should and would be the extent and consequences of sanctions. There was also a variety of reasons why individual Governments supported sanctions.

In Great Britain itself, there was widespread public support for sanctions. The Labour Opposition had endorsed Hoare's September speech in Geneva and gave strong and virtually unanimous support to the sanctions programme. Left wing groups like the Independent

Labour party and the Socialist League accused the orthodox Labour party of supporting the Tories in an imperialistic programme. In contrast the Communist party supported sanctions. The extreme pacifist group represented by Mr. Lansbury and Lord Ponsonby found difficulty in approving forcible action. But the main body of the Labour party stood unwaveringly behind an enforcement of the Covenant though Attlee warned that the League should not be used as a cloak for imperialism. Lloyd George, on behalf of the Liberal party, expressed support of Hoare's speech in September but criticized the Government for applying economic sanctions so late.[79] To this Eden pointed out that sanctions could not be instituted under the Covenant until after aggression had occurred.[80] Among Conservative, non-ministerial groups, Mr. Churchill[81] and Sir Austen Chamberlain[82] supported the Government in its League action. The most trenchant criticism came from the right wing Conservatives like Mr. Amery, who felt that sanctions would not achieve their purpose, and declared, "I am not prepared to send a single Birmingham lad to his death for the sake of Abyssinia."[83]

This fear that action against Italy might result in an attack upon the obvious promoter of League action had led the British Government to undertake a precautionary strengthening of the British fleet in the Mediterranean as early as the middle of September. Despite Italian protests in October, and a French request, the British Government refused to reduce the Mediterranean Fleet to a normal footing until, it was reported,[84] Italian troops were withdrawn from Ethiopia. In addition to strengthening its forces, the British sought and secured French assurance of support in case of an unprovoked attack. These were made formal on October 10th, when the French Government pledged itself to "unlimited solidarity of action in the matter of military, air, and naval assistance" in the event of an attack by a Covenant-breaking state arising out of measures taken under Article 16.[85] At the same time, however, the British Government pledged itself not to take "the initiative in any measure against Italy which would not be in conformity with the decisions taken, or to be taken, by the League of Nations in full agreement with France." In this way, France secured the right of veto over any subsequent sanctions measures Great Britain might wish to institute. Valuable as was this pledged solidarity, it resulted in fact in restricting British freedom of action. Moreover, these moves and counter-moves helped to strengthen the fear in some quarters that action through the League might lead to an Anglo-Italian conflict.

This fear seems to have been particularly prevalent in Australia. When its Parliament reassembled on September 23rd, the Prime Minister had proposed that since neither Italy nor Ethiopia had yet violated the provisions of the Covenant, there should be no consideration of action which might be taken in future contingencies.[86] The Deputy Leader of the Federal Labour party, however, immediately expressed apprehension lest the Commonwealth Government should have already committed Australia "right up to the hilt" and thereby have "blundered" into a situation which might involve Australia in war. While not seeking to justify Italy's action, he hinted that imperialistic motives were at the basis of the concern over Ethiopia. His party, he declared, "wanted no war on foreign fields for economic treasure. It wanted Australia to be kept free of entanglements leading to a repetition of the horrors of 1914-1918." It opposed participation therefore. The Federal representatives of the Labour party of New South Wales were even more outspoken in their opposition to any move which might lead to war and in their suspicion that the League had become a political machine of the dominant powers. They favoured a policy of absolute isolation and strict neutrality. In particular they declared that they would not support "a war camouflaged as sanctions." They moved an amendment to the Prime Minister's statement noting their alarm that *H.M.A.S. Australia* with an Australian crew had been despatched by the British Admiralty "to the war zone" (i.e. to join the Mediterranean fleet). They requested its immediate recall (from its period of exchange with a British vessel), declaring that the application of sanctions would not be supported and that the neutrality of Australia should be formally announced.

Government spokesmen replying when the debate was resumed on October 9th made comparatively little effort to endorse the collective security system as such, but affirmed solidarity with Great Britain and the rest of the Commonwealth. Dr. Earle Page of the United Country party, part of the governing coalition, declared that it was a matter of "natural precaution" for Great Britain to take reasonable means to protect "their imperial interests." He questioned also whether the parliamentary statements of the two Labour leaders had in fact represented the feeling of labour throughout the country, noting that the Government had received letters from many labour organizations calling on it to take every step in co-operation with the British Government to prevent aggressive war, to preserve peace, and even to impose full sanctions. Curtin, leader of the Federal Labour party and soon to be acknowledged leader of a united Labour party, acknowledged that they could not be indifferent to the fate of Ethiopia and agreed that an economic boycott was the most effective means of preventing war. He believed, however, that such a boycott was unworkable as long as so many major nations were outside the League. Under the circumstances he maintained that Australia's primary obligation was to the Kellogg Pact which he interpreted to mean that its people should not take up arms in any event except the defence of their own position when attacked by an enemy. On behalf of the party, he submitted that an attempt to enforce the provisions of Article 16 would subject the League to a strain which it would be impossible to endure and which would prove detrimental to Australia, to the British Empire, and to the League of Nations itself.

To this challenge, the Government could do no more than threaten that failure to support Great Britain in case of war would mean secession. This would leave Australia isolated, declared the Attorney General, and overwhelmed by the effort necessary to ensure its own defence. When challenged on the right of Australia to declare war and peace for itself, Menzies declared that he denied "Australia's right to go mad." As long as the League policy was the right one for Great Britain, South Africa, and Canada, it was the right one for Australia.

The strength of the Labour opposition was indicated by the fact that on division the amendment was rejected only by 27 votes to 21. That the Government was right in thinking that this stand did not represent the unanimous opinion of Labour was evidenced by a subsequent declaration of the Tasmanian Labour party that Australia was morally bound to uphold the obligations of the Covenant.[87] "How can we demand sanctions when attacked," they asked, "if in time of difficulty and danger we leave the weaker League members to fend for themselves?" The New South Wales Labour Council divided between those who urged support of sanctions as the only possible means of preventing general conflict and the Lang group which successfully argued that Australia would gain nothing by a "foreign war."[88] It finally decided to support a policy of neutrality in the Ethiopian crisis and to define defence as resistance to actual attack. The actual outbreak of hostilities in Africa led the Federal and State Labour parties to unite, however, under the leadership of Curtin, on the platform of opposition to sanctions against Italy which it was believed would lead to war. In some concession to imperial unity, it was declared that war in defence of well-defined imperial interests was one thing, but that war to uphold the vague theories of the Covenant was quite another.[89]

This opposition and its own doubts and fears put the Commonwealth Government in a difficult position. On the outbreak of hostilities, Lyons stated publicly that Australians were "greatly disappointed" at the failure of Great Britain and the League to settle the Ethiopian dispute peacefully.[90] "All our efforts," he declared, "will be directed towards confining the trouble within the narrowest limits, simultaneously giving the League the fullest support to effect a peaceful settlement." When sanctions proposals were received from Geneva, the Government introduced a bill to make them effective. In moving the second reading on October 31st, Menzies declared that the freedom to accept or reject the recommendations for economic sanctions was "nominal rather than real."[91] He acknowledged that resistance to economic sanctions might involve conflict but maintained that if the "remote possibility of armed resistance" was to deter them from taking measures against an aggressor, they would have abandoned the principle of collective security and returned to a state of international anarchy. In any case, he pointed out, sanctions were collective and if other countries broke their obligations under the Covenant, those now willing to take action would be at liberty to reconsider their position.

The Labour party maintained its opposition, however, on the ground that sanctions were inevitably linked to war because resistance to economic sanctions would compel Great Britain to take military or naval action, and Australia would then be faced with the decision whether or not to support Great Britain in war. Since sanctions threatened "to plunge Australia into the perilous vortex of European conflicts," the Labour party would vote against the sanctions bill. It did so, and the bill was passed only by 30 votes to 24, becoming law on November 15, 1935.

Despite the unanimity of view of Australian Labour's political representatives, there was probably still considerable division of feeling within the ranks of labour at large. Early in October it was reported that while some felt that Australia's remoteness made it necessary not to do anything involving it in the dispute, others argued that if Australian workers did nothing, they could not expect support from workers in other countries in the event of a future war affecting Australia directly.[92] What influence the Catholicism of a large group of Australian labour had upon its opinions is difficult to ascertain. Probably more influential was the fear of war and the belief that League action was motivated by imperialist interests. Towards the end of November, the All-Australian Trades Union Congress voted 78 to 41 against the imposition of sanctions on the ground that they "committed organized labour to support the sending of armed forces overseas to take part in a capitalist war."[93] An amendment proposed by the Railwaymen's Union supporting the refusal of supplies to Italy was rejected as contrary to the Congress' neutrality policy. But by a large majority there was also rejected a proposal for a general strike in the event war broke out which involved Australia, though it was decided to urge workers to refuse to produce goods for use in a "capitalistic" war. The Federal Council of the

Returned Soldiers League, on the other hand, approved British action in supporting collective security as the only hope of world peace, and as the only possible justification for going to war in a conflict which did not touch Australia directly.[94]

Behind the uncertainties and extremist views on developments in this crisis was the lack in Australia of a well-developed sentiment in favour of the League of Nations.[95] Though among prominent newspapers, the *Sydney Morning Herald* (New South Wales) and *The Age* (Victoria) had generally supported the League system, other papers were sceptical of its value as constituted.[96] During the Italo-Ethiopian conflict, *The Bulletin*, for example, was avowedly hostile to the League. Though the press expressed a general belief in a collective system if it were effective, the actual efforts of the League seem to have met with comparatively little sympathy. Nor, though the actual imposition of sanctions roused some enthusiasm, were there groups within the country which had developed the kind of sentiment in Australia which was reflected in Great Britain in the Peace Ballot.

Even Government circles appear to have been concerned to support Great Britain rather than the League of Nations. None the less, when W. M. Hughes, a member of the Cabinet, published at the beginning of November a book entitled *Australia and War Today*[97] attacking the weaknesses of the League, declared world peace could not be maintained without armed force, and asserted that "economic sanctions are . . . either an empty gesture or war," the Prime Minister asked for his resignation. Though Hughes declared himself wholeheartedly behind the Act imposing sanctions against Italy, the fact that Labour members in their opposition to it had made effective use of his book led the Federal Council of the parties forming the Government to insist that he be made to retire. In the telegram requesting his resignation, Lyons declared that Hughes' statement regarding economic sanctions "strikes at the root of the Government's support of the League and also at its loyal discharge of the Covenant's obligations. . . ."[98] In February, 1936, Hughes was taken back into the Cabinet again after making a long declaration on his support of the ideals of collective security and of the Government's policy as directed towards these ends.[99] In fact, however, it would seem that the Commonwealth Government was chiefly influenced during the Italo-Ethiopian conflict by its fear lest the war should become general or spread more widely in the area of the Mediterranean or Suez Canal. While ostensibly supporting the British stand at the League, the influence of Australia was probably thrown on the side of restraining Great Britain from sponsoring too drastic a policy of sanctions against Italy.

In sharp contrast to the situation in Australia, there was comparative unanimity in New Zealand in support of collective security. The outbreak of hostilities and the decision regarding sanctions roused public opinion to an intense interest in the League of Nations and the particular circumstances of the conflict. A correspondent reported that "the Abyssinian question has stirred New Zealand from north to south. . . . The League and what will eventuate is the topic of conversation among all sections of the community. It seems universally accepted that the League of Nations must be justified and supported by all nations even at great cost."[100] When, because of early prorogation of Parliament, a bill was introduced on October 23rd to confer power on the Government to provide by Order-in-Council for the application of sanctions under the Covenant, the Prime Minister could point out that it had been prepared in collaboration with the Leader of the Opposition.[101] In this matter, he declared, there was no question of party politics or difference of opinion. Both British and New Zealand policies had no other aim than to preserve peace and prevent war. It could still be hoped that the collective system might prevent a recurrence of the anarchy of the past. He was endorsed heartily by Mr. Savage, leader of the Labour party and soon to become Prime Minister, who declared that Labour's passion for peace made it necessary for them to support the collective action of the League. Stopping supplies to the aggressor would bring them nearer "to the principles advocated by the Prince of Peace."

The bill included a specific provision stating that it did not authorize either compulsory training or conscription for service in New Zealand or abroad, and that it did not limit "reasonable criticism" of the Act. This had been drawn up, as Savage pointed out, with particular reference to unfortunate memories of experiences during the former war. While these provisions met with general approval in the House of Representatives, it is interesting to note that in the Legislative Council where the same general unanimity of opinion was demonstrated, several speakers felt that the bill should have made provision for New Zealand to participate in naval and military measures if these should become necessary. One member went so far as to say that "if the League is really in earnest to end the present war as soon as possible, why not bring into being its strongest weapon—the combined Military Forces of the rest of the world—against the aggressors. . . . Every country," he added, "that believes in the principles of the League should be prepared to conscript the whole of its manhood and wealth to make an example of those who break the principles of the League and so secure peace."[102] These suggestions that even stronger means should be used to enforce peace form an interesting background to later proposals by the New Zealand Labour Government for increasing the authority and effective power of the League. The debates in general demonstrated a new concern for the success of the collective system.

The Governments of South Africa and the Irish Free State had been the most outspoken in support of effective implementation of the Covenant in the early stages of the dispute. Both adopted sanctions when they were proposed. On October 9th, when the Assembly began discussion of action after war had broken out, the South African Government instructed its representative at Geneva to support whatever action was taken against Italy. On the same day, the Dominion party assured the Prime Minister of its full support in any action which the Government might take jointly with Great Britain and other members of the Empire in imposing collective economic sanctions on Italy.[103] Since Parliament was not in session, the Malanite party had no official opportunity to express the opposition which it was to make known so forcibly in January, 1936. Sanctions were instituted by Orders-in-Council and appear to have met with fairly general support. Feeling among the natives against Italy was reported to be high in Natal during October and the few Italian businesses were being boycotted.[104]

Speaking on Armistice Day, General Smuts hailed the spirit of activity of the League of Nations which had arisen out of the new sense of the grave dangers confronting countries.[105] He believed that the League was finding its feet and "would more and more stand forth as a determined foe to that Imperialism, that spirit of aggressive expansion and annexation characteristic of the old pre-War order, which it was fondly thought was killed in the Great War, but which was once more showing its horrid head in world affairs." The message of Armistice Day, he believed, was "Long live the League of Nations."

In the Irish Free State, though there was a surface agreement between the two major parties and the Labour party over the Act to make possible the application of sanctions, the debate on November 6, 1935, heard echoes of the recriminations which had been hurled at de Valera since his speech in the Assembly.[106] It had been charged that de Valera had pledged support to Great Britain, that he was blindly following the British lead and that he was threatening the Irish people with conscription in the interests of Great Britain. During the second reading of the bill, certain speakers declared that the Free State should have exacted concessions from Great Britain as the price of their support of the Covenant. But other speakers applauded the Government for not giving effect "to the old doctrine . . . that Great Britain's difficulty is Ireland's opportunity."

De Valera maintained a firm stand throughout the debate, asserting that the imposition of sanctions was an obligation entered into at the time when the Free State became a member of the League. However much he regretted it, he saw no alternative to taking action against Italy, since Italy had taken the law into its own hands. In regard to conscription, he stated categorically that "in my opinion, we have no legal or moral obligation to engage in military sanctions." The second reading of the bill passed with only three members dissenting and its final passage was opposed only by two members.

A subsequent attempt to rescind the sanctions order was made on November 28th on a motion brought forward by one of the Deputies who had opposed the bill.[107] Citing speeches against sanctions by Roman Catholic prelates (including the rector of the Irish college in Rome, Archbishop Mannix of Australia and Father Coughlin in the United States) to prove his point that the measures taken against Italy were iniquitous, he asked, "Are we going to do our little bit to starve the nation that has given Europe her civilization, the nation that has been the cradle of Christianity and the spiritual home of all Catholics in all ages?"[108] Moreover, he declared, public opinion was unanimously against sanctions. Others suggested that they involved the country in "a sort of war" and asked why Ireland should participate if the Great Powers were not serious enough to impose oil sanctions. Opposition to the motion was overwhelming, however, and only four Deputies voted for it. Mr. McGilligan of the Opposition gave the most biting comment, declaring there should be "no nonsense hereafter and no weakling attitude in respect of Italy on the grounds of religion."[109]

The far-sighted view taken by most of the deputies that collective security was an essential safeguard for a small country seems to have found little reflection in public opinion. No well-defined sentiment either in favour of or opposed to sanctions seems to have developed in the Irish Free State. But there was a kind of bewilderment among the Irish people that the Free State should be participating in measures against Italy, the home of their religion and the foreign country most familiar to them. Nor could they understand why for once they were on the same side of a dispute with Great Britain. It was with realization of these attitudes that de Valera had said to the Assembly that the issue of sanctions against Italy was perhaps more difficult for the Irish Free State than for any other League member. Yet he refused to compromise so long as there appeared any hope that sanctions could be successful.

In Canada, the parliamentary election was in the forefront of interest during October, 1935, but there had already been indications of divided reactions to developments at Geneva. Ontario C.C.F. candidates in the Federal election agreed in September that Canada should sever diplomatic, trade, and financial relations with Italy if it were declared an aggressor but opposed sending any troops to assist the League as constituted.[110] "The C.C.F. refuses to allow Canada to be involved in a war fought to make the world safe for capitalism," they declared. "It stands resolutely opposed to all imperialist wars, and at two national conventions has unanimously declared itself in favour of neutrality in the event of war." In contrast, the Canadian Trades and Labour Congress, meeting in Halifax two days later, ranged itself alongside the British Trades Congress in its support of collective security.[111] Only half a dozen of the two hundred delegates, representing more than a hundred thousand workers throughout Canada, did not endorse the resolution calling upon the Canadian Government to participate fully in support of the Covenant as a whole and in applying sanctions against Italy as a means of maintaining peace, and even in the event of war. As sanctions were speedily organized at Geneva during October, considerable respect was evidenced in many quarters and fresh hopes that League action could prove itself effective. The Conservative ministry, whose representative had taken such a firm stand in support of implementing sanctions once the decision to impose them had been made, immediately approved the sanctions proposal transmitted from Geneva.

Feeling was far from unanimous, however, in support of an active rôle in League action. The most bitter cause of division was over British policy towards Italy. Public opinion, though hostile to Mussolini and his régime, remained sympathetic towards the Italian people. "It is true in Canada, at any rate," wrote the *Winnipeg Free Press*, "that there is no animosity to Italy as a nation."[112] Internationalist groups, however, condemned its action and felt that the League decision had been inevitable. But many French Canadian newspapers, in contrast, supported Italy's action, criticized the stand taken by Great Britain, and opposed Canadian participation in sanctions. *La Renaissance*, a weekly published in Montreal, was particularly active in championing Italian policy and impugning British motives.[113] It reproduced at length attacks on Great Britain by the French Fascist and Royalist Press and argued that Canada should abstain from helping to coerce Italy. *Le Soleil*, a Liberal paper published in Quebec City, spoke of "haughty England" and of its determination to humble Italy, either by fear or by force and arrogance. *La Patrie* and *Le Devoir*, the organ of Bourassa, veteran Nationalist leader, also attacked British policy. On the other hand, *L'Evenement* of Quebec defended it.[114]

Nor were French Canadian papers the only ones sceptical of British motives, some English publications expressing the fear that British "interests are at stake in East Africa, and so she's got the League to pull her chestnuts out of the fire."[115]   To this the *Vancouver Sun* retorted editorially, "if it had not been for the League's spirit in the world there would have been another general war long before this. . . . Before they criticize Britain for using every available peaceful means to 'pull her chestnuts out of the fire' they should decide what the United States would do if Japan marched into California.   After all, they're Britain's chestnuts."

Unfortunately suspicion of British imperialism tended in some Canadian quarters as in Australia to overshadow the significance of the effort being made on behalf of collective security.   Among naturally isolationist groups, like the French Canadians, sympathies for Italy because of religious reasons embittered feeling towards League action. The not insignificant body of opinion intellectually convinced of the necessity of a strong system of collective security had not permeated the general public to anything like the same extent as in Great Britain. It remained to be seen whether the solid French Canadian bloc within the Liberal party and the anti-imperialist feeling which had marked its policy during a considerable part of the inter-war period would be reflected in the party's attitude towards sanctions, or whether support of collective security might be looked on as a counterbalance to the relation with Great Britain.   For the Federal election swept Mr. King into office at the end of October with one of the largest majorities which a Canadian Government had ever had.

On assuming office, King immediately announced that the Government would take the necessary steps to secure "effective application" of the economic sanctions against Italy proposed by the Co-ordination Committee.[116]   In maintaining "its continued and firm adherence to the fundamental aims and ideals of the League of Nations, and its intention to make participation in the League the cornerstone of its foreign policy in the general field" the Government had no doubt that it expressed "the overwhelming conviction" of the people of Canada.   At the same time, the Prime Minister emphasized that the Canadian Government did not recognize any commitment binding Canada to adopt military sanctions.   Moreover, he declared, "the Government's course in approving economic sanctions in this instance is not to be regarded as necessarily establishing a precedent for future action."   Such League proposals as had been made up to that time had been approved but there was no commitment to future action, particularly such as might involve the use of force.

In a subsequent declaration later in November in answer to a letter sent by the Italian Government to all States represented on the Co-ordination Committee the Canadian Government made clear its awareness of the significance of the decision it had made in imposing sanctions.[117] The Italian statement maintained that the Co-ordination Committee was not a League organ and placed direct responsibility on individual Governments for whatever measures they instituted. It called their attention to the gravity of the situation and asked for a precise statement of how they intended to apply sanctions. In reply, the Canadian Government declared that "they have always believed that their membership in the League of Nations implied the acceptance of the obligations set forth in the Covenant to which they have tried to make their conduct conform." In so interpreting their obligations, they declared further they were confident that "they are expressing the overwhelming conviction of the people of Canada." Mindful of Canada's long friendship with Italy, they "are anxious, so far as lies within their power as a member State of the League of Nations, to facilitate, at the earliest possible moment a settlement of the regrettable conflict now in progress." But they trusted that the Government of Italy "may yet see their way to view their obligations under the Covenant in the same light" as had the Assembly of the League and Canada "as a free and sovereign nation." It was, at the least, an indication of loyal support of existing commitments.

The varied responses within Commonwealth countries to the first attempt to organize sanctions in support of collective security reflected the wide differences in opinion among their peoples. Partly this was conditioned by strategic position, but perhaps more by traditional loyalties or fears. Overriding both in some instances was the conviction that collective security offered the best, perhaps only hope, for security in a world in which power politics was all too obvious. Countering this feeling even among many who believed in the general ideal of collective security was fear that with the League as constituted collective action would only lead to conflict. This dread of the ultimate implications of the course of action on which League members were embarking acted as a continual drag upon policy.

Yet despite all the doubts, hesitations, and actual opposition within Commonwealth countries, all of them instituted and enforced those sanctions against Italy which were proposed during October by the Co-ordination Committee. In this they were joined by many other League countries. The first great step had been taken to develop forcible action against an aggressor. Subsequent developments would determine its ultimate effect.

REFERENCES FOR CHAPTER VI

1. J. G. Latham, *Report of Geneva Conference*, reprinted from the *Parliamentary Debates, September 30, 1932* (Canberra, 1932).

2. *Cmd. 4827* of 1934.

3. *New Zealand, House of Representatives Debates*, 1935, 241: 79-83. See also *The Times* (London), February 20, 1935.

4. *The Times*, April 25, 1935 (Ottawa, April 24th).

5. *Otago Daily Times*, May 11, 1935, and *New Zealand Herald*, May 1, 1935.

6. *New York Times*, Sept. 7, 1935 (Bennett, September 6th).

7. MacManus, M. J., *Eamon de Valera* (Dublin, 1944), p. 324.

8. No. 69 of 1934. This Act substantially altered the South Africa Act, 1909.

9. *Cf.* an interesting description of South African political life by the special correspondent of *The Manchester Guardian* in South Africa, printed in the issue of March 9, 1935.

10. *O.J.*, May, 1935, Minutes of the Eighty-fifth (Extraordinary) Session of the Council, p. 551.

11. *Ibid.*, p. 558.

12. *Canada, House of Commons Debates*, Session 1935, 2: 1786-87.

13. *C. 175, M. 96*, 1935, VII.

14. *The Times*, March 22, 1935.

15. *Manchester Guardian*, May 1, 1935.

16. *The Times*, May 8, 1935.

17. *Ibid.*, May 10th, 24th, and 31st.

18. *Ibid.*, January 7, 1935. In the issue of February 12, 1935, an official statement issued in Australia on January 11th, was cited which denied that Hankey had urged reinstituting compulsory military service. *The Manchester Guardian*, January 25, 1935, reported a statement by Bennett that the Canadian Government had not authorized discussion of Empire defence with Hankey during his visit to Ottawa.

19. *Cmd. 4827*.

20. *The Times*, May 20, 1935.

21. *Ibid.*

22. *Manchester Guardian*, June 11, 1935 (Reuter despatch).

23. At a Mayoral luncheon at Capetown on June 10th, Hertzog asserted that "the predominant feeling among English-speaking people is that the ultimate destiny of the Protectorates is within the Union . . . but [they] hold that the natives should be educated to trust the Union before they come under its rule." *The Times*, June 11, 1935.

24. *Manchester Guardian*, June 11, 1935.

25. *Nazi Activities in South West Africa* (as stated in the report of South West Africa Commission, March, 1936). With a foreword by the Rt. Hon. Lord Lugard. "Friends of Europe" Publication No. 43, (London, 1936).

26. *O.J.*, 1923, Spec. Sup. No. 19, p. 15: *Fourth Assembly*, Sixth Committee, Fourth Meeting, September 19, 1923.

27. For a detailed account of this incident as well as of earlier and subsequent developments, *see* Arnold J. Toynbee, *Survey of International Affairs*, 1935, vol. II, *Abyssinia and Italy* (London, 1936).

28. To his Bournemouth constituents, August 30, 1935, *The Times*, August 31, 1935.

29. *E.g.*, in issues for June 7th, July 15th and 25th, August 5th ("The only thing for Britain to do is to get out of Geneva or we shall be manoeuvred into war overnight") and September 3, 1935.

30. *E.g.*, in issues for July 8th ("Sanctions and disarmament are bats which lodge in the same belfry"), and September 27, 1935.

31. Toynbee, *Survey of International Affairs*, 1935, II, 43.

32. *The Times*, August 17, 1935.

33. *New York Times*, September 7, 1935.

34. *Winnipeg Free Press*, September 9, 1935.

35. *The Times*, September 10, 1935.

36. *The Toronto Daily Star*, editorial, September 9, 1935.

37. *The Times*, August 26, 1935.

38. *New York Times*, August 27, 1935.

39. *The Times*, September 5, 1935.

40. *Le Temps*, Sept. 20, 1935.

41. *The Times*, Sept. 20, 1935.

42. *Ibid.*, Aug. 13, 1935.

43. Said during an interview. *Manchester Guardian*, Aug. 13, 1935.

44. *Ibid.*

45. *The Times*, Sept. 2, 1935.

46. *Ibid.*, Sept. 7, 1935. The Cape Federation of Trades stated that it believed its action had received the support of the vast majority of citizens in the Union. The incident raised the question of unofficial boycotts as expressions of public opinion.

47. *The Times*, Sept. 9, 1935.

48. *Ibid.*, Sept. 11, 1935.

49. *Ibid.*, Sept. 19, 1935.

50. *O.J.*, 1935, Spec. Sup. No. 138, pp. 43-46: *Sixteenth Assembly*, Third Plenary Meeting, September 11, 1935.

51. *E.g.*, *Report of the New Zealand Delegate to the League of Nations*, 1 (Wellington, 1936).

52. Statement by Laval in the Chamber of Deputies, Dec. 28, 1935. Quoted in Toynbee, *Survey*, 1935, II, 183-84. *See* also note on latter page.

53. *O.J.*, 1935, Spec. Sup. No. 138, pp. 51-53: *Sixteenth Assembly*, Fourth Plenary Meeting, September 11, 1935.

54. *Ibid.*, pp. 77-78: Eighth Plenary Meeting, September 14, 1935.

55. *Ibid.*, pp. 78-79.

56. *Ibid.*, pp. 81-82: Ninth Plenary Meeting, September 16, 1935.

57. *Ibid.*, pp. 66-67: Sixth Plenary Meeting, September 13, 1935. Smuts warned that the black races might be roused to nationalistic self-consciousness, in his interview on Aug. 12, *cf. The Times*, Aug. 13, 1935, as did Reitz, Minister of Agriculture, speaking in Capetown, Aug. 19, *cf. Manchester Guardian*, Aug. 20, 1935. Sir Abe Bailey, in letters to *The Times* in Oct., 1935, and the *Daily Telegraph*, Nov. 11, 1935, also drew attention to the danger of the militarization of the Blacks. A correspondent writing in the *Manchester Guardian*, Dec. 7, 1935, found widespread feeling of the danger of making the African natives familiar with the weapons of modern war.

58. *O.J.*, 1935, Spec. Sup. No. 138, p. 64: *Sixteenth Assembly*, Fifth Plenary Meeting, September 12, 1935.

59. *Ibid.*, pp. 57-59: Fourth Plenary Meeting, September 11, 1935, (Norway), and 62-64: Fifth Plenary Meeting, September 16, 1935 (Sweden).

60. *Ibid.*, pp. 73-74: Seventh Plenary Meeting, September 14, 1935.

61. *Ibid.*, p. 105: Fifteenth Plenary Meeting, October 10, 1935.

62. *Ibid.*, p. 106.

63. *Ibid.*, p. 114: Sixteenth Plenary Meeting, October 10, 1935.

64. *Ibid.*, p. 109.

65. There are frequent references to its work during the discussions through which the sanctions programme was planned. *E.g.*, *O.J.*, 1935, Spec. Sup. No. 145, pp. 37, 38, 80, 87, 106; and *O.J.*, 1935, Spec. Sup. No. 146, p. 55.

66. Although there is as yet no access to the minutes of the Committee of Thirteen and to the report it presented to the Council in September, 1935, the reports of its sub-committees (C.O.S.C.-6, June 28, 1935, and C.O.S.C.-7, (1) July 13, 1935), references to its work in subsequent meetings, and personal conversations have made it possible to gauge the general direction of its work.

67. The importance of the discussions of the Committee of Thirteen appears to have been overlooked by Toynbee who says: "The whole organization for studying and proposing the sanctions had to be improvised at a few hours' notice," and omits any mention of the earlier committee, from his list of factors contributing to the speed and success of the work of the Committee of Eighteen. *Survey*, 1935, II, 228-231.

68. *O.J.*, 1935, Spec. Sup. No. 145, p. 30: Dispute between Ethiopia and Italy, First Session, Committee of Eighteen, First Meeting, October 11, 1935.

69. *Ibid.*, p. 36. Second Meeting, October 12, 1935.

70. *South Africa, House of Assembly Debates*, 26: 515-16, 1936 (Feb. 11, 1936).

71. *Ibid.*, 27: 3098, 1935 (May 6, 1935).

72. *O.J.*, Spec. Sup. No. 145, p. 37: Dispute between Ethiopia and Italy, First Session, Committee of Eighteen, Second Meeting, October 12, 1935.

73. *Ibid.*, p. 87: Sub-Committee on Economic Measures, First Meeting, October 15, 1935.

74. *Ibid.*, p. 38, Committee of Eighteen, Second Meeting, October 12, 1935.

75. *See* below, p. 225.

76. *O.J.*, Spec. Sup. No. 145, p. 42: Dispute between Ethiopia and Italy, First Session, Committee of Eighteen, Second Meeting, October 12, 1935.

77. *Ibid.*, pp. 53-54. Fourth Meeting, October 14, 1935.

78. Toynbee, *Survey*, 1935, II, 235.

79. In London on October 21. *The Times*, Oct. 22, 1935.

80. In the House of Commons, October 23. *Ibid.*, Oct. 24, 1935.

81. In the House of Commons, October 24. *Ibid.*, Oct. 25, 1935.

82. Cited in *Paris Soir*, Oct. 16, 1935.

83. In speeches at Birmingham, October 8 and 16. *The Times*, Oct. 9 and 17, 1935.

84. *Ibid.*, Oct. 17, 1935.

85. *Cmd. 5072* of 1935, pp. 3-4. For a full account of negotiations *see* Toynbee, *Survey*, 1935, II, 248 ff.

86. This debate and subsequent ones, including that of November 1st, at which the Sanctions Act was adopted, are summarized in *J.P.E.*, 17: 58-73, January, 1936.

87. *The Times*, Sept. 26, 1935.

88. *Ibid.*, Sept. 27, 1935.

89. *The Observer*, Oct. 6, 1935.

90. *The Times*, Oct. 5, 1935.

91. *The Bulletin*, Sydney, N.S.W., Nov. 6, 1935, claimed that this evidenced the deceit of previous declarations of freedom of action.

92. *The Times*, Oct. 5, 1935.

93. *Ibid.*, Nov. 29, 1935.

94. *New York Times*, Nov. 24, 1935.

95. *See* review by R. T. E. Latham of *Australia and War Today* in *International Affairs*, XV, 1936, p. 586.

96. *See* E. A. Ferguson, "Australia's Attitude towards Collective Security," in *Australian Foreign Policy, 1935-1936* (1936), p. 18 ff.

97. W. M. Hughes, *Australia and War Today* (Sydney, 1935).

98. *The Times*, Nov. 4, 1935.

99. Hughes rejoined the Cabinet on Feb. 6 as Minister for Repatriation. His letter in reply to one from Lyons asking his attitude to the Government's League policy and to the League, stated: "I have always believed in the principles laid down in the Covenant. I am a firm believer in the rule of law and its extension to the domain of international affairs. I believe that security, which is the condition precedent to the settlement of disputes by peaceful means, is best assured by collective action by peace-loving nations and also that the League is the most effective, indeed the only, means whereby collective action is practicable. I believe that as a means of restraining aggression the League should impose such sanctions other than military as may tend to prevent or hamper warlike operations by an aggressor. Lastly as I believe that a strong British Empire is essential to the effective functioning of the League and also to the world's peace, I whole-heartedly favour such policy as will preserve its unity and increase its power for good. The Government's policy is inspired by those ideals and directed towards those ends, and I am entirely in accord therewith." *The Times*, Feb. 7, 1936.

100. *Manchester Guardian*, Oct. 19, 1935.

101. *New Zealand, Parliamentary Debates*, Fifth Session, 1935, pp. 497-506 and 518-528 for the discussions in both Houses.

102. *Ibid.*, p. 522 (The Hon. Mr. McIntyre).

103. *The Times*, Oct. 10, 1935.

104. *Manchester Guardian*, Oct. 23, 1935.

105. *The Times*, Nov. 12, 1935.

106. *Dail Eireann Debates*, 59: 482-539 and 603-634.

107. *Ibid.*, pp. 1677-1708.

108. *Ibid.*, p. 1685 (Mr. Belton). He had spoken in the earlier debate "as an Irishman and as a Catholic" against applying sanctions to Italy "who is going out to civilize and to Christianize a pagan race."

109. *Ibid.*, p. 1702.

110. *The Toronto Daily Star*, Sept. 18, 1935.

111. *Ibid.*, Sept. 20, 1935.

112. *Winnipeg Free Press*, Oct. 31, 1935.

113. *The Times*, Oct. 23, 1935.

114. *Ibid.*, Oct. 29, 1935.

115. *Vancouver Sun*, Oct. 21, 1935.

116. Statement given to the press by the Secretary of State for External Affairs, Oct. 29, 1935, included in Canada, 1936, *Documents Relating to the Italo-Ethiopian Conflict*, No. 17.

117. *Ibid.*, No. 18.

CHAPTER VII

OIL SANCTIONS AND THE RHINELAND CRISIS

By the end of October, the response of Governments to the sanctions proposals made it apparent that the great majority of League states were prepared to participate in the programme of collective security. Fifty Governments had accepted the arms embargo against Italy, forty-nine were ready to impose the financial ban, forty-eight had given some assurance that they would prohibit Italian imports and also stop export of certain key products which participating members controlled, and thirty-nine had agreed to consider measures of mutual support to lessen the loss and inconvenience resulting from the economic and financial measures.[1] Replies from non-League members indicated that the United States would not be able directly to support League action but was sympathetic and that Germany did not intend to offer obstruction. The way seemed open to apply pressure upon Italy which was driving ahead its attack upon Ethiopia.

From the beginning, however, the promotion of the sanctions programme to thwart Italy's aggression was paralleled by a second policy aiming to find a means of ending the Italo-Ethiopian conflict through conciliation. The latter was a continuation of Laval's earlier efforts to find a settlement. With Sir Samuel Hoare's consent, it led to the drawing up of plans by British and French officials whereby this might be achieved. On November 2nd, at the meeting of the Co-ordination Committee, Laval and Hoare noted their intention of seeking a solution to the dispute, a task in which the Council's Committee of Five had been unsuccessful. Laval declared that to seek an amicable settlement was "particularly imperative" for France because of its treaty of friendship with Italy. Hoare was more reserved and gave assurances that an agreement would have to be acceptable to the League, Ethiopia, and Italy. Enthusiastic support of their suggestion by van Zeeland of Belgium was taken to mean endorsement by the Committee which in fact had no legal basis from which to extend approval even if it had been felt in more measure than was indicated in the meeting. While to the French a settlement was the primary need, others felt it more important to support the principles of collective security.

At the same session, the latter line of policy was given concrete expression through the adoption of resolutions requesting Governments to bring the financial ban, the prohibition of Italian imports, and the embargo on exports into force by November 18th. The next most

216

obvious development was to increase the force of sanctions by placing an embargo upon additional products useful in Italy's war effort as the original proposal indicated would be done. Among such products, it was becoming obvious that oil was the most important.

Before enlarging the scope of sanctions, however, it was necessary to deal with objections and questions raised during the earlier sessions, and also in the replies of Governments, particularly in relation to the ban on Italian imports and the embargo on export of key products. In these discussions, both te Water and Riddell maintained a firm stand in line with their earlier attitudes. When Romania asked for exceptions because of clearing agreements with Italy, Riddell opposed granting them because he felt they would threaten the structure of sanctions and undermine solidarity.[2] He made it clear that in his view the ban on imports "represented the key of all the sanctions, the central column of the whole structure." Moreover, he knew from the discussions in the Committee of Thirteen that this measure was the one most opposed by Italy. So convincing was he that the Swiss delegate who had questioned the feasibility of the ban on imports withdrew his suggestion.

The embargo on exports to Italy of key products offered more difficulties because only a few materials were controlled by participating members of the League. In the effort to put the embargo into effect quickly, it had been decided to propose immediate action only on those key products whose production was controlled by participating members of the League, and to put on a second list for future consideration those products which were not controlled by the participating members alone and which required the co-operation of others before an embargo could be feasible. The division of products between List 1 and 2 was undertaken in a series of meetings in the Sub-Committee on Economic Measures beginning October 15th in which Riddell played an active part. Though the principle adopted made the division comparatively easy, it also raised practical problems which were to lead directly to subsequent suggestions involving oil sanctions.

As Riddell had been quick to point out in the Committee of Thirteen on Collective Security and stressed again in the Sub-Committee on Economic Measures, there were obvious difficulties involved in cases where the production of raw materials was controlled by one country and processing undertaken by another. While a country possessing a raw material might be prevented by the embargo from exporting it, another country could buy the raw material, make it into a finished article and sell it to the state against which the embargo on raw materials had been placed.[3] This might mean, in practice, that the embargo would prove ineffective. The provision that the participating state should be responsible for preventing its materials from being used in this way seemed to place an unfair burden upon it. In order to prevent injustices of this character and to make the embargo more effective, Riddell used the opportunity afforded by the consideration of nickel, which was placed on List 1 for immediate action to propose that some kind of qualifying statement should be made whereby derivatives of relevant raw materials would also be covered.

While not making a definite motion, Riddell suggested that the products on List 1 should be held to include:

(a) All forms of these materials, whether ores, scrap, alloys, products or derivatives, from which any of these materials may readily be extracted or derived;

(b) Such products or derivatives of these materials as represent a stage in the manufacture of war materials or implements of war, or any forbidden article or product;

(c) Such products or derivatives of these materials as may be utilized in the manufacture of war materials, implements of war, or any forbidden article or material.[4]

The chairman of the committee noted this suggestion as one which might be discussed later but no comments were made upon it at this time. However, on the next day when Riddell drew attention to the fact that he had raised the question of a general clause to cover all forms of the materials placed on the embargo list,[5] the chairman "recalled" that the Sub-Committee had already adopted this proposal and that it would be transmitted for consideration to the Drafting Committee and the Committee of Eighteen.

On the following day, October 19, the Committee of Eighteen considered the draft proposal, known as Proposal IV, for a ban on the export to Italy of articles which had been put on List 1 by the Sub-Committee on Economic Measures. The Spanish representative, Madariaga, objected to the fact that while iron ore and scrap iron were included on the list of products whose export and re-export to Italy was to be prohibited, iron and steel, the finished products, were not. The omission of the latter, he declared, made the inclusion of the former worthless. It was pointed out that products were included on this list because participating members could enforce the embargo and that iron and steel were not controlled by participating members while scrap iron and iron ore were. Riddell again raised the point which he had brought up in the Sub-Committee, noting that his delegation felt that any scheme of economic sanctions should be comprehensive and stressing the fact that all the responsibilities were being placed on the states producing raw materials. ". . . he hesitated to forecast the way in which his Government would receive the enquiry as to what measures it was prepared to take to control the export of crude minerals, . . . when it was informed that there would be no restrictions on the export of derivatives, semi-manufactured and manufactured forms of the raw material."[6]   Though he was "not in a position at present to make any definite proposal," he thought that the question should be very carefully considered.   After further discussion, it was decided to accept the list as it stood and to leave further comments to the home governments to which the proposals were then sent.

The point which Madariaga had raised regarding iron ore was endorsed by the Spanish Government's answer to the sanction proposals and was one of the special cases to be considered by the Committee of Eighteen on its reassembly.   Because it was connected so closely with the question of derivatives on which Riddell had spoken several times, it could be expected that he would make a further comment at this time.[7]   There had been no objection by the Canadian Government to his previous statements on this subject.   But the new Liberal administration had come into office after they had been made and it might be questioned whether King's statement of October 29th was intended to indicate that while existing sanctions would be enforced any further proposals would be considered on their individual merits. Because of this fact, Riddell apparently hesitated to repeat his earlier suggestion without specific approval and therefore wired for instructions.[8]

In view of the number of cases to be considered at the session of the Committee of Eighteen on November 2nd, the question of iron ore was not expected to come up before the afternoon.   But due to unusual speed in dealing with earlier cases, its turn for consideration came at twelve o'clock.   Riddell could have used delaying tactics, such as making an excuse to put the matter off to the afternoon meeting or leaving the meeting and giving his place to one of his younger colleagues.   If he chose to stay, he was faced with the dilemma of allowing the opportunity to pass, or of accepting the responsibility of bringing forward a proposal which might widen the basis of sanctions.

The Spanish reply had challenged the inclusion of iron ore on the sanctions list as a "question of logic and principle," pointing out that iron and steel were the products useful for arms and that if an embargo were not placed upon them, iron ore should be taken off the list.   The chairman declared that the Committee was not competent to modify the list adopted by the Co-ordination Committee, "It could only make additions to it, e.g. it could add iron and pig-iron, as the Canadian delegate proposed."[9]

Riddell took this opportunity to remind the Committee that it was entrusted with the task of making suitable proposals to governments on the subject of the embargo of certain exports to Italy.[10] It was evident that the list of key products was not complete, in as much as important products like "petroleum and its derivatives, coal, iron, and steel" were not on the list. The Committee had been successful in obtaining acceptances regarding the embargo as far as it went, and he now ventured to propose that the substances he had named should be added to the list "in principle" and that measures with regard to them should come into effect "whenever the Committee found that an embargo could be made effective." He hoped that the inclusion of iron and steel in this way would give satisfaction to the Spanish delegate. He then suggested that:

In execution of the mission entrusted to it under the last paragraph of Proposal IV, the Committee of Eighteen submits to Governments the following proposal:

"It is expedient to adopt the principle of the extension of the measures of embargo provided for in the said proposal to the following products: Petroleum and derivatives; Coal; Iron, cast iron, and steel.

"As soon as it appears that the acceptance of this principle is sufficiently general to ensure the efficacy of the measures thus contemplated, the Committee of Eighteen will propose to Governments a date for bringing them into operation."

This proposal did not suggest an immediate extension of embargo measures but picked out from List 2 certain products of particular importance for serious consideration in respect to a future extension of the embargo list. That this was understood by the Committee is evidenced by a later statement of the French delegate that the resolution was "a decision of principle, which was not to come into force pending the accession of the non-participating countries whose co-operation was required for the effectiveness of the measure proposed."[11] Thus the aim of the proposal was to meet the general problem of derivatives as it had been raised by Riddell in earlier comments and to indicate the direction in which extension of sanctions should go when feasible.

The proposal as formulated by Riddell was referred to the Sub-Committee on Economic Measures and, in a more specific form, was subsequently returned by the Drafting Committee to the Committee of Eighteen as Proposal IV (a). It read:

In the execution of the mission entrusted to it under the last paragraph of Proposal IV, the Committee of Eighteen submits to Governments the following proposal:

"It is expedient that the measures of embargo provided for in Proposal IV should be extended to the following articles as soon as the conditions necessary to render this extension effective have been realized: Petroleum and its derivatives, by-products, and residues; Pig iron; iron and steel (including alloy steels), cast, forged, rolled, drawn, stamped, or pressed; Coal (including anthracite and lignite), coke, and their agglomerates, as well as fuels derived therefrom.

"If the replies received by the Committee to the present proposal and the information at its disposal warrant it, the Committee of Eighteen will propose to Governments a date for bringing into force the measures mentioned above."[12]

In this form it was adopted as a statement of principle embodying action which might be taken if the Committee at a later meeting decided that the measures should be put into force. In a circular letter of November 7th, the Secretary-General of the League, in communicating to Governments the texts of the proposals which the Committee of Eighteen had adopted for recommendation during its second session, drew special attention to the last paragraph of Proposal IV (a), since subsequent action by the League committees on this proposal would depend on the extent of the support which it received.

In the meantime, Riddell found himself in an awkward position. In reply to his cable asking for instruction, the Government had wired that he was "to do nothing in the matter of extending sanctions."[13] This was not received, however, until after he had taken the initiative which resulted ultimately in Proposal IV (a). The similarity between his suggestion at this time and the earlier one to which no objection had been made had probably made him feel that instructions when they came would support his action. Moreover, by singling out iron, steel, coal, and oil with its derivatives for special attention, Riddell may well have thought that he was making it easier for his Government to agree to an extension of the embargo for these products had been freely discussed in earlier meetings and, in addition, it was well known that the Government of the United States, from which came the largest supply of oil to Italy from a non-League state, was attempting to limit American oil producers by moral pressure from increasing their exports to that country. On the other hand, another key product which had been placed on List 2 was cotton, and the attempt to impose an embargo on this might have created more ill-will in the United States. It is noticeable that at the meeting at which Riddell brought forward his suggestion, the Netherlands delegate had expressed a preference for prohibiting the export of all products on the second list. He did not see, he declared, "why, for instance, an exception should be made for cotton," which seemed to him just as important as coal. But at the meeting on November 4th, this proposal was officially withdrawn by the Netherlands delegate in favour of the products specified in Riddell's proposal.[14] These met with the general approval of the Committee and by the time Proposal IV (a) was sent out three days later, it was clear that it was a Committee proposal not that of a single member. In fact, the private character of the sessions of the Committee of Eighteen would under ordinary circumstances have provided anonymity regarding the initiating of a particular proposal. On an earlier occasion, te Water's proposal to break diplomatic relations with Italy had been looked on as the suggestion of a member of the Committee, not as being sponsored by the South African Government.[15] The difference with Riddell's proposal came out of the fact that he had wired for instructions and then acted before they came, that the proposal was accepted by the Committee and submitted to Governments, and that it received a great deal of publicity because of the inclusion of oil, which it was apparent by this time was the one product essential to the success of the Italian aggression in Ethiopia.

The first response of the Canadian Government was that though Riddell himself considered "quite rightly, that he was not in any sense to be regarded as acting for Canada, that he was simply acting as a member of the committee," he had "no right to take any step that was at all likely to be of importance in a critical situation . . . without specific instructions," and that he "had exceeded his authority."[16]   In a statement to the House of Commons in February, 1936, Mr. King declared that the Government had considered very carefully whether Riddell "should not immediately publicly repudiate his act." Such action had not been taken "only because we were most anxious not to take any step which might possibly embarrass the situation in Europe or might appear even remotely to indicate an exception on the part of Canada to what was being done by other parts of the British Empire."

It seems clear that the Canadian Government opposed the taking of initiative in this matter rather than the substance of the proposal itself.   The Prime Minister subsequently declared early in December that Canada might support "oil and any other sanctions" and that the "attitude of the Government towards the League and its objects has never changed, nor is it intended that it should be."[17]   Had there been no further complicating factors, the matter would no doubt have been allowed to rest.

Problems arose, however, when the press began to designate Proposal IV (a) as a Canadian proposal.   Word that Riddell had taken the initiative must have been given to the press fairly quickly, for the News Chronicle, The Observer, and the Daily Telegraph mentioned it in their issues of November 4th.   This publicity regarding the initiative of the Canadian representative on the Committee of Eighteen was one of the most unfortunate aspects of the situation for up until this time proposals had been accepted as being matters of collective responsibility as should have been done also in this case.

At the same time increasing prominence was given to the inclusion of oil in the proposal as it became apparent that an oil embargo would have serious repercussions on Italy, perhaps to the extent of forcing it to discontinue its aggression in Ethiopia. Enough favourable replies were being received to Proposal IV (a) to make it worth while to discuss putting it into effect, and on November 22nd, the Committee of Eighteen was convened for November 26th with the proposal upon its agenda.

Before it had met, however, Italian warnings that the imposition of an embargo on oil might be expected to have serious results on Franco-Italian relations led Laval to ask as a personal favour that the meeting should be adjourned.[18] After considerable hesitation and discussion with both French and British representatives, the chairman of the Committee consented to postpone the meeting until December 12th. Before that time, the Canadian Government had disclaimed official initiative of Proposal IV (a) and, shortly after, Sir Samuel Hoare meeting with Laval in Paris had agreed to what became known as the Laval-Hoare plan for the partition of Ethiopia.

Despite news of the adjournment of the meeting of the Committee of Eighteen, the Italian Government had continued to make obvious its alarm and resentment at the possible imposition of an oil embargo. While subsequent information tends to verify the fact that Italy would not have resorted to force against League powers in case an embargo on oil had been imposed,[19] troop movements within Italy and rumours of a possible air attack on the British fleet in the Mediterranean gave credence to the possibility. It was partly in the light of this situation, partly perhaps because of charges of initiative in oil sanctions levelled against Liberal members in the provincial campaign in Quebec,[20] and partly, the Prime Minister later said, because pro-sanction sources were pressing the British and other representatives to hasten action on an embargo on oil "because Canada was anxious and insistent in the matter,"[21] that the Canadian Government decided to state publicly that Proposal IV (a) had not been the result of official initiative but simply the suggestion of an individual member of the Committee of Eighteen.

This explanation was given to the press on December 2nd by M. Lapointe, Acting Secretary of State for External Affairs, in a statement in which he declared that the Government had not taken and did not propose to take the initiative in the extension of the embargo upon exportation of key commodities to Italy "particularly in the placing of a ban upon shipments of coal, oil, iron, and steel."[22] He emphasized that the suggestion which had been made by the Canadian member of the Committee of Eighteen "represented only his own personal opinion, and his views as a member of the Committee—and not the views of the Canadian Government." At the same time, he declared that Canada would continue to consider "the changes in the situation as they arise, including any proposal for the revision of economic sanctions," but made it clear that participation would be limited "to co-operation in purely financial and economic measures of a pacific character which are accepted by substantially all of the participating countries."

What was described as "a storm of considerable proportions" was stirred up in Canada by Lapointe's statement.[23] Prominent Liberals, including Newton W. Rowell and Sir Robert Falconer, former president of the University of Toronto, regretted that the Government had not taken the responsibility for the proposal of oil sanctions. The English-language press ranged from qualified approval to emphatic disapproval. The French Canadian newspapers without exception approved the Government's move. L'Action Catholique declared that it had "set an example of national pride which should be pursued in the future."

The Conservative press accused the Government of impairing the solidarity of the British Commonwealth during an international crisis and giving comfort to Mussolini.[24] The Globe, a Liberal paper, also vigorously assailed the Government's statement.[25] It declared that a united front by the whole Commonwealth was the greatest guarantee for the preservation of peace and that this division over sanctions policy made for disunity. It believed that Canada's action was being interpreted, rightly or wrongly, as official dissociation from the plan of checking Italy by sanctions, that it had brought cheer to Italy and that it suggested a break in the ranks of those striving for peace.

That a strong effort was made to capitalize on the Canadian statement was shown by despatches from Rome. Authoritative political quarters in Italy were reported on December 3rd to be expressing the opinion that the proposal for an oil embargo was dead. This optimism was supposedly based on the change in the attitude of the Canadian Government "in disowning the initiative of its delegate" in proposing the embargo.[26] The correspondent of Le Temps (Paris) reported that the Canadian move "est jugé à Rome comme ayant une véritable signification politique," and to have resulted in "un véritable optimisme."[27] Arnaldo Cortesi, New York Times correspondent in Rome, declared that it continued to monopolize the attention of Rome's political diplomatic circles, and quoted the foreign ministry's official spokesman as saying, "As the oil embargo has been repudiated by the Government supposed to have made it, we believe it must now be discarded, for the time being at any rate."[28]

After the first indignation subsided in Canada, newspaper comment tended towards more support of the Government's action, but with a suggestion that the situation could have been handled more wisely. Some papers considered that the Riddell action was contrary to the October 29th statement of Mackenzie King and in so far should not have been taken without specific instructions. Others felt that it was in conflict with the commitments of both parties against being drawn into war over the existing difficulties in Europe.[29]

It is clear that the Prime Minister who, though on vacation, had been consulted before the Lapointe statement was issued, believed it to have been essential. Subsequently he told Parliament that he was "not at all sure that, when the whole story comes to be told, it may not be discovered that, but for the action of the government of Canada in this particular matter, at that particular time, the whole of Europe might have been aflame today."[30]

Whether in fact the Canadian statement had such significance for the international situation is difficult to determine, particularly in view of other developments at the time. The work of the French and British experts on a peace plan had been completed and on December 4th, two days after the Canadian statement, a despatch to the *New York Times* by "Augur" gave a substantially correct outline of it.[31] On December 6th, Mussolini warned in a public address that an embargo on oil was calculated to prejudice the situation gravely. On December 7th, Sir Samuel Hoare, an ill man on his way to a vacation in Switzerland, stopped to talk with Laval in Paris at the request of the British Prime Minister. In Paris, Hoare was told by the French Premier that Mussolini threatened to launch an attack upon the British fleet in the Mediterranean in case oil sanctions were voted, and that it would take two weeks before the French could come to their support. Confronted with this veiled ultimatum, Hoare agreed to consider the peace plan drawn up by the French and British experts. With some modifications, not all to the advantage of Ethiopia, he accepted it subject to the approval of the British Cabinet. As a copy was carried to London, the night of December 8th, Hoare himself was travelling happily to Switzerland. Next morning, when Baldwin was reading the secret despatch, he learned to his dismay that the details of the plan had already been published in at least two French newspapers, undoubtedly in an effort to force the hand of the British Government.

The British Cabinet split over the plan, a minority led by Mr. Neville Chamberlain opposing it while the majority under Baldwin felt it necessary to support Hoare. But a rising tide of indignation in Great Britain against a proposal which threw away everything for which the Peace Ballot, League action, and the recent election had stood made it impossible even for Baldwin to maintain his stand. On December 18th, Sir Samuel Hoare tendered his resignation, a sacrifice in the interest of maintaining the position of the National Government which turned much indignation away from Hoare himself to Baldwin. The Government survived the crisis but the Laval-Hoare plan did not. It was rejected not only by public opinion but also by Ethiopia. But Laval had secured his purpose for the consideration of oil sanctions was indefinitely postponed.

The Laval-Hoare Plan provided for a partial partition of Ethiopia, giving to Italy practically all the territory it had been able to conquer up to that date. In return Italy was to cede a very much smaller strip of territory through Eritrea, giving Ethiopia access to the sea. The Italians were not only to gain territory but also to get exclusive economic rights in a zone of expansion and settlement largely consisting of fertile temperate highlands in the southern half of Ethiopia. This was the proposal which Laval and Hoare had decided should be communicated to the two belligerents with a note that the oil sanction would be held in suspension pending their decision. The implication, which unfortunately in practice proved to be correct, was that if Ethiopia refused to accept the plan, it would be penalized by receiving no further assistance from League members beyond that already being extended.

The reasons for Sir Samuel Hoare's acceptance of this plan were in part disclosed by him in his speech to the Commons following his resignation.[32] The fear of war, either "an isolated war between Italy and Great Britain" or a "European conflagration," obviously stood first in motivating his action. War, he believed, would almost inevitably follow from the imposition of oil sanctions. The plan offered an alternative to voting for or against these sanctions though Hoare did not put it in this way. Moreover, it was apparent that Hoare believed that without an embargo on oil (perhaps even with it) Ethiopia was doomed. The strength of the Italian army, the leadership of Marshal Badoglio, the inability of the Ethiopian Government to secure munitions abroad due to its lack of funds made its position hopeless in his view. "I have been terrified with the thought," he declared to the House, "that we might lead Abyssinia on to think that the League could do more than it can do—that in the end . . . Abyssinia would be destroyed altogether as an independent state." The Laval-Hoare plan would at least save something for Ethiopian sovereignty. Another influence may have been his doubts that the Government of the United States would be able to restrain American oil producers from meeting the Italian demand left by cutting off supplies from Romania, the Soviet Union, the Netherlands, and Iraq, which customarily supplied about 75 per cent. of Italy's oil and by December 12th had indicated their readiness to consider the embargo.[33]   A further factor in his decision might have been the Canadian statement disclaiming official initiative for an oil embargo.   When Hoare spoke in his *apologia* of an isolated attack being launched upon "one Power (Great Britain), without, it may be, the full support of the other Powers," he may have been thinking not only of France but also of Australia and Canada.

On the other hand, it is only fair to say in respect to the Canadian statement that it was a repudiation of initiative not of willingness to support oil sanctions as such or to stand behind Great Britain if it should come into danger as the result of League action against Italy. King subsequently made it known that the Canadian representative was instructed to vote for oil sanctions if they became a practical possibility.[34]   Moreover, there would seem to be little doubt that both Canada and Australia would have supported Great Britain if an Anglo-Italian war had broken out.   Nor, though the timing of the Canadian action was undoubtedly unfortunate from the point of view of united League support for a measure affecting oil, is there any evidence that the move itself was directly interrelated with the developments which gave rise to the Laval-Hoare Plan.   On the contrary, at the time the statement was issued, Hoare does not seem to have been aware of the proposal Laval was to make in Paris.   If either Canada or Australia were influential in his decision to accept the Laval-Hoare Plan, it was rather because their known reluctance for more forcible measures and their fear of war coincided with his own.

News of the Laval-Hoare plan was greeted with indignation not only in Great Britain but also by many groups in the Dominions, though others approved it.   In Canada much of the criticism of Lapointe's statement was shifted to the Laval-Hoare plan while those groups which had supported the statement found justification for their stand.   The extreme Conservative press, which had slight influence, had consistently opposed sanctions and favoured the proposed settlement as a means of avoiding European war.   The *Montreal Star*, a typical paper of this group, considered that the Baldwin Government was taking the line of conciliation through "a stern sense of duty," feeling it essential for the peace of the world and the safety of the British Commonwealth.[35] The isolationists, comprising practically the whole French Canadian group, found the proposals an unanswerable proof of their argument that Canada should not engage in foreign commitments, either for the League or for the Empire. Most of the Liberal newspapers were very critical of the plan, however, and of the British Government. *The Toronto Daily Star* declared that the proposed settlement had regard only for the immediate security of France and Great Britain and was drafted without concern for the paramount consideration of making the League a dependable instrument for affording collective security.[36] The plan would make the League, which was moving slowly towards the fulfilment of its pledge of protection for Ethiopia, a party to a crime of spoliation. The *Winnipeg Free Press* expressed the current doubts of the sincerity of the Baldwin Government.[37]

In Australia, though opinion was reported to be unanimously against Italy's gaining an advantageous position as a result of its aggression against Ethiopia, absence of information about the circumstances prompting the Laval-Hoare proposals caused emphatic criticism to be withheld.[38] In a leading article, the *Argus* declared that "The League of Nations is not the slightest use as an instrument for promoting peace if the weaker nations cannot rely on it to defend them against powerful nations." It pointed out that "events now or later may disturb the complacent notion that Australia and New Zealand can remove themselves from the current of international trouble." Other papers saw the plan as reinforcement of their criticisms of the League. But the plan had been repudiated by the Baldwin Government before opinion had time to consolidate.

From New Zealand, equally limited in news, came no direct comments. Savage, the new Labour Prime Minister, speaking to a group of governmental officials, affirmed continued solidarity with the Commonwealth.[39] "We have no desire to sever connection, even if we could, with the people of the British Commonwealth," he declared. "We are bound to the British people by unbreakable ties of blood, to say nothing of trade. We can build in New Zealand and we can lend a hand to the British Commonwealth at the same time." It was not a new attitude but it had significance as a statement of policy by the leader of a party which had always been independent in its reactions to British policy.

The strongest opposition to the Laval-Hoare plan appears to have been roused in South Africa. Despite the growing tension in the international scene, both Smuts and Jan Hofmeyr, Minister of the Interior, had affirmed the Union's support of League action. At a meeting in Pretoria at which Hertzog also appeared, Smuts maintained on December 4th that he did not believe there was danger of war, but that if it came, the Government would consult Parliament before taking action.[40] Support of the League was continued, he declared, not because of hatred for Italy but because "they were realizing the power of the League to protect the small nations." On the same day in Johannesburg, Hofmeyr asserted the Government's determination that "nothing shall interfere with the carrying out of our obligations under the League Covenant."[41] When the Laval-Hoare plan became known, opposition was widespread. The general view was that while a formula or compromise might bring partial peace, none of the smaller nations would continue to have faith in the League if it permitted Italy to gain by its aggression.[42] The League should not endeavour "to satisfy Signor Mussolini's appetite," wrote the *Cape Times*, "but . . . to prove to the Duce and to everybody else that no nation will in future be permitted to make a profitable bargain out of an aggressive war."[43] News of the rejection of the Laval-Hoare plan and of the overwhelming opposition to it in Great Britain was received with great satisfaction. There was reluctance to be critical of the good faith of the British Government[44] but a strong feeling that collective League sanctions should be enforced without delay.[45]

In general, opinion in Commonwealth countries had reacted against the Laval-Hoare plan and news that it was no longer supported by the British Government met with approval. But the heart had been taken out of the League effort to enforce collective security. In the face of a threat by Mussolini to regard an effective sanction as a cause for war, the two most powerful countries in the League had at least temporarily considered offering the aggressor more than it had achieved up to that time by force of arms. Doubts about the sincerity of purpose of the British Government were reinforced by this experience. The smaller countries became more reluctant to commit themselves lest they be left "holding the bag." Doubts and divisions succeeded the rejection of the Laval-Hoare plan instead of an all-out effort to make the League action effective.

In Australia, *The Bulletin*, most consistent opponent of the League, ridiculed its impotence in the Italo-Ethiopian conflict. ". . . it has failed to prevent war; it has failed to stop war; it has failed to make peace," it wrote in January, 1936.[46] From Canada came a more thoughtful evaluation of the situation by a prominent Conservative, J. M. Macdonnell, who pointed out the need for "clear and unequivocal evidence that Great Britain is really supporting the League."[47] Dividing Canadian opinion into the isolationists, the imperialists, and the collectivists, he affirmed convincingly that only a strong League policy by Great Britain could unite the two latter groups as they had been united in support of Sir Samuel Hoare's speech at the Assembly and after the imposition of sanctions. Despite the uprising of British feeling against the Laval-Hoare proposals, there had been "a good deal of uneasiness at the revelation of double-dealing on the part of the United Kingdom," he declared, "and people were especially upset by the part played by Mr. Baldwin." This feeling not only existed in Canada but was "almost universal" in the United States, and it would take "a long period of honest and consistent conduct to banish it."

Developments after the Laval-Hoare plan had been discarded gave little encouragement to the idea that the British Government intended to support a more effective League policy henceforth. In regard to the safety of its own Mediterranean fleet and possessions, it was successful in securing pledges of support on January 22, 1936, from Greece, Turkey, and Jugoslavia which made formal the engagements undertaken by these countries in December, 1935.[48] These pledges were the more valuable in that they were made after consultation with Romania and Czechoslovakia, and stood in sharp contrast to the very restrained and vague response made by Spain. But despite the appointment as Foreign Secretary of Mr. Eden, who had played such an active rôle in organizing sanctions in October, British policy in support of Ethiopia was, in comparison with its efforts on its own behalf, halting and ineffective. No doubt Eden was made too conscious of the wide responsibilities of his new office to feel that he could concentrate at once upon efforts through the League. At least considerable time was allowed to lapse during which the Italians made unexpectedly successful advances in Ethiopia.

In January, the Council found itself unable (or unwilling) to extend financial assistance to Ethiopia to enable it to buy war materials with which to defend itself. Since at the same time the Council found no likelihood of securing an agreement between the parties to the dispute, the way was open for the Committee of Eighteen, meeting January 22nd, to deal once more with the subject of oil sanctions. This it did but only to the extent of setting up a Committee of Experts to give information regarding the probable effectiveness of this measure. Their report issued on February 12th made it clear that oil sanctions if combined with no more than normal exports by American oil producers would still have a serious, possibly crippling effect on Italy's war effort.[49] Under this spur, the Committee of Eighteen reassembled on March 2nd to consider the issue.

In the meantime, there had been few formal expressions of opinion in the Dominions except in South Africa, where Parliament reconvened on January 24, 1936, after having been adjourned since March 4, 1935.

On January 31st, Malan, leader of the Nationalist Party, moved a resolution opposing "any steps, including the application of military or economic sanctions which may tend towards extending the sphere of operations" of the Italo-Ethiopian war and expressing the view that "subject to its duty of self-defence in case of attack, South Africa should strictly refrain from participating in any war between other nations."[50] This point of view, maintained by a small but vocal minority, served mainly to throw into relief the positive support of League action by the Government and the small Labour party in the House.

Malan argued that developments had served to demonstrate that neutrality was not an academic question, that the identification of South Africa with British foreign policy was very unfortunate, that sanctions would be justifiable only if the League were a world organization and that with its existing constitution, sanctions might not only cause a new world disaster but destroy the League itself. His seconder, Dr. Van der Merwe, accused the Communist movement and British imperialism of being responsible for carrying sanctions to such an extreme and asserted that collective security was only a cloak for the means whereby England held its Empire together.

Hertzog and Smuts maintained an uncompromising front to this attack. Hertzog pointed out the danger to a small nation like South Africa if countries seeking additional space for their population were to be at liberty to go and take it. He moved an amendment supporting the policy of the Government in loyally carrying out its obligations as a member of the League of Nations. Smuts refused to endorse a proposal by Colonel Stallard, leader of the Dominion party, that safety could be found only through a united Empire defence, any more than the Malan view that South Africa could stand and fight alone. There was no defence any more in the world except through co-operation, he maintained, no security except through the help of friends and no alternative before South Africa except fidelity to their engagements and loyalty to the League of Nations. Only in collaboration with the British Commonwealth and the League of Nations could he see safety for South Africa.

Going even farther than the Government, the small Labour party in the House moved a further amendment urging on the League "the necessity for the imposition of oil sanctions and any other economic sanctions that may be calculated to bring the Italo-Abyssinian conflict to an end as speedily as possible." This was a reiteration of a resolution passed by the Labour party at a special conference and subsequently endorsed at the annual meeting even before Italy had been declared an aggressor. It smacked too much of independent action for the Government, however, and received only the four votes of the Labour party.

The original resolution was defeated by 98 votes to 14, and the Prime Minister's amendment supported by 93 votes to 14. It was evident that, despite the shock given by the Laval-Hoare plan, South Africa remained staunchly behind the sanctions programme.

In another legislative session on February 24, 1936, shortly before the Committee of Eighteen met in Geneva, Labour and Liberal members of the British Parliament pressed the Government to apply oil sanctions. Despite rather general replies by Eden and Cranborne, the Government was giving the question serious attention. When Eden went to the meeting of the Committee of Eighteen on March 2nd, it was with the endorsement of the Cabinet for the general tightening up of measures against Italy and for the imposition of oil sanctions.

At Geneva, however, Eden encountered the same French arguments that Hoare had met in Paris, though Laval had been replaced by Flandin. The latter had apparently been threatened by Mussolini with Italian withdrawal from the League and abrogation of the Franco-Italian Pact if oil sanctions were imposed.[51] Under this threat, Flandin asked a further postponement of the vote on oil sanctions while one more effort was made at mediation between the belligerents. Though Eden had behind him in support of .oil sanctions not only his own Government but also the overwhelming majority of the Committee and in addition received specific assurances of support from the Soviet Union, Turkey, Romania, and Jugoslavia, he consented to Flandin's plea for a brief postponement of action. A time limit of March 10th was set for the answers of the belligerents to an appeal from the Council looking to a speedy cessation of hostilities and restoration of peace. But before the time limit had been met, the entry of German troops into the demilitarized zone of the Rhineland on March 7, 1936, had breached not only the Treaty of Versailles but also the freely negotiated Locarno Treaty. Attention was thereby effectively distracted from the Italo-Ethiopian conflict, which was to continue henceforth to its disastrous conclusion. The "Stresa Front" became of too much concern once more to permit thoughts of extending punitive action against Italy.

German remilitarization of the Rhineland swept away the one remaining element of the safeguards whereby France had been persuaded at the Peace Conference to give up its demands for the detachment of this area from Germany. By opening the way for fortification of Germany's western borders, it threatened to block France's most effective means of exerting pressure on behalf of its eastern allies. Implicit in the development was a new alignment of power in Europe whereby encirclement of Germany by France and its allies would be replaced by the isolating of France itself.

As with the announcement of rearmament the year before, remilitarization of the Rhineland was a unilateral *fait accompli* in a situation whose revision had already been the subjects of extensive negotiations. As before, the treaty violation was accompanied by proposals for a new basis of peace in Europe. Once again France and Great Britain differed in the weight they put on these two aspects of the issue and once again France yielded to British pressure for negotiations rather than action.

Under both the Treaty of Versailles and the freely negotiated Locarno Treaty, German remilitarization of the Rhineland permitted or even called for military action by the other signatories. Such measures, it is now believed, would almost undoubtedly have caused the withdrawal of German troops from the area. But France, though prepared to share in collective action, was unwilling to act alone, and Great Britain was strongly opposed to forcible intervention. The Council, meeting in London on March 14th, condemned the German breach of international obligations and referred it to the Locarno powers. Subsequent negotiations with Hitler served but to postpone action until it became too late to initiate it.

Behind the British reaction to the Rhineland crisis lay fear of war and hope of a general European settlement. Much of the British public still had faith in Hitler's professions. The reassertion of full German sovereignty in territory indubitably German met a sympathetic response undisturbed at first by recognition of the implications of the move for the European balance of power. The Government, more aware of the potential dangers of the new situation, as Eden's speech to the House on March 9th disclosed, was no more ready for military action.

In this attitude, the British Government was at one with other Commonwealth Governments. On March 10th, Prime Minister King emphasized in the House of Commons that Canada had no obligations under the Locarno Treaty.[52] He coupled this declaration with the assertion that Canada had given no commitments to Great Britain in regard to its defence programme. As a member of the League he stated that Canada was responsible only for "those steps they had taken on their own behalf." To the challenge of Mr. Bennett that they should be bound by League action as such, he replied briefly that the Government would consider new obligations as they arose in the light of existing circumstances.

This caution also marked King's further comments on the situation on March 23rd in which he again stressed that Canada was not a party to the Locarno Treaty.[53] Bennett accepted the assurance that the Government was being kept informed by the British of the course of events and said he would not precipitate a debate which might "lessen or imperil" British efforts to preserve world peace in the face of serious difficulties. Woodsworth of the C.C.F. was less easily satisfied, however, and demanded a statement on Canada's attitude both to Great Britain and the League. To this, King replied in a statement strongly characteristic of the Liberal Government's policy. ". . . in a word the attitude of the government is to do nothing itself," he declared, "and if possible to prevent anything occurring which will precipitate one additional factor into the all-important discussions which are now taking place in Europe." Canada's first duty both to the League and to the Empire "with respect to all the great issues that come," he added, "is, if possible, to keep this country united." It was a clear indication of his hope that there would be no development which would face Canada with the awkward alternative of participating in action or not.

In South Africa, the tone was rather of rejoicing that the British Government was averting the danger of war and of hope that the removal of the last signs of inequality in Germany's position might pave the way for "a solid and lasting peace." Smuts, speaking in Capetown on March 22nd, applauded Great Britain as a peacemaker and said, "We are tremendously proud of the way she has stood in the breach when the world looked like being precipitated into war."[54] As to the German action, he believed it had brought to an end "The spirit of inequality, subjection, and bondage in which the Peace of Versailles was concluded." With this removal of the last provision of inequality, he held out hope that "a perfect peace" might be achieved through negotiations which would "take Hitler at his word." In this, he was applauded by *The Cape Times* which believed all nations including Germany desired to see a new order established in Europe.[55]

Leaders in the Pacific Dominions were less vocal but the same attitude appeared to prevail. New Zealand's Labour Government declared through the Governor General's speech on March 26th that "in general," it endorsed British policy up to that time.[56] New Zealand's influence would be used "always in the direction of peace," and at the same time in support of "maintaining the inviolability of international engagements voluntarily accepted." In Australia, no formal statement was made but *The Bulletin's* comment that "There is a large body of sensible opinion here that does not want war on any account, short of actual attack upon Britain and the Empire,"[57] was probably fairly typical of opinion. Bruce, acting as President of the Council, was directing his efforts towards ensuring negotiations and conciliation in the crisis. Commonwealth countries found it easier to be unanimous in opposition to any measures which might precipitate conflict than to agree upon positive action.

In the meantime, while attention was concentrated upon the Rhineland crisis, the Italian armies, equipped with modern weapons and using poison gas, were racing towards Addis Ababa. Despite the desperate appeals of the Ethiopian Government, no serious consideration was given to the situation between March 8th when the Italian Government agreed in principle to open negotiations leading to a settlement and April 20th when at last the Italo-Ethiopian conflict was allowed to share a place with the Rhineland crisis on the Council's agenda. In the interval, general Ethiopian resistance had practically come to an end. The hope of effective League action on Ethiopia's behalf was no less at an end, despite a few scattered efforts to rally it.

In Great Britain, Liberal and Labour members still pressed for a continuation of measures against Italy in the face of growing anti-League sentiment in the Conservative party. In the latter, there was fear lest Britain lose the position of arbiter in Europe coupled with doubt that the League was an adequate means through which to preserve peace. None the less Eden retained the pledge of the Government that it would support an intensified programme of sanctions, as he made known at the Council meeting on April 20th.[58] Paul-Boncour, however, under pressure from Italy, declared his belief that the essential task was to find a settlement so that Italy could be associated as soon as possible in the League's work of "European reconstruction."[59] And the Australian Government also represented on the Council had already made known its uneasiness lest the British attempt to exert further pressure on Italy.

Early in March, the *Sydney Morning Herald*, a long-established conservative Australian newspaper, had summed up prevailing sentiment on League action in the Italo-Ethiopian conflict in saying that "it had been shown again that without adequate force diplomacy can effect little."[60] The *Courier-Mail*, an anti-Labour paper with wide circulation in Queensland, pointed on April 17th to the ineffectiveness of sanctions and urged that the best terms possible should be sought for a country "that trusted too implicitly in the strength of the League."[61] The day before the opening of the Council session, it was reported that the Australian Federal Cabinet, deeply concerned over the European crisis and its possible repercussions on Australia, had called for a special report from the Deputy Prime Minister, Dr. Earle Page, then in London, on Eden's policy regarding sanctions.[62] At the same time the proposal to extend sanctions was stated to be causing serious concern.

In the Council session, which ended with no more than a "supreme appeal" to Italy to reach a settlement with Ethiopia in the spirit which the League should be able to expect from one of its permanent members, Bruce spoke in words clearly representative of the sentiment of his Government. He regretted the failure of recent efforts at conciliation but felt that the same line of action must be continued in the hope that it might eventually "meet with success."[63]   But this, he believed, was not enough. The result of experience with collective security demanded a re-examination of the system. ". . . to allow nations to be lulled into a false belief of security where, in fact, there is no security," he declared, "and to allow them to rely upon assistance which will not be forthcoming, is not a contribution to the peace of the world but is a menace to it." They were words not unlike those with which Hoare had defended his efforts to find a settlement lest Ethiopia be misled into expecting more assistance than in fact it would receive. They summed up the fear that had been present in some Australian minds since the beginning of the conflict, that to become involved in ineffective collective action was to court war and have no other result than unjustifiably to encourage the victim of aggression to resist.

As League action had been carried out, the verdict was not inappropriate. Not enough hindrance had been offered to Italy's aggression or enough help to Ethiopia to change the pattern of events. On May 5, 1936, the Italian army entered Addis Ababa. Two days before, the Emperor had left the country to become an exile in Great Britain. On May 9th, the decree of annexation was published by Mussolini and the following day, in a supreme gesture of contempt, a copy of the decree was handed to the Secretary-General of the League of Nations.

The League had failed to carry out the purpose to which fifty-one of its members had pledged themselves. It remained to be seen what response would be made to the failure. Would sanctions be retained in the hope of eventually forcing Italy to relinquish its hold on Ethiopia or lifted in despair at its success? If lifted, would the Italian conquest be recognized or would the one slight sanction of non-recognition evolved under American initiative in the Sino-Japanese conflict be maintained?

Among League countries, the most steadfast in support of implementation of the sanctions programme was one of the smallest members of the Commonwealth, South Africa. Writing to Gilbert Murray in a letter published May 7th, Smuts declared, "I am for hanging on grimly to sanctions, even if it prove impossible to add further sanctions. . . . If sanctions cannot end the war they could and should secure a decent peace, even if Italy goes bust in the process."[64]   He warned prophetically, "If Italy succeeds in 'getting away with it,' we are up against a crisis as grave as has ever been faced since 1914. For if she does, the thing will be repeated on a much vaster scale than that of Abyssinia." That this was not an isolated opinion was borne out by the unanimous backing it received from leading newspapers in Cape Province.[65] Commonwealth Governments were urged to support the League in its time of crisis and to maintain sanctions "until the new law of the world is respected."

During the debate on estimates for external affairs on May 6, Hertzog endorsed the belief that the League should maintain sanctions, even if it took years to achieve their purpose. "Is it permitted in society that the person who steals shall retain the result of his theft and booty?" he asked. "The Government became a member of the League of Nations for no other reason than to prevent international robbery, and the Government wants to stand by that."[66] If the nations would not continue sanctions, then the League of Nations would be dead, he maintained, "but we must not go and give instructions now to our representative to co-operate in killing the League of Nations." If it did maintain its stand, then he believed it would exist in the future with strength and even greater prestige. Smuts, in a public statement the following day, saw no less drastic an alternative.[67] If sanctions were continued, he believed that not only would the League be saved, but the peace of the world maintained for many years to come. "The choice is not between this League and another League," he said to those who preached revision of the Covenant, "It is between this League and chaos and destruction."

Even a month later, Hertzog, speaking in the Senate, still asserted his belief that the League could meet its trial successfully.[68] If its members would be "willing to incur the necessary risks which go with the obligations" they had assumed, it could maintain peace. If not, the biggest nations of the world would be masters and the smaller nations the objects of their mastery. Every nation would have to arm to the utmost in the effort to protect itself. In the final vote showing the degree of his support, "unqualified approval of the Government's support of the League of Nations during the Italo-Abyssinian crisis" was given by 25 votes to nine.[69]

In New Zealand, there was a unanimous feeling of disappointment in Parliament coupled with a good deal of general support for the conception of collective security. In the debate on May 15th on renewing the Sanctions Order, some difference of view showed between the Opposition, which felt that since sanctions had been ineffective there was no point in keeping them in operation, and the Labour Government, which saw them as the only means of achieving collective security.[70] Confessing himself an idealist, Prime Minister Savage declared he still believed that a League of Nations composed of idealists "prepared to face up to the realities of the situation" could make progress towards realization of the ideal of peace on earth.   But he agreed that whatever action was taken must be collective and that the Commonwealth "standing together, not separately" should take the lead in reorganizing the League which he still believed to be "our only hope."   Others added the Empire connection, British rearmament and measures for New Zealand's own defence.

But where the South African Government had indicated strong backing for continuation of measures against Italy and the New Zealand Government moderate support, the Governments of Australia, Canada, and the Irish Free State favoured lifting sanctions.   Among the three, the sharpest change was in the attitude of de Valera as expressed in the *Dail* on June 18th.   He had said from the first that the League would have its last opportunity in the Italo-Ethiopian conflict to show whether or not collective security was practical.   He was now convinced that the League as organized was incapable of fulfilling this purpose.[71]   To the military action which he was now convinced was a necessary corollary to a programme of sanctions, he was unwilling to pledge his country. He believed in the future, therefore, that the League should be used only as a forum for conciliation and arbitration.   Though the Opposition criticized him for being discouraged so quickly and some deputies felt that complete economic and financial sanctions might have had the desired effect, de Valera refused to modify his stand.   "If we had the choice tomorrow of continuing with the old League of Nations as it was or withdrawing from it," he said, "the advice I would give our Government would be to withdraw."   In the immediate situation, he secured agreement that sanctions having failed to fulfil their purpose should be withdrawn.

The view of the Canadian Government was not dissimilar.   In a statement in the House also made on June 18th, King declared that the raising of sanctions would be supported.[72]   The Government had participated in League sanctions in the spirit of his statement of October 29th and had been ready to concur in any proposal regarding oil which was generally supported.   But no appreciable number of countries were ready to continue measures of compulsion against Italy including war. "Collective bluffing cannot bring collective security," he pointed out, "and most countries have shown that they are not prepared to make firm commitments beyond their immediate interests."   For the future, while he believed the League to be an indispensable agent for organizing and strengthening the forces of good will, it was clearly impossible for Canada to make binding commitments to use either economic or military force. Situations might arise in which military action was necessary but that would be for Parliament to decide in the light of the given situation. Bennett asked whether Canada would not stand beside South Africa in support of sanctions but hastily withdrew the suggestion when King insisted it would mean being prepared to support the stand with military sanctions. The Conservative leader felt the greatest assurance for the maintenance of peace lay in strengthening the ties of Empire. Woodsworth of the C.C.F. maintained on the contrary that Canada's trouble had been its tendency to follow Great Britain. He favoured a declaration of neutrality to let Britain know that it could not count on Canada's aid if it became involved in war, and felt that participation in the League should only be on the terms of not participating actively in any overseas conflict whatever. That the general trend, except among the Conservatives, was towards isolation and separate action was evidenced by King's emphasis that the decision on sanctions had been taken before any indication was given regarding British action in the matter.

Most eager of all the Dominion Governments for the raising of sanctions seems to have been that of Australia. A hint of its attitude was given as early as May 14th in the statement by the Minister of External Affairs, Senator George Pearce, in the Senate, in which he declared that the subject was being seriously considered by the Government which also believed that the Covenant and "existing League machinery to establish collective security and to maintain the rule of law in international relations" should be re-examined.[73] On June 5th, it was reported from Melbourne that a considerable portion of Australian public opinion and the press favoured raising sanctions, the more so because Australian commerce was suffering from loss of the Italian wool market.[74] Word leaked out on June 16th that a message had been sent to the British Government through Bruce indicating the Australian view that sanctions should end immediately.[75] Two days later, Lyons formally announced that he had instructed Bruce to favour lifting of sanctions and a re-examination of the Covenant.[76] The continuation of sanctions, the Government believed, would not restore Ethiopia's position and only serve to preclude Italian participation in peace measures, presumably in Europe.

In comparison with this relative unity of opinion on the future of sanctions within individual Dominions though not between them, opinion in Great Britain was sharply divided between those who felt that the defeat of Ethiopia made their intensification the more necessary and those who maintained that the only alternative to calling them off was to risk war. As early as April 30th, Winston Churchill called for the abandonment of sanctions.[77]   From then on a vigorous contest was waged in press, public meetings, and parliament by the pro- and anti-sanctionist groups.   The Government reiterated its support of League action until it became apparent that there was no longer the force behind the pro-sanction drive which had caused the defeat of the Laval-Hoare plan.   On June 10th, Neville Chamberlain, Chancellor of the Exchequer, broke the pattern of innocuous statements with a speech in which he declared that to continue sanctions would be "the very midsummer of madness."[78]   The functions of the League should henceforth be limited to accord with its real powers, he declared.   Challenged in the House by Attlee next day, Baldwin would neither deny nor confirm that the words represented the policy of the Government as a whole.   But on June 18th, formal announcement was given by Eden that the British Government would recommend the raising of sanctions at Geneva. Despite vigorous protests, Labour and Liberals could muster only 170 votes on June 23rd for a measure of censure as compared with 384 votes against.   The force of the British drive behind sanctions had spent itself.

The British Government had taken the lead in organizing action through the League.   It had been returned to office in November, 1935, with a large majority which reflected the general satisfaction at its wholehearted support of sanctions.   With the Australian and Canadian Governments, it now led the way in making official announcement of intention to support their abandonment.   The simultaneous announcement by the three Governments of their decisions suggests a measure of consultation but the decisions themselves can almost certainly be said to have been the result of independent considerations.   In varying degrees, the three Governments had always been sceptical of the potentialities of League action and fearful of being placed in a situation which might lead to conflict.   The Baldwin Government had undergone a temporary conversion under the stimulus of the Peace Ballot, the pressure of Mr. Eden, and an impending election.   But the reception of the Laval-Hoare plan by the Prime Minister and subsequent developments showed that his heart was not in the sanctions effort.   The Australian Government had been dubious from the first but anxious to support Great Britain at least in public.   But its own fear of British conflict with Italy had been reinforced by the active opposition to League action of the Labour party.   The Canadian Liberals had long sought to withhold themselves from active commitments abroad. Coming into office after League action had been brought under way, the King Government had sought a middle road of support for existing sanctions coupled with an assertion of no commitments to adopt a more stringent programme. The potential threat of conflict over oil sanctions had led it to somewhat the same reaction as Hoare and Baldwin had to the same apparent danger. All three Governments placed the immediate fear of conflict higher than the long-range hope of an effective international organization through which war might be banished.

These similarities of governmental attitude did not reflect comparable sentiments in their respective countries. There was a vigorous and well-organized body of opinion in Great Britain which offered strong support for a League programme. In Canada, opinion on behalf of League action was less well organized, less pervasive, but within its own circles exerted considerable influence. In Australia, sentiment on behalf of the League was weakest, the more so because its natural supporters in labour were too isolationist and anti-imperialist to appreciate the potential value of what was being undertaken. But in one unfortunate respect, there was a strong similarity in the operation of public opinion in the three major countries of the Commonwealth. The flare-up of indignation over the Laval-Hoare plan appeared to exhaust its positive force on behalf of League action. Thenceforth, despite periodic demonstrations in favour of curbing Italy, governments were left to take almost any decisions they would. Opinion remained more vocal in Great Britain than elsewhere but even there its effectiveness had gone.

Reactions in the smaller countries of the Commonwealth followed a different pattern. From the first, South Africa had maintained an unwavering stand in support of sanctions and even after the decision of the British Government, it did not change. The New Zealand Government would have liked to support continuation of sanctions but preferred to maintain solidarity with the majority of Commonwealth countries and of League powers. The Irish Free State Government came closest in its response to those of the larger Commonwealth countries but by a different route. De Valera had believed as the Governments of the other two smaller members of the Commonwealth still did in the overriding necessity of building an effective international organization. He had given convincing evidence of his belief. It was disillusionment which now led him to change. The chief difference between the attitudes of the Irish and the South African Governments was that the former gave in when it became convinced that sanctions had failed to fulfil their purpose while the latter was prepared to maintain its stand to the end, and even beyond the end. In this, however, the South African Government was alone not only within the Commonwealth but also within the League.

The day after the British Government gave notice of its intention to support the raising of sanctions, the French Government signified its agreement. A sudden accession of concern for the League had resulted from the coming into power of the Blum Government and popular indignation at the Italian annexation of Ethiopia. But it came too late to change developments, or at this stage to affect the British Government, which could say with justice that every effort it had made in the earlier part of the conflict had been sabotaged by former French administrations. Belgium associated itself with the decision on June 22nd; the Scandinavian countries, on June 25th; and three Latin American countries and Poland, the following day. On June 27th, Poland took steps to drop sanctions as Haiti and Ecuador had already done. American neutrality restrictions had been withdrawn on June 20th. When the Assembly reconvened on June 30th, as the Argentinian Government had requested it should, there was no doubt about what action it would take regarding sanctions. The only questions were in what terms the decisions would be publicly stated and whether or not Italy's conquest would be recognized.

In the Assembly, Eden reaffirmed the thesis of the British Government that nothing short of military action could now change the situation and that sanctions should be withdrawn because they could no longer achieve the purpose for which they had been instituted. Many of the other delegates during the four-day debate coupled their regret at the failure of sanctions with proposals for the revision of the Covenant. For some it was merely a face-saving expedient. Others like the French and Russians made it obvious that they wished a League strong only in regard to their particular purposes. But for many of the smaller states, it was reflection of the belief that the Covenant which they had looked on as a safeguard now seemed to embody a threat to their existence. So long as the Great Powers were unwilling to stand steadfastly behind them, its coercive provisions appeared to have implicit within them the danger which they were designed to prevent.

Conspicuous for its outspoken condemnation of the policies of the Great Powers which had "let down" the League, te Water's speech was, with the exception of that of the Emperor of Ethiopia, the most impressive made during the Assembly. Speaking on the opening day, he recalled bitingly the "lofty protestations" of the British and French statements at the September meeting.[79] Today, he pointed out, "Fifty nations, led by three of the most powerful nations of the world, are about to declare their powerlessness to protect the weakest in their midst from destruction." Was the successful resistance of Ethiopia "a condition precedent to the fulfilment of their collective obligation?"

The South African Government found justification for no such argument. And he asked, "Where are the great Powers leading us, who have not the faith to persevere?"

Te Water's appeal from his Government for retention of sanctions found support only from New Zealand, whose representative declared that his Government "still favours sanctions . . . their maintenance and intensification."[80] If "an effective majority" of League powers had agreed to this, it would have supported such measures. But with that majority on the other side, Sir James Parr believed "Their maintenance, with any chance of success, is, therefore, impossible." He agreed to the removal of sanctions but only on the understanding that there would be a thorough consideration of the Covenant in September to which he felt all nations of the world should be invited. That unlike the representatives of most other small states, he favoured strengthening rather than limiting the functions of the League was made clear in his closing words that "the all important question" was "how best to make the League really efficient in deterring any future aggressor against the world's peace."

In contrast, de Valera, eloquent of the humiliation the League had suffered, believed that commitments must be "rigidly restricted . . . to those we know can be loyally carried out."[81] He pointed out that no small nation could but feel that "what is Ethiopia's fate today may well be its own fate tomorrow, should the greed or the ambition of some powerful neighbour prompt its destruction." War was even then threatening in Europe if its causes were not removed. In such issues, peace was now dependent upon the great Powers. All that was left to the small powers was "resolutely to determine that they will not become the tools of any great power," he declared, "and . . . resist with whatever strength they may possess every attempt to force them into a war against their will." It was a declaration of isolation born of the feeling of helplessness.

In a stiff and formal statement, the Hon. Vincent Massey, Canadian High Commissioner in London, associated his Government with the move to raise sanctions. Though "deeply regretting the failure of the joint attempt to protect a weak fellow-Member of the League," it found no "practical alternative" to their abandonment.[82] Even were they continued, he added, there was no certainty that their objective might not "soon be lost sight of in the very serious disturbances that might arise," a strong hint of the fear which Eden had also expressed that Germany might fish in the troubled waters. As to the future, he declared that Canada's action in participating in the sanctions programme was not to be regarded "as necessarily establishing a precedent."

In particular, the Government recognized no commitment to adopt military sanctions without prior consent of Parliament. It was potentially another declaration of isolation, characteristic of the growing strength of this sentiment on the North American continent.

From Australia came a more careful analysis of the situation which had caused the League's failure but equal opposition to the continuation of sanctions. The achievement of their goal could be secured only if the nations were prepared "to meet force with force," declared Bruce.[83] Full application of economic, financial, and military sanctions would undoubtedly have stopped Italy's aggression despite the lack of universality of the League. But the nations had not identified such action closely enough with national interest to be willing for the sacrifices involved. Sanctions of the type imposed and with the limitation that they should rule out the risk of reprisals must inevitably fail. Was it not fairer to Ethiopia to declare this openly? "Have we not misled that unfortunate nation long enough?" he asked. He pledged Australia's co-operation in future reconsideration of the Covenant but with the warning that if some method of "remedying the defects which have been shown in the existing system" were not found, "the League will inevitably be destroyed."

Despite the contrast in their emphases, te Water, de Valera, and Bruce were not far apart in their analysis of the situation. All three were aware that the real failure of the League had been the unwillingness of its members, particularly the Great Powers, to identify national and international interests. South Africa and the Irish Free State, small countries with limited responsibilities, had been willing to do so. Australia had not. Great Britain for all its early leadership had interpreted international interest always in national terms. On such a basis, threat to national security would always be the Achilles heel of international action.

Where success in League action would have silenced doubts on the value of internationalism, failure tended to intensify them. New Zealand's Government was to be almost alone in its subsequent attempts to make the League a forceful international body. For the most part both within and without the Commonwealth, the experience was to reinforce concern with regional security. The British Conservatives traditionally followed this emphasis. So did the Canadian Liberals which now drew back temporarily into North American exclusiveness. Australian concern focussed on the Pacific while South Africa reconsidered its position in its own continent. National defence programmes came to the fore. So, too, in some parts of the Commonwealth, did questions of co-ordinated defence plans.

The experience with League action was in some measure to press Dominions like South Africa back into dependence upon the British Navy for defence. It was not without significance that during the debate on May 6th in the South African House of Assembly, in which Hertzog reaffirmed the Government's support of sanctions, the Minister of Defence announced that he was leaving shortly for England to consult with the British Government and the Committee on Imperial Defence.[84] True, he pledged to those who feared involvement in British wars, that "We shall take part in no war except where the true interests of South Africa make such a participation inevitable. . . ." but the implication of closer contacts was clear. In another way, however, the experience was to loosen the bonds of Commonwealth which depended not only on interest but also on confidence and respect. In his letter to *The Times* in April, 1936, Mr. J. M. Macdonnell had pointed out that if "the feeling widely held in certain quarters in Canada that Great Britain merely uses the League when it finds it convenient is confirmed, then the movement in this country away from any co-operation with Great Britain will be greatly intensified."[85] British policy in support of League action had united imperialists and collectivists within the Dominion. Its failure made a sharper split between them than had existed before the temporary alliance had been forged.

After the Assembly debate had registered the views of member states, they faced the necessity of taking positive action. The Ethiopian delegation pressed for a clear-cut declaration of non-recognition of Italy's conquest and for a substantial loan. After unsuccessful attempts to reconcile this challenge with the general desire for an innocuous declaration, a resolution was evolved by the Belgian delegate which committed the Assembly to nothing except ending sanctions and a future reconsideration of the Covenant. It was declared, however, to embody the intention of the Ethiopian resolution on non-recognition of Italian annexation for which Eden also had asked in his Assembly speech. Though in fact non-recognition was not mentioned in the Assembly declaration, the device made it possible to avoid a direct vote on the subject. The resolution passed with only the Ethiopian vote against and four abstentions, including that of South Africa. In the end there was even a less precise statement on non-recognition in this conflict in which League sanctions had been imposed than in the earlier Sino-Japanese dispute. The issue remained to complicate the proceedings of the next Assembly, and to be one of the bones of contention in subsequent international relations.

In the face of this vacillation and weakness, it may be asked whether anything constructive had been accomplished by the imposition of sanctions. For the time being the results seemed only negative but in the long view it had significance as a demonstration that nations could act collectively. Moreover, despite the criticism of economic sanctions, evidence of their operations shows that they had a definite effect, particularly in the field of exports to Italy. In reports on the application of Article 16 sent to the Secretary-General in accordance with a resolution adopted by the Co-ordination Committee on July 6, 1936, the overseas Dominions indicated the effect sanctions had had upon their trade.[86] New Zealand, which normally had relatively little commerce with Italy, estimated that the loss to that country would amount to about £200,000 (New Zealand £). The value of Australian exports to Italy dropped from £991,483 (£A) in 1934-35 to £363,705 in 1935-36. South African imports and exports were affected markedly; the imports dropping from a value of £451,412 for the first six months of 1935 to £45,190 for the comparable period of 1936, and the exports to Italy from £544,502 to £141,270 in the same periods though there was an increase in exports to Italian possessions which amounted to about £162,000.

The Canadian Government reported that Italian imports sank from a value of $1,523,685 in the eight months between November, 1934, and June, 1935, to $726,836 in the comparable period during which sanctions were in force. Exports to Italy were practically halved, the difference being between $2,189,957 and $1,193,115. The most decisive difference was in the specific products subject to sanctions, scrap iron or steel, aluminium, other metals, and nickel which dropped from a value of $604,107 to $679. The most significant of these products was nickel because of Canada's predominant position as a producer in this field. Stock piling by Italy just before sanctions were imposed and substantial increases of American and German imports from Canada immediately thereafter suggest that Italy did not feel the effect of the embargo immediately.[87] In his speech of June 18th, however, Prime Minister King declared that both Canada and Great Britain had been concerned to ensure that no nickel would reach Italy and said that none had been sold in the United States for export to other countries.[88]

This information from the overseas Dominions on the effect of sanctions, the most detailed contained in the reports supplied to the Secretary-General, demonstrated that in fact economic sanctions could have a great effect on the economy of a country. General comments indicated the need of putting them into effect more swiftly and it was clear that the influence took some time to show. By the spring of 1936, however, Italy, which had already adopted severe economic and financial controls due to earlier economic difficulties, was being forced to intensify them drastically.[89] It was, in fact, true that if Ethiopia had been able to hold out to anything like the same extent that China did in the earlier dispute, economic sanctions even limited to the types adopted would have almost certainly achieved their purpose.

This aspect of the experience was to have almost no publicity. The general view, not surprisingly, was that economic sanctions had failed and would always fail if not backed by force. This verdict was probably correct unless the adversaries were fairly equally matched in strength, in which case there would seem little doubt but that economic sanctions would turn the balance.

Where the experience in the Sino-Japanese dispute left League members uneasily aware that in a future challenge to collective security they would have to act or abdicate, that of the Italo-Ethiopian conflict convinced all but a few that League action was ineffective and potentially dangerous. The original hope in the Dominions that collective security would gain its effectiveness from the self-restraint of nations had vanished with the outbreak of trouble in the Far East. The later hope of the collectivists that the application of sanctions would ensure an ultimate peace seemed to disappear with their failure to preserve Ethiopia. Only the willingness to risk war to save peace might have stopped the descent into still more troublous times. In failing to face the risk, not only the League but the Commonwealth itself had been placed in jeopardy.

REFERENCES FOR CHAPTER VII

1. For the official texts, *see O.J.*, 1935, Spec. Sup. No. 150, pp. 2-12. By December 12, 1935, proposal 1 had been put into force by 50 Governments; 2 by 47 Governments; 3 by 43; 4 by 45; and 5 by 46. Others had indicated their intention to do so.

2. *O.J.*, 1935, Spec. Sup. No. 146, pp. 22-27 and 52-59. Dispute between Ethiopia and Italy, Second Session, Committee of Eighteen, Second Meeting, October 31, 1935, and Sub-Committee on Economic Measures, First Meeting, November 1, 1936.

3. *O.J.*, 1935, Spec. Sup. No. 145, pp. 93-94. Dispute between Ethiopia and Italy, First Session, Sub-Committee on Economic Measures, First Meeting, October 1, 1935.

4. *Ibid.*, p. 104. Third Meeting, October 17, 1935.

5. *Ibid.*, p. 115. Fourth Meeting, October 18, 1935.

6. *Ibid.*, p. 80. Committee of Eighteen, Seventh Meeting, October 19, 1935.

7. It is interesting to note that the *Montreal Gazette*, Dec. 9, 1935, wrote in an editorial that Dr. Riddell had sponsored the resolution "at the request of his fellow delegates. As Dr. Riddell is dean of Geneva's diplomatic corps, his selection as mover of the resolution before the Committee of Eighteen was a natural gesture and a logical part of procedure." There is no other evidence to support this point.

8. *Canada, House of Commons Debates*, February 10, 1936, I, pp. 92 ff. (Mr. Mackenzie King).

9. *O.J.*, 1935, Spec. Sup. No. 146, p. 37. Dispute between Ethiopia and Italy, Second Session, Committee of Eighteen, Fourth Meeting, November 2, 1935.

10. *Ibid.*, pp. 37-38.

11. *Ibid.*, pp. 61-62. Sub-Committee on Economic Measures, Second Meeting, November 4, 1935.

12. *Ibid.*, p. 46. Committee of Eighteen, Seventh Meeting, November 6, 1935.

13. *Canada, House of Commons Debates*, February 10, 1936, I, pp. 92 ff. (Mr. King).

14. *O.J.*, 1935, Spec. Sup. No. 146, p. 61. Dispute between Ethiopia and Italy, Second Session, Subcommittee on Economic Measures, Second Meeting, November 4, 1935.

15. *See* above, p. 199.

16. *Canada, House of Commons Debates*, 1936, I, 92 ff.

17. *The Daily Telegraph*, Dec. 7, 1935.

18. For a detailed account of these and subsequent developments, *see* Toynbee, *Survey, 1935*, II, 277 ff.

19. de Bono, Emilio, *The Conquest of an Empire*. With an introduction by Benito Mussolini. (London, 1937.)

20. *The Manchester Guardian*, Dec. 3, 1935, reported that: "isolationist sentiment in the Dominion, notably in Quebec, has been thoroughly aroused by the suggestion that the Canadian Government is leading a drive for the extension of sanctions and a statement was regarded as necessary to meet these criticisms . . ."

21. In his speech to the House, Mr. King cited *The Spectator* (London) of Nov. 22, a Canadian Press despatch dated London, Nov. 26, and a Canadian Press-Havas despatch dated Geneva, Nov. 26. *House of Commons Debates*, 1936, I, 92 ff. There may also have been some embarrassment in seeming to take the lead regarding a product of which Canada produced little.

22. *Canada, 1936, Documents*, No. 19.

23. *New York Times*, Dec. 4, 1935.

24. *The Times*, Dec. 5, 1935.

25. *The Globe* (Toronto), Dec. 4, 1935.

26. *The Manchester Guardian*, Dec. 4, 1935.

27. *Le Temps* (Paris), Dec. 5, 1935.

28. *Montreal Gazette*, Dec. 4, 1935. He also quoted Virginio Gayda writing in the *Giornale d'Italia:* "The granite block of imperial will here displays the most noticeable fissures," and *La Tribune* which said: "The common action ship is beginning to take water. Canada has been brought face to face with her responsibilities for initiative which was capable of bringing an Italian reaction that would profoundly trouble the already delicate European political condition."

29. *The Toronto Daily Star*, Dec. 4, 1935. Its comments and those of the *Saturday Night* (Toronto), quoted in the *Winnipeg Free Press*, Dec. 9 and 10, 1935, together with comments from the *Vancouver Province*, the *Saskatoon Star-Phoenix*, the *Ottawa Citizen*, the *Ottawa Journal*, and the *Mail and Empire* (Toronto).

30. *Canada, House of Commons Debates*, 1936, I, 92 ff.

31. *New York Times*, Dec. 5, 1935. It appeared in *The Manchester Guardian*, Dec. 6, 1935.

32. *Great Britain, House of Commons Debates*, Vol. 307, cols. 2007-2017: First Session of the 37th Parliament, Dec. 19, 1935.

33. Toynbee, *Survey*, 1935, II, 276 and 243 ff.

34. *Canada, House of Commons Debates*, 1936, 72: 4185-4221 (unrev. ed.).

35. *Montreal Star*, Dec. 13, 1935.

36. *The Toronto Daily Star*, Dec. 12, 1935.

37. *Winnipeg Free Press*, Dec. 14, 1935.

38. *The Times*, Dec. 18, 1935.

39. *The Daily Telegraph*, Dec. 12, 1935.

40. *The Times*, Dec. 5, 1935.

41. *Ibid.*

42. *New York Times*, Dec. 13, 1935 (despatch from Bloemfontein, South Africa).

43. Quoted in *The Times*, Dec. 11, 1935.

44. *E.g.*, the *Johannesburg Star*, quoted in *The Times*, Dec. 18, 1935.

45. *E.g.*, *The Cape Times*, quoted in *The Daily Telegraph*, Dec. 21, 1935.

46. Ferguson, "Australia's Attitude towards Collective Security," *Australian Foreign Policy, 1935-1936*, p. 19.

47. Letter to the Editor, dated April 9, 1936, *The Times*, Apr. 21, 1936.

48. *Cmd. 5072* of 1936.

49. Toynbee, *op. cit.*, p. 331 ff.

50. *South Africa, House of Assembly Debates*, 1936, 26: 30-167, for the whole debate.

51. Toynbee, *op. cit.*, p. 336 ff.

52. *Canada, House of Commons Debates*, March 10, 1936.

53. *Ibid.*, March 26, 1936.

54. *The Daily Telegraph*, Mar. 23, 1936.

55. *The Cape Times*, Mar. 23, 1936.

56. *New Zealand, Parliamentary Debates* (Legislative Council), 1936, First Session, p. 6.

57. Quoted in Ferguson, "Australia's Attitude towards Collective Security," in *Australian Foreign Policy, 1935-1936*, p. 19.

58. *O.J.*, 1936, No. 4, Pt. II, pp. 337-9: Ninety-first Session of the Council, Tenth Meeting, April 20, 1936.

59. *Ibid.*, pp. 379-80.

60. *Australian Foreign Policy*, p. 23.

61. *Ibid.*, p. 21.

62. *The Observer* (London), Apr. 19, 1936.

63. *O.J.*, April, 1936, II, pp. 385-86: Ninety-first (Extraordinary) Session of the Council.

64. *The Manchester Guardian*, May 7, 1936.   The letter was written April 19.

65. *New York Times*, May 6, 1935.

66. *South Africa, House of Assembly Debates*, 1936, 27: 3145-3146.   The debate extends from col. 3089-3159.

67. *The Daily Telegraph*, May 7, 1936.

68. *South Africa, Senate Debates*, 1936, pp. 234-6 (June 2).

69. This was the amendment moved by the Government to the original motion calling for amendment of the Covenant by removing the obligation of Article 10 and by limiting League activities "in the interest of world peace, to the application of pacifist measures."

70. *New Zealand, Parliamentary Debates*, 1936, First Session, pp. 149-184.

71. *Dail Eireann Debates*, 62: 2649-2801.   Earlier proposals for revising the Covenant were included in his Assembly speech, October, 1935.   *O.J.*, 1935, Spec. Sup. No. 138, pp. 81-82.

72. *Canada, House of Commons Debates*, 1936, 72: 4185-4221 (unrev. ed.).

73. *J.P.E.*, 1936, XVII, 544.

74. *Le Temps*, June 7, 1936.

75. *The Times*, June 17, 1936.

76. *Ibid.*, p. 463.

77. Toynbee, *Survey*, 1935, II, 455.   *See* section XIII of this volume for a careful consideration of British reactions to the Italian victory.

78. *Ibid.*, p. 463.

79. *O.J.*, 1936, Spec. Sup. No. 151, pp. 31-33: Plenary Meetings, Pt. II, Annex III.

80. *Ibid.*, p. 49.

81. *Ibid.*, pp. 47-49.

82. *Ibid.*, pp. 33-34.

83. *Ibid.*, 38-40.

84. *South Africa, House of Assembly Debates*, 1936, 27: 3098-3159.

85. *The Times*, April 21, 1936.

86. *League Document C.L. 216*, 1936, II, A.   Co-ordination of Measures under Article 16 of the Covenant, Annex, II, New Zealand (Sept. 5, 1936), Annex III, Canada (Sept. 21, 1936), Annex VI, South Africa (Oct. 8, 1936), Annex VII, Australia, (Oct. 16, 1936), United Kingdom (Oct. 31, 1936).

87. Canadian exports to Germany increased from a value of $158,000 in Oct., 1935, to $425,000 in Nov., 1935.   Exports to the United States increased by $6,000,000 to make a total of $26,000,000.   *New York Times*, Dec. 19, 1935.   In the month of October, 1935, before sanctions were imposed, Italy bought 12,779 cwt. of nickel valued at $558,712, almost twice the amount of this commodity bought by Italy during the whole of 1934.   *The Times*, Nov. 22, 1935.

88. *Canada, House of Commons Debates*, 1936, 72: 4185-4221 (unrev. ed.).   In October, 1935, Mr. R. C. Stanley of the International Nickel Company of Canada had declared that "The Company does not sell any nickel in the United States for subsequent export therefrom, and will continue to adhere to that policy.   All nickel for European consumption is sold to British concerns. . . ."   *The Financial News* (Toronto), Oct. 18, 1935.

89. H. V. Hodson, "The Economic Aspects of the Italo-Abyssinian Conflict," in Toynbee, *Survey*, 1935, II, 435-42.

CHAPTER VIII

POLICIES IN A TIME OF DIMINISHING
SECURITY

To avoid war and to find a new basis of peace became the key-notes of the period succeeding the failure of League action in the Italo-Ethiopian conflict, a period in which international strains grew not less but greater. It opened with new developments at both ends of the Mediterranean, the Turkish appeal for revision of the Straits Convention and civil war in Spain, soon to become a European battleground. In the middle of 1937, the second Sino-Japanese war broke out in the Far East. Despite all efforts at appeasement, Italy left the League later in 1937, and joined the anti-Comintern Pact avowedly aimed at the Soviet Union. In March, 1938, Austria was annexed. In the fall, Czechoslovakia was threatened with German invasion. At each stage of these successive crises were posed the issues: could peace be preserved at that moment and could a foundation be found on which more lasting arrangements might be built?

More desperately than ever before in the inter-war period were answers offered to these questions. Some favoured a new basis for collective security by making commitments automatic. Others insisted the emphasis should be put upon universality and hence on conciliation rather than force. Those who mistrusted the general approach through the League preferred more limited commitments through regional arrangements. Almost all countries began or intensified rearmament programmes for their own defence and among the Great Powers to increase their international influence. At the same time means were sought through economic or territorial adjustments to satisfy the demands of the aggressive powers for an improved position.

It was a Great Powers' period in which the smaller countries had but little to say in the complicated negotiations centring around specific issues. They could attempt to strengthen the hand of the particular Great Power with which they had closest relations or to separate themselves from what was going on in the hope of not being involved if war should come. They could press for one kind of League policy or another, for the League was still a platform for a minor power. They could strengthen their defences but without much hope of their effectiveness unless some more powerful country was prepared to come to their support.   To be a small country in a period of continual crises was to be torn by apprehension with little chance to affect the outcome of events. Even to be a Great Power seeking peace was an unhappy state.

To the Commonwealth, the time brought dark memories of the period before 1914.   But the analogy was far from exact.   Great Britain was relatively much weaker in the time from 1936-39 than from 1911-14.   Its potential enemies in Europe were stronger, its allies less sure than in the earlier period.   Its naval position, even in Europe, was weaker and the country lay open to the assault of a new weapon, air power, which was unhindered by the traditional barrier of the English Channel.   In the Far East the defence of its interests in the earlier time, the Anglo-Japanese Alliance, had been replaced by paper arrangements of which the naval limitations and restrictions on fortifying bases were denounced by Japan early in 1936.   The United States had retreated into isolation behind the Neutrality Act.   Nor within the Commonwealth itself was there as much unquestioning support as in the earlier period.   Slow as they had been to develop individual pro- grammes in international affairs, there had emerged within the Dominions in the period after 1919 points of view which were gradually crystallizing. There were divisions of opinion on international issues within each Dominion as there were between them.   They had become intensified during the Italo-Ethiopian conflict and in some instances coupled with mistrust of British intentions.   The Commonwealth in the inter-war period had always been in fact, as in theory, a group of independent states held together by common ideals and purposes and acting jointly only as the result of decisions independently considered and adopted. The difference at this time was that conditions were resulting in new interpretations of interests and aims, which might or might not lead to unanimity in a time of ultimate need.

As always, impending danger tended to force the more dangerously situated members of the Commonwealth, Australia, New Zealand, and South Africa, into closer alignment with Great Britain.   Equally typical was the Canadian reaction towards isolation and closer relations with the United States.   Yet in no case was there a unified national move. Nor could the old clear-cut division between isolation and participation in imperial policies exist while membership in the League of Nations remained a reality.   For those most prepared for a close imperial relation, League principles provided a touchstone by which British policy could be judged.   Those most reluctant to be involved in imperial affairs were hesitant to drop their League activities which inevitably ran somewhat parallel to general British policy.   More indication of the desires of Dominion Governments is probably to be found in their League utterances than anywhere else.   But perhaps more indication of future courses of action was to be gleaned from rearmament programmes and responses to British policies.

Within the general period from 1936 to the outbreak of the war, the first year and a half were decisive for future courses of action. Aspirations were tested against realities in this time.   The overseas Dominions began to see more clearly the implications of events.   Though they struggled to maintain their distinctive policies, the increasing immediacy of danger began pressing them back into solidarity with Great Britain in the face of the common menace of war.

In response to the obvious weakness of the League and the growing power of the Fascist states, the movement for rearmament within the Commonwealth was intensified early in 1936.   On March 3rd, a British White Paper[1] indicated the progress made in defining defence requirements for navy, army, and air since the original statement issued a year before on the eve of the announcement of German rearmament. In the same month, the Australian Government declared that the existing state of unrest would make it necessary to undertake a further three-year defence plan[2] after expiration in 1937 of the programme for naval increases and improvement of army equipment, port defences, and air strength announced September 25, 1933.[3]

The Government based Australian defence on "an efficient and powerful Empire Navy," despite unofficial British warnings against depending on substantial naval support in the Far East in case Australia found itself in danger[4] and the views of some Australian observers that preparation for the defence of Australia itself rather than of its trade routes was the primary need.[5]   Since dependence on naval strength continued to mark the Commonwealth Government's defence programmes, the corollary as the Minister for Defence, Mr. Parkhill, pointed out in December, 1935, was that mobility of British naval power must be safeguarded "by freedom of passage through the Suez Canal, naval bases along the sea routes and an adequate base in Eastern waters," at Singapore, then approaching completion.[6]   That imperial solidarity in defence played a considerable rôle in Australian thinking, was evidenced by the satisfaction with which British plans for rearmament were greeted in the press[7] and by Parkhill's assurance at the launching of a new ship on March 29th that "Australia's part in the empire defences will never be repudiated or refused."[8]   Nor was it without significance that early in August, 1936, the Prime Minister urged Australians to take a greater intellectual interest in Imperial foreign policy for its greatest anxieties lay outside its own borders, that W. M. Hughes declared that "In practice the Empire remains a complete entity," and

Pearce, Minister of External Affairs, called for the establishment of an Imperial Secretariat to co-ordinate policies regarding trade and defence.[9] Though there was still considerable lassitude in the country on the subject of defence and some active opposition by the Labour Party to the emphasis on the navy, the Government insisted it was Australia's first line of defence and thereby implicitly endorsed dependence on British support as the basis of Australian security.

South Africa, stirred by Italian aggression in its own continent, also emphasized defence needs in the spring of 1936. A statement by Pirow, Minister of Defence, on April 27th, followed shortly by announcement that he would leave for England for discussions on South African defence, made it clear that British naval power was depended on for protection from a sea attack.[10] An extension of the coastal defence system, which was governed by the 1928 agreement with the Committee of Imperial Defence, was under consideration and Pirow pledged maintenance "in the spirit as in the letter" of obligations undertaken in the Smuts-Churchill Agreement of 1922 to assure the land defences of the British naval base at Simonstown. Emphasis in the five-year defence programme inaugurated in 1934 had been placed on the army and air force as means of repelling land invasion and Pirow hinted that in due course it might be necessary to concert common defence measures with South Africa's northern neighbours in British Africa. To subsequent Nationalist objections that the Government might be committing itself in a future British war, Pirow asserted that "We are not bound directly or indirectly to take part in any war in Africa or elsewhere. We shall take part in no war except where the true interests of South Africa make such a participation inevitable."[11] It was obvious, however, that South Africa had no means of protection from sea attack except such as the British Navy afforded. Smuts pointed out on June 25th that "We do not possess a single ship which could ward off those aircraft-carriers that could land enough aeroplanes on our shores to wipe out our large cities in a few hours."[12] Moreover, the thought that Cape Town might again become the half-way house to the East for British shipping if the Mediterranean route were threatened was not distasteful to South Africans.

Spurred by Australia's example, the New Zealand budget presented August 4, 1936, showed increased provision for "the defence of the Dominion and the maximum co-operation with the British Commonwealth in its policy for this purpose."[13] Subsequent discussions on August 19th showed the Nationalist Opposition more in favour of building up defences than was the Labour Government, but Prime Minister Savage agreed that there should be "a common policy" with

Great Britain and Australia.[14]   There was general acceptance that the Navy was the first line of defence but appreciation that air forces and harbour defences were essential corollaries.

Even in Canada, the general movement towards rearmament found an echo.   Like other countries, Canada had seriously neglected its defences in the inter-war period.   It considered their strengthening not in terms of co-ordinated imperial defence arrangements, however, but of responsibilities for North American security.   Even before President Roosevelt declared at Chautauqua on August 14, 1936, "We can defend ourselves, and we can defend our neighbourhood," the Canadian Government recognized the necessity of assuming a share in continental defence though the first practical steps were not taken until 1937.[15]   Unlike the other overseas Dominions, Canada's concern with defence developed less under the spur of necessity than of self-respect, for it had the assurance of American support in time of danger on which no other Dominion could count.

The increase in armaments noticeable in the overseas Dominions and the renewed emphasis on imperial defence in Australia, New Zealand, and South Africa indicated tendencies rather than policies.   Behind them lay the tension engendered by the Sino-Japanese dispute, the Italo-Ethiopian conflict, League intervention and failure, and Germany's aggressive policy, first in rearmament and then in remilitarization of the Rhineland.   Whether these tendencies would harden into specific courses of action leading to a new solidarity was dependent on subsequent events.   Whether, if such solidarity were achieved, it would include Canada was even more problematic.

In the late spring of 1936, there were hopes that a calmer European situation would be secured through appeasing Italy by raising sanctions and through negotiations with Germany aiming at a new Western Pact. But these hopes foundered on fresh challenges to the balance of power in the Mediterranean through the Turkish demand in April, 1936, for revision of the Straits Convention and the outbreak of the Spanish civil war in July.   The period had opened in which crises were no longer the exception but the rule.

The weakness of the League and growing rearmament were the justification offered by the Turkish Government for proposing revision of the Convention by which the freedom of the Straits and demilitariza-tion of adjacent shores and islands had been secured in 1923 under international supervision.   The proposal for negotiated change was welcome but behind it lay the potential threat that if it were not accepted the Convention might be torn up as Germany had torn up the limitations on its freedom of action.   Haste was made, therefore, to agree and on June 22, 1936, a conference opened at Montreux to consider a new settlement. Represented were all the signatory powers of the Treaty of Lausanne except Italy. Each of the Dominions had been invited[16] but the Governments of Canada,[17] South Africa, New Zealand, and the Irish Free State did not send representatives. They agreed, however, to accept the conclusions of the Conference. The Australian Government decided to participate since the Near East was "an area in which they were directly concerned by reason of vital Empire communications both by air and sea," as the Minister for External Affairs pointed out.[18]

The British, and implicitly the Australian, interest at Montreux was to prevent any impairment of British naval power in the eastern Mediterranean whereby it controlled the Suez Canal route to the East and the approach to the Iraq oil fields. To this, the original Turkish proposal for remilitarization of the shores of the Dardanelles offered no threat. At the Conference, however, the powers were confronted by a further demand that entrance to the Black Sea through the Straits should be drastically restricted while exit was left free.[19] This would have greatly strengthened the naval position of the Soviet Union and it disturbed British negotiators lest Germany be provided with an excuse for overthrowing the Anglo-German Naval Treaty of June, 1935. But the sentiment of the Conference was generally against them. The final compromise provided for free exit through remilitarized Straits in time of peace but no movement of warships in either direction in a war in which Turkey was neutral unless in fulfilment of Covenant obligations. This settlement was to the advantage of the Black Sea powers, particularly the Soviet Union and Turkey itself, though not to the extent of the Turkish proposals. But the Australian Minister of External Affairs was perhaps not making an overstatement when he declared the results of the Montreux Conference to be "very satisfactory." However the British might feel about the terms of the settlement, they succeeded in achieving close relations with Turkey which they recognized as being the key to the new situation.

There is no evidence that Australia itself played a particular rôle at the Conference though its representative, Mr. Bruce, had the honour of being selected President. His chief public statement reflected gratification at assurances of continued facilities for the war graves at Gallipoli. But he doubtless felt that there was no reason to take an open stand on the general issue. In this situation, Australian interests were clearly identical with those of Great Britain.

In another matter affecting Empire communications, relations with Egypt, Australia was also vitally concerned. It was with special satisfaction that it noted that these were put on a firmer basis than at any previous time in the inter-war period through the signing of the Anglo-Egyptian Treaty on August 26, 1936.   This agreement permitted British troops to remain in the vicinity of Alexandria for eight years and provided them with sufficient freedom of movement within Egypt for the purposes of training or of war.   The Australian Government was "in closest touch" with that of Great Britain "both before the initiation of the negotiations and throughout their proceedings," Sir George Pearce told the Senate, "and each detail of their development was carefully followed."[20]   He concluded that "Everything has been done to ensure the continued security of those Empire communications through Egypt which meant so much to us in Australia."

The Montreux Conference spanned the Assembly during which sanctions against Italy were lifted.   It might well have resulted in a more settled state of affairs in the Mediterranean had not its final Convention coincided with the outbreak on July 17th of civil war in Spain through the revolt of General Franco.   What appeared at first sight to be a domestic struggle between the Popular Front groups which had just acquired governmental power and a group of military conservatives became all too quickly an international war with strong Italian and German aid for Franco and less effective help for the other side from the Soviet Union.

Under the fear that general war[21] might result from the Spanish conflict, the British Government agreed to a proposal by the French Premier, M. Blum, for general non-intervention in Spain in the hope of isolating the conflict.   By the end of August, the principal European countries, including Germany, Italy, and the Soviet Union, had signed a non-intervention agreement.   Germany, France, Great Britain, and other states in principle agreed to prohibit export of arms and war materials to Spain, thereby abrogating the customary rule of supplying arms to the legitimate government.   But these apparent drastic means to prevent the spread of war foundered on the actual participation of Germany and Italy on the side of Franco, thereby proving in practice to be mainly handicaps to the Government side alone.   They did little to ease the tension which had gripped Europe and which formed the atmosphere within which the Seventeenth Assembly convened in Geneva in September to consider revision of the Covenant in the light of the failure of collective security on behalf of Ethiopia.

At its very outset, the Assembly was confronted with the issue it had dealt with so indirectly in June, its attitude towards the conquest of Ethiopia.   Any hope that it would not arise again vanished with the decision of the Ethiopian Emperor to send a delegation to the Assembly.   The certification of credentials forced a decision and the

Assembly, confronted by the necessity of registering its opinion in open vote, agreed by a large majority to seat the Ethiopian delegation though with the proviso that it was not setting a precedent. The Italian delegation thereupon left the Assembly which proceeded in an unhappy frame of mind to consider the future of the Covenant.

Despite the undermining of confidence in the collective system through its failure to save Ethiopia, the members of the Commonwealth had reacted seriously to the issue of Covenant revision posed by the special Assembly in July. Opinion within their countries, with the possible exception of Australia, was still too strongly in favour of the League to permit too obvious a divergence from its principles. But at the same time, the need for change seemed obvious. In what direction should it be pointed?

Unique in the Commonwealth and indeed among League members was the stand taken as early as July, 1936, by the New Zealand Government in favour of automatic commitments and of providing the League with means to implement its recommendations. "We are prepared to accept, in principle," they wrote, "the provisions proposed for the Geneva Protocol of 1924 as one method of strengthening the Covenant as it exists.[22] We are prepared to take our collective share in the application, against any future aggressor, of the full economic sanctions contemplated by Article 16," they continued, "and we are prepared, to the extent of our power, to join in the collective application of force against any future aggressor." They argued that to be effective, sanctions must be made "immediate and automatic," include a full boycott and be supported if necessary by force. For that reason they advocated placing an international force or a proportion of the armed forces of member states under the control of the League, and, to ensure popular support for this plan, the holding of national plebiscites as early as possible to secure their assent. Regional pacts they did not favour but were prepared to agree that military commitments should be limited by this means if economic sanctions had "immediate and universal application." But though emphasizing the necessity for putting force behind the collective system, it was not for the purpose of stratifying the *status quo*. ". . . adequate machinery for the ventilation and, if possible, rectification of international grievances" should be set up, they believed, and in particular the status established by the peace treaties reconsidered. To such deliberations and those on the application of the Covenant or "of any other universal method of collective security that may be proposed in its stead," they wished all nations to be invited in the hope of making a move towards gaining the universality essential to a fully satisfactory system.

Far reaching as these proposals were, they represented in the judgment of two leading newspapers, the *New Zealand Herald*[23] and the *Otago Daily Times*,[24] the general view of New Zealanders. The Government itself felt that such a policy if adopted "in its entirety" would considerably minimize the possibility of war.[25] With the exception of the inclusion of the obligation and means to restrain an aggressor by force, the New Zealand memorandum embodied something of the same point of view which the South African Government had supported implicitly in its actions during the sanctions period. With the same exception, it was in part the approach suggested by de Valera in the Assembly a year before when he had asked that the Covenant be separated from the Peace treaties, that economic and colonial adjustments should be made and that in the atmosphere of good will thus engendered a measure like the Geneva Protocol should weld the nations in the "common purpose of self-preservation."[26] Neither the South African nor Irish Free State Government presented a proposal for revision of the Covenant or spoke in the Seventeenth Assembly on the subject. Both were disillusioned about pressing for a course of action which experience seemed to have shown to be unable to command the support of other League countries. The New Zealand Government answered the same sense of failure by putting forward a clear-cut programme which went further than any country had yet been willing to go in implementing the provisions of the Covenant. It was the reflection of a genuine intellectual conversion to the principles of collective security. Though it had no practical effect at this time, it served to provide a landmark for the exponents of stronger League action in many countries.

What the Government of a million and a quarter people isolated in the Pacific Ocean was willing to undertake, the Governments of Great Britain,[27] Australia, and Canada felt impractical in the given circumstances. Eden's speech in the Assembly, September, 1936, echoing his earlier one in the House of Commons,[28] stressed the need for universality, for "more energetic and effective" action in the earlier stages of a crisis, and for consideration of grievances.[29] To achieve universality, he believed obligations under the Covenant would have to be reconsidered as well as League support for an order with which some Governments were not content. To secure speedier action, he favoured removing the unanimity rule from Article 11 under which threatening situations could be considered before outbreaks occurred, specific statements at an early stage on the measures Governments were willing to undertake in a given case, and regional pacts with military commitments of the type which Great Britain hoped to organize in Western Europe. To meet grievances, he supported separating the Covenant from the peace treaties, improving financial and economic conditions, facilitating access to raw materials and general reduction of armaments but only if war mentality were laid aside as well as weapons.   It was a careful, reasonable programme reintroducing the traditional Conservative support of regional arrangements without overthrowing League obligations.   It emphasized what experience had demonstrated that action should be taken at an early stage of a crisis.   It reflected the experience of defections during the imposition of sanctions in his request for positive commitments in a given case.   It made clear his belief that a whole-hearted effort to meet the expressed grievances of the aggressive powers was an essential preliminary to peace.   But it made little or no mention of the use of force to support collective security.   Perhaps partly for that reason it received general support within the Assembly and in particular from the representatives of Australia and of Canada, which had sent a powerful delegation including the Prime Minister.

Both Bruce and King in their speeches gave first place in the preservation of peace to the efforts of the Great Powers within Europe itself to find a satisfactory settlement of their differences.   Both opposed formal amendment of the Covenant.   Both drew the conclusion from experience during the Italo-Ethiopian conflict that in a non-universal League "to attempt to implement in full the Covenant involves the danger of spreading the area of conflict" and thereby might negate "the ideas embodied in the Covenant by its founders."[30]   Both felt general recognition should be given to existing practice regarding Article 16, that is, that financial and economic sanctions be not considered automatic, that there should be consultation before action and that action must be on a co-operative basis.   Both approved separating the Covenant from the peace treaties and giving a more prominent place in League deliberations to Article 19 providing for revision of treaties which had become inapplicable.   Mr. King went so far as to suggest that these latter provisions were "in form and fact an essential complement to the provisions of Article 10 for the maintenance of the territorial *status quo*."[31]   They thus agreed that European problems could be best met by European powers, that League commitments were not automatic and that conciliatory action towards dissatisfied powers should be promoted.

In other respects, the Australian and Canadian speeches reflected the particular geographical features of their countries.   Bruce supported the British view on regional pacts.   As his Government pointed out in a parallel statement in the Australian House of Representatives, the Pacific was the area in which they were most vitally interested.[32]

Though the absence of the United States and Japan from the League made it impossible to plan for a regional pact inside the League structure, they favoured "promotion of a regional understanding and pact of non-aggression for Pacific countries, in the spirit of the League undertakings." It was the first public introduction of their 1937 proposal for a Pacific Pact.

Prime Minister King went even farther in underlining the characteristic attitudes arising out of the particular position of the country he represented. He began by stressing the contrast between the international outlook in Europe from whose problems he explicitly held himself aloof and that in North America where "friendly relations with our neighbours" was the rule. Regional agreements he felt applicable only in Europe and warned against letting them degenerate into "old-fashioned military alliances." To supplement them with automatic economic sanctions would be to "strengthen and perpetuate the existing one-way tendency in the application of sanctions"; to impose no obligations on European nations in regard to Asia or America while asking action by outside countries in "the European pact areas." Citing the Canadian statement of 1928 on the relation of the Covenant and the Kellogg Pact,[33] he pointed out that forceful support of the *status quo* had never been considered the primary function of the League by Canada. He called instead for emphasis on its conciliation and mediation functions as the means whereby a more universal League might be achieved. It was the appeal of the secure and fortunate that others might meet their own problems by pursuing the same policies as had worked so well for Canada.

This stress upon conciliation stood in some contrast to Bruce's endorsement of the British proposal for removing the unanimity rule from Article 11 and for securing specific pledges of action in given cases of violation of the Covenant. Bruce did not go as far in his Assembly speech, however, as did his Government in its statement on the same day to the Australian House of Representatives. In the latter, the Australian proposal was said to include recommendation of automatic economic and financial sanctions in case the Council found a member state to be an aggressor with only the limitation that each state should be its own judge as to whether the aggression had taken place. In such a case, it was felt that there should be automatic prohibition of export of arms and munitions of war and of raw materials useful thereto including metals and oils or alternatively prohibition of all exports, and imports, and refusal of loans and credit facilities. Behind the recommendation of these drastic measures, it was disclosed, lay the impressive evidence which the Commonwealth Government had secured of the "constant and cumulative" effect of sanctions upon the economic life of Italy.[34] Had the Australian proposal been transmitted in these terms to the Assembly, there would have been a far sharper contrast with the Canadian stand than appeared in practice. The European situation was probably the reason why Bruce modified them, and it is noticeable that when his report was laid before the Australian House of Representatives the following June, his emphasis was accepted without question.[35]

The distinction suggests that despite the apparent similarity in general view of the Australian and Canadian representatives at the Assembly, there was in fact a sharp difference arising out of strategic position. In December, 1935, the Minister of Defence in a statement on Government defence policy had pointed out that the security of Australia lay "within three successive safeguards."[36] Of these, the widest, he declared, was the Covenant of the League and supplementary Treaties like the Four and Nine Power Treaties and Locarno. Next came co-operation in Imperial Defence and, lastly, the defence forces of the Commonwealth. "The guarantees of national security consist of a blending of these three safeguards," he pointed out, "The degree to which reliance can or must be placed on each having been determined, a basis exists for the National Policies relating to the League, Imperial Co-operation, and Defence." Despite its lukewarm response to sanctions, the Australian Government even at that time was not unaware of the potential advantages of League support in a moment of crisis. In September, 1936, it appears to have been ready to support a strong programme of economic and financial measures if it could reserve freedom of decision as to whether aggression had occurred or not. It is not outside the bounds of possibility that the increasing tension in the Far East which was to flare into hostilities the following year may have been a conditioning factor in this decision, the more so because of the ill-advised trade diversion policy towards Japan which had been embarked on, probably thoughtlessly, in an effort to stimulate imperial trade.[37] But confronted at Geneva by the tense situation in Europe arising particularly out of the Spanish civil war, the Australian representative seems not unnaturally to have trimmed his statement to conform with that of Great Britain. Where a League programme and solidarity with Great Britain appeared to conflict, there was little doubt that Bruce and the existing Commonwealth Government would support the latter.

No such inhibitions were reflected in Prime Minister King's speech. It was born rather of disillusionment and mistrust regarding the League's use of "collective coercion" and of pressure from very substantial groups within his own party for withdrawal from involvement in European politics. Both were reflected in his emphasis on the conciliatory functions of the League and on European peoples knowing their own problems best. Moreover, King no doubt sincerely believed ‘that "it was wise at this time not to precipitate anything into the discussions of the Assembly which would add to their [European peoples] embarrassment and difficulties."[38] None the less, the speech put forward a clear-cut distinction between the affairs of Europe and those of North America, and stressed conciliation to the extent of virtually excluding any forceful support of collective security.

The speech received by no means unanimous support in King's own country, where pro-League and pro-Commonwealth groups interpreted it as implying an unwarranted aloofness from international affairs. "Canada is part of a big World; we cannot sit and fold our hands and say 'it concerns only Europe,' " Sir Robert Falconer, former President of the University of Toronto, was quoted as saying.[39] The *Winnipeg Free Press* declared Mr. King was permitting the League to continue in existence "providing it agrees not to recognize or act upon the principle that is the reason for its existence."[40] *The Toronto Daily Star*, customarily a strong supporter of the Prime Minister, acknowledged that he had perhaps not allowed sufficiently for the warlike preparations and aggressive acts of the Fascist powers or that an international system of law and order required a backing of force. But it pointed out that the Great Powers had been unwilling to accept the risk of war on behalf of the Covenant when their own direct interests were not involved. The policies enunciated by King were those which both parties had voiced consistently for fifteen years. "If these policies are mistaken and unrealistic, as we fear they are," the *Star* editor wrote, "it is because this country is in a position of peculiar detachment; not because it lacks courage or devotion to the cause of peace." It was a significant statement because it suggested that even at the moment when disillusionment appeared to be accentuating traditional Canadian policies of separateness from the affairs of Europe, there was recognition that the aggressive acts of dictators might nullify any real freedom of action.

But though questioned by a few groups in his own country, King's speech in its emphasis on conciliation instead of coercion probably represented a broad body of opinion in Canada. At Geneva it was paralleled by those of representatives of the Scandinavian states. In general, the Assembly discussions showed support for lessening commitments, and particularly for watering down the obligations of Article 16. The hope was to avoid danger, but the effect was largely to nullify the influence of smaller states.

In the end, no more was done than to set up a Committee of Twenty-Eight to study the proposals for revision of the Covenant and problems connected therewith. On the urging of the New Zealand representative,[41] the committee was empowered to propose a special session of the Assembly if it considered it advisable to do so. In fact, although discussions were continued during the next two years, no formal decisions were ever taken which affected the form of the Covenant. Nor did the League become again, except rarely, an important centre for international deliberations and decisions. The chance of developing international policies based on principle which might override interest was nearly at an end. The absence of adequate support for the League combined with increased concentration on the hazardous game of power politics was to exclude small states henceforth from effective influence on foreign affairs except within limited circles.

For more than a year and a half, following its outbreak in July, 1936, the Spanish civil war appeared to offer the prime danger of plunging Europe, and perhaps the world, into a general war. Germany and Italy actively aided General Franco's forces at first with material and soon with men. Substantial though less considerable support came to the Loyalist Government from the Soviet Union. This outside participation made the struggle in Spain even more clearly an ideological one. To the fear of general war and to the strategic implications of a struggle for power in an area dominating the entrance to the Mediterranean, was thus added bitter divisions of sympathy within outside countries. To an unusual extent, strategic or other arguments justifying one policy or another became in fact the reflection of attitudes towards the two parties within Spain.

In Great Britain, the Government eagerly followed the lead of France in establishing non-intervention. Labour, strongly pro-Loyalist, found itself unable to oppose non-intervention but focussed its attacks on the obvious breaches in the system made by Germany and Italy. New Zealand's Labour Government had much the same view and was to have the opportunity through its membership on the League Council to voice it. In South Africa, there seems to have been little active feeling for either side though its attitude was coloured by a slight fear of communism and a general desire to avoid implication. In Canada, sentiment divided as in European countries with Catholic Quebec almost unanimously in support of Franco, both because of religious and ideological sympathies. Australian Labour with its large percentage of Catholics was affected by its social viewpoint and arrived at no clear-cut stand. The most unanimous view was probably in the Irish Free State where virtually all groups united in supporting Franco. The

Labour party, though torn between its religious and social sympathies, finally split with its fellow-Labourites in England and came out for Franco. The Catholic hierarchy publicly affirmed its sympathy with "Catholic Spain" on October 13, 1936.[42] The Opposition, the United Ireland party, adopted the cause as their own. Even participation was undertaken. In August, it was announced that a battalion of the Blueshirts, under General O'Duffy, would fight on Franco's side, which they did between November, 1936, and June, 1937. In contrast, there were volunteers on the Loyalist side from all the overseas Dominions. But despite these variances of view, all the Commonwealth countries supported non-intervention as a policy and probably only the New Zealand Government would have considered changing to intervention.

The Irish Free State Government adhered to the Non-Intervention Agreement in August, 1936. Prime Minister Lyons on September 11, 1936, stated the traditional policy of non-interference in the internal affairs of other countries and asked the Australian people not to contribute to appeals for funds for either party.[43] This attitude was reaffirmed in the House of Representatives several times during October. The Canadian Government followed that of the United States in seeking to avoid entanglements.

In a move designed to force attention to its situation, the Spanish Government appealed under Article 11 on November 27, 1936, for League consideration of the armed intervention of Italy and Germany which were in fact pouring in an increasing number of "volunteers." Nine days before, these two countries had announced their recognition of Franco's régime as the government of Spain and Franco himself had proclaimed a blockade which the British refused to recognize as legal since they had not granted belligerent rights. At the same time, British ships had been forbidden by their own Government to carry arms to Spanish ports. The aim had been to tighten non-intervention so as to decrease the risk of incidents likely to be caused by the new developments. But the Spanish Government's appeal seemed likely to bring all the embarrassing facts into the open. The British Government feared that it might complicate their negotiations with Italy for a Mediterranean understanding. None the less, reluctant as they were, the Council members found themselves unable to deny the Spanish appeal which was placed on the agenda of the Council for the session of December 10th.

In order to make the meeting as much as possible a mere formality, none of the Foreign Ministers of Great Britain, France, or the Soviet Union were present. The Italians refused to come. The meetings which were otherwise largely characterized by colourless comments aiming only to support the non-intervention procedure were signalized by one outspoken statement by Mr. Jordan, delegate of New Zealand, in support of the Spanish Government and of the view that it was the "business" of the League to examine the situation within Spain.[44] Speaking for his country, he declared that "We are prepared to examine the cause of the trouble, and if necessary to act in accordance with the requirements of the situation." It was a statement in line with the stand the New Zealand Government had taken in its memorandum on the Covenant but it found no echo in the Council. The meeting ended with a compromise declaration which affirmed the duty of states to refrain from interfering in the internal affairs of other states but without specifically referring to what was going on in Spain.

The seriousness of the situation caused by increasing numbers of foreign troops, especially German, stimulated the British and French Governments, however, to seek an answer to it through agreements by interested countries not to permit further "volunteers" and subsequently to withdraw those already in Spain. By December the Soviet Union was ready to agree to limit volunteers, but Germany and Italy withheld consent, still feeling the advantage to be on their side. Italy held back its troops for a while pending the Anglo-Italian Agreement which was announced January 2, 1937, but which made no mention of Spain. In January, the German Government, impressed by the stronger stand being taken by the French especially over Morocco, began to limit sharply the support it was giving Franco and left the burden to be carried by the Italians, who took it up. Detailed negotiations finally resulted by February 21, 1937, in agreements by all countries concerned to stop the enlistment or despatch to Spain of volunteers. Considerable time was to elapse, however, before a satisfactory system of control was organized and on the issue of withdrawing volunteers it was to prove far more difficult to reach agreement. Almost to the end there were to be elements in the Spanish situation which threatened to precipitate general war.

Partly for the purpose of setting a good example, partly to avoid involvement, the United States and Great Britain took the lead in adhering strictly to the line advocated by the Non-Intervention Committee. The British Government banned the enlistment of volunteers on January 10th by bringing into force the Foreign Enlistment Act which made it a punishable offence for British subjects to engage in operations on either side in the Spanish war. The Labour party criticized the imposition of the Act before securing assurances that Germany and Italy would follow suit but not in other respects. In the United States where moral suasion by the Government had proved ineffective in restraining profit-making through selling war materials to the participants in the Spanish civil war, action had been taken even a little earlier, through an amendment extending the Neutrality Act to cover civil war. This included penalties for enlistment and became law on January 8, 1937.

Since the Foreign Enlistment Act which the British Government had brought into effect was an imperial statute of 1870, its effect extended throughout the Empire except in as far as separate Dominion action was taken in accordance with the Statute of Westminster, 1931. This provided that any Dominion had the legal right to re-enact, repeal, or amend any imperial statute relating to it. Both in the Irish Free State and in Canada such action was taken, largely because of their interest in separate forms and also no doubt because feelings were more highly engaged in these two countries than in Australia, New Zealand, or South Africa.

The Irish bill was introduced on February 17, 1937, on the same day on which general agreement had been reached in the Non-Intervention Committee. It received opposition only in as far as the United Ireland party urged, as it had done before in November, 1936,[45] that diplomatic relations be broken off with "the Caballero Government," in Spain, "the Government of anti-Christ" as they called it. They demanded also that "the Franco Government" be formally recognized.[46] But de Valera successfully maintained his earlier stand that recognition should not be a matter of sympathy with a particular type of policy but of response to a factual situation. This attitude of non-partisanship in a situation in which feelings were deeply engaged was to mark de Valera's policy throughout the Spanish war with the possible exception of the stand he was to take at the 1937 Assembly.

The Canadian measure was not introduced until March 19th, but it was accepted immediately. It seemed agreed that the British statute had referred to Canada up till that time. The C.C.F. leader regretted the introduction of Canadian legislation on the subject on the somewhat curious grounds that it might "easily involve" Canada "in those European entanglements" which it was sought to avoid.[47] This seemed almost an attitude of colonialism but it was probably intended to reflect the party's support of neutrality. The Canadian Government's action was in fact in line with the conception of separate legal status which should have appealed to the C.C.F. party. So, too, should the wide powers governing the sale of goods to Spain which were in practice approved by the C.C.F. so long as their operation did not give advantage to Franco's side. There was much sympathy for the Loyalists but even more desire not to be involved in the conflict.

The C.C.F. leader, Mr. Woodsworth, had already expressed in January the belief of a good many of his party's members that Canada should adopt a formal policy of neutrality. In a formal resolution introduced in the House of Commons, it was proposed "That under existing international relations, in the event of war, Canada should remain strictly neutral, regardless of who the belligerents may be."[48] It was as Woodsworth made clear, a gesture of hopelessness, both in relation to war settling anything and to Canada being able to engage in war without being split "from stem to stern." In this latter fear, he was not alone. The resolution also opposed profiteering and favoured action "to discover and remove the causes of international friction and social injustice."

In a statement significant for gauging Canada's future course of action, the Prime Minister endorsed these last two points in principle if not in the extreme form in which they were presented. But the first, as he pointed out, would tie the hands of Parliament in a manner which could not be justified. That Parliament should meet to decide Canada's action in a given situation, he reaffirmed. "I want to make it clear," he continued, "that we will not necessarily become involved in any war into which other parts of the British Empire may enter, simply because we are part of the British Empire." Canada must decide its policy in relation to its own interests. What it could do at the moment, he felt, was to work for universality in the League and to remove causes of international friction and injustice. But he warned, also, "that forces of evil were present in the world, fighting against the forces of good. As long as there was this conflict, those who wished to see the good triumph must take every possible means to prevent evil from gaining control." It was a shrewd acknowledgment of the danger involved in supporting a policy which would play into the hands of aggressive forces. There was even a hint that Canada might have to align itself with other Commonwealth countries, not because it was "part of the British Empire" but because they formed part of "the forces of good."

The direct impact of international politics, which even Canada could not avoid, was being felt more acutely by the other overseas Dominions early in 1937 because of intensified German agitation for the return of territories lost at the end of World War I. This claim which had been pressed early in 1936 and suggested by Nazi spokesmen to be the alternative to further German expansion in Europe affected South Africa, Australia, and New Zealand directly because of their mandates. These they had claimed originally because of their strategic importance to the respective Dominions and demands for their return raised fears and opposition. On the other hand, there was appreciation of the need to remove causes of international friction in the interests of maintaining peace.

The Australian Government made known its opposition to the return of its mandated territories to Germany as early as March 13, 1936,[49] and Hertzog took the same attitude on May 6, 1936.[50] Both stressed the strategic argument and justified their continued control of the territories by their success in developing them. The Australians sought an answer to German claims through economic adjustments though they emphasized that they could be made only in a non-warlike atmosphere and should be carried out within the framework of the League. Hoare's reference at the Assembly, September, 1935, to freer access to raw materials seemed to them to provide the right approach to the problem. They approved, therefore, the establishment of the Committee for the Study of the Problem of Raw Material set up on British initiative by the Council early in 1937 in pursuance of a resolution passed by the Assembly, October 9, 1936.[51] In this way, they hoped to meet the legitimate grievances of the "have-not" powers without playing into the hands of aggressive forces.

South Africa faced the problem in a different context because of the active Nazi activity being carried on in South-West Africa which threatened to undermine the position of the Union in that area.[52] The efforts to assimilate the Germans remaining in South-West Africa had been moderately successful during the twenties but increasing influence from Germany on the younger groups, particularly after 1933, served as a constantly disturbing factor. But to return South-West Africa to Germany would be to endanger the Union itself. Hence the hope of South Africans that if territorial concessions were made, it would be in areas which were not vital to their security.

From within the Union, the Nationalist leader, Malan, proposed at an early date a general redistribution of colonies from which South-West Africa should be omitted. Pirow at that time suggested that he would not be averse to such a development, as long as Tanganyika remained in British hands because of its strategic importance to the Union,[53] an attitude which he was not long to maintain. In the same period, the Union Government was considering the importance of initiating common action among the countries composing the southern half of Africa in support of their mutual defence needs. As tension grew in the spring of 1936 with Italy's increasing success in Ethiopia, more attention was given both to affirming the necessity of retaining mandated territories and of building a common front within Africa against a possible attack.

But even if the Union itself stood against such territorial concessions to Germany, might Great Britain not attempt to satisfy German
demands in a way which would affect South African interests? This
fear was raised by rather indiscreet statements made by Pirow in July,
1936, on his return from visiting London. Feeling "in influential
quarters" in Great Britain, he declared, was that there would be no
settlement of the colonial issue unless Germany were given "adequate
territorial compensation" in Africa.[54] But this story which raised
some excitement in South Africa created even more of a stir in London.
Anxious questions were asked in the House of Commons.[55] To these,
the Government asserted that they "have not and are not considering
the handing over of any British colony or territory held under mandate."[56] Continued questions over the future of Tanganyika, led its
Governor to comment on August 6, 1936, that if the British Government's
good faith were doubted, at least to believe in its sanity.[57] It was
unthinkable, he believed, that such "an insane surrender" would be
made.

This attitude of concern over territorial changes in Africa tended
to solidify resistance to German claims and make the advantages of
solidarity in southern Africa appear still greater. Speaking to the
delegates at the Southern African Transport Conference on September 7,
1936, Smuts was careful to disclaim any intention of a South African
domination of the communities to the north.[58] "It is the first intention
of the Union to be to you not a grasping but a helping hand," he declared.
Pirow sent a message emphasizing the importance of holding together
for joint defence, and two days later, Hofmeyr, Minister of the Interior,
went so far as to say that "If Mr. Baldwin was right in saying that
Britain's frontier is now the Rhine, then it is also correct for the Union
of South Africa to say its frontier is the Kenya-Abyssinia border."[59]
Moreover, he declared that there was no justification "for thinking or
speaking of handing over African communities as though they were
bales of goods or parcels of merchandise. The nations have no right
to juggle with the map of Africa as if piecing together bits of a jigsaw
puzzle." There seemed general support in the press for these points
of view though as in Australia there were some suggestions that adjustments regarding raw materials would be important.[60]

The increasingly urgent demands of Nazi officials in the spring
of 1937 led to even a hardening of attitude. The *Rand Daily Mail*
commented in February that the move for return of colonies seen in
the perspective of the Nazi observation that Germans preferred guns
to butter suggested that "it is raw material for guns rather than food-
stuff she is seeking."[61] A month later the *Cape Times* characterized

von Ribbentrop's alternative solutions to Germany's problem of return of colonies or "by means of the German people's own strength," as "almost insolent." It remarked that guns still seemed regarded "as better than milk and honey."[62] The *African Observer* commented editorially that "As an armed force, in *esse* or in *posse*, he [the German] must be opposed at every point of the compass by all who wish well by the African Continent."[63] Criticized by Malan for appointing an Administrator for South-West Africa with dictatorial powers to deal with aliens, Hertzog acknowledged that it was a "police measure" but asserted that though there was no "change of disposition towards Germany or the German population . . . we can no longer continue to act in a friendly way . . . when we find it does not lead to the welfare and benefit of the population, but to the retardation of the interests of the country."[64] It was a declaration of determination to maintain Union control in South-West Africa.

In the spring of 1937, Australia, too, was agitated by the fear of danger if an aggressive Germany were provided with a strategic position close at hand through return of former colonies. W. M. Hughes charged in January that German claims for colonies were propaganda aimed to distract attention from the failure of the Nazi dictatorship to solve the economic problems of Germany.[65] He asserted also that Australia had done more to develop New Guinea than Germany had ever done. The *Sydney Morning Herald* foresaw that German claims might turn Australia back to closer relations with Great Britain.[66] When Lord Elibank, while visiting Australia, suggested that the Commonwealth would not seriously oppose the return of New Guinea to Germany, he was publicly rebuked by Sir George Pearce, Minister for External Affairs.[67] As the *Australian National Review* commented, both Australia and New Zealand had "reason to remember the menace in the last war of the *Scharnhorst* and the *Gneisenau* which had their bases in these former German islands." A member of the Legislative Council at Rabaul voiced the belief in March that "If Australia handed over the Mandated Territory of New Guinea to Germany, there is nothing more certain than that in time, if not immediately, the territory would become a naval base overshadowing Singapore" and constantly menacing "our all-important trade routes."[68]

Australia was concerned not only by the potential threat of Germany but also of Japan, the more so after the latter country denounced the Washington Naval Treaties. When efforts to replace them failed in 1936 the American Government let it be known that it considered that the non-fortification agreement had also ceased to be binding. But Congress was to restrain its efforts to develop the defences of the Pacific bases. Japan, in contrast, was suspected of building up armaments in its mandated islands. At once there disappeared such feeling of security as had been induced in Australia by the broad area between itself and Japan to which the non-fortification agreement applied. Almost equally disturbing was the American decision of 1936 to withdraw ultimately from the Philippines, which some Australian circles interpreted as an attempt to isolate the United States from developments in the Far East. Because of their position in relation to Hong Kong, Singapore, and the Dutch East Indies, the Philippines were considered of vital strategic importance to Australia. Lessening of American responsibility for their safety seemed to remove one of Australia's chief safeguards.

Out of this concern came the proposal for a Pacific Pact which was put forward by Prime Minister Lyons at the 1937 Imperial Conference. This would have provided for "a regional understanding and pact of non-aggression by the countries of the Pacific, conceived in the spirit of the principles of the League"[69] as had been suggested at the time of the Assembly. As he explained to the Foreign Press Association on June 7th, "Australia does not ask for special commitments but that every country concerned shall renounce war as a means of settling differences, and agree to meet round a table if difficulties cannot be overcome, in the first place, by diplomatic means."[70] Its purpose, in fact, was probably to ensure that Japan would not secure control of the Philippines. The proposal as such never became particularly significant both because neither Great Britain[71] nor New Zealand[72] took it seriously and because of Japan's subsequent aggression against China. Subsequent criticisms stamped it as vague and unrealistic[73] or as an election dodge with an eye to the coming campaign in Australia that autumn. But however it was ultimately used, the original proposal seems to have reflected the fear of American withdrawal from the Far East and the hope that it might still be possible to come to some arrangement with Japan which would safeguard the southern Pacific. What was clearly unrealistic was to expect Japan to welcome such a political proposal in the light of the economic conflict precipitated by the Australian trade diversion policy and far from settled by the *modus vivendi* of January 1, 1937.[74] Perhaps it was even more so to expect that a self-denying pledge could provide a practical solution in a time in which power politics was the dominant feature of international relations.

When the Imperial Conference opened on May 14, 1937, at the time of the Coronation of King George VI, it was in an atmosphere dominated not only by fear that the conflict raging in Spain might yet overleap the frontiers of that unhappy country, but also by anxiety over German colonial claims and concern for the future of the Pacific.

These issues tended to draw Australia and South Africa[75] closer to Great Britain. New Zealand's Government found itself both compelled towards Great Britain by the sense of urgency induced by the situation and repelled by its concern lest the British Government was prepared to sacrifice principle on the altar of expediency. Mr. King as so often stood between. To those who feared lest he bind Canada to British policy, he had maintained in Parliament, when challenged on the modest defence measures introduced in 1937,[76] that there were no commitments to Great Britain nor would the Government commit Canada to anything at the forthcoming Imperial Conference.[77] None the less he was well aware that events themselves might well remove the freedom of action of countries. The fifth Dominion (if such it could still be called following the adoption of a new constitution which removed the King from all participation in internal affairs though an Act declared that Eire (Ireland) was in "external association" with the British Commonwealth of Nations[78]), did not attend.[79] It was the outward and visible sign of a division which had long existed. The Commonwealth in practice, if not in theory, had returned to its original numbers.

Little is known of the actual discussions which took place within the Imperial Conference between May 14th and June 15, 1937. While the Conference was still in session, Mr. Baldwin gave place to Mr. Neville Chamberlain as Prime Minister of Great Britain but without leading to a change in Government, or according to all indications, to any essential shift in policy. Attention at the Conference was concentrated on foreign affairs and defence and resulted in very general resolutions on these subjects. Many commentators have believed that the discussions out of which these came were as platitudinous as the resolutions might be interpreted to be.[80] But subsequent evidence suggests that it was at this Conference that the Commonwealth forged the unity which it was to exhibit when faced with the challenge of war in 1939.

Specifically stating that nothing therein diminished the right of the individual Governments to pursue the policies advocated by them at the Assembly, September, 1936, the resolutions on foreign affairs placed the preservation of peace as the primary objective, reiterated support of the aims and ideals of the Covenant, and approved regional agreements including the Australian proposal for a Pacific Pact in as far as these did not conflict with the Covenant.[81] In the spirit of conciliation, they favoured separating the Covenant from the Peace Treaties, avowed willingness to remove barriers to international trade and to general improvement of standards of living, and asserted that "differences of political creed should be no obstacle to friendly relations between Governments and countries, and that nothing would be more damaging to the hopes of international appeasement than the division, real or apparent, of the world into opposing groups." At the same time, they declared that the respective Governments "are bound to adopt such measures of defence as they may deem essential for their security, as well as for the fulfilment of such international obligations as they may respectively have assumed." This was combined, however, with a statement regarding subsequent co-operation. "Being convinced that the influence of each of them in the cause of peace was likely to be greatly enhanced by their common agreement to use that influence in the same direction," the resolution read, "they declared their intention of continuing to consult and co-operate with one another in this vital interest and all other matters of common concern."

Were these mere generalities or were they declarations of common purposes? Were they indications that the Commonwealth was separating in the face of common danger or coming closer together? The answer probably lies between these two extremes. The need for each member of the Commonwealth to take steps to meet its special needs and aims was accepted. But in the light of international danger, the reality of common purposes was recognized more clearly by all.

There seems no question but that the Dominion Prime Ministers put forward as pointedly as possible the strategic problems of their countries and also the points of view of their Governments. In his opening speech, Mr. Savage had declared that New Zealand held "definite views" on many of the subjects the Conference would consider and that he would express them "as cogently, indeed as forcibly" as he could. It is said that he strongly opposed granting belligerent rights to Franco in Spain or recognizing the conquest of Ethiopia. It was on his insistence that the note regarding the statements of policy made to the Assembly, September, 1936, was inserted.[82] He appears to have pressed strongly for "such readjustment of the economic causes of war as to make international conflict highly improbable," referring in the main to freer trade.[83] Though the smallest and weakest member of the Commonwealth, New Zealand carried weight out of the definiteness of its convictions. Temporarily at least the British Government was ready to modify its policy in order to secure unanimity within the Commonwealth.[84]

Granting that principles of collective security and general support of the League were upheld and the fullest possible co-operation sought with the United States, New Zealand's Labour Government was ready for closer Commonwealth relations in defence and foreign policy.[85]

The Australian and South African Prime Ministers appear to have come to the Conference ready for such solidarity. In his opening speech, Lyons made an open plea for "a consistent and unified Empire policy," and "for a common understanding . . . between the British Nations as to the manner in which measures should be concerted between them for the maintenance of their common ideals."[86] Hertzog echo:d Baldwin's words that "we must now try to co-ordinate our policies of action in such a way that we shall be as mutually helpful as possible." He pointed out that South Africa was realizing more and more "how closely she is implicated in the fate of Europe and in the fate of the world" and expressed his "hearty appreciation of the manner in which the British Government has succeeded in steering through these difficult times."[87] These seemed invitations to plan joint policy. The question marks concerned how far Mr. King would be willing to go, and how far in fact joint defence and joint consideration of policy within the Commonwealth were practical.

As far as defence was concerned, the key-notes became those of separate responsibility for local means of protection, and of strengthening the Navy. Local areas were to be made as self-sufficient as possible by establishing industries to provide for local armament needs. Reports current in Australia during the Conference that proposals had been made by the Australian delegation for pooling the defence resources of the Dominions and placing Australian forces under the control of the British Imperial Staff were indignantly denied by Government officials.[88] "The conference decided that there should be less dependence by the dominions on munitions produced in the United Kingdom," reported the Acting Minister of Defence on June 16th, "and that the concentration of resources for manufacture of munitions in any area liable to attack should be avoided as far as possible." This was confirmed by Parkhill and Lyons following the conclusion of the Conference. "Australia has been committed to nothing incompatible with complete local control and determination in any emergency," declared the Prime Minister.[89] Parkhill described the aim of the coming period of co-operation in defence "as decentralization of the Empire's productive resources of munitions." Both stressed, however, the value of the adoption of the principle of the development of Empire civil aviation.[90]

As far as defence was concerned, therefore, the decision seems to have been to combine an emphasis on individual responsibility with the maintenance of the possibility of collective support. That the overseas Dominions should provide for their own means of defence in a moment of crisis was a necessity in view of the likelihood that Great Britain would be forced to concentrate almost all its forces in Europe in the event of a general war.   It did not contradict the impulse motivating Churchill's statement regarding Australia and New Zealand, "We shall go to their aid as long as there is breath in our bodies," which was quoted approvingly by *The Times* during the Conference with the comment that it believed the sentiment would be reciprocated.[91]   On the contrary, it merely recognized the difficulties arising out of the widespread geographical distribution of the Commonwealth.

In practice, these lines of policy in defence were to be followed fairly exactly by the overseas Dominions.   In Australia, though defence programmes were to be dictated more by local considerations than heretofore, they continued to meet the criticism of the Labour party. It urged concentration upon the air force rather than the navy which Lyons insisted was still Australia's first line of defence.[92]   This division of opinion was to be an issue in the autumn elections though never faced squarely by the Australian people who returned Lyons to office largely on personal grounds.   This development meant that Australian defence policy would be continued on the two-fold basis, building up local armaments but maintaining the navy as the dominant part of the services.   New Zealand was to follow the same line.   South Africa emphasized land defences and protection of coastal areas.   Canada in a somewhat similar line gave first place to the air force and fortification of coastal areas on the Pacific and Atlantic and second to the navy. In addition, the non-permanent militia was reorganized along more modern and realistic lines.   Even those modest programmes met challenge, particularly in Canada by C.C.F. members and Quebec Liberals.   In comparison with what was being done by other countries, they might well have been criticized for not going far enough.

What the programmes confirmed, however, was that the agreement reached at the Imperial Conference was for defence through individual efforts plus such two-way support between individual Dominions and Great Britain as might be possible.   What was new in the situation was that the problem was presented to Dominion statesmen on the assumption that Great Britain might be fighting an almost isolated war with one or more enemies.   "The only alliance taken for granted," wrote an acute observer, "was the French and that only in the limited zone of joint British and French interests in Western Europe."[93]   In this perspective, what attitude did the Dominion statesmen take in regard to common policy or to support of Great Britain should it become involved in war?

Though the information in this field is even more scarce than in regard to defence, it appears that on these vital issues there was a greater degree of solidarity than has generally been thought.   It seems clear that the British Government spared no effort to put before the Prime Ministers of the overseas Dominions the full measure of the crisis as they saw it and the full details of the negotiations by which they had sought to avoid general war. In general, their policies of the past seem to have been approved except perhaps by New Zealand. The programme of non-intervention in Spain to which Commonwealth countries had already acceded appears to have had the approval of at least Great Britain, Canada, Australia, and South Africa. It was noticeable that Hertzog in his closing address to the Conference stressed the fact that war should be resorted to "only as a measure of self-defence in the hour of despair."[94] This may be taken to have been the attitude general within the Conference. But if, as Kingsley Martin, editor of *The New Statesman and Nation*, wrote, an understanding was reached "that in no circumstances would England become involved in any way which all the Dominions did not approve," then it was no doubt equally valid to say as he did that "equally in the event of such a war, Britain could rely on the co-operation of all members of the Commonwealth."[95] The wheel was turning full round again. In the face of the threat of a militant Germany, Great Britain was pledging itself to fight only if the need were so clear and pressing that all the Commonwealth members would be equally aware of it, and in turn the Prime Ministers of the overseas Dominions were indicating that in such a situation their countries would come to its support.

Whether more precise considerations were entered into cannot be determined. Foreign papers were full of rumours as to whether the Dominions limited their solidarity with Great Britain to a direct attack in the west. The *Berliner Tageblatt* felt it was likely that "the Dominions will stand by England through thick and thin in Western Europe, but make reservations with regard to Eastern Europe."[96] The *Prager Presse*, on the other hand, found it striking that no one at the Conference had declared "that England should limit her commitments in the European peace system to Western Europe."[97] There may well have been some division on this point for Hertzog was subsequently to show himself reluctant for outright support of Great Britain in a conflict arising in eastern Europe. Though his was the most outspoken opposition on this point, it was probably shared in general by the other overseas representatives who recognized the difficulty of making their own people aware of their direct interest in such a conflict. This feeling of remoteness, which was not absent from British public opinion either, helps to explain the appeasement policy of the succeeding period.

But granting the overwhelming desire to avoid war, there seems yet to have been reached at this Conference a general acceptance of the fact that if Great Britain became involved in war through the aggressive action of Germany, the overseas Dominions would come to its support.   At a civic reception on his return, Prime Minister Savage declared that there had been much plain speaking at the Conference and many divisions of opinion among the members.[98]   ". . . but if Great Britain were in a difficulty tomorrow," he asserted, "I do not think there would be much division.   I think about the same would happen as happened last time."   Though Prime Minister King could hardly be expected to make so open a statement at home in view of sentiment within the Liberal party, the comment that his "isolationist bark is worse than his bite" and largely for home consumption was not without justification.[99]   For King, about whose attitude there had been the most questioning before the Conference, took the far-reaching step on its conclusion of letting it be known in official German and British quarters that if Germany should attack Great Britain, Canada would come to its support.

For the specific purpose of ensuring that the Nazi Government should not be left in any doubt about this fact, King went to Germany in June, 1937.   As he told the House of Commons on August 11, 1944, "my visit had as its objective to make it perfectly clear that, if there was a war of aggression, nothing in the world would keep the Canadian people from being at the side of Britain."[100]   Not only was this said to the German Government but the British Government was fully informed of his action, Mr. King made clear.   That it felt the move to be a valuable contribution to the cause of peace was evidenced by Eden's speech to the Canadian House of Commons on April 1, 1943, when he declared that he for one could never be too grateful for what Prime Minister King had done.[101]

Though the object of his visit to Germany was kept secret until long after war was in progress, King did give voice to his feelings on behalf of solidarity in a speech at the Canadian Pavilion of the Paris Exhibition early in July, 1937.   Though the Reuter account of his most striking statement, "We like to manage our own affairs but any threat to England would immediately bring Canada to her side,"[102] was subsequently questioned, his general meaning was hardly open to doubt.   Some who were present during the speech said that he had used the words "British Commonwealth" instead of England.   The Canadian Press account was longer and more general.   "We like to manage our own affairs," it reported him as saying, "we co-operate with other parts of the British Empire in discussing questions of British interest.   The fact that we have our own representation in other countries is evidence of that liberty and freedom which above all we prize and, were it imperilled from any source whatever, would bring us together again in preservation of it."[103]   But though the meaning was more veiled in this latter account, the implication of unity in the face of aggression seemed clear.   Taken in conjunction with the reason behind his visit to Germany, it seems fair to conclude that King was voicing what he well knew would be the fact, that Canada would come to Great Britain's support if it were attacked.   In the light, however, of the isolationist tendencies in his own party as well as in the C.C.F.,[104] it was hardly surprising though perhaps somewhat dangerous that he left it to events to bring a similar awareness to Canadians as a whole.

The Imperial Conference of 1937 became in fact one of the decisive meetings in the history of the Commonwealth, not because of any formulation of theoretical principles such as made the 1926 Conference so significant, but because it united its participants in an awareness of common danger.   What threatened in Europe was not merely a challenge to imperial interests over which the Dominions might differ in attitude but a threat to Great Britain itself which no one of them could face with equanimity either in the light of their own security or of the sympathies of those of British stock among their own peoples. Such a threat challenged the security of the North Atlantic on which Canada's safety rested as obviously as that of South Africa, of Australia, and of New Zealand depended on maintaining contact by sea with a great naval power.   For the first time in the inter-war period, the motive of self-preservation acted directly upon the Governments of all the overseas Dominions to induce a common attitude.   There was to be no slackening of the efforts to avoid war.   But should aggression threaten them directly, then the nations of the Commonwealth could be expected to stand united in the face of common danger.

REFERENCES FOR CHAPTER VIII

1. *Cmd. 5107* of 1936.

2. A. J. Toynbee, *Survey of International Affairs*, 1936, pp. 136-37.

3. *Statement of the Government's Policy regarding the Defence of Australia* delivered at Sydney by the Minister for Defence (Senator the Rt. Hon. Sir George Pearce, K.C.V.O.), 25.9.1933 (Melbourne).

4. *E.g.*, Authorities cited by John Sandes in "The Defence of Australia," *Australian Quarterly*, Dec., 1933, pp. 11-27.

5. *E.g.*, Observer, "Australian Defence Policy," *ibid.*, June, 1935, pp. 65-74, and "Albatross," *Japan and the Defence of Australia* (Melbourne, 1935).

6. *Statement of the Government's Policy regarding the Defence of Australia*, delivered at Mosman, N.S.W., by the Minister for Defence (The Hon. Archdale Parkhill, M.P.), 2nd December, 1935 (Canberra), p. 10.

7. *The Argus* and *The Age* cited in *The Times*, Feb. 12, 1936 (Melbourne).

8. *New York Times*, March 30, 1936 (Melbourne, March 29).

9. *The Times*, Aug. 7, 1936 (Brisbane, Aug. 6).

10. *J.P.E.*, 1936, XVII, 626-29.

11. *Ibid.*, pp. 610-12 (May 6, 1936). He also answered criticisms on May 14, *ibid.*, 1937, XVIII, 167-71. He left for England on May 22.

12. *The Times*, June 26, 1936 (Kroonstad, Orange Free State, June 25, Reuter).

13. *J.P.E.*, 1936, XVII, 811.

14. *Ibid.*, 1937, XVIII, 134-44.

15. F. H. Soward, "Politics," *Canada in World Affairs, The Pre-War Years* (Toronto, 1941), pp. 34 and 51 ff.

16. *J.P.E.*, 1937, XVIII, 96 (Sir George Pearce in the Australian Senate, Sept. 11, 1936).

17. For Canadian reaction to the signing of the Treaty of Lausanne, *see* above, p. 90.

18. *J.P.E.*, 1937, XVIII, 96.

19. For details *see* Toynbee, *Survey*, 1936, p. 613 ff.

20. *J.P.E.*, 1937, XVIII, 96. For earlier Australian reactions to British policy in Egypt, *see* above, p. 83.

21. *Ibid.*, p. 222 (Eden citing M. Blum in the House on Mar. 2, 1937).

22. *C. 347, M. 223*, 1936, VII.

23. Sept. 3, 1936. It spoke of the League as "a wounded but neither helpless nor hopeless crusader, needing only the rallying of wisely brave endeavour to achieve success," and felt "it would be necessary to go farther than had the Geneva Protocol."

24. Sept. 5, 1936. It felt the sanctions experiment had "sufficiently demonstrated the futility of lukewarm adherence to the cause of peace . . ."

25. *New Zealand Parliamentary Papers*, 1936, 1st Session, p. 874 (Prime Minister Savage in the House of Representatives on Oct. 21, 1936, in answer to a question regarding Jordan's speech to the Assembly (*O.J.*, 1936, Spec. Sup. No. 155, pp. 78-80: *Seventeenth Assembly*, Tenth Plenary Session, Sept. 29, 1936) which reiterated the points raised in the New Zealand statement on revision of the Covenant).

26. *O.J.*, 1935, Spec. Sup. No. 138, pp. 81-82: *Sixteenth Assembly*, Ninth Meeting, September 16, 1935.

27. On Dec. 16, 1936, Mr. Eden declared in answer to a question that the British Government had not been consulted regarding the terms of the New Zealand memorandum and did not consider the proposals to be "practicable at the present time." *Great Britain, House of Commons Debates*, cols. 2431-32.

28. *J.P.E.*, 1936, XVII, 727-28 (July 27, 1936).

29. *O.J.*, 1936, Spec. Sup. No. 155, pp. 44-47: *Seventeenth Assembly*, Sixth Plenary Session, Sept. 25, 1936.

30. *Ibid.*, pp. 74-77 (Bruce): Tenth Plenary Session, Sept. 29, 1936. Cited as expressing his own and the British point of view by Mr. King in a speech on "The Seventeenth Assembly of the League of Nations" at the National Peace Action Week Dinner of the League of Nations Society in Canada, Ottawa, Nov. 9, 1936, *Supplement Monthly News Sheet*, League of Nations Society in Canada, March, 1937.

31. *O.J.*, 1936, Spec. Sup. No. 155, pp. 67-70: *Seventeenth Assembly*, Ninth Plenary Session, Sept. 29, 1936.   In his statement of Oct. 29, 1935, on assuming office, King had declared, "In the future, as in the past, the Government will be prepared to participate in the consideration of the most effective means of advancing the aims of the League through the adjustment of specific controversies, the lessening of the rivalries based upon exaggerated economic nationalism, the renewal of the effort to stem the rising tide of competitive armament, and such other policies as are appropriate for a country in the geographic and economic position of the Dominion, and as will ensure unity and common consent in Canada as well as the advancement of peace abroad."   Canada, 1936, *Documents Relating to the Italo-Ethiopian Conflict*, No. 17.

32. *J.P.E.*, 1936, pp. 93-95 (Sir George Pearce, speaking in the Senate on Sept. 30, 1936).

33. *See* above, p. 126.

34. *Australia, Annual Report of the Department of External Affairs* for the year ended 31st December, 1936 (Canberra, 1937), p. 25.

35. *J.P.E.*, 1937, XVIII, 850-52 (Sir George Pearce in the Senate, June 18, 1937).

36. *Government's Policy regarding the Defence of Australia*, Mosman, N.S.W., by the Minister for Defence, 2nd December, 1935, p. 6.

37. Jack Shepherd, *Australia's Interests and Policies in the Far East*, pp. 43-62.

38. King, "Seventeenth Assembly," *Monthly News Sheet*, March, 1937.

39. *The Globe and Mail*, Sept. 30, 1936.

40. Quoted in *The Toronto Daily Star*, Oct. 8, 1936, which answered the accusation.

41. *O.J.*, 1936, Spec. Sup. No. 162, pp. 24-25: Special Main Committee.

42. Toynbee, *Survey*, 1937, II, 218.

43. Australia, *Report of Department of External Affairs*, 1936, p. 40.

44. *O.J.*, January, 1937, pp. 14-16: Minutes of Ninety-fifth (Extraordinary) Session of the Council, Third Meeting, Dec. 11, 1936.

45. *J.P.E.*, 1937, XVIII, 172-74.

46. *Ibid.*, pp. 438-41.

47. *Ibid.*, pp. 312-16.

48. *Ibid.*, pp. 302-09 (January 25, 1937).

49. *Ibid.*, 1936, XVII, 305-07.

50. *Ibid.*, p. 613.

51. Its report was published Sept. 7, 1937. *League Document, A 27*, 1937, IIB.

52. *Nazi Activities in South West Africa* (as stated in the Report of South West Africa Commission, March, 1936) with a foreword by the Rt. Hon. Lord Lugard. "Friends of Europe" Publication, No. 43 (London, 1936).

53. Eric A. Walker, *A History of South Africa* (2nd ed. London, 1940), p. 670.

54. *The Times*, July 15, 1936.

55. *J.P.E.*, XVII, 731-32 (July 16, 1936).

56. First stated by the Colonial Secretary on Feb. 12, 1936, *ibid.*, p. 208, and reaffirmed on Apr. 6, 1936, *ibid.*, p. 195 and Apr. 8, *ibid.*, p. 449.

57. *The Times*, Aug. 6, 1936 (Sir Harold Macmillan).

58. *Manchester Guardian*, Sept. 8, 1936 (Johannesburg, Sept. 7, Reuter), and *The Times*, Sept. 9, 1936.

59. *The Daily Telegraph*, Sept. 10, 1936. Reitz, Minister of Agriculture, said much the same in regard to mandates a month later. *Ibid.*, Oct. 13, 1936.

60. In the *Bloemfontein Friend*, cited in the *Manchester Guardian*, Sept. 12, 1936. It also quoted from the *Cape Times* and the *Johannesburg Mail*.

61. Quoted in *The Daily Telegraph*, Feb. 1, 1937 (Johannesburg).

62. *Ibid.*, Mar. 4, 1937 (Cape Town).

63. *The African Observer*, VII, Mar., 1937, p. 12. *See* also the article on "Tanganyika—British or Foreign," by Churusi, pointing out the dangers of returning this territory to Germany.

64. *J.P.E.*, 1937, XVIII, 613-14.

65. *The Daily Telegraph*, Jan. 29, 1937.

66. Quoted in *ibid.*, Feb. 4, 1937.

67. *Australian National Review*, Feb., 1937.

68. *Sydney Morning Herald*, Mar. 25, 1937 (Mr. Grose).

69. Imperial Conference, 1937, Summary of Proceedings, *Cmd. 5482*, p. 53.

70. *The Daily Telegraph*, June 8, 1937.

71. Toynbee, *Survey*, 1937, I, 166-67.

72. *Contemporary New Zealand: A Survey of Domestic and Foreign Policy* (Auckland, 1938), p. 226. As is pointed out, New Zealand had a definite prejudice against regional agreements, mainly lest they degenerate into "alliances of the old type."

73. *E.g.*, J. W. Crawford, "Australia as a Pacific Power" in *Australia's Foreign Policy*, ed. by W. G. K. Duncan (Sydney, 1938), p. 106 ff. "Austra" in "A Pacific Pact," *Australian National Review*, June, 1937, pointed out the difficulty of securing an agreement between Japan and the United States and Great Britain whose interests in China were in conflict and ended, "Pact or not Pact, it is to Australia's interest to cultivate the friendliest possible relations with the United States and Japan."

74. *See* "Australia's Trade Relations," *Data Paper for the Institute of Pacific Relations* (Melbourne, 1939). *Le Temps* reported on May 21, 1937, that a number of Japanese papers including *Ayashi* declared that questions relating to raw materials and trade agreements should be settled before a Pacific Pact was taken under consideration.

75. When Malan objected to the Prime Minister going to the Imperial Conference, Hertzog replied that the fear that he would compromise the Cabinet was one of the contingencies with which every country had to reckon. *J.P.E.*, 1937, XVIII, 615.

76. As described by the Minister of Defence, *ibid.*, 319-20.

77. *Ibid.*, pp. 319 and 324-25.

78. The Act providing for the Constitution was introduced and passed on the same day, Dec. 11, 1936, on which action was taken on the abdication of Edward VIII. The Executive Authority (External Relations) Act was introduced the same day and passed Dec. 12, 1936. *Ibid.*, pp. 178-186.

79. After hedging on questions for some time, de Valera declared on March 31 in the *Dail* that in his opinion "in the existing circumstances, it would be of no advantage to our country to be represented at the Imperial Conference." *Ibid.*, p. 445.

80. *E.g.*, Comments cited by F. H. Soward in "Politics" in *Canada in World Affairs: The Pre-War Years*, p. 69.

81. *Cmd. 5482*, pp. 14-16.

82. *Contemporary New Zealand*, p. 181.

83. *Cmd. 5482*, p. 68. *See* also his speech on the Conference to the House of Representatives, *J.P.E.*, 1938, XIX, 121-23. For general moves in this direction *see* Toynbee, *Survey*, 1937, I, Part II.

84. Rumours were current that the British Government attempted to persuade Mr. King to take the lead at Geneva for the elimination of Article 16 but with no success. The editorial in *The Times*, June 14, 1937, referring to his brusqueness, may or may not refer to this.

85. *Contemporary New Zealand*, p. 181.

86. *Cmd. 5482*, pp. 52-54.

87. *Ibid.*, pp. 58-59.

88. *Sydney Morning Herald*, June 17, 1937.

89. *Ibid.*, July 21, 1937.

90. *Ibid.* and *The Times*, July 29, 1937 (Sydney, July 28).

91. *The Times*, June 14, 1937.

92. *See* Jack Alexander, "Australia at War," in *The British Commonwealth at War*, ed. by W. Y. Elliott and H. Duncan Hall (New York, 1943), p. 368 ff.

93. Kingsley Martin, "Is the British Empire in Retreat?" *Yale Quarterly*, Autumn, 1937.

94. *Cmd. 5482*, p. 69.

95. Martin, *Yale Quarterly*, Autumn, 1937, p. 28.

96. *Berliner Tageblatt*, June 17, 1937.

97. *Prager Presse*, June 17, 1937.

98. *The Times*, July 29, 1937 (Wellington, July 28).

99. *Sydney Morning Herald*, June 9, 1937.

100. *Canada, House of Commons Debates* (unrevised), 1944, LXXXII, 6420.

101. *Ibid.*, April 1, 1943, LXXXI, 1765.

102. *The Times*, July 3, 1937.

103. *Canadian Press Despatch*.

104. The Trades and Labour Congress passed a resolution at their fall convention declaring themselves unalterably opposed to war and maintaining that there should be no declaration of war by the Government until the people had been consulted by a referendum. *The Times*, Sept. 18, 1937.

CHAPTER IX

COMMONWEALTH RESPONSE TO THE THREAT
OF WAR

THE Imperial Conference of 1937 answered one vital question by reaffirming the solidarity of the overseas Dominions with Great Britain in case of unprovoked aggression. But it left unanswered the equally, if not more, important issue of what positive policies should be pursued to lessen or eliminate the danger of an outbreak of general war. For solidarity pledged for a time of ultimate need was conditioned by the understanding that every effort would be made to prevent this contingency from arising.

On one but probably only one line of positive policy was the Commonwealth united. This was on the need for closer relations with the United States. The Anglo-American Trade Agreement of 1938, specifically endorsed by the Imperial Conference, provided tangible evidence of this development. When seen in the context of Canadian participation in Commonwealth affairs, one of its most promising signs was the joint pledges on defence exchanged between the leaders of the United States and Canada in August, 1938. This was the most encouraging aspect of a period which was marked increasingly by vain hopes and humiliating compromises.

On the more difficult issue of how to prevent the crisis which all dreaded from coming to pass, there were and remained wide differences. One alternative was appeasement, originally hailed as synonymous with conciliatory action though ultimately with the passage of time to acquire the connotation of "peace at any price." Another line far less widely supported was the maintenance of a firm stand behind principles to which collective support could be given. This was generally felt to entail dangers which outweighed its potential advantages at this stage of international relations. Others stressed aloofness but this was to be found more possible in theory than in practice.

From the fall of 1937 to the spring of 1939, the British Government, with the tacit and sometimes explicit support of the Australian, Canadian, and South African Governments, followed the road of appeasement. The premise on which it was based was that many aims of the aggressive powers were legitimate. The hope behind it was that if they were satisfied, the urge to conquest would disappear. To yield a little to avoid war became the maxim. However distasteful was the process when looked at in perspective, it must be recognized that at least in Europe appeasement was looked on as a conditional process: thus far and no farther. Yet as always when yielding began, it became more difficult to set a halt. In this, New Zealand's Government was clearly right that only fixed principles of international action provided standards behind which nations could take a united stand. Barring this, there was only security as a guide and security could be only a matter of individual interpretation. As a road to security, appeasement found more general support, however, than formal alliances. It seemed to offer the hope of easing dangerous situations without necessitating commitments which would remove freedom of action for the future. For this reason it appealed to most members of the Commonwealth. Only New Zealand's Government stood out against it openly.

Not till March, 1939, with the annexation of Czechoslovakia, did the British Government become convinced that the appeasement policy had failed. It then undertook a sudden and startling reversal of traditional policy. Limited liability confined to western Europe was replaced by large-scale commitments in eastern Europe extended under the view that European peace was indivisible. That these heroic measures failed ultimately to keep, the peace does not indicate that they were basically unsound but rather that they were undertaken too late. The tragedy of the years immediately preceding the outbreak of war was that most public opinion within democratic countries did not become convinced of the necessity of a firm stand against the fascist powers until the moment had passed when such a stand could be effective.

In this period, marked by the outbreak of the second Sino-Japanese war, by the dragging out to its unhappy conclusion of the war in Spain, and above all by the growing menace of Germany, Commonwealth countries with the exception of New Zealand proved no more alert than other democratic powers in mobilizing against the coming danger. Along the road of appeasement, the Chamberlain Government was to be supported with varying degrees of enthusiasm by the Australian and Canadian Governments. The New Zealand Government, as could be expected, resisted as far as it could.[1] Only gradually and somewhat reluctantly did it come back to solidarity with Great Britain in the fall of 1938 with the new crises. The South African Government trod the middle road, taking little active stand either for or against what was developing. Eire, acting independently, was treated in fact if not in theory as outside the Commonwealth.

Within the overseas Dominions, there were still greater divisions over what policies should be. The Canadian Conservative party supported a common policy for the Commonwealth reached by discussion[2] and pressed for increases in the Navy. But even the measures obviously designed for home defence met stringent opposition from some members of the Liberal party and even more from the C.C.F. Though there was little open support of the League on the floor of the House, its adherents were not without influence in the country and needled Prime Minister King when they felt he was letting down its principles. In Australia, the Labour party, defeated in the elections of October, 1937, partly at least because of uncertainty over its confused foreign policy of the previous years, continued to oppose the emphasis on building up the navy[3] and at the same time accused the Government of being subservient to Downing Street and to fascist interests at home and abroad. In New Zealand, it was the Opposition which pressed for strong support for Great Britain at all times. In South Africa, the division between Hertzog and Smuts became wider as events centred outside the area which the former felt directly affected South African interests. Hertzog began once more to flirt with ideas of neutrality though he never went as far as Malan. In contrast to his fellow leader of the Fusion party, General Smuts continued to maintain that peace was indivisible and unity with Great Britain essential. Nor did Hertzog seem to consider this difference of opinion to be destructive of the unity of the party. On being challenged by Malan after the election of May, 1938, as to whether the Government would follow him or Smuts in case Great Britain should be in danger, he replied that, "When the time came, the people would decide; and it would all depend on who had the most authority and whom the people trusted most."[4] It was an important foreshadowing of what actually occurred in September, 1939.

These divisions of opinion, healthy in themselves, yet complicated efforts to build strong national policies or to develop constructive programmes of common action. Almost to the end unity could be secured only in opposition to war. In the time of paper plans the emphasis of Commonwealth countries had been on security *against* war. It was still only an essentially negative line of policy which could command support. As the danger points shifted between the Far East and Europe, the policy of avoiding involvement commanded the support of the major members of the Commonwealth.

In July, 1937, there was added to the other causes of international concern a fresh outbreak of large-scale conflict between Japan and China. During the interval of uneasy truce beginning in 1934, China had acquired a greater degree of unity under the leadership of Chiang Kai-shek. In Japan, the old split between the moderates and the young, aggressive military groups had widened again. Once more the latter decided to take affairs in their own hands and attempt to create a situation which would lead the Japanese people to support an increase of Japanese forces in China. Such an incident was staged at Lukouchiao on July 7, 1937. It led to rapid Japanese advances and an increasing number of incidents. Shortly after the arrival of a squadron of Japanese warships off Shanghai, large-scale hostilities began on August 13, 1937. Despite resistance, the Japanese pushed ahead rapidly and by the end of the year had acquired control of the Yangtze River and of Nanking. In comparison with the first Sino-Japanese conflict which aimed at cutting off certain provinces from Chinese control, the war which began in 1937 appeared directed towards domination of the whole of China.

The United States and Great Britain were still obviously the natural leaders in any efforts to restrain Japan in its aggressive course. American executive action was hamstrung, however, by the new Neutrality Act of 1937. This permitted discretion only in determining whether or not a war was taking place, not as to the embargoes and prohibitions which could be imposed and which would automatically affect both belligerents alike. In the effort to avoid handicapping the Chinese, the President did not bring the Neutrality Act into operation in this conflict as he had done during the Italo-Ethiopian and the Spanish civil war. But he was left with few formal means of affecting the outcome. From the British side, there was obvious willingness "to go as far and as fast as the United States, but no faster."[5] Though the Labour Opposition pressed at intervals for more vigorous action in support of the principles of collective security,[6] there was never any serious possibility that League members in general and Great Britain in particular would take more drastic steps than the United States was prepared for.

In 1937, public opinion in Canada,[7] New Zealand,[8] and Australia[9] assumed a far more active antagonism towards Japan than in the earlier dispute, and in each country there were plans for or attempted boycotts of Japanese goods. But there is no evidence that any Dominion Government other than that of New Zealand favoured forcible action. On the contrary, the Australian Government appears to have continued to preach moderation to the British Government in any policies adopted in the Far East lest they have unfortunate repercussions on the Pacific Dominions.[10] Similarly the Canadian Government maintained its customary reserve.[11]

Except for one brief moment of excitement following President Roosevelt's "quarantine the aggressors" speech at Chicago on October 5, 1937, there was little hope that collective action would affect the course of the conflict. The pattern of means used to restrain Japan was at all times unspectacular and ineffective. The American State Department urged Japan and China to find an amicable settlement following the first incident in July. Subsequently it circulated among sixty Governments Mr. Hull's statement on July 16, 1937, of his Government's position on international problems and situations. This afforded Commonwealth countries the opportunity to point out the similarity of their views, the Australian Government citing the Imperial Conference declaration on foreign affairs as evidence that the Commonwealth attitude corresponded "in all material respects" to that of the United States.[12] In September, the President forbade American merchant ships to transport implements of war to China and Japan in the effort to avoid incidents arising out of Japan's "pacific blockade" of the China coast. At the same time it protested against Japanese bombing of open cities. But there was no indication that a more positive policy might be used to give effect to such protests.

Early the same month, the Chinese Government in the effort to force attention to its plight appealed to the League under Articles 10, 11, and 17 since Japan was no longer a member. The appeal was referred to the Far Eastern Advisory Committee which had been set up by the Assembly Resolution of February 24, 1933.[13] The Committee included among its twenty-one members, Great Britain, the United States, Canada, and New Zealand, and at its first session Australia was also invited to participate in its work. At the same time invitations were extended to China, Japan, and Germany, but only China and Australia accepted.

On the same day, September 21st, on which it was decided to offer a place on the Committee to Australia, its representative, Mr. Bruce, asked in his Assembly speech that China should not be misled "into believing that she can rely on forms of assistance which may not be forthcoming."[14] It was the same point of view he had put forward regarding Ethiopia during the Italo-Ethiopian conflict. When he became a member of the Advisory Committee, Bruce maintained his cautious attitude but at the same time sought to prevent issues from being side-tracked. It was a reflection of Australia's interest and concern over the issue coupled with perhaps oversensitiveness as to the difficulties and potential dangers of pillorying Japan.

The first matter which the Committee considered was a protest against Japanese bombardment of open towns. Bruce, supported by Cranborne, proposed that the condemnation of such practices be left in general terms without specific reference to Japan. He met sharp criticism from Jordan of New Zealand, and the final resolution specified attacks by "Japanese aircraft."[15] But subsequently Bruce showed more concern for a definite statement of attitude, pressing that the proposal to appoint a sub-committee to consider recommendations for Assembly action should be to expedite matters, not "to let the problem remain somewhat in suspense. . . ."[16] He himself became a member of the sub-committee and, on the proposal of Litvinov, Jordan was added to its number.

During the discussions of the sub-committee, Jordan distinguished himself by asking for specific measures against Japan. He urged that the report to be presented to the Assembly should recommend that members of the League "should consider how, or use their influence, or endeavour to deter Japan from continuing its present form of aggression."[17] But, put to a vote, Jordan's amendment was supported only by two other states which were unofficially reported to include the Soviet Union. It was opposed by four, reported to be Great Britain, Australia, Holland, and France, while six refrained from voting.[18] The report, as accepted by the sub-committee, and the Far Eastern Advisory Committee, merely recommended that the League members which were parties to the Nine-Power Treaty should meet with other states having special interests in the Far East to concert proposals and that the Assembly should remain in session to receive them. Together with another report reviewing the facts which stamped Japan as a violator of its treaty obligations, in particular the Nine-Power Treaty and the Kellogg Pact, it was accepted by the Committee on October 5th and presented to the Assembly the same day.

Up to that point, there had been little reason to suppose that the United States would be prepared to support any direct action but on the evening of October 5th, the Assembly was electrified by reports of President Roosevelt's "quarantine" speech. There was no longer opportunity to strengthen the report nor was such a suggestion made. In the light of the importance of the issue, however, many delegations, including the Canadian[19] and South African, wished to get the approval of their home countries. To make this possible, the Assembly was held in session one more day and with only the abstentions of Poland and Siam the resolution was adopted unanimously on October 6, 1937.

In the light of the President's speech, much was hoped for from the subsequent meeting of the "Washington powers" in Brussels for which the Assembly resolution had called. Eden reasserted that Great Britain would go as far as would the United States. But by the time invitations went out, adverse reactions in that country to the "quarantine" speech had led the American Government to put its emphasis once more on mediation. Japan refused to attend the Conference. Despite this snub, no important power proved willing to take any initiative. Jordan protested once more against the infringement of Chinese sovereignty and pleaded for action against Japan.[20] But the first resolution of the Brussels Conference was only a little more specific than the report adopted by the Assembly. The final report and declaration on November 24, 1937, went even less far. Once more aggression was allowed to go unchecked.

In 1938, as the Spanish war reached its climax and Germany began the series of external aggressions which were to culminate in war, the second partner of the Berlin-Tokyo-Rome Axis was well on its way towards domination in the Far East. Having failed to secure the concessions hoped for from its initial blows, Japan concentrated in 1938 on destroying the resistance of General Chiang Kai-shek's Nationalist party by capturing Hankow and cutting communications between South-Eastern and Central China. In October, 1938, Canton was taken. Despite its fairly steady record of military successes, the Japanese army was still far from being in control of the country. That such was its ultimate aim was made clear, however, at the end of the year with the announcement that it was establishing a "new order" which would replace the old system marked by the "open door" and protection of China from domination by a single power.

Such a development, which also carried with it threats to and violations of foreign concessions, was not regarded with equanimity by western countries. But as always there was question regarding the means to take to support China. The obvious way was through the League. But fear of the implications of collective action blocked this route, though the issue was raised again and again. In the end aid to China was extended individually, the British Government following closely the example of the Government of the United States.

In the Council meetings in which the Chinese delegation again appealed for League support, New Zealand did not take an open stand opposed to that of Great Britain. But it probably urged action in private. When Japan's refusal to treat with the League was declared in September, 1938, to lay it open to the coercive penalties of Article 16, New Zealand was reported to be supporting collective sanctions.[21] As President of the Council at that time, Jordan maintained an impartial attitude in the public meetings but the report that he opposed the British view that imposition of sanctions should be "optional" would indicate a continuation of his earlier attitude. In opening the Nineteenth Assembly in his rôle as President of the Council, Jordan pointed out that "If the League fails, it will be the failure of Governments," and cited his Government's belief that "the Covenant forms the minimum of any real system of international co-operation to secure peace."[22] In January, 1939, and again in May, Jordan pleaded for an embargo on

exports of oil and airplanes, "articles of indiscriminate slaughter," as
he called them.[23]   In this later meeting, he maintained that the least
that League members should do would be to secure the facts about
bombing of civilians, to formulate measures of aid to China and means
to deter Japan and "lastly to implement the resolutions which have
already been adopted by the League."[24]   But he found little or no
support for collective action.

None the less, Great Britain did not ignore in this period the
injunction of the Assembly to consider how far aid could be extended
individually to China.   A British loan to China announced at the end
of 1938 and implemented early in 1939 followed similar American aid.
Also no obstacles were put in the way of building the Burma Road to
provide a southern supply route to China though it gave rise to serious
anti-British feeling in Japan.   In a similar situation, the French
apparently limited the supply of goods moving to China through Indo-
China though the action was not taken officially.   In other ways, less
directly concerned with aiding China than with protecting their own
rights, the British attempted to restrain Japan's progress towards
domination of China.   They joined with the United States and France
in demanding the reopening of the Yangtze River in November, 1938,
in attempting to safeguard the Chinese Customs Administration and in
declaring themselves unwilling to accept the Japanese conception of a
"new order."   In the latter *démarche*, they put themselves even more
openly than the other countries behind the doctrine of the integrity of
China.

In this middle of the road policy, Great Britain was going less
far than the New Zealand Government would have liked but almost too
far for the Australian Government.   Its old fear of a Japanese drive
south was intensified by the occupation of Hainan and subsequently
of the Spratly Islands.   Though the general embargo on the export of
Australian iron ore which was imposed July 1, 1938, had almost the
look of a sanction against Japan whose war programme it affected
adversely, it was apparently not so intended.[25]   Early in 1939, the
Australian Government established one of its first two legations in Tokyo.
In May, the new Minister of External Affairs made an open gesture of
friendship in asking, "Why, in the event of war, or even in these days
when we live under the shadow of war, should Japan prefer its new
friends in the Anti-Comintern Pact, to its far older friends through
the British Empire?"[26]   When the British concession in Tientsin was
blockaded and British citizens suffered indignities at the hands of the
Japanese, Australia appeared torn between concern and wrath on one
side and fear that Great Britain would be tempted into drastic measures

on the other.   During the period of special tension in June, 1939, the Australian Government amicably continued its negotiations for renewal of the Australian-Japanese trade agreement.   Reports indicate that it was Australia which urged the British Government to come to some understanding with Japan, perhaps of the character of the "Tokyo agreement," recognizing the special position of the Japanese army in China which was announced July 24, 1939.[27]   At least Prime Minister Chamberlain in a speech early in August referred to the difficulties confronting positive action in the Far East because of the necessity of consulting the Pacific Dominions.[28]   Since members of the New Zealand Labour party openly criticized the agreement and the Government declared it had not known of the terms until they were published,[29] there is an unmistakable implication that Australia was a factor in this introduction of "appeasement" into British policy towards Japan.

From its own side, however, events in Europe had long since determined that Great Britain would not take forceful action in any quarter of the globe where it could be avoided.   Throughout this time, Europe formed the real centre of its concern.   To prevent the Spanish war from spreading outside that country, to re-establish good relations with Italy as a safeguard for the all-important Mediterranean route and a possible counterbalance to Germany, to restrain the latter from moves which would precipitate general war were its primary aims.   On these, its attention was chiefly concentrated.

While the Imperial Conference was still in session, attacks on non-intervention patrol and other ships, including the German battleship *Deutschland* and brutal Nazi reprisals by shelling a Spanish town, had temporarily frustrated the attempt to secure an agreement on withdrawal of "volunteers" from Spain.   Behind the German and Italian refusal to negotiate further on "volunteers" probably lay also the deeper calculation that their presence was mainly an aid to Franco's side alone.   The Loyalist Government was being hard pressed by the forces brought against it and was suffering from lack of supplies.   Its defeat appeared nearer than in fact it was.

In the summer of 1937, the degree of Fascist intervention in Spain was beginning to cause concern in quarters previously convinced of the merits of non-intervention.   The Liberals, in particular, and Winston Churchill began to preach the danger to Great Britain's strategic position if Gibraltar should be threatened.   The Conservatives seemed deaf to their favourite watchword.   But in August and September, 1937, indiscriminate attacks on shipping in the Mediterranean roused the British Government to action.   In a series of meetings of Mediterranean powers and the Soviet Union which took place simultaneously with the Assembly and largely overshadowed the latter, the decision was reached on September 14th to set up a naval patrol which would run down the piratical underseas vessels.[30] Germany and Italy, which had refused to attend the meetings, found themselves outmanœuvred for once. Italy so acknowledged by signing a supplementary agreement[31] at Geneva on September 30th and ultimately joining the patrol. By that time the danger, generally believed to have been caused by Italian submarines, had virtually ceased. Action in this case had more than justified itself.

It did little or nothing, however, to aid the situation in Spain. The Spanish Government had appealed once more to the Council and to the Assembly in September, 1937, requesting recognition of Italian and German aggression. It asked for measures to end their intervention, for withdrawal of foreign combatants and for freedom to buy war materials once more. To the Council it protested at not being invited to the Nyon Conference, and at the exclusion of its shipping from the protection of the naval patrol. But to its appeal, only the New Zealand and Soviet representatives on the Council responded wholeheartedly. Desperately seeking some means whereby Spain could freely settle its own destiny, Jordan asked again as he had done in May[32] whether the country could not be placed temporarily under an "A" mandate.[33] It was a sincere if naïve proposal. It received no more serious consideration than did the Spanish appeal which was answered with another resolution couched in the most general terms.

Aware that there was great anxiety in the Assembly as to whether non-intervention was achieving its purpose or not, the Spanish Government had decided to refer to it rather than the Council the specific issues of aggression and of the "volunteers." Here they had more success in securing a resolution drafted in forcible terms but it encountered strong opposition in which de Valera took an active part. Though the resolution ultimately failed to secure the necessary unanimity, the strength of its support showed the deep concern over continued foreign intervention in Spain.

That this concern existed also in home countries was evidenced by the sharp reaction in pro-League circles in Canada, including the *Winnipeg Free Press*,[34] caused by a journalist's report that Canada had cast its vote against Spain[35] when the latter's appeal for re-eligibility to membership on the Council had been turned down by the Assembly along with that of Turkey. The rumour was not based on fact as the Prime Minister subsequently made known by taking the unusual step of making public the Canadian vote. No official instructions had been issued on the matter, he said, but in fact Spain's request for re-eligibility had been supported.[36]   "The Canadian Delegation did not feel," wrote Senator Dandurand in the letter quoted by the Prime Minister, "that the calamity of war in Spain could justify the Members of the League to inflict upon this unhappy country the further humiliation of the loss of her seat on the Council."   He took pains to make it clear, however, that the action was not intended to be partisan and was without reference to "what Government would represent her, today or tomorrow."

In the Sixth Committee to which the formal Spanish appeal was referred there was general concern that foreign "volunteers" had not yet been withdrawn from Spain.   Though only the Mexican and Soviet representatives proposed any specific types of action, the resolution as drafted for submission to the Assembly spoke openly of "veritable army corps on Spanish soil, which represents foreign intervention in Spanish affairs."   It joined its appeal to Governments to take new and earnest efforts in this regard with the warning that "if such a result cannot be obtained in the near future, the Members of the League which are parties to the Non-Intervention Agreement will consider ending the policy of non-intervention."[37]

It was in regard to this last section that de Valera raised his objections, maintaining both in the Committee[38] and in the Assembly[39] that approving such a declaration was inconsistent with the intention of the Irish Free State to maintain non-intervention no matter what happened.   Though the British and French delegates insisted that the resolution left individual countries complete freedom of action, he continued his opposition.   "There is a danger, in the present condition of Europe," he told the Assembly, "that the League of Nations, as it now is, may degenerate into a mere alliance of one group of States against another group.   That would be the end of our hopes for a real League, and I consider that the smaller States of the League, in particular, should resist from the beginning every tendency in that direction."   Though some have thought that in this instance de Valera was not adhering strictly to the non-partisan attitude he had followed before,[40] and did not want to approve action he believed detrimental to the interests of Franco, his objection and fears may well have been sincere.   Support for this view comes from the fact that South Africa adopted much the same stand.   Its representative abstained from voting in the Committee pending receipt of instructions.   In the Assembly, he announced his Government's opposition to the paragraph referring to foreign intervention in Spain as "not a sufficiently clear and comprehensive statement of the facts of the situation."[41]   The section to which de Valera objected, they declared capable of being "construed as containing a threat, possibly not conducive to the necessary co-operation" and felt that "States voting for it might be regarded as associating themselves in advance with a policy of the eventual application of that threat." In this situation the South African Government may also have been somewhat swayed by its dislike of radicalism but more especially it seems to have been motivated by its fear that trouble would be provoked.[42]

Though both the Irish Free State and South Africa only abstained along with twelve other states from voting on the resolution, Albania and Portugal prevented it from receiving the unanimity necessary for adoption. But abstention was in itself sufficient indication of opposition. Answering Labour party criticism in the House of Commons for not doing more, a Government spokesman pointed out that the utmost effort had been made to find a declaration which would enable the League "to present a united front to the world" but without success.[43] Citing specifically the abstentions by South Africa and Eire, Cranborne concluded that "it was clear that the League could not and would not at the present time take action in the Spanish dispute."

Nor was it to have another opportunity for from this time on consideration of the Spanish situation centred outside the League. Fresh hopes of securing an agreement on "volunteers" grew dim as belligerent rights for Franco were demanded as the price of withdrawal. This price was never granted. But in British efforts to reach an agreement on volunteers and other matters with Italy which in November, 1937, resigned from the League and joined the Anti-Comintern Pact one price was paid ultimately: the recognition of its conquest of Ethiopia. In the Anglo-Italian Agreement of April 14, 1938, the Italians agreed to a proportionate withdrawal of "volunteers" from Spain and the British pledged themselves to take steps at the May Council meeting to remove any obstacles to recognition of Italian sovereignty over Ethiopia. In this they succeeded, though not without running the gauntlet of criticism by the representatives of New Zealand, China, the Soviet Union, and Bolivia. Action was withheld, however, pending satisfactory assurances of withdrawal of Italian "volunteers." These were provided by Mussolini during the Munich Conference. On November 16, 1938, the British Government officially recognized the Italian conquest of Ethiopia. By this time, it may be added, the future of Spain was no longer in question and on February 17, 1939, Great Britain and France recognized General Franco's administration as the legitimate Government of Spain. A military dictatorship which had acquired its position through Fascist and Nazi aid was in control of the country flanking the entrance to the Mediterranean.

In Great Britain itself, this development led in February, 1938, to the resignation of Anthony Eden as Foreign Secretary. He had opposed opening conversations with Italy looking towards an Anglo-Italian Agreement until something specific had been done by that country to show its good faith. He was overruled by the Cabinet, which seems to have entertained the vain hope that the Stresa Front might be re-established before Hitler undertook to seize Austria. His resignation led to substantial criticism of British policy in Commonwealth countries. But in Australia, most nearly affected by the issue, the Chamberlain Government was supported by the Lyons administration as adhering to the "essential aims and ideals of the League" in its policy.[44] Early in February, revealed Lyons, he had wired Chamberlain that "We agree that the present situation calls for action, and we feel that the re-opening of conversations with Italy is of the utmost importance." The Agreement itself was welcomed by the Commonwealth Government both in the hope it would generally improve Anglo-Italian relations and that its specific provisions would relax tension in the Near East and safeguard the Suez Canal. In November, the Australian Government indicated its belief to the British that "the sooner the Agreement was implemented, the better it would be for both Great Britain and Italy and probably for the general peace of the world."[45] On February 28, 1939, it followed the British lead in extending recognition to the Franco Government.[46]

While the Australian Government approved British policy towards Italy and Spain in terms of the safety of "an essential artery between Australia and its principal markets," and the British Government itself believed it to be "an essential feature of a general appeasement,"[47] the Government of New Zealand was outraged at the suggestion of recognizing Italian sovereignty over Ethiopia. The British argument that many states including members of the Council had already granted recognition and that Eire had been among the first,[48] had no effect on the New Zealand attitude. When the matter came before the League Council on May 12, 1938, Jordan took an uncompromising stand in which he was matched only by Litvinov. "In our view, the League of Nations should not divest itself of the responsibility by leaving the issue to individual Governments," he declared.[49] ". . . for that is a direct denial of the collective responsibility which is fundamental. . . . The New Zealand Government cannot support any proposal which would involve either directly or by implication approval of a breach of the Covenant." But despite the force of his statement, the sense of the meeting was interpreted to be in support of the British request for freedom of action in the question of recognition. In fact, hardly anything else could have been done in the face of the number of States which had already granted recognition without waiting for even such a reference to a League organ as Great Britain had made. But it was worth noting that not even the one collective sanction on which League members had agreed in the Sino-Japanese dispute was maintained to indicate their moral disapproval over the more blatant case of aggression against Ethiopia.

Where the Australian Government had strongly encouraged the British Government's efforts to reach an understanding with Italy and New Zealand's Government had been equally strongly opposed to the recognition of Italy's conquest of Ethiopia, Canada and South Africa had refrained from committing themselves. But it was indicative of its general attitude that the Canadian Government quietly announced on December 22, 1938, that it had asked the British Ambassador in Rome to inform the Italian Government of its recognition of the King of Italy as Emperor of Ethiopia.[50] If concessions even over principle might bring an improvement in relations with a country whose customary importance in Mediterranean affairs was being enhanced by developments in Spain, then the major members of the Commonwealth were ready to make the attempt.

Behind this policy of conditional appeasement of Italy lay the far more critical relations with Germany. In the face of its growing military strength, no continental or other coalition was being forged. The French system of alliances had been rendered ineffectual by the remilitarization of the Rhineland which in fact rendered the western powers impotent to prevent forcible changes in eastern and central Europe. France, itself, was weakened by internal division over social and economic changes. The Nazi "fifth column" technique of stirring up internal divisions was at work in eastern and central European countries. Much of this was still veiled in 1937. Public opinion found itself confused by inability to gauge how far the Nazi demands were conditioned by real needs, how far by desire for prestige and how far by strategic considerations aiming at ultimate European or even world domination. The progress of events was to demonstrate, however, that every gain was merely the signal for further demands. And behind these demands was a steadily growing superiority of military might.

The appeasement of Germany by economic concessions, particularly raw materials and freer trade, had come into consideration at an early date. Sir Samuel Hoare proposed this at the 1935 Assembly which met on the eve of the Italo-Ethiopian conflict. Eden echoed it at the 1937 Assembly.[51] Bruce devoted much of his speech at the latter Assembly[52] to the issue of raw materials on which the League report had been presented,[53] and to the related matter of improved standards of nutrition to which the Australian Government henceforth devoted a considerable amount of attention.   But at all points the economic issue had been related by German spokesmen to the question of colonies. This in turn was declared to be interrelated with Germany's need for expansion in Europe.

Towards the end of 1937, intensification of German propaganda and the visit of Lord Halifax to Berlin gave rise to the belief that a general settlement was being attempted.   That this included consideration of the colonial question was confirmed by a British *communiqué* issued November 30th.[54]   In South Africa and Australia the issue was to the fore again.   The New South Wales Congress of the Returned Soldiers' League voted in September that New Guinea should be incorporated in Australia.[55]   Similar feeling was general in South Africa regarding South-West Africa.   Though the Congress of the Transvaal Nationalist party, followers of Malan, declared in October, 1937, that "We Afrikaaners will not fire a single shot against the Germans if they try to get their former colony back,"[56] Malan himself was not willing to go so far.   But he felt "moral support" should be given "to a scheme that will satisfy Germany's colonial needs."[57]   The *Johannesburg Star* thought there would be support for a general plan if coupled with assurances "against Nazi proselyting and attempts to foment discord as in Czechoslovakia, and Austria, Spain, and elsewhere. . . ."[58] Smuts made it clear early in December that the Government felt Germany had legally renounced all claims to South-West Africa in 1923 and that the issue could not be reopened again.[59]   None the less, there was no disposition to object to general discussions with Germany looking towards a broad settlement.   The Australian Government specifically expressed its hopes that the exchange of views would "make it easier to find a solution, by means of conciliation and co-operation, of those problems which today menace the peace of the world."[60]

Any hope that they would do so ended abruptly with the forcible annexation of Austria in March, 1938.   Both the act itself and the way in which it was carried out proved a rude shock to those who thought in terms of conciliation and adjustment.   The British defence programme was accelerated.   At the same time, Prime Minister Chamberlain endeavoured to restrain Germany from further advances by making clear on March 24, 1938, that Great Britain would go to the defence of France and Belgium in case of unprovoked attack, had obligations to Portugal, Iraq, and Egypt, and in addition might help a victim of aggression in a case arising under the Covenant.[61]   Though not giving specific assurance that France would be supported if it were called upon to implement its obligations under the Franco-Czechoslovakia Treaty, he warned that "The inexorable pressure of facts might well prove more powerful than formal pronouncements." It might lead to the involvement of other countries than the parties to an original dispute, he pointed out and found this "especially true" in the case of Great Britain and France.

This speech, of which the Australian Government had been apprised before it was delivered, received its agreement "on all vital issues," Mr. Lyons made known on April 27, 1938.[62] None the less there was little indication that it wished a strong stand made on behalf of Czechoslovakia, which seemed next on the Nazi programme of expansion. On May 25th, W. M. Hughes, Minister for External Affairs, reassured the House of Representatives on British responsibilities towards Czechoslovakia.[63] Citing recent press statements regarding the agitation of Sudeten Germans and reported movements of German troops, he declared, "I emphasize that the British Government has assumed no new commitments in regard to Czechoslovakia during the past few days." He welcomed the representations of the British and French Governments to the Czechoslovak Government looking towards an easing of the situation and hoped optimistically "that it will be possible to find a peaceful solution of this question which has so long been a disturbing factor in European politics."

In Canada, there was a less direct but no less significant commentary on events in Mr. King's statement of May 24, 1938, on ways in which Canada might become involved in war. In regard to the League of Nations, he pointed out that though various League powers including France, the Soviet Union, Czechoslovakia, and New Zealand were convinced that sanctions were workable, Canada was not. "As far as the Canadian Government is concerned, the sanctions Articles have ceased to have effect by general practice and consent," he declared, "and cannot be revived by any State or group of States at will."[64] As for Great Britain, he acknowledged that no course which it adopted "can fail to have repercussions, great or small, upon Canada and the other members of the Commonwealth of Nations." Because of this some had advised following any policy Great Britain adopted, and others those policies which were consonant with League action. Still others favoured advising the British Government what course it ought to follow. Some even wished to adopt the extreme position of neutrality regardless of developments. None of these did the Prime Minister feel satisfactory, in as much as they bound either Canada or Great Britain in an unwarranted manner. The course of action he himself supported though he acknowledged it to have unsatisfactory features was to allow Parliament to "decide upon our course when and if the emergency arises, in the light of all the circumstances at the time." It was the traditional middle of the road policy, avoiding commitments but not separating Canada from the impact of events which affected Great Britain. In the light of the divisions still obvious within his own party and within Parliament there seemed no other line which could have been followed. Nor was it clear in fact what the British Government itself was prepared to do.

In July, 1938, following further outbreaks in the Sudeten areas and threatening troop movements in Germany, the Czechoslovak Government mobilized its forces and succeeded in restoring the semblance of calm once more. Thereafter it agreed to accept Viscount Runciman as an unofficial mediator with its Sudeten minority whose leadership at least was strongly Nazi in sentiment. But his work did little to ease the situation. By the end of August, tension ran as high as ever. German troops were massing. There were inflammatory declarations on both sides of the border. On September 13th after serious rioting, the Czech Government imposed martial law. To observers, it seemed that it might be the step which would lead to a German attack.

In this crucial situation the Commonwealth stood united in the desire to avoid war. On September 2nd, the Australian Government wired strong support of the British refusal to commit itself to go to war if an act of aggression were committed against Czechoslovakia.[65] It also favoured representations to the Czech Government to secure an immediate public statement of the most liberal concessions it could make. On September 6th, Prime Minister Hertzog declared that there had been no consultation with Great Britain over what policy to pursue in the German-Czech crisis and that South Africa would not be bound to give support if Great Britain became involved in war as the result of its policy.[66] The following day, Pirow pointed out that there was nothing fixed about South African policy and that they might or might not fight on the side of Great Britain if it became engaged in war.[67] New Zealand pledged support but also endorsed the attempt to preserve peace. The Canadian Government, kept in touch with day-to-day developments, was said by King to have supported the efforts of Mr. Chamberlain.[68]

Fearful of the consequences of the Czech act in the light of the German Government's attitude, Chamberlain took the unprecedented step on September 15th of flying to Berchtesgaden to undertake direct mediation with Hitler. At the same time, strong Anglo-French pressure was exerted on Czechoslovakia to make concessions. Recognizing that no Great Power would come to its support, since the Soviet Union would not act unless France and the League did and France would not act without the guaranteed support of Great Britain which was not forthcoming, the Czech Government gave in. On September 21st, it agreed to accept a Franco-British proposal for cession of the Sudetenland. But at once Poland and Hungary added demands, and Hitler increased the severity of his terms. In the face of this development, the Czech Government ordered general mobilization on September 23rd. Chamberlain, who had returned to Germany to confer with Hitler at Godesberg, strove for amelioration of the new German terms. On September 26th after his return to England, he announced jointly with the French Government that Czechoslovakia would be supported if attacked by Germany. Hitler in turn threatened war if his full demands were not accepted by October 1st. President Roosevelt now added his appeal for further negotiations and Chamberlain offered to return to Germany for a last effort to preserve peace. On the proposal of the Australian Government, Mussolini, appealed to also by Roosevelt, was asked to make a personal plea to Hitler, which he did.[69] On September 29th, Chamberlain, Daladier, Mussolini, and Hitler met at Munich. On the same day, the Munich Agreement, involving only minor changes in Hitler's latest demands, was signed. Peace had been secured at the expense of a partition of Czechoslovakian territory. In the process Germany had become by far the largest state in Europe west of the Soviet Union.

The Munich Agreement, the high point of the appeasement policy, met an immediate and joyful response throughout the Commonwealth which showed how heavily the threat of war had lain upon its countries. In Great Britain itself, Chamberlain's "peace in our time" met with widespread rejoicing, untinged at first by the sense of guilt and humiliation which was soon to follow. King wired his congratulations beginning with the words, "The heart of Canada is rejoicing tonight at the success which has crowned your unremitting efforts for peace," and ending with the hope that "a turning point in the world's history" had been reached.[70] Dr. Earle Page, Acting Leader of the House, in tabling the Munich Agreement in the Australian House of Representatives on October 5th, declared that "The whole world welcomed with relief the outcome of the negotiations, and owed a deep debt of gratitude to those who had made the success of the negotiations possible."[71]

The very intensity of the relief was evidence that if Great Britain had gone to war in September, 1938, most of the Dominions would have supported it. When Curtin challenged the Government to say whether it would have committed Australia to war if Great Britain had been involved, Hughes, Minister of External Affairs, answered, "If war had occurred it would have required no committal. We should have been committed to war and no power could have saved us from it."[72] Reports indicated that the Canadian Cabinet was unanimously in support of participation if Great Britain were drawn into war,[73] though there were fears that the country would be badly split.   There was no doubt about New Zealand despite the divergent stand it had taken in the League.   The chief question mark (if Eire is omitted from consideration) was South Africa, and there the division between Hertzog and Smuts which developed in September, 1939, might well have been duplicated a year earlier, though it was reported that the "inner Cabinet" favoured neutrality.[74]   The Commonwealth countries stood on the verge of war in September, 1938, and at least their Governments were aware of the fact.

The post-Munich period was marked by intensification of defence arrangements, and by disillusionment that appeasement could bring a stable peace.   Though the shock of coming so close to the brink of war stimulated action on armaments, the hope in the overseas Dominions that appeasement had done its work lasted longer than in Great Britain. Early in November, the Australian Labour party fought the defence increases of the greatly accelerated programme as being "an utterly unjustifiable and hysterical piece of propaganda" after the Munich Pact.[75]   Even Mr. King was mildly optimistic up to March, 1939, though he interspersed his more encouraging remarks with indications of the potential seriousness of the situation.   But preparations in case of war were not allowed to lag.   In 1939, the Canadian defence estimates were twice as high as for the year before.   Though not substantial, they at least prepared Canada better against attack than in any previous time of peace.   The Australian plans were far more ambitious and, though aiming for co-operation with Great Britain through the navy, reflected also the need for self-sufficiency in defence in the emphasis on the militia and air force.[76]

Early in December, the Australian Minister of Defence warned that "events since Munich had not taken them very far along the road to peace."[77]   Already the distastefulness of watching what happened in the partition of Czechoslovakia had wiped away much of the relief gained through avoidance of war at Munich.   Nor was Germany's conduct such as to encourage hope that any final settlement had been achieved.   Pirow, South African Defence Minister, undertook a tour of European capitals in November, 1938, supposedly for the purpose of considering colonial concessions to Germany which might ease the situation, but if this was its motive, the trip had no direct results.[78] As late as June, 1939, Pirow asserted that German colonial demands must be considered[79] though not in relation to Tanganyika or South-

West Africa.   It was a sign that continued concessions were still looked on as a means to buy peace though the reservation of territories strategically important to the Union laid it open to cynical surmises.   Some of Canada's isolationists and former collectivists reacted to the situation by attempting to separate themselves from its implications and pressed for neutrality in any future war.   But the Prime Minister almost casually raised doubt on January 16, 1939, as to whether Canadian neutrality would be respected by other countries even if declared.   Though affirming as always that Parliament must decide whether Canada participated in a war in which Great Britain was engaged, he accepted also Laurier's statement, "If England is at war, we are at war and liable to attack."[80]

Whatever hopes still remained that appeasement might have done its task vanished with the German annexation of Czechoslovakia on March 15, 1939.   There vanished with it the Chamberlain policy of appeasement.   As the Prime Minister forecast on March 17, 1939, in a speech in Birmingham, there was soon to be in existence a new British policy, diametrically opposed to the one pursued up to that time; a policy of commitments in eastern Europe.   Throwing overboard in the face of continued German aggression the long-maintained insistence on limited liability in western Europe alone, the British Government extended a guarantee to Poland on March 31st and to Greece and Romania on April 13, 1939.   Negotiations were opened with the Soviet Union looking towards a united front against further Nazi aggression.   It was a heroic effort to redress the balance of power in Europe by treating it as a unit whose peace was indivisible.   That it failed was due less to the merits of the plan than to the lateness at which it was adopted.

Immediately after Chamberlain's Birmingham speech of March 17th and before the specific guarantees had been extended, Dr. Manion, the new leader of the Canadian Conservative party, proposed that "liberty loving democracies" make clear "their determination to stand together in a solid front against the tyranny of the Hitlerian dictatorship."[81] On March 20th, King added his criticism of Germany's "wanton and forcible" occupation of Czechoslovakia.[82]   Indicating his willingness for the consultations which Chamberlain had suggested, the Prime Minister maintained that it was necessary to see developments before a course of action could be adopted.   But in one of his most definite forecasts of future action, he differentiated between "a dispute over trade and prestige in some far corner of the world" in which he suggested Canada would not be concerned, and an unprovoked attack on Great

Britain. "If there were a prospect of an aggressor launching an attack on Britain, with bombers raining death on London," he said, "I have no doubt what the decision of the Canadian people and parliament would be. We would regard it as an act of aggression, menacing freedom in all parts of the British Commonwealth."

Though English-speaking Canada widely endorsed his view, there were strong protests from French-speaking Canada at King's statement. To their objections against being involved in another European war, the Prime Minister showed himself sympathetic in a further statement in the House on March 30th.[83]   He cited without disapproval the view that it was "a nightmare and sheer madness" for a country "which has all it can do to run itself" to feel "called upon to save, periodically, a continent that cannot run itself. . . ."   But he reasserted his assurance of co-operation with other members of the British Commonwealth in any war of unprovoked aggression.   His chief French Canadian lieutenant, Lapointe, went still farther in pointing out that the very danger they were most eager to avoid, the splitting of Canada asunder under the strain of divergent policies, would be inevitable if strict neutrality were attempted in a war threatening Great Britain's existence.[84]

Though there was no evidence that the Dominions took an active part in framing the new British policy of barring German aggression in eastern and south-eastern Europe by specific guarantees to dangerously placed countries, they were kept fully informed[85] and can hardly have made any serious protests.   In Canada, it provoked no greater concern than had the background situation precipitated by the German annexation of Czechoslovakia.   Gradually the logic of argument and event was bringing the country together in agreement that if Great Britain were brought into war through its policy of restraining aggression, Canada would come to its support.   It was equally agreed that the character and degree of its aid would be a matter to be determined by itself.   It was generally accepted that it would be largely economic and there were pledges against the imposition of conscription for overseas service. Events were to change radically the initial conception of the Canadian war effort, but the agreement at this time was of the greatest value.

In Australia, the new policy met wholehearted response as an essential move of defence against aggression.   "If . . . in pursuance of this policy, the Government of Britain is at any moment plunged into war," declared the Minister of External Affairs on May 9, 1939, "this Government will on behalf of the Australian people, make common cause with the Mother Country in that war."[86]   Though Curtin, as leader of the Labour Opposition, was careful to emphasize "that the

Governments of the Dominions must themselves decide, in the light of circumstances, how and to what extent they will be participators in a war," he also acknowledged "a common concern for peace, and a common interest in the security of the English-speaking race" which acted as a bond of Commonwealth.[87]   In New Zealand the traditionally imperialist Opposition and the more radically-minded Government met in common agreement on the need to support Great Britain in the policy it had adopted.[88]   South Africa was torn by a division of views which was to come into the open when the British Government declared war in fulfilment of its pledge to Poland.   Few can have expected Eire to participate.   Nor in view of its guarantee to deny its ports to an enemy of Great Britain and of its value as a source of food, would it have been of special advantage to Great Britain in the early days of the war had it done so.

Among the overseas Dominions, the two which might expect their own safety to be placed in jeopardy with the outbreak of war were Australia and New Zealand.   In April, 1939, a Pacific Defence Conference was held in Wellington on the initiative of the New Zealand Government to work out common defence plans with Australian and British representatives.   Behind these and other deliberations was the fear that the existence of the anti-Comintern Pact and the close relations between Germany and Japan would precipitate a Pacific war at the moment when conflict broke out in Europe.   Though there is no indication that Australia attempted to block in any way the Anglo-French negotiations with the Soviet Union looking towards a common front against Germany, its Government apparently pressed that no move should be taken which would antagonize Japan.[89]   The news which stunned western Europe on August 24, 1939, of the German-Soviet Non-Aggression Pact acted paradoxically to relieve the tension in Australia for it made far less likely Japan's participation in a war which subsequently broke out in Europe.   From an ideological point of view, the German-Soviet Pact probably acted also to influence French Canadian and perhaps even some South African sentiment in favour of solidarity with Great Britain.

News that the British Parliament would meet to consider the crisis precipitated by the German-Soviet Pact, generally believed to be the prelude to a German attack on Poland, led Mr. King to inform the leaders of the opposition parties of the seriousness of the situation. He received from them assurances of full support and promised to call Parliament as soon as all hope of maintaining peace had disappeared. On August 25th, the Prime Minister emulated President Roosevelt in appealing to Hitler and to the President of Poland to settle their differences by mediation.[90]   Canada, he declared, was ready to join with other members of the Commonwealth in seeking a fair solution of the problems with which the nations were faced.   Another message to Mussolini urged that he use his influence on the side of peace.   At the same time, mobilization was ordered of part of the non-permanent militia to aid permanent forces in defending key points within Canada.

The German invasion of Poland on September 1, 1939, precipitated the crisis which it had been hoped to the last could be avoided.   The Canadian Parliament was called for September 7th and Mr. King announced that if Great Britain became involved in war in the effort to check aggression, the Government would seek authority for effective co-operation at its side.   On September 3rd, Great Britain and France declared war in support of their pledges to Poland.   One hour after the British declaration, the Australian Federal Executive Council approved a proclamation that Australia was in a state of war with Germany. New Zealand's Cabinet took an equally rapid decision and pre-dated its proclamation to have effect at the moment of the British declaration. Both Governments were unanimously upheld in their decisions by their Parliaments.[91]

In South Africa, the long-expected split between Hertzog and Smuts broke into the open on September 4th.   On behalf of himself and five colleagues, the Prime Minister asked the House to approve his policy of continuing existing relations with the various belligerent countries "as if no war is being waged."[92]   At the same time it was understood, he said, that South Africa would carry out its obligations to defend the British naval base of Simonstown and such relations and obligations as would result from its League membership or "impliedly from the free association of the Union with other members of the British Commonwealth of Nations."   This attempt to straddle the problem of neutrality he justified as being based on a policy of friendship towards Great Britain and a belief that "we are concerned here with a war in which the Union has not the slightest interest."   Germany's series of aggressions he interpreted as being the results of "the monster of the Treaty of Versailles" and not the outcome of the urge to "world domination" against which he himself would "fiercely advocate" opposition.

To Smuts, who led the rest of the Cabinet in an appeal for active participation in the war, it was the belief that the German drive was for world domination which gave power to his argument.   After Danzig would come the demand for South-West Africa and thereby a direct threat to South Africa itself, he maintained.   In this sense the war was South Africa's war. Nor did he believe that the middle position advocated by Hertzog was feasible; they had either to be fully neutral or fully a participant. Overseas service for their forces might not be expected but South Africa should at least take all necessary measures to protect its own safety and interests. In his conviction that the Union had direct concern in the war and that therefore it should participate actively, Smuts was upheld by the House which voted in favour of his amendment. When the Assembly met three days later, it was under the leadership of a new Government formed by General Smuts when the Governor General refused Hertzog a dissolution. In the new Government were represented both English and Afrikaans-speaking leaders from the former United party and also the leaders of the Dominion and Labour parties.

On the same day that Smuts appeared as Prime Minister and war leader before the South African House of Assembly, the Canadian House of Commons met to consider Canada's participation in the war.[93] Though true to the Government's pledge, formal entry into war was delayed for the action of Parliament, preparations for conflict were under way. The War Measures Act, which had never been repealed, had been brought into effect and orders-in-council had begun the process of bringing the country to a war footing. In this atmosphere and with knowledge of opinion in their own constituencies and throughout Canada, its parliamentary representatives gravely debated the situation. On September 9th it was made known that acceptance of the Speech from the Throne would be regarded as approving immediate participation in the war. It was adopted that evening. Immediately following adjournment, the Cabinet met and approved an Order-in-Council authorizing the Prime Minister to advise the King to approve the proclamation declaring a state of war.[94] On Sunday morning, September 10th, just one week after the British declaration of war, Canada was formally at war with Germany.

Despite all its efforts to avoid war, the Commonwealth had been plunged once more into a world conflict whose full scope no one could yet imagine. The long search for security after the first world war had ended. In the place of hopes, plans, and compromises were the clear-cut ends of war. Yet faced with the final test, the overseas Dominions and Great Britain stood united. All that could be done was to meet aggression squarely and to carry on till peace was won again. Thereafter it would be their task to begin building the foundations of security once more with the wisdom and urgency of experience to guide them.

REFERENCES FOR CHAPTER IX

1. In his report to the House of Representatives on the Imperial Conference, Prime Minister Savage endorsed the need for a Commonwealth policy based on common understanding but added that by the time that was secured "there was, at times, not much left of principle." *J.P.E.*, 1938, XIX, 122. The Debate extends from pp. 121-30. For general consideration of New Zealand's policy in this period *see* F. L. W. Wood, *New Zealand in Crisis—May, 1938-August, 1939*.

2. *Ibid.*, p. 564 (Mr. Bennett, May 24, 1938).

3. *See* debate on the Prime Minister's report on the Imperial Conference and the defence programme which had temporarily been in abeyance until after the Conference. *Ibid.*, 1937, XVIII, 852-64.

4. *Ibid.*, 1938, XIX, 909 (Aug. 25, 1938).

5. *Ibid.*, p. 11 (Viscount Cranborne, Under-Secretary of State for Foreign Affairs, in the House of Commons, Oct. 28, 1937).

6. *See* Toynbee, *Survey*, 1937, I, 286, n. 2.

7. A. R. M. Lower, *Canada and the Far East—1940*, p. 23 ff., and for press comments, p. 39 ff. The campaign reached its height late in 1937. In December, 1937, the leader of the provincial C.C.F. party introduced a resolution in the Manitoba legislature denouncing Japan's action which, shorn of its protests against export of war materials to Japan lest this intrude on the Dominion sphere of action, was duly passed. *J.P.E.*, 1938, XIX, 75-76.

8. In New Zealand, dockworkers refused to load cargo for Japan for a brief time in October, 1937. *J.P.E.*, 1938, XIX, 141.

9. Prime Minister Lyons in October warned Australian organizations planning boycotts that "they would prejudice collective measures taken for a settlement and might have a far-reaching effect on future relations with Japan." *The Times*, Oct. 19, 1937 (Melbourne, Oct. 18).

10. Ball, W., Macmahon, and Foxcroft, E. J. B., "The Australian Attitude Towards British Policy in the Far East," *Data Paper* for Meeting of the Institute of Pacific Relations, Nov.-Dec., 1939 (Sydney, 1939), pp. 3-4. It quoted the Prime Minister as saying in April, 1939, "in the Pacific we have what I might call primary responsibilities and primary risks. . . ."

11. Mr. King declared on Feb. 14, 1938, that Canadian policy in relation to the Sino-Japanese dispute was "to maintain a strict neutrality and, in collaboration with other Governments, to contribute, as opportunity afforded, to movements designed to restore peace in the Orient through methods of conciliation." *J.P.E.*, 1938, XIX, 301.

12. Mr. Hull's statement and the comments of foreign Governments are printed in *International Conciliation*, 1937, No. 334, pp. 733-97. The Australian statement is on pp. 735-37.

13. *See* above, p. 162.

14. *O.J.*, 1937, Spec. Sup. No. 169: *Seventeenth Assembly*, Eighth Plenary Meeting, Sept. 21, 1937, pp. 75-79.

15. *O.J.*, 1937, Spec. Sup. No. 177: Sino-Japanese Conflict, Appeal by the Chinese Government, II. Minutes of the Third Session of the Far East Advisory Committee, Second Meeting, Sept. 27, 1937, pp. 15-16.

16. *Ibid.*, p. 20.

17. *Ibid.*, p. 25.

18. Ian F. G. Milner, *New Zealand's Interests and Policies in the Far East* (New York, 1939), p. 87. The report is from the *Dominion*, Oct. 7, 1937. Canada was reported to have supported the New Zealand amendment but was not on the sub-committee.

19. The Canadian representative abstained from voting on the report in the Advisory Committee as he had had so little time to study it. He also asked delay in the Assembly to consult his home Government. The initial abstention was criticized in the *Winnipeg Free Press*, Oct. 14, 1937. Mr. King subsequently justified it in the House, pointing out that the delegation had acted properly in wiring for instructions and that these had been sent immediately. *J.P.E.*, 1938, XIX, 297-98 (Feb. 21, 1938).

20. Milner, *op. cit.*, p. 88, and *Contemporary New Zealand*, p. 202.

21. Milner, pp. 88-89.

22. *O.J.*, Spec. Sup. No. 183: *Nineteenth Assembly*, First Plenary Meeting, Sept. 12, 1938, pp. 29-31.

23. *O.J.*, February, 1939, pp. 100-01: 104th Session of the Council, Fifth Meeting, Jan. 20, 1939.

24. *Ibid.*, May-June, 1939, p. 254: 105th Session, Second Meeting, May 22, 1939.

25. Jack Shepherd, *Australia's Interests and Policies in the Far East*, p. 87 ff.

26. Quoted in *ibid.*, p. 128. The debate is printed in *J.P.E.*, 1939, XX, p. 682.

27. *Bulletin of International News* (London), Aug. 26, 1939, 16, 858.

28. *Great Britain, House of Commons Debates*, Vol. 350, cols. 2868-69: 37th Parliament, 4th Session, Aug. 4, 1939.

29. Quoted in Milner, *op. cit.*, p. 90. For debate, see p. 91.

30. The Agreement was printed in *Cmd. 5568* of 1937.

31. *Cmd. 5569*.

32. *O.J.*, May-June, 1937, pp. 325-26: Ninety-Seventh Session of the Council, Fifth Meeting, May 28, 1937. He did not specify an "A" mandate in this meeting but asked that the League should assist Spain so peace could be restored more quickly. In September, however, he said he was repeating his suggestion of a mandate. This is the speech regarding which an unsubstantiated story printed in *The Daily Worker* was circulated that Eden had "blue pencilled" certain portions during the Council meeting.

33. *O.J.*, December, 1937, pp. 917-99: Ninety-Eighth Session of the Council, Third Meeting, Sept. 16, 1937, pp. 917-19. When asked in the House whether this proposal for an "A" mandate for Spain had been approved by the Government and whether other Commonwealth members were consulted before it was made, Prime Minister Savage replied that the Government: "approved of any attempt to resolve the Spanish difficulties by a reference of the questions at issue to the unfettered decision of the Spanish people themselves, and will be prepared to support any plan that offers prospects of successful action along these lines. The High Commissioner's speech appears to have been in accordance with these principles. The High Commissioner also takes every opportunity for informal consultations with other representatives of the British Commonwealth upon matters of importance which are on the agenda of the League and, while no definite information on this point is available, the Government has no reason to believe that this custom was departed from in the present instance." *J.P.E.*, 1938, XIX, 114 (Sept. 29, 1937).

34. *Winnipeg Free Press*, editorial, Oct. 14, 1937.

35. Grant Dexter, "Vital Votes," *ibid.*, Oct. 12, 1937.

36. *J.P.E.*, 1938, XIX, p. 298 (Feb. 21, 1938).

37. *O.J.*, 1937, Spec. Sup. No. 175, pp. 66-7: *Eighteenth Assembly*, Sixth Committee, Tenth Meeting, Sept. 30, 1937.

38. *Ibid.*, pp. 67, 68, 69, and 70.

39. *O.J.*, 1937, Spec. Sup. No. 169, p. 100: *Eighteenth Assembly*, Eleventh Meeting, Oct. 2, 1937.

40. Toynbee, *Survey*, 1937, II, 218.

41. *O.J.*, 1937, Spec. Sup. No. 169, p. 102: *Eighteenth Assembly*, Eleventh Meeting, Oct. 2, 1937.

42. On April 7, 1937, Hertzog had declared that "the question of Spain interested him vastly, but it was for that reason that his policy with regard to Spain was to have nothing to do with it." *J.P.E.*, 1937, XVIII, 618. Smuts expressed concern about the crisis in the Mediterranean early in September. Cited in *Neue Frie Presse* (Vienna), Sept. 9, 1937.

43. *J.P.E.*, 1938, XIX, II (Oct. 28, 1937).

44. *Current Notes on International Affairs* (Canberra, Australia), May 1, 1938, pp. 206-12. Statement by the Prime Minister in the House of Representatives, Apr. 27, 1938. In the ensuing debates, Mr. Curtin approved the Anglo-Italian Agreement but questioned Australian adherence to British defence principles, *see J.P.E.*, 1938, XIX, 637 ff.

45. *Current Notes*, Dec. 1, 1938, p. 289. Statement by the Prime Minister, Nov. 16, 1938.

46. *Ibid.*, Mar. 15, 1939, p. 111. Statement in the House by the Prime Minister on the same day.

47. *J.P.E.*, 1938, XIX, 472 (May 2, 1938).

48. De Valera maintained that in accrediting the new Irish Minister to the "King of Italy and Emperor of Ethiopia" *de jure* recognition was not involved but the point was hardly tenable. *Ibid.*, p. 143 (Dec. 14, 1937).

49. *O.J.*, May-June, 1938, pp. 345-46: 101st Session of the Council, Sixth Meeting, May 12, 1938.

50. Soward, *Canada in World Affairs*, p. 119.

51. *O.J.*, Spec. Sup. No. 169, pp. 64-66: *Eighteenth Assembly*, Sixth Plenary Meeting, Sept. 20, 1937.

52. *Ibid.*, pp. 75-9: Eighth Plenary Meeting, Sept. 21, 1937.

53. *Doc. A. 27*, 1937, II, B. (L.O.N.P. 6).

54. *Germany's Claim to Colonies*, (R.I.I.A., 1939) p. 66.

55. *Sydney Morning Herald*, Sept. 25, 1937.

56. *The Times*, Oct. 8, 1937 (Johannesburg, Oct. 7, Reuters).

57. *The Observer* (London), Oct. 10, 1937 (Klerksdorf, Transvaal, Reuters).

58. *The Times*, Oct. 29, 1937 (Capetown, Oct. 28, Reuters). The comment was provoked by a leading article on Germany's colonial claims in *The Times*.

59. *Current Notes*, Jan. 15, 1938, pp. 12-13.

60. *Ibid.*, Dec. 15, 1937, p. 373. Statement by the Minister of External Affairs, Dec. 3, 1937.

61. *J.P.E.*, 1938, XIX, 188-189.

62. *Current Notes*, May 1, 1938, p. 209.

63. *Ibid.*, June 1, 1938, p. 255.

64. *J.P.E.*, 1938, XIX, 557-62.

65. *Ibid.*, 851 (Mr. Lyons on Sept. 28, 1938). The speech is printed in full in *Current Notes*, Oct. 4, 1938.

66. *Ibid.*, 1939, XX, 389 (cited by Mr. King in the Canadian House of Commons, Mar. 30, 1939).

67. *Ibid.*, 1938, XIX, 913.

68. *Ibid.*, 1939, XX, 388 (Mar. 30, 1939).

69. *Current Notes*, Oct. 4, 1938, pp. 191-93.   Statement by Mr. Lyons to the House of Representatives on Sept. 29.

70. Private copy.

71. *J.P.E.*, 1939, XX, 116.   *See* also press statement issued by the Prime Minister on Sept. 30.   *Current Notes*, Oct. 4, 1938, p. 194.

72. *Ibid.*, p. 118.

73. Soward, *Canada in World Affairs*, p. 115.

74. Lucretia Ilsley, "The Union of South Africa in the War," in *The British Commonwealth at War*, p. 431.

75. *J.P.E.*, 1939, XX, 126 (Nov. 3, 1938).

76. *See* Shepherd, *op. cit.*, p. 104 ff.

77. *J.P.E.*, 1939, XX, 427 (Dec. 6, 1938).

78. *Germany's Claim to Colonies*, pp. 70-73.   On Feb. 7, 1939, Pirow denied that he had ever given the interview in which these intentions were described.   *J.P.E.*, 1939, XX, 449.

79. *New York Times*, June 25, 1945 (Lydenburg, Transvaal).

80. *J.P.E.*, 1939, XX, 375.

81. Cited by Soward in *Canada in World Affairs*, p. 126.   Dr. Manion's press statement of Mar. 19 was repeated in the House the following day.   *J.P.E.*, 1939, XX, 387-88.

82. *J.P.E.*, 1939, XX, pp. 386-87.

83. *Ibid.*, pp. 388-92.

84. *Ibid.*, pp. 393-95.

85. *Ibid.*, p. 288.   (Mr. Chamberlain in the House of Commons, Mar. 31, at the conclusion of the announcement of the pledge to Poland.)

86. *Ibid.*, p. 684.

87. *Ibid.*, p. 685.

88. F. L. W. Wood, *New Zealand in the World* (Wellington, 1940), pp. 121-23.

89. Shepherd, *op. cit.*, p. 129.

90. *Canada in World Affairs*, p. 150.

91. *J.P.E.*, 1939, XX, pp. 930-33 and 944-45.

92. *Ibid.*, pp. 968-71.   Smuts' speech and ensuing debate follow immediately.

93. *Ibid.*, pp. 891-905.

94. *Ibid.*, pp. 905-06.

CHAPTER X

CONCLUSION

In the inter-war period, the peoples of the overseas Dominions learned that there was no return to normalcy. In a period of experimentation, they, too, had been empirical. But the apparently wavering line of their policies was in fact motivated by two types of need—the need to maintain their internal unity which demanded independent and popular decisions in any marked changes in social, economic, or political policies, and the need for world security within which they could develop their potentialities.

Collective security through the League might have provided an answer for both needs had it become effective without placing too heavy demands upon its members. But at no time in its history did the League provide the type of international organization which they found necessary to meet the needs of world security. The absence of the United States undermined their confidence in it from the beginning. Its lack of clear distinction between general and limited responsibility frightened countries which felt they needed to concentrate their major attention on their own development. Its comparative inflexibility was looked on as a serious weakness. The continual extension of its functions in non-political fields ran counter to their belief that its energies should be concentrated on the all-important issue of preserving peace. Perhaps, above all, they were never convinced that its other members wholeheartedly supported its security programme.

None the less, the Dominions must take their share of responsibility for the failure to establish collective security. Their opposition to general or regional guarantees helped to weaken faith in the League as a guardian of peace. Their insistence on a *liberum veto* reinforced the nationalistic attitude of others. Their denial that the movement of goods and people was an issue for international consideration forced an artificial distinction between causes of friction and the procedures which sought to prevent friction from developing into war. Their criticism of the League as an instrument of world security took too little account of the long, slow processes needed in building international solidarity. Finally, Australia and Canada had shown themselves reluctant to face the ultimate implications of collective action though the smaller members of the Commonwealth had been ready to do so.

312

But for the Dominions, the League was never the only alternative to isolation. The Commonwealth offered a grouping which was deeply interested in their particular problems. By sharing the special knowledge of Great Britain, they avoided the chief disadvantages of being small countries, without facing, except through ultimate implication, the responsibilities usually associated with such special knowledge. In the Commonwealth, they were early accepted as being "middle powers," that is, as having equality of status coupled with differentiation of function conditioned by relative strength.

Could this compensate for the obvious weaknesses of the Commonwealth as a general security agent? To this the answer was not clear till late within the inter-war period. The world-wide possessions and interests of Great Britain seemed more likely to lead to conflict than the limited and more isolated ones of the Dominions. There was fear that if general war should be precipitated, it would be in Europe rather than in some other part of the world. Out of this came their anxiety over British commitments in Europe except the limited ones necessitated by its strategic position. But the very concern of the Dominions over British commitments was a measure of their adherence to the British connection.

During the inter-war period several specific steps were taken to remove signs of Dominion inferiority in status within the Commonwealth. The Balfour Report, 1926, and the Statute of Westminster, 1931, despite the reluctance of New Zealand, had general effect except in as far as specific reservations to the latter were drafted by Australia, New Zealand, and Canada. South Africa, where there was great interest in legal forms, established a separate seal and passed a statute to provide for the right of neutrality in a British war. But no overseas Dominion established separate nationality. Far more important, no overseas Dominion attempted to abrogate the arrangements extending special facilities to the British Navy in certain of its ports, such as Halifax and Esquimalt in Canada, and Simonstown in South Africa. These were tangible evidences that the Commonwealth relation was still looked on as a means of providing security.

As a guarantor of general security, the British Commonwealth connection had obvious weaknesses after 1918. Yet the British Navy, while no longer unrivalled in strength, remained one of the most powerful striking forces afloat with a far greater mobility than any other fleet because of its world-wide port facilities. The provision of some of these port facilities, the maintenance of small Dominion navies, armies, and air forces, and the acceptance of common standards for training and equipment were the only active contributions made by the Dominions to the Commonwealth as a security system, except in a time of ultimate need. In the stage of development of their peoples in the inter-war period, preoccupied as they were with their own concerns and unwilling for unified policies, the Commonwealth answered their needs surprisingly well. Its amazing flexibility enabled the Dominions to pursue co-operation without specific commitments, to act like the small states which their populations indicated them to be and yet to have the share in world affairs to which their area and resources entitled them. On the basis of accepted purposes, a wide degree of co-operation was developed which formed a sound basis for whatever subsequent action might be decided upon. This was the strength of the Commonwealth. Yet co-operation in specific action was conditional upon maintaining a clear relation between Commonwealth policy and general security needs.

For the unity of the individual Dominions, the backbone of their ultimate security, the British Commonwealth connection was both a consolidating and a divisive influence. It provided a wider focus of interest and a larger stage on which local clashes lost something of their intensity. On the other hand, economic, social, or racial divisions in Canada, Australia and South Africa were accentuated in times of extreme stress by the division between those who interpreted their country's interest in local terms and those who believed it was best served by group action. The resolution of such conflicts came only when the locally rooted group became convinced of the necessity of action from the point of view not of purely British interest but of general world security.

This need to maintain a relation between British policy and policies contributing to genuine world security had given a special significance to the attempt of the Covenant of the League of Nations to harness foreign policy to justice. British deviations from League standards were in general unpopular in the Dominions. It is not without reason that the Laval-Hoare Plan was followed by more proposals from within the Dominions for neutrality in future British wars than appeared at any other point in the inter-war period. Even a New Zealander wrote in 1938, following New Zealand's decision to take the League seriously, that imperial loyalty was complicated by international morality. For the satisfactory working of the Commonwealth system, it needed to be linked to the general ends of world security. It was the belief that this relationship had been re-established that brought the overseas Dominions unanimously into war in September, 1939.

The six years of war from September, 1939, to August, 1945, heavily underscored the need of world security. In June, 1940, Great Britain faced the threat of invasion by the forces which had overrun the continent. For a year, the Commonwealth fought almost alone against Germany and its satellites, battling to keep the supply lines open to the isolated outpost of western Europe on whose defence rested the safety of the North Atlantic. Canada increased its flow of men and materials and joined with the United States in a formal partnership of defence and of economic aid to Great Britain. South Africa became the half-way house to the Far East and with war once more in its own continent, sent troops to aid the defence of Egypt, threatened by the German drive across Africa and down through the Balkans. From the Pacific came a steady flow of military and economic aid from Australia and New Zealand to the Middle East and to Great Britain itself.

Then early in 1942, after savage German and Japanese attacks had brought the Soviet Union and the United States into the war, Australia itself faced the threat of invasion as Great Britain had done eighteen months before. The Japanese forces spreading relentlessly into the south-west Pacific found no effective block in Malaya or Singapore or the Dutch East Indies. Such British naval reinforcements as could be sent went down without affecting the issue. Only Japan's overstrained lines of communication and the potential resistance of Australian and American forces seem to have checked the southward drive.

For three and a half years thereafter the United Nations battled to win back the positions they had lost and ultimately to drive their way to the heart of Nazi and Japanese power. The countries of the Commonwealth became part of a far greater coalition pledged to unity in war and to concert common measures for the ultimate maintenance of peace.

Under Anglo-American leadership, this coalition began the shaping of new international organization before the war was over. The San Francisco Conference on the United Nations Organization for International Security was in session at the time that Germany surrendered unconditionally. Its plans were being considered by the individual members of the United Nations when Japan's capitulation brought to a close the titanic struggles of World War II.

In the course of the long conflict, the overseas countries of the Commonwealth became mature members of the world community as in 1919 they had become partners within the British circle of nations. Canada and Australia claimed the position of "middle powers" internationally as the just recognition that their contributions in the war had been only a little less than those of the Great Powers. All took an active share in shaping the formal structure of the United Nations which reflects far more than did the League of Nations their conception of differentiated responsibilities.

Three alternatives faced them as the war came to an end: to unite with Great Britain to form a British Commonwealth and Empire which could take its place side by side with the super-powers of the United States and the Soviet Union; to translate independence into separatism; or to combine the Commonwealth relation with the new international organization of the United Nations. To the first, all their instincts for separate decisions and against power politics gave an emphatic denial. For the second, the bonds of partnership forged in peace and war were too strong. To subscribe to the third was not difficult. It was the natural outgrowth of the past. To reaffirm the bonds of Commonwealth, as did the Prime Ministers' Conference in May, 1944, in terms of "free association" and "inherent unity of purpose" was no limitation on independence nor on the interdependence for which the United Nations stood.

The future of the Commonwealth as an agent of security will be dependent on events. The war demonstrated that it can provide mutual defence only in a localized conflict. It can never again be as powerful a force as it was in the inter-war period. Even then it had obvious limitations. Nor can it again provide as complete a centre of interest as in the inter-war period for even its smaller overseas members. Canada's partnership with the United States in mutual defence extends inevitably into the post-war period. Australia and New Zealand recognize the predominant position of that country in the Pacific. Perhaps only South Africa is bound more strongly by ties of security to Great Britain than to the United States. But there is no either-or in this situation. It is rather that the common strategic interests of the United States and the countries of the Commonwealth have become more apparent.

Ultimately it must be hoped that international organization will fulfil its purpose and collective security become a reality. At that moment the burden of security will be lifted from more limited groupings like the Commonwealth which will be left free to pursue such other common purposes as its members desire. But to bring this about, the United Nations will have to receive from all its members more support than the overseas Dominions were generally willing to give in the inter-war period. For this their peoples may well have been prepared by the sacrifices of war and the experience of the past.

Between 1919 and 1939, the peoples of the Dominions developed an awareness of the issues in international political life. They grew quickly from adolescence to maturity. In the Commonwealth and in the League, their leaders faced some of the most complicated issues of the day. In this period the bridge was finally made between characteristic attitudes born of internal developments and the needs of external policy.

To the problems of the future, Canada, Australia, New Zealand, and South Africa can bring a varied experience in international working together and a world-wide point of view. Though their interests are regional, they can never in the nature of things be exclusively so. They link the old world and the new, bound to Europe through Great Britain more closely than other independent overseas countries have been, yet responding to all the forces which characterize the frontier areas of western civilization. Out of this background, their people can with self-confidence take up again the search for security which can be fully realized only with the development of a world community.

INDEX

Abyssinia, 191, 226, 237, *see also* Ethiopia, Italo-Ethiopian conflict
L'Action Catholique, 224
Adatci, M., 115
Addis Ababa, 235, 236
Ador, Gustave, 22
African Observer, 271
The Age, 205
Albania, 25, 26, 197, 295
All-Australian Trades Union Congress, 204
Allen, Sir James, 17, 18
Allenby, Lord, 83
Alsace-Lorraine, 81
American Naval Act 1916, 40
American Note on Demilitarization, 75
American Treaty of Guarantee, 77
Amery, Leopold, 201
Anglo-American Naval Parity Proposals, 41-43
Anglo-American Trade Agreement 1938, 284
Anglo-American Treaties of Guarantee, 75
Anglo-Egyptian Treaty 1936, 257
Anglo-French Alliance, 80, 109
Anglo-French Treaty *see* British Treaty of Mutual Guarantee
Anglo-German Naval Agreement, 178, 186, 187, 189, 256
Anglo-Italian Agreement 1937, 266, 295, 296
Anglo-Japanese Alliance, 37, 40, 41, 42-47, 51, 52, 55, 252
Anti-Comintern Pact, 251, 291, 295, 305
Arbitration Commission on Ethiopia, 188, 189
Argentina, 198, 242
Argus, 228
Armenia, 20, 21, 25
Attlee, Clement, 201, 240
Australia
  and defence, 39, 54-64, 253-4, 286
  and disarmament, 39, 109, 176, 286
    Washington Conference, 58-61
  and European affairs, 77, 81, 89, 94, 112-3, 273, 275, 277, 279, 284-5
    Germany, policies to, 4, 9-11, 234, 269, 271, 298-300, 304-5
    Italo-Ethiopian conflict, 179, 191, 194, 196, 201-5, 235, 239, 244-6, 296
    Laval-Hoare plan, 228
    Locarno Treaty, 93-5
    Munich Agreement, 301
    Spanish civil war, 264
    war declared, 306
  and Far Eastern affairs, 37, 39, 44, 60, 137, 292

Anglo-Japanese Alliance, 42-3
  Far Eastern Advisory Committee, 288
  Pacific Pact, 260, 261, 272
  Sino-Japanese dispute (first), 147, 155-6, 160, 164-5, 166
  Sino-Japanese dispute (second), 287, 289, 291
  Washington Conference, 46-7, 50-55
and the Kellogg-Briand Pact, 125
and the League of Nations, 167, 229, 241
  Covenant, 3-9, 10-16, revision proposed, 260-63
  Draft Treaty of Mutual Assistance, 108, 112, 113, 122
  First Assembly, 16-30, rules of procedure, 18
  General Act for the Pacific Settlement of Disputes, 128
  Geneva Protocol, 115-6, 119-22, 127, 128
  mandates, 4, 5, 9, 21, 53, 269
  Optional clause, 120, 124, 127
  Resolution XIV, 109
  sanctions, 179, 201-5, 239, 244, 246
and Near Eastern Affairs,
  Chanak incident, 73-4, 82-3, 85-6, 87, 88
  Egypt, 82-3, 256-7
  Montreux Conference, 256-7
  Treaty of Lausanne, 91
Australian-Japanese Agreement, 292
Australian National Review, 271
Austria, 25, 190, 197, 251, 296, 298
Austro-German Customs Union, 135
Axis powers, 290

Badoglio, Pietro, 226
Baldesi, Digno, 22
Baldwin, Stanley, 178, 225, 226, 230, 240, 270, 273, 275
Balfour, A. J., 21, 51, 52, 55, 58, 59, 112
Balfour Report, 181, 313
Baltic States, 25
Beatty, Admiral, 55
Belgium, 47, 62, 111, 124, 196, 216, 242, 245, 298
Beneš, Edouard, 26, 114, 161
Bennett, R. B., 136, 154, 165, 186, 190-1, 233-4, 239
Berliner Tageblatt, 277
Blankenberg, Sir R., 25
Blueshirts, 265
Blum, Leon, 242, 257
Bolivia, 175, 177, 197, 295
Bonin Islands, 55
Bonsal, Col. S., 7

319